The Social Life of Coffee

BRIAN COWAN

The Social Life of Coffee

THE EMERGENCE OF THE BRITISH COFFEEHOUSE

Yale University Press
New Haven &
London

Published with assistance from the Annie Burr Lewis Fund.
Published with the assistance of the Frederick W. Hilles Publication Fund
of Yale University.

Set in Sabon type by Keystone Typesetting, Inc.

The Library of Congress has cataloged the hardcover edition as follows:

Cowan, Brian William, 1969–
The social life of coffee : the emergence of the British coffeehouse / Brian Cowan.
p. cm.
Includes bibliographical references and index.
ISBN 978-0-300-10666-4
1. Coffeehouses — History. 2. Coffee — History. I. Title.
TX908.C68 2005
647.9509 — dc22
2005043555

ISBN 978-0-300-17122-8 (pbk.)

A catalogue record for this book is available from the British Library.

Contents

Acknowledgments

The history of coffee has been on my mind for almost a decade now, and over the course of this time I have had many opportunities to share these thoughts with a number of individuals in a variety of locations. I am acutely aware of just how fortunate I have been to work with so many interesting people along the way.

I began working on this book at Princeton University, where Peter Lake offered his indomitable support, advice and encouragement at every step along the way. The rest of the historical community at Princeton also played an important role in shaping the ways in which I began to think about the rise of British coffee. Robert Darnton's graduate seminar on the social history of eighteenth-century ideas first inspired me to pursue this topic and he has continued to be an important source of guidance and encouragement. Lawrence Stone enlivened my first thoughts on this topic and they will be forever poorer for lacking his continued insights; the magnificence of his historical imagination remains an example to us all. I was also fortunate to study British history along with a remarkable cohort of historians including Susan Whyman, Alastair Bellany, David Como, Margaret Sena, Ethan Shagan, Ignacio Gallup-Diaz, John Hintermaier, and Brendan Kane, each of whom encouraged me to think more clearly about this project in numerous discussions.

The argument of this book is based on a wide reading in archival sources on both sides of the Atlantic. I am particularly grateful to the archivists, librarians, and staff at the British Library; the Public Record Office (now the National Archives); the London Metropolitan Archives; the Corporation of London Record Office; the London Guildhall Library; the archives of the Royal Society; the Department of Prints and Drawings at the British Museum; Dr. Williams Library; the National Art Library at the Victoria and Albert Museum; the Westminster Archives Centre; the National Library of Scotland; the Bodleian Library; and the Cambridge University Library. In the United States, I am indebted to the staff at Princeton University's Firestone Library, especially the late John Henneman. At Yale, the staff at Sterling Library, especially Susanne Roberts; the Beinecke Library, especially Stephen Parks; the British Art Center, especially Lisa Ford and Elisabeth Fairman; and Maggie Powell at the Lewis Walpole Library have been immensely helpful and supportive. The Huntington Library, the William Andrews Clark Library, and the Folger Shakespeare Library have offered substantial research support and source materials which have been immensely helpful.

Research for this book was made possible by a Leverhulme Foundation Fellowship at the University of Kent at Canterbury in the year 2000. The University of Sussex in Brighton, England, and Yale University in New Haven, New England both offered welcome bases from which I was able to continue to refine my arguments as well as begin my teaching career. I am particularly grateful to Master John Rogers and Associate Master Cornelia Pearsall for welcoming me as a Resident Fellow of Berkeley College and providing me with a wonderful set of college rooms in which I was able to rethink and rewrite the bulk of this book. My new colleagues in the Department of History at McGill University have received this work enthusiastically, and I look forward to working with them in the years to come.

The arguments presented here have been discussed and debated with countless excellent scholars. I have received particularly useful advice and assistance from Tricia Allerston, John Demos, Paul Freedman, Tim Harris, Negley Harte, Michael Hunter, Adrian Johns, Jane Kamensky, Newton Key, Lawrence Klein, Peter Mandler, Neil De Marchi, David Ormrod, Nicholas Phillipson, Steven Pincus, James Rosenheim, David Harris Sacks, John Styles, Keith Wrightson, and several anonymous readers for Yale University Press. I have also presented versions of many of the chapters to audiences at Warwick University; the Berkshire Women's History Conference in Rochester, New York; the Institute of Historical Research at the University of London; the Victoria and Albert Museum; the University of Utah; Harvard University; the University of Leeds; Edinburgh University; the North American Conferences on British Studies in Cambridge, Massachusetts, and in Toronto; Emory University; Stanford University; and the Melbern G. Glasscock Humanities Center at Texas A&M University. I am grateful to all of the participants in these seminars for their helpful comments and questions.

Grants from the Whitney Humanities Center and the Huntington Library helped expand the research base upon which my arguments have been based. Funding for the illustrations has been kindly supported through the assistance of the Frederick W. Hilles Publication Fund of Yale University.

Portions of this book have been previously published in earlier form as: "What Was Masculine About the Public Sphere? Gender and the Coffeehouse Milieu in Post-Restoration England," *History Workshop Journal* 51 (2001); "The Rise of the Coffeehouse Reconsidered," *Historical Journal* 47:1 (2004); and "Mr. Spectator and the Coffeehouse Public Sphere," *Eighteenth-Century Studies* 37:3 (2004), although each of these articles has a separate historiographical point to make that is distinct from the wider argument of this book. I am grateful to the publishers of these journals for permission to reprint excerpts from these articles here.

Yale University Press has been an exemplary publisher for this book and I must thank my editors Lara Heimert and Molly Egland as well as Keith Condon for their help in bringing this book into print.

The most important debts are often reserved for last, and this is no exception. The book is dedicated to my parents, William and Beverly Cowan, who have unstintingly supported my studies from the very beginning.

A Note on Styles and Conventions

The Social Life of Coffee refers extensively to early modern source material in various media, printed, manuscript, and visual. My quotations from these sources attempt to capture the character of the original sources without sacrificing readability. To the latter end, abbreviations have been expanded, the punctuation has often been silently altered, and characters such as *u, v, w, i,* and *j* have been modernized except in book titles.

Until 1752, Britain recognized the "old-style" Julian calendar, which was ten days behind the "new-style" Gregorian calendar used by most of the rest of Europe. I have retained old-style dates throughout this work. The legal year began in late March, but I have followed standard convention in modernizing all dates so that the new year is understood to begin on 1 January.

References to Acts of Parliament are given by the regnal year as well as the session, chapter, and pertinent section numbers. The statutes can be found in a number of reference works. References to the royal proclamations of James VI and I and Charles I may be found in the 1973 and 1983 editions of James F. Larkin and Paul L. Hughes. References to post-Restoration royal proclamations are identified by their numeral in the older work of Robert Steele, ed., *Bibliography of Royal Proclamations of the Tudor and Stuart Sovereigns* (1910).

The longstanding conflation of "British" and "English" identities has come under serious scrutiny in the current age of devolution and growing European union. For the majority of the period under consideration here, the term "British" with reference to the multiple monarchies of England and Scotland is anachronistic. Nevertheless, I continue to use the word as a heuristic means of referring to the various different areas ruled by the Stuart monarchs and their post-1688 successors. While this study has taken Scottish and Irish evidence into consideration in its account of British coffee culture, the preponderance of its evidence concerns the English case. One of the main reasons for this is that the history of British coffeehouses is intimately related to the urban history of metropolitan London, a city whose cultural predominance loomed large over all of the British Isles. The legal City of London, located within the walls and governed and administered by the Lord Mayor and Aldermen of the City, is always referred to with capital letters in this work. The metropolitan city of London encompassed a much larger area and had no formal governing structures, but rather fell within various jurisdictions, such as the City of Westminster and the counties of Middlesex and Surrey. References to this broader city are never capitalized.

The notation convention of Adrian Johns's *Nature of the Book* (1998) and several other works has been adopted here. Full bibliographical details of all works cited in the notes are in the bibliography.

Introduction

Hard as it is to believe today, there was once a world without coffee. Coffee was entirely unknown before the middle of the fifteenth century, when it began to make its way into the drinking habits of the peoples living in the Red Sea basin. After its discovery, the rise of coffee seems to have been inevitable. It became one of the great success stories of the changing consumer habits that reshaped the early modern world. Although it was controversial in every society into which it was introduced, coffee soon found its place alongside more traditional drinks such as beers, wines, waters, and juices. This book focuses on the development of this new taste for coffee, and the emergence of a new social institution, the coffeehouse, in the British Isles.

Coffee drinking spread from the Red Sea region throughout the Ottoman Empire over the course of the sixteenth century.[1] But what induced the British peoples to adopt the custom of a foreign, and even non-Christian, land during the seventeenth century? Why did coffee and related hot drinks, such as tea and chocolate, succeed where so many other exotic drugs and consumables failed? What accounts for the emergence of an entirely new social institution, the coffeehouse, as the primary place in which these new drinks were consumed? The answers to these questions will take us deep into the mental, political, social, and economic structures of everyday life in a world which only gradually came to recognize a life accentuated by coffee and populated by numerous coffeehouses.

The history of coffee and coffeehouses offers a new perspective on some of the major themes in recent historical writing on early modern Britain. This is a period which has often been characterized as experiencing a "consumer revolution" as well as the rise of a "public sphere" of critical debate beyond the regulation of the monarchical state.[2] If the late seventeenth and eighteenth centuries saw something like the birth of a consumer society, then the rise of the new coffee-drinking habit is a good indicator of this phenomenon. To learn why and how seventeenth-century English consumers came to desire a strange new drink such as coffee can take us a long way toward understanding the origins of the consumer revolution of the long eighteenth century. Concomitantly, the notion of a public sphere, first articulated by Jürgen Habermas, has always held up the coffeehouse as the prime example of the sort of institution that characterized this new social world. In this account, the coffeehouse has been understood to be a novel and unique social space in which distinctions of rank were temporarily ignored and uninhibited debate on matters of political and philosophical interest flourished. If there was a relation between the birth of a consumer society and the rise of a public sphere, then the best way to understand it is through a thorough study of the origins of coffee drinking and coffeehouse society.

The Social Life of Coffee revisits and revises both the consumer revolution and the public sphere paradigms. It looks for the reasons for the spread of new consumer practices such as coffee drinking and it traces the relation between these new tastes and the development of new modes of social organization. In both cases, novelty had to be made legitimate. Neither the commercial success of coffee nor the social success of the coffeehouse was a given. The early modern world without coffee had to be coaxed into accepting the hot black broth and the places in which it was drunk. The rise of the coffee-drinking habit required a great deal of persuasive work on the part of its earliest proponents, and the legitimation of the coffeehouse required that people think differently about the role of public association in the social order.

Curiosity, commerce, and civil society provide the three major themes through which this book explores the rise of coffee and coffeehouses. The crucial social legitimacy for both the coffee commodity and the coffeehouse was provided by the unique combination of a genteel virtuoso "culture of curiosity" and a rapidly growing commercial world centered in London.[3] Civil society in early modern Britain developed as a product of this mixture of gentlemanly curiosity and urban commerce. The virtuosi provided the catalyst that spurred the initial commercial interest in coffee and the development of the coffeehouse as a significant social institution, but this initial interest was then seized upon and transformed by the exigencies of urban sociability. Coffee culture began with virtuosity and quickly became an integral part of urban living. Just as coffee drinking was transformed by its move from a relatively restricted circle of gentlemanly elites to a much broader and diffuse urban milieu, so were the social lives of the virtuosi and the city dwellers who drank coffee and frequented coffeehouses.

Dramatic changes in British consumer preferences and in British public life did accompany the rise of coffee drinking and coffeehouses in the later seventeenth century, but these changes did not happen automatically; they were accompanied by trepidation and often outright resistance. British coffee culture developed slowly, and its ultimate success was achieved less through rapid and radical change than through its gradual insinuation and adaptation into the basic structures of everyday life. The supposed early modern consumer revolution was less revolutionary than it was *evolutionary*, and the rise of the coffeehouse public sphere was accepted by the British old regime only when it was clear that coffeehouse politics would not upset the status quo. The making of the British coffee world cannot be understood as a telling example of the inexorable process of the making of the modern world. The rise of coffee did not inaugurate the "creation of the modern world"; coffee and coffeehouses were received and popularized by an old regime and a pre-industrial society.[4] Coffee and modernity did not emerge in tandem. The story told in this book is therefore a resolutely *early* modern one: the first coffeehouses in the British Isles were not today's global Starbucks corporate empire writ small. They were the product of a world in which novelty was not a sales pitch, but something to be looked at askance. Similarly, early modern coffeehouse politics did not prefigure the rise of modern liberal democracy: the first coffeehouses were shaped by the prejudices of a world in which kings and queens were still thought to rule through some sort of divine sanction and the participation of the common people in political action was something to be feared rather than celebrated.

Insofar as it emphasizes the traditional as much as it recognizes many of the incipiently modern aspects of the reception of coffee in early modern British society, this book contributes to a "post-revisionist" history of the seventeenth and eighteenth centuries which remains as yet incomplete and often contradictory.[5] Whiggishly optimistic and triumphalist paradigms such as the consumer revolution and the rise of a public sphere do not do justice to the fitful and uncertain acceptance of coffee in early modern Britain and this work joins revisionist critics of these whig views in rejecting their anachronistic and teleological anticipations of the modern present in the early modern past. Nevertheless, the social fact of coffee's acceptance must be recognized, as most "revisionist" histories of the period have stubbornly refused to do. *The Social*

Life of Coffee offers an account of the rise of coffee and coffeehouses in which their success is not assumed but explained.

The chronological scope of this study covers the long Stuart century from the last years of Elizabeth's reign around 1600 until the opening years of George I's reign around 1720. It begins in the early seventeenth century with the first few discussions of coffee and coffeehouses in the English language, but for the first half of this period (c. 1600–1660) coffee was primarily noticed and consumed by a select group of English virtuosi. After the Restoration, the efflorescence of coffeehouse culture changed all of this and therefore much of the rest of the work focuses on the latter half of the "long seventeenth century." The end point of the study around the year 1720 has been chosen because by that time both the coffeehouse and coffee consumption had become firmly entrenched within British society. A social template had been set and it was not to change greatly for the next hundred years. At the same time, the 1720s saw the growing popularity of two important competitors to coffee in the English beverage market: tea and gin. The phenomenal success of tea in insinuating itself into British consumer preferences as the national drink began with the opening of the Canton trade to China on a regular basis by the English East India Company in 1717.[6] At nearly the same time, gin also took hold of the popular palate, and the 1720s are well known as the decade in which gin drinking and its regulation became the objects of intense public scrutiny.[7] The third decade of the eighteenth century did not see a great qualitative or quantitative transformation in the nature of British coffee culture, but by this time coffee and coffeehouses had been so thoroughly assimilated into the fabric of British society that they had ceased to be controversial. The Anglicization of oriental coffee was complete.

PART I

Coffee: From Curiosity to Commodity

In a letter from Aleppo, written in 1600, the clergyman William Biddulph became the first Englishman to write about coffee. He noted that the Turks' "most common drinke is Coffa, which is a blacke kinde of drinke, made of a kind of Pulse like Pease, called Coava, which being grownd in the Mill, and boiled in water, they drinke it as hot as they can suffer it." Ten years later, George Sandys put his own observations on this strange Turkish beverage in print; he found it "blacke as soote, and tasting not much unlike it." For both Biddulph and Sandys, coffee was an unfamiliar and rather unappealing drink. Along with chocolate and tea, coffee was bitter, drunk hot, and utterly unlike the ales, beers, or even the continental wines that were, as Keith Thomas put it, "built into the fabric" of pre-industrial English social life.[1] Nevertheless, these drinks had become just as tightly woven into that fabric less than even a century after Biddulph first introduced his compatriots to the mysterious Turkish drink.

Coffee is most definitely an acquired taste, as the behavioral psychologist Robert Bolles has observed:

> Coffee is one of the great, marvellous flavours. Who could deny that? Well, actually, anyone drinking coffee for the first time would deny it. Coffee is one of those things that [have been] called innately aversive. It is bitter and

characterless; it simply tastes bad the first time you encounter it. By the time
you have drunk a few thousand cups of it, you cannot live without it. Children
do not like it, uninitiated adults do not like it, rats do not like it: nobody likes
coffee except those who have drunk a fair amount of it, and they all love it.
And they will tell you it tastes good. They like a mediocre cup of coffee, they
relish a good cup of coffee, and they go into ecstasies over a superb cup of
coffee.[2]

Henry Blount made much the same observation in the 1650s, when he remarked upon how "universally [both tobacco and coffee] take with mankinde,
and yet have not the advantage of any pleasing taste wherewith to tempt and
debauch our palat, as wine and other such pernicious things have, for at the
first tobacco is most horrid, and cophie insipid, yet do they both so generally
prevail, that bread it self is not of so universall use." Drinking coffee is a habit
that must be learned and assimilated into one's dietary consumption routine in
a manner not unlike the process Howard Becker has described for marijuana
smoking.[3] Acquiring a taste for such products requires a process of socialization and habituation in which the novice user learns to make sense of, and
enjoy, their psychoactive effects and their taste.

The successful introduction of coffee into English drinking customs was by
no means an easily achieved victory. Beyond the initial strangeness of the drink
and its taste, there were also substantial entrenched interests and ideologies
that made the acceptance of coffee consumption no easy matter in the English
market. First, there was no reason for the English to look favorably upon any
new Turkish custom. In the early seventeenth century, the Ottoman Empire
was often regarded as a vehicle for the forces of the Anti-Christ, and this fear
of the Turk could occasionally be strong enough to prompt quixotic calls to
engage the Ottomans in a holy war against the infidels. Even in the later
seventeenth century, the Turks continued to be feared for their martial prow-
ess and the despotism of their political system, a view expressed even by those
who had lived and worked with the Turks for years in the service of the Levant
Company. Paul Rycaut tersely summed up his view of Turkish society by
declaring quite simply: "Tyranny is requisite for this people." Second, many
Paracelsian-inspired writers expressed a profound distrust of exotic medicines
and imported foodstuffs and argued that local products were sufficient for
English consumption. Furthermore, the dominant seventeenth-century economic paradigm of mercantilism stressed the deleterious effects of excessive
spending on foreign imports, especially nonessential "luxury" items, on the
national economy.[4]

How, then, did coffee come to be received favorably by English palates? The
answer lies in looking carefully at the significance given to the new and exotic

coffee commodity by its first seventeenth-century English consumers. Coffee is an important case to study precisely because it was a new and exotic commodity. Understanding the reasons why it gained favor with English consumers sheds light on the general expansion of early modern consumer demand that is often called the "consumer revolution." To that end, I will review and evaluate the respective merits of previous explanations for changes in consumption habits before proceeding to elaborate on the specific reasons for the successful reception of coffee in England.

The extraordinary success of coffee and other related exotic "soft drugs" in insinuating themselves into European culture between the sixteenth and the eighteenth centuries has commonly been explained through four general lines of argument: the profit-maximizing motive of neoclassical economics; social emulation theories; functionalist explanations; or subjective motivation from ideological or cultural impulses. While each of these perspectives has its own particular strengths and weaknesses, it is ultimately the subjective motivations articulated by the earliest consumers of coffee in England that provide the best means of understanding the reasons why they began to drink coffee in the first place.

Classical economics has been unconcerned with the reasons why changes occur in the demand structure of a society. Economists of this ilk rarely dare to offer a mirror into the souls of consumers, and thus they remain content to notice that a new sort of demand has in fact appeared and then proceed to chart the further consequences of the changing tastes of consumers on the rest of the economy. The impact of variables such as "custom, institutions, political power, and socialization" on demand is usually bracketed.[5] The consumer is thus presumed to be a relatively unconstrained, rational, and self-interested maximizer. The origin of demand for new commodities is really a nonproblem for the classical economist, because it is assumed that supply creates its own demand — consumer desires are infinite and thus limited only by prices and one's ability to pay them.

This is the perspective adopted by Ralph Davis in his influential studies of England's late seventeenth-century "commercial revolution." For Davis, demand for novel commodities was "created by sudden cheapness . . . which introduced the middle classes and the poor to novel habits of consumption," and this demand "once realised, was not shaken by subsequent vicissitudes in prices, but continued to grow rapidly." Similarly, Jan de Vries has noted that the late seventeenth-century rise in real wages and decrease in import prices in northwestern Europe created "favorable demand conditions" which do much to explain "the enormous expansion of tobacco, sugar, coffee, cocoa, and tea imports to Europe."[6] Demand in this view remains merely a function of price: if a commodity is cheap enough, it is assumed that purchasers will snap up more of it.

Jordan Goodman offers a variant on this line of argument in his important study of the development of the European market for tobacco in the early modern era. His account of the initial reception of tobacco stresses the profit-seeking motivation of early modern Europeans, and especially the Spanish colonizers of the New World, to find suitable medicinal substitutes for their expensive imports of oriental drugs. It was this initial drive toward import substitution, he suggests, that provided the crucial original receptiveness toward accepting new drugs like tobacco into the traditional European pharmacopoeias. Goodman's argument is particularly persuasive because he recognizes that tobacco could not have immediately served as an import substitute without first being fit into European medical paradigms. Thus he stresses that tobacco and similar exotic "soft drugs" found a European market only through a process he calls "the political economy of Europeanization," by which exotic drugs were adapted to pre-existing medical concepts and were thus made understandable and desirable to European consumers.[7] In his focus on this complementary process of "commodity indigenization," Goodman moves beyond the neoclassical assumption that demand is a natural response to the price-mediated vicissitudes of supply and seeks to explain the reasons why *any* previously unknown or exotic commodities should have been accepted by early modern consumers.

The social emulation, or "trickle-down," theories first articulated by Thorstein Veblen and Georg Simmel are akin to and compatible with the neoclassical paradigm, for they also propose to reveal rational and consistent motivations behind the apparent frivolity and vagaries of changing fashions and consumer tastes for nonessential goods.[8] The most important insight provided by these arguments is that consumer preferences are integrally related to the exercise of, and competition for, social power. Taste is recognized to be a symbolic marker of social status, and the pace of fashionable change is thought to be set by social elites, whose taste is constantly emulated by their ambitious inferiors. Elite consumption must therefore remain variable in order to prevent their tastes from being adopted wholesale by the masses.

Many historians have accepted this sort of emulation theory, and assert that exotic hot drinks such as coffee were adopted first and foremost by the upper classes and that later mass consumption was spurred by attempts to emulate elites. This view was expressed as early as the late seventeenth century by the French physician Daniel Duncan. Unfortunately, these accounts are as uninterested as the neoclassicals in exploring the reasons why certain commodities, and not others, should have been adopted by those elites in the first place. To state that "part of the initial appeal of coffee and tea was that they were novel, exotic and thus fashionable" is simply to beg the question of why coffee and tea specifically, rather than say betel nuts and marijuana — both of which were both also introduced to Europeans at about the same time as coffee and tea — first caught the fancy of the upper classes.[9]

A common means of resolving this dilemma is through postulating a certain functional "fit" between a given social order, or a social class, and its characteristic consumption habits. Such arguments focus attention on the ways in which consumption preferences reinforce a given social order or a given social identity. The strength of these arguments thus lies in their focus on the specific uses, and the cultural meanings attributed to the uses, of consumer goods.

For example, some writers have associated the appeal of the new exotics with the requirements of court societies to make extensive expenditures on luxury items as a conspicuous display of their dominant social status. This view is most forcefully expressed by Werner Sombart, and is entirely consistent with Norbert Elias's emphasis on the importance of "social display, elaborate ceremonial and virtuoso consumption" in court societies. Another variant on this theme has been offered by Piero Camporesi in his study of the culinary preferences of Italian elites in the later seventeenth and eighteenth centuries. He claims that Enlightenment culture was accompanied by "a new taste, a new poetics and a new style" in which a Baroque "poetics of hyperbole and heaping high . . . [in dietary matters] were replaced by refined sobriety and by rationally balanced and didactically pragmatic 'good taste.' " Exotic hot beverages were thus well suited for this new "enlightened" diet.[10]

Woodruff D. Smith, in contrast, has associated the success of coffee and tea with their ability to move beyond their original elite consumers and eventually become the "central material features of the emerging pattern of [bourgeois] respectability," a culture that welcomed these exotic drinks' "promotion of health, sobriety, moderation and rationality."[11] The putative sobering effects of coffee, in particular, have led many observers to associate the rise of stimulant beverages with a concomitant rise of a "bourgeois" or "capitalist" ethic.[12] Peter Stallybrass and Allon White have perhaps expressed this view most explicitly in their claim that coffee provided "a new and unexpected agency in the prolonged struggle of capitalism to discipline its work-force." Sidney Mintz's remarkable study of the changing role of sugar from elite luxury to ubiquitous staple in British consumption habits also offers a profoundly functionalist argument in its claim that industrial capitalism required both a growing consumer demand and a workforce whose diet was appropriate to the regular discipline of factory labor.[13]

The major shortcoming to these functionalist arguments is that the supposed "needs" of a given culture or social class are more often assumed than actually demonstrated or sufficiently explained. Furthermore, the wide variety of functionalist claims — in which coffee is said to have been well suited for everything from court culture to bourgeois capitalism — suggests that further explanation is required to trace the various ways in which coffee, tea, and similar new commodities were received by different consumers in different contexts. That is precisely the promise held out by the final set of arguments I want to consider: those that take seriously the subjective motivations for consumption expressed by the consumers themselves.

The most articulate and persuasive proponent of this approach to the study of consumer culture has been Colin Campbell, who has suggested that "it would seem essential to any proper process of historical explanation to accord a central role to those motives and intentions which actually served to prompt individuals to act."[14] In his own assessment of the "the spirit of modern consumerism," Campbell finds its origins most clearly in a long eighteenth-century "Romantic ethic" which legitimated consumer desire for novelties by viewing such consumption as a mode of individual soul-searching, indeed a specifically modern mode of hedonism in which "the essential activity of consumption is . . . not the actual selection, purchase or use of products, but the imaginative pleasure-seeking to which the product image lends itself." The argument self-consciously diverges from Weber's emphasis on Protestant asceticism and capitalist accumulation while also preserving a Weberian methodology in which the guiding principles of ideal typical "ethics" provide the fundamental motivation for social action.[15]

Campbell's thesis is much more ambitious than the one offered here, but the mode of argumentation is similar. Like Campbell, I am also interested in locating the ideological origins of consumer demand and I will also argue that the initial desire for new commodities like coffee came from a specific cultural ethic, or an "ideal of character." In this case, however, I want to focus this attention on a rather different sort of cultural avant-garde, seventeenth-century England's virtuoso community, and their "ethic," as it were, of curiosity.

Who were these virtuosi? The label virtuoso was Italian in origin and it referred to individuals with an interest in promoting an interest in arts and antiquities in mid-sixteenth-century Italy. The term had migrated to England by the early seventeenth century and it makes its first appearance in print in Henry Peacham's gentlemanly courtesy manual, *The Compleat Gentleman* (1634).[16] The English gentlemen who chose to identify themselves with the Italian word virtuoso were seeking to associate themselves with an international world of elite cultural interests strongly rooted in knowledge about classical antiquity and Italianate Renaissance learning. This interest in the classical past quickly expanded to encompass many more objects of inquiry. More than anything, these English virtuosi shared a distinct sensibility, a set of attitudes, habits, and intellectual preferences that they labeled "curiosity." The virtuosi held an almost limitless curiosity about the wider worlds around them. This curiosity "was an attitude of mind involving a fascination for the rare, novel, surprising and outstanding in all spheres of life," and it was the preserve of "a self-declared, cosmopolitan elite."[17] According to Walter Houghton's seminal study of the virtuosic sensibility, the virtuosi had "an insatiable appetite for the strange and the ingenious" in all things, from works of art to natural wonders and mechanical inventions. Appreciation for the novel and the bizarre thus constituted an identifiable "aesthetic of rarity" with its own discourse and its own codes of sociability and individual conduct that clearly defined the members of this international community. Intellectual curiosity and an admiration for the rarities of art and nature were considered by the virtuosi "to be an outright virtue and an essential quality of the cultivated gentleman."[18] Collecting these rarities from all over the world and developing a body of knowledge about them became the primary activities that defined virtuoso culture. As we shall see, coffee was one of the curiosities that captured the fancy of England's virtuoso community.

Virtuoso culture was formed at the margins of the English social elite. It owed much to the cosmopolitan ideals and rigid codes of civility and politeness that were characteristic of the Renaissance courts, but the English virtuosi, unlike their continental brethren, were not courtiers. The two founding fathers, as it were, of English virtuosity were Thomas Howard, the fourteenth earl of Arundel, whose stoic tastes and religious proclivities alienated him from the courts of the early Stuart monarchs, and Francis Bacon, an ambitious courtier under James I whose career was famously cut short by impeachment before the House of Commons in 1621. After Bacon's fall, his fellow travelers in the pursuit of the advancement of new learning would shirk from seeking too much solace in the world of Whitehall. Although the Royal Society, which became the primary focus for the social and intellectual life of the English virtuosi in the later seventeenth century, obviously gloried in its royal charter, the fellows did not see themselves as primarily courtiers, but rather as independent and universal champions of the pursuit of true knowledge.[19]

As with the courts, so it was with the universities. It was part of the very character of a virtuoso to be learned and wise without being pedantic or scholarly. The education of a virtuoso ideally occurred in an academy or with a private tutor, and it was never confined to the subjects taught at the universities.

John Evelyn found "it is impossible to redeeme [the universities] from pedantry, for want of that addresse and refinement of a more generous conversation."[20] And since breadth of knowledge and catholicity of interest were paramount, virtuosity tended to value the quantity of one's learning over the quality. This meant that a virtuoso was often open to being criticized for dilettantism. Thomas Shadwell's play *The Virtuoso* (1676) was only the most popular of a persistent series of satiric attacks on the frivolity and uselessness of virtuoso pursuits such as collecting curiosities and performing scientific experiments.[21] The physician and polemicist Henry Stubbe scoffed at the naiveté of the foreign inquiries and armchair speculations made by the incipient Royal Society, calling them "newe speculators" with little experience of foreign lands or cultures.[22] The virtuosi would remain the butt of many jokes throughout the Augustan era, especially as they became embroiled in the war of high culture fought between the ancients and the moderns. The advocates of polite antiquity valued "classical" standards of beauty and rhetoric above all, whereas the "modern" virtuosi preferred to apply their inelegant, but exhaustive, scholarship in an effort to establish true knowledge. At issue were not only what should be acceptable standards of taste in literature and science, but also the values of genteel culture as a whole. In such a contest, an earnest but rhetorically challenged virtuoso such as Dr. John Woodward was no match for the satiric skills of Jonathan Swift, Alexander Pope, and their fellow Scriblerians.[23]

Even modern scholars have shared some of the scorn that the Augustan wits heaped upon the virtuosi, as they lament the unfortunate coexistence of "a Baconian impulse to instructiveness and utility and a proneness to inconclusiveness and frivolous curiosity" which demeaned the "more serious aspects" of virtuoso learning. Thus Houghton concluded that the ultimate purpose behind the virtuosic sensibility was not the advancement of learning in any real sense, but simply the advancement of a gentleman's social reputation, and Robert Frank, Jr., defined the Oxford virtuosi as "men who did little original scientific work themselves, but were eager participants in, and followers of, the activities of their more gifted peers." Frank's virtuosi were not real scientists, but merely fellow travelers. A very different perspective on this question has been offered by Steven Shapin, who has argued convincingly that, far from being in any way opposed to the "real" work of scientific learning, gentlemanly codes of conduct and modes of sociability provided the necessary foundations upon which such work was accomplished and made credible.[24] What is often lost from view in this argument, however, is the way in which the prestige which accrued from the pursuit of scientific endeavors could in itself become a means by which one might stake out a claim to gentlemanly status. For Samuel Pepys, for example, virtuosic curiosity might provide an entryway into the rites of gentlemanly sociability rather than merely being the end product of those rites.

It is, after all, only through the benefit of hindsight that we are allowed to distinguish the unserious dilettantes from the committed champions of the advancement of learning: all virtuosi professed such a commitment, and Baconian empirical investigation was by its very nature unfocused. It did, however, establish an important "ideal of factuality," as Lorraine Daston has argued, in which each piece of evidential datum could be valued in itself as a "nugget of experience" entirely "detached from theory." And it was this ideal which "stamped the characteristic new methods of science that emerged with the culmination of the Scientific Revolution."[25] It should be no wonder, then, that the most detailed attention to virtuoso culture has come from the ranks of historians of science.[26]

Economic historians might also usefully explore the mental world of England's virtuosi. For along with all of their professions of allegiance to the reformation of learning, the virtuosi also consistently insisted upon the practical and utilitarian aims of their endeavors. Elias Ashmole stated that he donated his famous collection of curiosities to Oxford University "because the knowledge of Nature is very necessarie to humane life, health, and the conveniences thereof . . . and to this [end], is requisite the inspection of Particulars, especially those as are extraordinary in their Fabrick, or useful in Medicine, or applyed to Manufacture or Trade." Similarly, John Evelyn answered those who thought the Royal Society and the new science wasted time in frivolous pursuits by declaring, "there is nothing meane in nature, nor has she produced any thing in vaine."[27] It was the responsibility of the scientific virtuoso to discover the purposes, and the uses, behind all of nature's various "particulars." Such discoveries would, of course, result in a substantial and steady augmentation of the wealth of the nation.

This was indeed a major theme of Charles Webster's important work, *The Great Instauration* (1975), although even Webster attributed the utilitarian focus of the neo-Baconian scientists to their supposed puritanism rather than to their virtuosity. Webster found it hard to take the virtuosi seriously, and he tried to clearly distinguish "the traditional motives of self-interest and gentlemanly curiosity" of the "orthodox virtuosi" from the committed humanitarian utopianism of his puritan Baconians—a view which ironically replicates the contemporary critique of the virtuosi as "gentleman dabblers." Yet Webster's study—especially his account of the projects and ideals of the Hartlib circle—provides important insights for the history of early modern economic culture.[28] These proponents of the new science were extremely interested in the economic implications of their studies, and they called for the increased exploitation of what they regarded as the "natural wealth of the earth," legal reforms to assist the development of native industries, and a more centralized means of collection and distribution of economic information, most notably through the establishment of an "Office of Address" and the compilation of a history of trades.[29] Such concerns remained high on the agenda of the founding members of the Royal Society.[30]

It was the virtuosi who led the way in spurring consumer interest in coffee. The virtuoso travelers and, even more so, the virtuoso readers of travel literature and accounts of the commodities of exotic cultures, were the first Englishmen to learn about, write about, and indeed to drink coffee. Furthermore, many virtuosi publicized and promoted the widespread use of the new commodity, even when its medical virtues were called into question by neo-Paracelsian dictates against the use of exotic drugs and its consumption was disapproved by mercantilists afraid of excessive foreign imports. Without the culture of virtuosity to nurture it in its infancy, coffee drinking may have remained little more than an odd Turkish habit with only a few English practitioners.

The chapters in this section detail the gradual development of a commercial interest in coffee. The story begins with the virtuoso discovery of coffee in the early seventeenth century and the gradual acceptance of the drink by the English medical community in the latter part of the century. In the second chapter, we look at the peculiarly positive reception of coffee as an exotic, mood-altering substance in the medical marketplace of early modern England. Coffee succeeded where many other foreign drugs failed. Due to the particular ways in which it was originally endorsed by the virtuosi, coffee gained a valuable reputation as a sober alternative to the alcoholic drinks that had dominated English drinking habits up to the mid-seventeenth century. Coffee's journey from an object of virtuoso curiosity to a valued international commodity ends with the reception of coffee by the English overseas trading community. English merchants in the Levant and the Indian Ocean region did not go abroad seeking the profit potential of new and hitherto unknown commodities. For this reason, they were slow to recognize that coffee could be a valued addition to their trade. Chapter 3 studies the ways in which coffee gradually insinuated itself into the mercantilist mindset of the early modern British trading community.

By tracing the complex reception of coffee by a wide variety of people in early modern Britain, we can better understand the nature of economic culture in the period. Economic activities are never separate from other social relationships, and historians of the early modern economy have come to realize just how important nonmonetary conceptions of value such as credit, honor, and trustworthiness were in a world in which there was not enough monetary specie to mediate all of the exchanges of goods and services required in the early modern marketplace.[31] We will never understand the success of coffee through econometric analyses alone. Coffee did not automatically find a place in the British economy simply because overseas merchants developed the capacity to buy it abroad and bring it back to Britain for sale at an affordable price. A market for the commodity had to be created; consumer demand for it had to be stimulated. Coffee became a desirable commodity because it successfully adapted to the various wants and needs of diverse constituencies in the British marketplace.

An Acquired Taste

The Discovery of Coffee: Virtuoso Travelers

The first printed reference to coffee in a European text occurred in a medical text by the French scholar Carolus Clusius (or Charles de l'Écluse in his vernacular) entitled *Aromatum et simplicium aliquot medica-mentorum apud Indos nascientum historia* (1575). Clusius himself had learned of coffee several years before, perhaps as early as 1568, when his fellow botanist Alphoncius Pansius in Padua described the strange new plant in a letter along with some sample seeds. At nearly the same time that Clusius was introducing the coffee plant to the European medical community, the German physician Leonhard Rauwolf was traveling in the Levant in search of the foreign and exotic plants he had read about in the works of Theophrastus, Pliny the Elder, and Galen during his education at the University of Montpellier. In the introduction to the account of his travels titled *Aigentliche Beschreibung der Raiss inn die Morgenlaender* (1583), Rauwolf stated, "from my infancy I alwaies had a great desire to travel into foreign parts, and to enquire out learned and famous men, that I might get something out of them to encrease my stock of knowledge." This desire was later directed toward the Levant when he learned from his texts that "several rare plants of great use in physick . . . were said to grow in Greece, Syria, and Arabia, &c. . . . and from thence" he claimed, "I was enflamed with a vehement desire to search out, and view such plants growing spontaneously in their native places, and propounded also to my self to observe the life, conversation, customs, manners, and religion of the inhabitants of those countries."[1] Rauwolf's journey was funded by his brother-in-law, Melchior Manlich, a prominent Augsburg merchant whose firm was already involved in the Levant trade and wanted Rauwolf to return with information about Eastern "drugs and simples, and other things convenient and profitable for his trade."[2] The result was his extremely well-received *Aigentliche Beschreibung,* a travel narrative in which he claimed to include only "what I have seen, experienc'd, observ'd and handl'd my self." His narrative also follows the pilgrimage trope inspired by the travels of Galen, "the proto-type of the physician traveler," that was a common refrain in the writings of the *curiosi.*[3] Rauwolf's professed Wanderlust, his familiarity with the ancient authorities on exotic materia medica, his desire to verify these texts with his own experience, and finally his close relationship with the overseas merchant community all were characteristic of the English virtuosi.

Rauwolf's work was indeed well known by the English virtuosi. Although it was not translated into English until 1693, and the only printed copy was to be found in the Arundelian Library at Gresham College, various manuscript copies of it had been available long before that, and the work was used as an important authority by English botanists. The Gresham copy of the book was in high demand among the members of the Royal Society, as Dr. Daniel Cox learned when he raised the ire of his fellows by borrowing the work from the library without returning it for nearly two years.[4]

In this work, they found the first description by a European of coffee drinking and the social rituals surrounding it in Ottoman culture. The Turks, Rauwolf observed, "have a very good Drink, by them called *chaube* (coffee), that is almost as black as ink, and very good in illness, chiefly that of the stomach." Rauwolf's observations on coffee were soon to be accompanied by those of nearly every other traveler to the Ottoman, Persian, and Mughal empires of the early seventeenth century.[5] Europeans first learned about coffee in travel narratives that described the exotic customs of the peoples living in the large "oriental" empires of Asia. These early reports about coffee and the social rituals surrounding its consumption made it appear at once both strange and familiar. While they expressed wonder at the notion of drinking a dishful of a hot black liquor, the travel writers inevitably attempted to draw comparisons between coffee consumption and more familiar European drink culture, especially the alcohol-centered rituals of the tavern or the alehouse.

A common refrain was the bitter and unpleasant taste of the coffee drink itself. Adam Olearius described "a certain black water, which [the Persians] call *cahwa,* made of a fruit brought out of *Ægypt,* and which is in colour like ordinary wheat, and in tast like Turkish Wheat, and is of the bigness of a little bean. . . . They make this drink thereof, which hath as it were the tast of a burnt crust, and is not pleasant to the palate." George Manwaring found coffee to be "nothing toothsome, nor hath any good smell," but he admitted "it is very wholesome," and similar remarks may be found in the accounts of Thomas Herbert and James Howell.[6] Because these travelers could not recognize the tastefulness of coffee, the salutary effects of the drink were emphasized instead as the primary reason for consuming it. William Lithgow thought coffee was "good to expell the cruditie of raw meates." William Finch believed coffee was "good for the head and stomacke," and Herbert was told by the Persians that "it expels melancholy, purges choler, [and] begets mirth." Some, like William Parry, thought coffee drinking "will intoxicate the brain, like our Methleglin,"[7] a spiced sort of mead of Welsh origin, often used for medicinal purposes.

The most familiar analogy made was in fact one between coffee and the alcoholic drinks of Europe. The coffeehouses of Asia were sometimes likened to European taverns or English alehouses, and Samuel Hartlib called the earliest English coffeehouse a "Turkish alehouse."[8] But the coffee consumed there was often mentioned with, and compared to, other well-known but exotic psychoactive drugs in these travel narratives. Herbert noted that the Persians commonly drank their coffee along with "tobacco suckt through water," and this led him to observe that they also commonly used opium. There is substantial evidence to suggest that Turkish coffeehouses were indeed popular centers of opium consumption. George Sandys thought that the Turks took opium because they are "giddy headed, and turbulent dreamers," and he added, "perhaps for the selfe-same cause they also delight in Tobacco." Along with these accounts of intoxicated fantasies, travel writers often noted that the Asian coffeehouses were centers of licentious behavior: the Turkish "Coffamen" kept "beautiful boyes, who serve as stales to procure them customers," and the Persian coffeehouses "keep young boys: in some houses they have a dozen, some more, some less; they keep them very gallant in apparel; these boys are called Bardashes, which they do use in their beastly manner, instead of women."[9]

These stories reinforced traditional European beliefs, obtained primarily from a familiarity with ancient Roman writings on the Asian origins of corrupt vices, in the luxurious, effeminate, and corrupt nature of oriental societies. Yet they also echoed another well-entrenched trope, the public "tippling" house as a source of vice and unwholesome social gatherings. The association was so clear that Robert Burton declared that the "Turkes in their Coffa-houses, which much resemble our Tavernes . . . will labour hard all day long to be drunk at night . . . in a tippling feast."[10] The "curious-ness" of coffee and coffee consumption lay in the ways in which the drink and the means of drinking it were bizarre to customary European sensibilities and yet nevertheless ultimately recognizable as akin to those same sensibilities.

But what was the purpose behind these accounts of unfamiliar Asian drinking customs? Did the writers intend merely to titillate their readers with stories of foreign vices and oddities, or did they have a different, perhaps pedagogical, aim? The literature of exotic travel in the early modern era differed from that of the Middle Ages, which was filled with fabulous tales of the exotic creatures and opulent wealth which were thought to be abundant in the orient. The new exotic travel literature also failed to follow the predominant themes of standard English virtuoso travel literature, which served as veritable guides for prospective virtuoso grand tourists and thus focused on the more accessible travel sites in France and Italy above all, as well as Germany or the Low Countries. But there was no such thing as an oriental grand tour, a fact well known to Thomas Browne when he told his son, "beleeve it, no excursion into Pol[and], Hung[ary], or Turkey addes advantage or reputation unto a scholar."[11] So the exotic travel narratives were concerned less with adumbrating the proper etiquette governing polite sociability abroad than with demonstrating the usefulness of the information they conveyed to the advancement of learning and the promotion of the national interest.

Henry Blount claimed that he set out on his Turkish travels in order to gain a better understanding of "humane affaires," which he thought "advances best, in observing of people, whose institutions much differ from ours; for customes conformable to our owne, or to such wherewith we are already acquainted, doe but repeat our old observations, with little acquist of new." He desired to find out for himself whether "the Turkish way appeare absolutely barbarous, as we are given to understand, or rather an other kinde of civilitie, different from ours, but no lesse pretending." After enjoying the hospitality of his Turkish guests, which included an introduction to the practice of coffee drinking, Blount's conclusions inclined toward the latter. Thus one should not find it too surprising that upon Blount's return to England he became one of the earliest proponents of coffee drinking, and a habitué of the first coffeehouses. Indeed, John Aubrey wrote that Blount "dranke nothing but water or coffee."[12]

Others could find an even loftier purpose in distant travel. Thomas Coryate's translation of Hermanus Kirchnerus's remarkable oration in praise of travel invoked the justification of divine providence:

> [God] hath by his divine will & heavenly providence so disposed this Universe, and so prudently distinguished it with that admirable diversity & order,

that one country is more fruitfull then others; so that in one and the selfe same reigon all and the same things do not grow: as Arabia is more plentitfull of Frankinsence and spices then other countries; one territory yeeldeth plenty of wine, another of corne, another greater store of other things. . . . So also those copious and admirable wits, so arts, sciences, and disciplines, which make us more human, or rather more divine, are not included in one place, in one province, or one house . . . but are divided and dispersed throughout the whole compass of the earth. . . . If we will be partakers of these such exellent gifts, covet to enjoy these so great riches and delights, and desire to be beautified with these so singular ornaments of learning, we must needs undertake journeyes & long voyages to those renowned places, wherein this fragrancy and most heavenly plenty doth harbor.[13]

This was a contentious position, for providence could just as well be invoked to justify the self-sufficiency of each land's natural provisions. But Kirchnerus's defense of cosmopolitan learning and the benefits of international commerce provided sufficient justification to those virtuosi and merchants who desired to seek out the diversity of natural and artificial goods beyond the seas.

John Davies's dedication of the translation of Olearius to the Russia Company similarly invoked the economic benefits that might accrue from a knowledge of foreign cultures and exotic commodities "in as much as this Kingdom, especially this City [i.e., London], begins to disperse its industrious inhabitants, and spread the wings of its trade into the most remote cantons of the world."[14] In the eyes of their authors, the proto-ethnographies of the exotic travel narratives were both "curious" and potentially useful, perhaps even profitable to the wealth of the nation.

Exotica and the Advancement of Learning

Knowledge of foreign, and especially exotic, cultures was central to virtuoso culture. Rarities from overseas, especially the Americas or the East Indies, were de rigueur in any serious virtuoso cabinet of curiosities, and the customs and commodities of exotic peoples were the subject of many a cabinet conversation or an epistolary disquisition. Although a cynically formalist understanding of the virtuoso fascination with the exotic might well emphasize that the primary function of these items and the knowledge about them was simply to provide plentiful opportunities for the virtuoso gentleman to show off the breadth of his learning, and indeed the genuineness of his curiosity, to his peers, we should not ignore the professions of the virtuosi themselves of their commitment to an ultimately utilitarian project for the advancement of learning and the national interest.

A major source of inspiration for the virtuosic interest in exotic cultures and their commodities lay, as with so many other aspects of virtuoso culture, in the writings of Francis Bacon.[15] Bacon's vision of a comprehensive natural history, which came to dominate his thinking toward the end of his life, stressed the need for the diligent collection of reliable observations about the products and workings of the natural world. Such a natural history therefore required extensive knowledge of the plants and commodities of exotic cultures. The strangest data were indeed the best, as "Baconian facts were handpicked for their recalcitrance, anomalies that undermined superficial classifications and exceptions that broke glib rules." The utopian Salomon's House described in Bacon's *New Atlantis* (1627) contained "dispensatories, or shops of medicines" which held "such variety of plants and living creatures more than you have in Europe." The breweries and kitchens also contained "drinks brewed with several herbs, and roots, and spices . . . some of the drinks are such, as they are in effect meat and drink both," as chocolate was said to be. Other foods there allowed men to fast for long periods of time.[16]

Travel writings were an important source of data for Bacon's natural histories. He tried to incorporate as much information as he could about every new exotic drug or commodity that he was aware of into his encyclopedic accounts in the *Sylva Sylvarum* (1627) and the *Historia Vitae et Mortis* (1638). Many of these were classified together: coffee, betel roots and leaves, tobacco, and opium Bacon thought were all "medicines that condense and relieve the spirits" even though "they are taken after several manners," coffee and opium being consumed as liquids, tobacco as smoke, and betel by chewing. He was impressed by the reports that the Turks claimed that coffee drinking "doth not a little sharpen them both in their courage and in their wits." Although "if it be taken in a large quantity, it affects and disturbs the mind; whereby it is manifest," Bacon concluded, coffee "is of the same nature with opiates." Noting that the Greeks, the Arabians, and the Turks all commended the use of such opiates for medicinal purposes, and that they may be conducive to "the prolongation of life," through "condensing the spirits," he thought it advisable that opiates be consumed at least once a year after adolescence.[17]

Bacon's immediate successors seem to have agreed with him as well. Edward Jorden cited the authority of Lord Bacon in recommending the use of hot drinks "both for the preservation of health, and for cure of many diseases" in his 1633 tract on the medicinal use of natural baths and mineral waters. John Parkinson's *Theatrum Botanicum* (1640), "the last great English herbal," incorporated the coffee plant for the first time into English botanical studies. In his last section, devoted to "strange and rare plants," Parkinson included an entry on "the Turkes berry drinke," coffee. His account was based on previous writings on the plant by Rauwolf, by Prosper Alpinus, a Venetian botanist, and by Paldanus's commentaries on the English translation of the Dutch traveler Jan Huygen van Linschoten's narrative of his observations in the East Indies. Parkinson also managed to add a plate containing the first pictorial representation of the coffee plant in an English work. This image would soon find itself repeated in numerous later natural histories of coffee (Figures 1 and 2). Parkinson concluded that the coffee drink "hath many good physical properties therein: for it strengtheneth a weake stomacke, helping digestion, and the tumours and obstructions of the liver and spleene, being drunke fasting for some time together."[18]

Walter Rumsey, who was a judge in Wales and a virtuoso in his own right, published a small pamphlet in 1657 entitled *Organon Salutis* which promoted the medicinal use of coffee in the form of an "electuary." This concoction consisted of a thick paste full of honey and coffee powder which was to be ingested so as "to make the stomach more apt to vomit, and to prepare the humors thereunto before you eat and drink." Rumsey realized that his method of taking coffee differed from the Turkish drink, but he thought the electuary a "less loathsome and troublesome" means of taking the medicine.[19] Clearly, Rumsey had not yet learned to relish coffee for its own sake, but rather saw it as an alternative to the harsher purgatives often prescribed by apothecaries. Rumsey's book on coffee met with great approval from the virtuoso community of mid-seventeenth-century England. It was published with prefatory letters of praise from the virtuoso travelers Henry Blount and James Howell and was highly commended by the gregarious virtuoso John Aubrey. Readers of the flourishing Interregnum national press were likely to happen upon the advertisements for Rumsey's work. Indeed, demand for the book was sufficient to warrant the printing of a second edition just two years after its initial publication as well as a third edition in 1667.[20] Howell's letter to Rumsey elaborated on remarks on coffee he had originally made in a familiar letter of 1632 to the Lord Cliff; here Howell reiterated the benefits that may accrue from a curiosity about, and judicious imitation of, the consumer habits of foreign lands: "Surely [coffee] must needs be salutiferous, because so many sagacious, and the wittiest sort of nations use it so much; as they who have conversed with Shashes and Turbants doe well know." Although Howell also concurred with George Sandys's hypothesis that the first coffee drinkers were in fact the ancient Spartans, who were said to have imbibed a "black broth" in Plutarch's *Alcibiades* and other classical texts.[21]

At the same time that Rumsey was promoting the medicinal virtues of coffee, oriental scholars at Oxford were also engaged in investigating the properties of the plant and the drink. Edward Pococke, who had been

Arbor Bon cum fructu suo Buna.
Turkes berry drinke.

Figure 1. Coffee, the "Turkes Berry Drink" (1640). This was the first illustration of the coffee plant in an English text. Engraved woodcut in Parkinson, *Theatrum Botanicum* (1640), 1623; Beinecke shelfmark Si8 0185. Courtesy of the Beinecke Rare Book and Manuscript Library, Yale University.

appointed by William Laud to hold the first chair in Arabic at Oxford University in 1636, translated and published an Arabic manuscript by Dawud ibn Umar Antaki entitled *The Nature of the Drink Kahui, or Coffe* (1659). Pococke may have been encouraged to complete this translation at the behest of the distinguished Oxford physician William Harvey, who was a great admirer of Turkish culture and, according to Aubrey, "was wont to drinke coffee; which

Of Coffee. 9

The Coffee Tree.

The Inſtrument.

Figure 2. Coffee tree and coffee grinder (1685). Engraved woodcut in Dufour, *Manner of Making of Coffee, Tea, and Chocolate* (1685), 9; Beinecke shelfmark UvL12 C6 685. Courtesy of the Beinecke Rare Book and Manuscript Library, Yale University.

he and his brother Eliab did, before Coffee-houses were in fashion in London." Harvey himself was probably introduced to coffee through his family's engagement in the Levant and East India trades.[22] Pococke's translation allowed for the assimilation of coffee into the humoral paradigm of Galenic medicine, as it identified the natural properties of coffee to be both hot and dry in the second degree, thus indicating that it shared the properties of both food and medicines. Indeed, the text claimed that coffee "allayes the ebullition of the blood, is good against the small poxe and measles, and bloudy pimples; yet causeth vertiginous headache, and maketh lean much, occasioneth waking . . . and asswageth lust."[23] The existence of this Arabic precedent, which was both accessible via orientalist scholars like Pococke and comprehensible due to the shared Galenism of orthodox medicine in the Arabic and European traditions, allowed for the speedy assimilation of coffee into the English materia medica.

Oxford was in fact the location for the first coffeehouse in the British Isles, which was opened in 1650 by a Jew named Jacob, and called by him the Angel. According to Anthony Wood, it was frequented "by some who delighted in noveltie," and thereafter became a favorite haunt for many of the university's scholars. Some coffee may well have consumed privately for some time in Oxford before this time, however, for John Evelyn recorded in his manuscript memoirs that around the year 1637 "there came . . . [to Balliol College, Oxford] one Nathaniel Conopios out of Greece . . . and was the first that I ever saw drink caffè, not heard of then in England, nor til many yeares after made a common entertainement all over the nation."[24] But until the 1650s, it remained a curious and difficult-to-obtain drink, which was valued more for its medicinal properties than for its taste.

Thomas Willis, who had begun his medical practice at Oxford in the 1640s and 1650s, seems to have been introduced to the medicinal potentials of coffee in this milieu. His own eyewitness observations of the effects of coffee on his patients led him to break with Bacon's original classification of the plant with other opiates, and caused him instead to identify coffee with sobriety rather than intoxication: "There is almost none but understands well enough by experience its efficacy and virtue for the driving away of sleep," he declared, and added that he found it "highly efficacious for the driving away the Narcosis or stupefyingness." For "as to the affects of the brain or nervous stock," Willis claimed, "I do frequently prescribe this drink sooner than any thing else for their cure, and therefore am wont to send the sick to the coffee houses sooner than to the apothecaries shops."[25]

Although Oxford, with its unique combination of orientalist scholarship and a vibrant experimental scientific community, seems to have provided the most fertile ground for introducing coffee consumption to Britain, it was not confined there for long. A coffeehouse had been opened in London by 1652, and the national English virtuoso community began to eagerly investigate the properties of this strange new beverage. In 1654, Samuel Hartlib had noted in his "Ephemerides," a collection of useful and curious information that he shared with his correspondents, the erection of "a cuphye-house or a Turkish, as it were ale-house . . . neere the Old Exchange [in London]. It is a Turkish kind of drink made of water and some berry or Turkish beane. . . . It is somewhat hot and unpleasant but a good after relish and caused breaking of wind in abundance."[26] Hartlib also copied Pococke's translation in manuscript form, having received it from Robert Boyle. Since Pococke would "suffer very few [copies] to be printed," presumably because his translation had not been originally intended for an extra-university audience, Hartlib took it upon himself to circulate the manuscript to those virtuosi who were curious about the new drink, such as John Worthington at Cambridge. Hartlib was clearly providing a valued service to the republic of letters, for the translation continued to be in high demand among the curious even more than a decade later, as the Hamburg physician Martin Vogel and the Oxford mathematician John Wallis each tried to obtain copies from Henry Oldenburg. Wallis thought the work was important enough to the European scholarly community at large that he undertook to translate Pococke's English rendition into Latin.[27]

Perhaps the most enthusiastic virtuoso of Hartlib's circle was the Herefordshire gentleman John Beale. Beale was deeply interested in botanical and hortulan affairs and wrote a short book entitled *Herefordshire Orchards* (1657), but he also maintained a sustained correspondence on these matters with Hartlib, John Evelyn, Robert Boyle, and the Royal Society. In a letter to Hartlib, Beale remarked that "the Turkish Coffa, which is soe much praysed by my Lord Bacon . . . is nowe brought into public sale." He thought that the speedy publication of the receipts for making coffee, Turkish sherbet, and "other wholsome drinkes" should be undertaken in order "to advance your publique informations in Oeconomics" — a probable reference to Hartlib's plans for an Office of Address. Beale expressed his hope that "this variety . . . may bee a meanes to put drunkennes out of countenance, which is in thiese wilde parts too prevalent," for he thought "T'were better wee were somewhat desultory in the choice of divers kinds of drinkes, then immoderate in adhering to the excesse in any one kind."[28] Beale thought that expanding the horizons of the English diet was an integral part of the Baconian program for the reconquest of nature. He told William Brereton,

> I lately had it under my pen to shewe some [hundreds] of kinds of rich, pleasant or wholesome drinkes, and more kind of bread and foode (for many parts of the world doe scarsely use bread at all) cordiall, nutritive, and vigorous, which might bee made of rootes, plants and other supplyes. And this is a part of Lord Verulams [i.e., Francis Bacon's] directions, and belong to the amplification of Gods Table for the releefe of Mankinde. But I see, that some are apt enough to prosecute this argument faster than my pen can direct it. Witnesse. Coffa, Thee &c. And wee see that smoke is become an aliment entertainment, and the meanes to sustaine the livelihood of many millions, and many newly planted nations. In this I see the Mystery of Gods providen-

tiall expedition in increaseing knowledge, commerce, and mutuall accommodations, all over the world.

Beale's endorsement of the expansion of knowledge about, and consumption of, new foodstuffs from overseas was attenuated by a mercantilist apprehension about the increasing reliance on foreign imports.[29]

The answer for Beale lay in the project of imperial expansion, and especially the establishment of tropical plantations that could supply the new commodities directly to the English metropole. "For thiese curiosityes are but a wantonesse in England, but a reliefe in a forreigne plantation," he averred to Hartlib, adding, "I should rather wish our supply [of coffee came] from our owne plantations, than from Turkye," whereby "our vanityes & luxury by Gods providence, are diverted to sustaine our forreigne brethren." Thus he urged that attempts be made to grow the coffee plant in the three plantations of New England, Virginia, and Jamaica. This theme echoed the earlier proposals of Benjamin Worsley, another fellow traveler in Hartlib's circle and the principal architect of the first Navigation Act.[30] Beale continued to press the issue after the Restoration as a Fellow of the Royal Society, when he urged investigating the possibilities of transplanting East Indian plants to the West Indies, as well as attempting the cultivation of new foreign plants on English soil. The worthiness of this mercantilist enterprise was, Beale thought, obvious to all save perhaps "the gallants of Covent Garden," from whom he feared "the greatest obstructions . . . by their debaucheries and apishness."[31] For the fashionable, nothing but the truly foreign and truly exotic would do to keep themselves à la mode, and no colonial substitutes could suffice.

These sorts of projects and inquiries were in fact central to the activities of the early Royal Society, the consummate gentleman's club for England's virtuosi. High on the agenda of the first fellows was an attempt to gather as much data as possible on the bizarre aspects of the natural world overseas. The society coordinated a series of queries which were then sent to merchants, mariners, and other fellow travelers resident abroad. The point of these investigations was the Baconian one of compiling the data necessary for "a Natural History in general," which would include especially "what is to be observ'd in the production, growth, advancing, or transformation of vegetables."[32] The fellows also wished to receive further confirmation of the accounts they had read in travel literature in order to distinguish true curiosities "from fictitious and ungrounded wonders, and give to discreet philosophers true matter of fact to exercise their reason upon." The reliability of travel narratives was, as Steven Shapin has argued, crucial to doing any substantial natural history in an age when long-distance travel was not easy.[33]

One of the objects of the Royal Society's inquiry was coffee as well as other exotic drugs and commodities. The question of possible harmful side effects of coffee drinking had been raised in a paper presented to the Society (apparently at the request of the king) by Dr. Jonathan Goddard, and it occasioned some debate among the fellows thereafter. Perhaps to resolve the issue, Dr. Harpur, a physician resident in Aleppo, was asked by the Fellows of the Society whether he could verify from his observations of the Turks whether the overconsumption of coffee could lead to apoplectic fits or paralysis. Although Harpur apparently never responded to the query, Paul Rycaut, a Levant Company factor in Smyrna, wrote to Henry Oldenburg, the Secretary for the Society, about the medicinal properties of coffee in skeptical terms. "Coffee is observed to work little effect," he noted, "especially in those that use it most, and yet because most Turks dye with a paine in the stomach, many physitians attribute it to their excesse in coffee, which drank in great quantity foules and bakes in the pit, or peslorus of the stomach."[34]

The coffee plant and its berries were themselves considered to be rarities worthy of the Society's collections, although they were unable to obtain a living specimen or even its seeds. The monopolist practices of the Arabian coffee merchants stood in the way of the advancement of learning in this respect. Dr. Tankred Robinson complained that "the Arabians are as careful in destroying the germinating faculty of the coffee fruit or seed . . . as the Dutch of the Moluccas are in their nutmegs." Research sailed ahead nevertheless; Anton van Leeuwenhoek began to scrutinize the structure of the coffee bean under the lens of his microscope, and the Society was soon treated to his discourse on the properties of the coffee bean and the best way to make an excellent cup of coffee. Leeuwenhoek's report was further augmented by even more detailed studies made by Richard Waller and Hans Sloane, the latter eventually being published in the Society's *Philosophical Transactions*.[35]

Perhaps the greatest coffee enthusiast in the Royal Society was John Houghton, an apothecary by trade who was also a coffee and tea merchant as well as a publishing entrepreneur; he is probably best known as the founder of the innovative financial weekly, *A Collection for Improvement of Husbandry and Trade* (1692–1703). In 1699, Houghton published his own "Discourse of Coffee" in the *Philosophical Transactions* which purported to give a history of the early coffee trade in England along with a natural history of the plant. Houghton also included an account of "the political uses of coffee," which amounted to an endorsement of the coffee trade for the economic benefits it brought to the kingdom. He focused especially on the value of the re-export trade in coffee and the ways in which increased coffee consumption had contributed to the growth in the trades of several related commodities, including "tobacco and pipes, earthen dishes, tin wares, news-papers, coals, candles, sugar, tea, chocolate and what not?" This was due, he recognized, to the ways in which the coffeehouse had developed as a central institution for the consumption of coffee and complementary goods as well. Thus, Houghton concluded, the "coffee-house makes all sorts of people sociable, they improve arts, and merchandize, and all other knowledge."[36]

Houghton could at times become overzealous in his advocacy of the benefits resulting from increased consumption of coffee and other luxury goods. Upon reading Houghton's article in the *Transactions,* John Evelyn recalled indignantly how "The author of this discourse did seriously [en]traite with me to ingage some greate persons to perswade the late Queene [Mary], to take tobacco, which by her example would bring it to be taken by all the women in England, [and thus] advance the publiq Revenu to a mighty improvement." Evelyn could not have approved of this scheme, for he had elsewhere lamented that the government fisc had been "reduc'd . . . to such streites, that smoke, & exotic drinks, were the greatest branches of the revenue."[37] Both Houghton and Evelyn undoubtedly exaggerated the importance of the coffee excise to the national treasury, but their concerns are indicative of the ways in which the new exotic consumables had become linked to the monetary sinews of power in the minds of England's virtuosi by the close of the seventeenth century.

By the late 1600s, virtuoso curiosity about the exotic was no longer mere idle speculation, and commodities like coffee were no longer just topics fit for cabinet banter. Coffeehouses had become a central fixture of London life, and they no longer catered exclusively to the esoteric tastes of a few odd gentlemen and scholars, as Jacob's in Oxford had done. As the strange had become familiar, so had the early centrality of virtuosity to the English understanding of coffee now become peripheral.

That the virtuosi were clearly fascinated by coffee and other exotic commodities appears indubitable, and some might even think it all too obvious. Travel literature and similar accounts of foreign lands would naturally be where we would expect to find the first references to new and exotic substances such as coffee, tea, and tobacco because these travelers were indeed the first people to witness the consumption of these products and they would be expected to make comments upon them. Yet we have seen that the actual comments made by these travelers were shaped by the discursive conventions and rhetorical expectations of virtuoso culture. The ever-curious virtuosi were the primary readers of these travel narratives and they were the ones who recognized the potential medical and ultimately, the commercial, significance of the new exotics.

One might wonder, if the virtuosi were so important in developing the initial market for coffee in Britain, why coffee drinking also took hold in other countries as well. Coffee consumption had begun in Venice well before it did in England, while France and the Netherlands also developed a small market for coffee almost contemporaneously with their neighbors across the channel. By 1700 it was known throughout central Europe.[38] Virtuosity was also a Europe-wide phenomenon. Although local conditions may have altered some of the particulars involved in the introduction of coffee into each new host environment, it seems that in each case figures equivalent to the English virtuosi were crucial in bringing attention to the new drink. The gentlemen scholars Prospero Alpino in Venice, Charles de l'Écluse in Antwerp, Leonhard Rauwolf in Augsburg, and Jean de Thévenot in Paris all were part of an international republic of letters that shared similar interests and social conventions. Works on coffee were published by continental virtuosi and reviewed in the journals of the emergent republic of letters, including the *Journal des Sçavans* as well as Pierre Bayle's *Nouvelles de la République des Lettres*.[39] An interest in coffee was no peculiarity of the English.

Yet no other country took to coffee drinking with quite the same intensity that Britain did in the seventeenth century. London's coffeehouses had no rival anywhere else in Europe save perhaps Istanbul. In 1700, Amsterdam could boast of only thirty-two coffeehouses, while London had at least several hundred. English visitors to eighteenth-century Paris immediately noticed that there were fewer, "and much more expensive," coffeehouses there than in London.[40] The reasons for this lay perhaps in the unique ways in which English virtuosity was able to fuse with the opportunities created by a dramatic expansion of overseas trade and the growth of a highly urbanized metropolitan capital unrivalled by any other city in western Europe.[41] Britain experienced a particularly intense combination of genteel curiosity, mercantile commerce, and metropolitan civil society in the seventeenth and eighteenth centuries. It was this unique combination of circumstances that made the British Isles so exceptionally receptive to the introduction of coffee consumption.

Coffee and Early Modern Drug Culture

Stupefacients, foods, or medicines, these were great factors destined to transform and disturb men's daily lives.
— *Fernand Braudel*

If the virtuosi were the first to introduce coffee to the palates of early modern English consumers, it did not remain confined to their select circles for long. Coffee was quickly assimilated into the fluid and diffuse "medical marketplace" of seventeenth-century Britain which promoted the commercialization of new and exotic cultural products. Its use was promoted by apothecaries, physicians, retailers, and most important, by the consumers of health-care products themselves. In a buyer's market for medicine, where the demand for effective drugs and services was great and the supplies of such were so various as to be virtually unregulated, new products which made claims to possess salutary qualities, such as coffee, could be eagerly assimilated into English health-care repertoires. At once, English consumers were introduced to coffee as both a new medicine and a new commodity beverage. Although it was advertised and promoted as a medicine, its distribution was not limited to the medical establishment, and it became simultaneously an integral part of the quotidian social ritual of London's urban culture as well as a new ingredient to the seventeenth-century English pharmacopoeia.

The dual appeal of coffee as a medical cure and a newly desirable consumer pleasure lay in part in the way in which coffee could maintain the oriental mystique of other exotic drugs while also remaining mostly free from the negative associations attached to more powerful psychotropic drugs such as "bang" (a marijuana-like hemp product) and opium — all of which were fairly well known to early modern English physicians and virtuosi, but were not accepted by English consumers. The central question this chapter addresses is thus: why did coffee, along with such related hot drinks as tea and chocolate, succeed in finding a broad and growing consumer market while many other similarly exotic substances did not?[1] While the virtuosi may have been almost indiscriminately interested in all sorts of strange and curious drugs, other consumers were far more discerning and less adventurous. It took more than a few overzealous virtuosi to make coffee a success in the seventeenth-century marketplace.

The commercial success of the coffee commodity arose from the particular, and indeed the quite peculiar, ways in which it was perceived by English consumers. Coffee offered a new social beverage which could be drunk in public settings in a manner akin to alcoholic beverages like ales, beers, or wines, but it could be consumed without fear of consequent intoxication. Furthermore, it had the added appeal of other exotic, mind-altering substances, but without the fearful associations with unreason and illicit sexuality that, as we shall see, plagued many of the other foreign drugs that English travelers and virtuosi introduced to their countrymen. Coffee drinking ultimately came to be seen as associated with sober and civil conduct and as such it became a key part of an ethic of "respectable" behavior shared by both the middling and elite classes.[2] These factors, in conjunction with the existence of a permeable and widespread medical marketplace, can account for the successful spread of coffee drinking beyond its initial virtuoso milieu.

Allurements to Other Naughtiness: Early Modern Perceptions of Exotic Drugs

When a European suffers some misfortune, he has no resource but to read a philosopher called Seneca; but Asians, showing more sense and a better knowledge of medicine, take drinks which can make a man cheerful and dispel the memory of his sorrows.
— *Montesquieu*, Lettres Persanes, *Letter 33 (1721)[3]*

Far from being devoid of psychotropic drugs, early modern European societies were in fact already awash with a substantial array of mind-altering substances, and they were always open to adding still more to their pharmacological repertoire — if we are to believe the provocative studies of Piero Camporesi, for whom the intoxicating potential of a number of indigenous medicinal or psychotropic substances, such as henbane or ergot, were commonly used as both as folk remedies and as a brief respite from the toils of daily life through intoxication. On this account, the "political strategies" of an elite interested in maintaining social control over the populace were "allied to medical culture" in order to "lessen the pangs of hunger or to limit turmoil in the streets." In other words, drug use was another means of social control. Following this line of argument, one might well conclude that the speedy and widespread adoption of coffee was therefore an easy accomplishment: Europeans were already accustomed to incorporating various different drugs that promised to offer some sort of relief from the inexorable miseries of undernourishment and disease.[4] Whether such relief came from homegrown *pane ollopiato* ("opiated bread"), from the fantastic *nepenthe* of classical myth, or from foreign drugs such as tobacco or coffee, this made no difference to a society in desperate need of medical, alimentary, and psychological solace.[5] This argument supposes that early modern society had a strong need to provide an escape from the daily grind of a barely subsistence-level economy.

There are many reasons to believe that recourse to this sort of functionalism is not appropriate, at least in the British Isles.[6] Alcohol seems to have been all but unchallenged as the intoxicant of choice for the people of early modern Britain. It is remarkable that English writers often used the verb "to drink" a means to describe the new practice of smoking — an indication perhaps of the hegemonic grip in which alcohol fastened early modern notions of the experience of mind-altering drugs. Although the "numming, soporiferous medicine" called *coculus India,* the dried berries of a climbing plant found on the Malabar coast, was sometimes used to increase the intoxicating power of beer, it was taken only in small quantities and the practice was ultimately forbidden by Parliament in 1701. Jerome Friedman's claims for the popularity of marijuana consumption during the Civil War era are based entirely on satires of tobacco smoking, while similarly hostile sources are used by Christopher Hill to support his claim that "the use of tobacco and alcohol was intended to heighten spiritual vision" among the radical Civil War sects.[7]

The virtuosi and their fellow travelers were rather extraordinary in the extent to which they eagerly explored the potential political economy of new and exotic drugs. To be sure, although virtuoso interest in mind-altering drugs was distinctive in the early modern era, it was not unprecedented. The author of pseudo–Albertus Magnus's late thirteenth-century *De mirabilibus mundi* included a recipe for a hallucinogenic substance "touted as capable of making people think that anyone they saw was an elephant."[8] But the mere fact that travel writers were surprised to find psychotropic substances in other cultures, and that the closest analogy they could find for the altered states of consciousness provoked by them was alcoholic drunkenness, suggests that nonalcoholic intoxication was generally unfamiliar, at least to the European social elite. Furthermore, virtuoso enthusiasm for these drugs rarely translated into market success for these substances. Much of Camporesi's best source material for an early modern interest in exotic intoxicants is found in the writings of the Italian virtuosi, people such as Ulisse Aldrovandi and Lorenzo Magalotti. Most novel or exotic drugs did not take hold as mass market commodities, and the reasons why they were not so well assimilated had much to do with the different stories told about these substances by travelers, the virtuosi, and the medical writers who first encountered them.

Orthodox medicine, which on the whole remained wedded to the Galenic paradigm, was not averse to accepting new and foreign drugs into its pharmacopoeia. The "new worlds" brought to the attention of early modern Europeans were often portrayed as abundant in natural wealth; they were a veritable "Land of Cockaigne" that could now be located geographically "West of Spain," so it was only natural to expect these lands to be rich in useful medicines as well. The early herbals of John Gerard and John Parkinson mentioned the medicinal virtues of plants not native to England or to Europe in their enormously influential works. Parkinson noted in 1640 that "most of the chiefest drugges in our apothecaries shops . . . come to us from forraigne parts," and thought that such "strange and rare plants . . . growing in the East and West Indies, and those parts neere unto them, . . . have beene observed by those that in their travells saw them, and brought many of them into Europe, that wee may contemplate the wonderfull workes of God, that hath stored those countries with such differing herbes and trees from ours."[9] In this view, exotic plants were seen as a part of God's bounty which could, and indeed should, be legitimately harvested by the English in their pursuit of personal health, national profit, and general piety. Further knowledge of such hitherto unknown medicines was indeed "joyful news out of the new found world," as John Frampton titled his 1577 translation of the Spanish text of Nicolas Monardes's description of the myriad of newly discovered cures in the Americas. The newly privileged Worshipful Society of Apothecaries was, in particular, eager to promote and profit from the use of new drugs from the East and West Indies, as were the initial merchant venturers in the East India trade.[10] Although India merchants such as Thomas Mun were quick to point out that catering to "the moderate vse of wholesome drugges and comfortable spices" was not intended "to surfeit, or to please a lickorish taste" among the English but rather to supply "things most necessary to preserve their health, and to cure their diseases." The number of imported drugs was at least twenty-five times greater at the end of the seventeenth century than it had been in 1600.[11]

This enthusiastic embrace of exotic remedies by the Galenic medical orthodoxy did not go unchallenged. There had been a longstanding fear in England that foreign medicines were at best an expensive superfluity, and at worst, a dangerous substance which could wreak harm on native constitutions. The import of Italian drugs was frowned upon as early as the fifteenth century, and not long after the new cures from the Americas began to make their way into England in the sixteenth century, Thomas Paynell thought that "no man woude lyghtly go unto a medicine, that came from so strange a place." By the later sixteenth and seventeenth centuries, an increasing number of critics of Galenic medicine — many of whom were inspired by Paracelsian notions to reject it as "a decadent heathenish tradition" which was not suitable for either Christians or Englishmen — began to vehemently oppose any recourse to foreign plants and drugs as a means of curing the ailments of the English people.[12] Many such Paracelsians came to suspect that the Galenic remedies supported by adherents to the medical orthodoxy such as the College of Physicians were often either ruses foisted upon patients whose lack of classical learning or access to the classic texts prevented them from knowing any better, or else expensive substitutes for remedies which were more easily, and cheaply, found in England itself. These writers thus desired to replace the esoteric medical monopoly derived from pagan pharmacopoias with their own, intuitive knowledge of the virtues of domestic plants, and to make this new learning accessible to the general public through writing in the vernacular.

According to the English Paracelsians, the unchallenged authority of Galen must give way to Dr. Reason, Dr. Experience, Mother Nature, and Dr. Dilligence, as Nicolas Culpeper proclaimed. Culpeper, who was perhaps "the most aggressive and prolific medical editor" of the mid-seventeenth century, complained bitterly that the herbals of both Gerarde and Parkinson "intermixed many, nay very many outlandish herbs, and very many which are hard, nay not at all to be gotten . . . for love nor money," while he proudly noted that his herbal referred only to easily obtainable, cheap, domestic plants. Even Gerarde himself had derided those physicians who preferred foreign remedies in place of domestic ones of similar efficacy. Thomas Fuller apparently agreed, for his enormously popular late seventeenth-century collection of the "worthies of England" included a careful catalogue of all of the medicinal herbs and mineral waters to be found in each county of England. For a writer like Henry Pinell, there would never be a reason to resort to exotics, for he thought that

"God created an inexhaustible supply of medicines, and distributed to every country sufficient for it selfe."[13]

For some, exotic drugs were not merely expensive and superfluous, but dangerous as well. Timothy Bright wrote his *Treatise . . . of English medicines, for cure of all diseases* (1580) in order to convince his fellow countrymen that "English bodies, through the nature of the region, our kinde of diet and nourishment, our custome of life, are greatly divers from those of strange nations, whereby ariseth great varitie of humours, and excrements in our bodies from theirs," and thus "the medicines which help [foreigners] must needes hurt us." Bright found it particularly galling and "absurde, that the health of so many Christian nations should hang upon the courtesie of those heathen and barbarous nations, to whome nothing is more odious then the very name of Christianitie." The popularity of such drugs, he added, was due to the malicious imposition of greedy overseas merchants, who sought gain in the sale of expensive commodities, the supply of which was in their monopoly control. More than a century later, John Evelyn's daughter Mary similarly lamented that before "foreign drinks and mixtures were wantonly introduced" into the English diet, "the scurvy, the spleen, &c. were scarce heard of." Even well into the late eighteenth century, one can find individuals such as Lord Rokeby, who declined to take any coffee, tea, or sugar because he thought England was "by means of its productions, competent to the support of its inhabitants."[14]

Such medical nativism could easily be reinforced by an early modern language of economic morality which frowned upon restrictive monopolies and excessive foreign imports. Indeed, English Paracelsianism may well be understood as the medical equivalent of mercantilist economics. These "protectionist" discourses retained their vigor throughout the seventeenth century and indeed persisted into the eighteenth century, despite the fact that they were ineffectual in preventing the rapid rise in popularity of such new exotic drugs as coffee, tea, and tobacco. Some authors sought to ban the importation of the new exotics outright on the mercantilist basis that they "greatly hinder the consumption of barley, malt and wheat, the product of our land." Occasional pleas to substitute native substances for the new exotics could be made in which coffee might be made out of burnt wheat, rye or barley, or a native tea made from the lemon balm plant.[15] One author recommended that concoctions made of juniper and elderberries might be "more universally agreeable to all tempers, palates and cases, than perhaps any other two simple medicines," and thus should be properly offered for sale in England's public houses. He noted, however, that such a project would not only draw the ire of Levant and East India merchants, but would fail to convince those "young ladies, and little sparks, who scorn to eat, drink, or wear any thing, that comes not from

France, or the Indies," for "they fancy poor England is not capable of bringing forth any commodity that can be agreeable to their grandeur and gallantry." Even the virtuosi of the Royal Society could be sympathetic to these schemes, as when they eagerly listened while Robert Hooke presented them with a sample of Lancashire sweet willow, which he proclaimed to be "a *succedaneum* of thee."[16] None of these schemes worked too well.

Perhaps one reason why they failed is that they lacked the foreign mystique of the new exotics, for despite the constant stream of moralized laments against the use of these imports, the exotic origins and natures of these plants were hardly concealed by their proponents — indeed they extolled them. How could exotic drugs be so appealing and yet so threatening at the same time?

The simplest answer to the critics of exotic remedies was to declare "nature gave it, and nature doth nothing in vaine," as Edmund Gardiner did in his 1610 defense of the medicinal use of tobacco. Gardiner's argument from natural design became ever more commonplace over the course of the seventeenth century. Sylvestre DuFour thought that it was "in contempt of the sacred rules of divine providence" to hold "that every country ought to be content with the sole use of its own drugs." By the early eighteenth century, Joseph Addison's praise of English commerce in the *Spectator* could declare uncontentiously that "Nature seems to have taken a particular care to disseminate her blessings among the different regions of the world, with an eye to the mutual intercourse and traffick among mankind."[17] Appeals to providence were thus a double-edged sword: in the absence of any empirical evidence one way or the other, one could just as easily claim that the diversity of the natural world was ordained for the good of man, as to claim that every land was endowed by God with remedies sufficient for its native inhabitants.

The biggest problem faced by the new exotics was that when they were introduced to the English consciousness, many of the new drugs were associated with licentious sexuality or disorderly intoxication. Jan Huygen van Linschoten's influential late sixteenth-century account of the Portuguese East Indies described the consumption of "bangue," or marijuana, as a substance that the Indians "useth most to provoke lust" or "to make a man drunke or in a manner out of his wits." The appeal of this drug certainly could not have been enhanced by Linschoten's observation that it was popular mostly among "the common people," prostitutes, soldiers, and slaves. Over a hundred years later, Louis Lémery reported virtually the same details in his *Traité des Aliments* (1702). John Fryer's late seventeenth-century account of his travels in the East Indies mentioned bang as a powerful intoxicant used by querulous sailors, dissolute fakirs, and Indian princes who desired to punish criminals with temporary madness.[18]

Perhaps the only good words for bang came from the virtuosi. James Howell reported to the curious that "in the orientall countries, . . . there is a drink call'd *Banque* which is rare and precious, . . . like that *Nepenthe* which the poets speak so much of."[19] Robert Hooke, who was curious about bang's putative abilities to stimulate the appetite as well as "to intoxicate without any ill symptom following upon it, and . . . to ease the sense of hard labour," treated the Royal Society to a short discourse of his own on the drug. When Hans Sloane brought a dried specimen of the plant in his famed collection to the attention of the Fellows, these inquiries provoked some to wonder, just as James Howell had, whether bang was not in fact the famed *nepenthe* of classical myth. The more astute botanist Dr. Plunkenet, however, more correctly identified Indian *bang* as "a true and genuine *hemp,* tho' . . . specifically distinct from our *European* sort."[20]

The indiscriminate culture of curiosity fostered by the virtuosi allowed them to investigate all sorts of bizarre drugs, medicines, and even poisons from the East and West Indies. Robert Boyle's "Considerations Touching the Usefulness of Experimental Natural Philosophy" (1663) included a substantial discourse on the various beverages of the West Indies, Russia, and China. The Royal Society's "Enquiries for the East Indies" of November 1662 included numerous queries about the qualities of plants as varied as the betel nut, the *arbor triste,* the poisons of Macassar, Lignum Aloës, the best region for harvesting tea, and the notorious Malabar intoxicant, *datura* (thorn apple), among many others. Daniel Colwall's response to some of these queries recommended that an Indonesian plant, the "Seree-boa" which was reputed by the natives of the island of Celebes to "giveth a more pleasing taste and maketh a fragrant breath," could well be "eaten in England" and still "have the same operation."[21] This proposal to introduce a new breath freshener to the British Isles may have come to naught, but it illustrates well the eagerness with which the virtuosi pursued such possibilities.

Some of the extremely curious even took to experimenting upon themselves with these new drugs, as when Sir Philiberto Vernatti ingested an infusion of datura with some of his fellow medical students at the University of Leiden in 1649. The effects, he thought, were remarkable: "We stood all four, and stared and laught at one another, like innocents or mad-men (as hath been told us by the people of the hour) for none had any remembrance of what past at that time. . . . Home I came that night, but how God knows, for I do not, neither could any body tell me; in the morning I awaked betimes, and perceived that I had (saving your respect) vomited most excedingly." Datura was known from the accounts of Linschoten and many others to be a powerful intoxicant often used in "a sort of drink much beloved by [Chinese] soldiers and mariners called *Suyker-bier* which makes them raging mad, so that it is forbidden strictly under a great penalty to make use of the same."[22] Datura was also commonly reputed to be popular among lascivious Indian wives who wished to drug their husbands to unconsciousness whilst they engaged in adulterous affairs.[23] It was not widely used in England as either an intoxicant or a medicine, but it remained the object of intense virtuosic curiosity.

An even better known, and perhaps even more notorious, foreign intoxicant was opium. The dangers of addiction to this narcotic were clear to Linschoten, who affirmed that he thought it was "a kinde of poyson," and observed once again that the Indians "use it most for lecherie: for it maketh a man to hold his seede long before he sheddeth it, which the Indian women much desire, that they may shed their nature likewise with the man." Paul Rycaut noted that opium consumption made the Turks "fly out either into a kind of phrensy, or into the wild actions of drunken persons." Opium was also thought to be used by thieves to make their victims unconscious before committing their crimes. John Hammond believed that while opium might be suited to Turkish constitutions, for the English it was even "but in a very small dose . . . [a] manifest poyson," and "onely long use and familiar practise hath made [opium] not vnconuenient for [Turkish] bodies."[24]

There was room for some consideration of the medicinal use of opium, however. Thomas Herbert thought it could be "of great use and vertue . . . [when] taken moderately," and he rather admired the way in which the drug putatively made the Turks "strong and long in Venus exercises." Francis Bacon, as we have seen, also commended its medical potential, although he cautioned that opiates "obtain a good effect from a bad cause."[25] The physician Henry Stubbe was so effusive in his praise of opium that he wrote Latin verse on the topic, and he prescribed it readily, without bothering to measure the doses, to his patients as well as himself while he practiced medicine in Jamaica. The virtuosi William Petty and Robert Southwell referred to "opium" as a sort of slang code word for happy occurrences in their correspondence. Even Culpeper included a short mention of some (presumably indigenous) poppy varieties, which he recommended "to procure rest and sleep, and to ease pains in the head as well as in other parts," in his herbal.[26] But on the whole most writers warned against the overuse of opium, for its addictive qualities were well known; Lémery remarked that frequent users "become dull, stupid and weak" and thought that Europeans "ought to shun the making our selves to be slaves to [such] habits."[27]

Virtuoso inquirers were above such warnings, and they ventured where others were loath to go. Robert Boyle proudly averred that "the naturalist may add to the *materia medica,* not only by investigating the qualities of unheeded bodies, but also by gaining admittance for divers, that, though well enough known, are forborn to be used upon the account of their being of a poisonous nature: for by . . . skilful ways of preparation, the philosophical spagyrist may so correct divers noxious, nay poisonous concretes, unfit in their crude simplicity for the physicians use . . . as to make them useful and effectual remedies." Even arsenic, Boyle thought, could be decocted into an effective medicine.[28] Philiberto Vernatti's East Indian gifts to the Royal Society's collection of curiosities included a sample of "Macassar poyson." Now poisons were not to be handled blithely in early modern Britain—associated as they were with popery, witchcraft, and political assassinations—and it was only the virtuosic claims to the disinterested cause of the advancement of learning which seems to have kept these activities above reproach from their critics.[29] Whereas most of their contemporaries might have been too squeamish to investigate the properties of exotic drugs and notorious poisons, the virtuosi were unafraid and indeed eager to learn about, to collect, to experiment with, and sometimes even to ingest such things.

Coffee, and the related hot drinks, chocolate and tea, were the major exceptions to this story. Unlike betel nuts, bang, datura, opium, or Asian poisons, these drugs quickly became profitable commodities in their own right and they were assimilated with relative ease into the dietary regimes of the wider British populace. Resistance to caffeinated beverages in seventeenth-century Britain was not based on anxieties about the health risks they might have posed, but was rather almost entirely a function of political anxieties about the rise of the coffeehouse as a new social institution.

What then made these drinks different from the rest? Unlike most other exotics, coffee and its "fellow travelers," as it were, had the distinct advantage of not being associated with licentious sexuality or with drunken disorder, while at the same time they were, as beverages, able to be assimilated into the preexisting drinking customs of early modern Britain. Put simply, coffee offered seventeenth-century consumers a drink with some of the familiarity of alcoholic wines, beers, and ales, but without the intoxicating effects of those drinks. Furthermore, the caffeinated hot drinks retained the attractive mystique of other exotic drugs, but they lacked any of the usual negative connotations associated with those substances. In the drink culture of seventeenth-century Britain, coffee and its near kin had the best of both worlds.

Wakeful and Civil Drinks: Sobriety and the Body Social

Coffee was so far from being associated with licentious sexuality that it was considered by many to be an anti-aphrodisiac of such potency that it could render men impotent and women barren. The association of coffee with a vitiated libido began with the very earliest accounts of the drink in English. Edward Pococke's translation of an Arabic medical text on coffee included among its many other medicinal properties the observation that coffee "asswageth lust." The reason for this, most writers agreed, was that coffee, being a substance hot and dry in the second degree, has the tendency to dry up the body's "radical moisture." "A hot and dry temperament and climate are least proper for fertility," the Montpellier physician Daniel Duncan declared.[30] The consequence of over-frequent consumption of such a drug was thus impotence in men and barrenness in women.[31]

Another source for the myth of coffee's anti-libidinal properties was the same sort of virtuoso travel literature which often reported stories of lascivious Indian women using intoxicating drugs to incapacitate their husbands before engaging in their adulterous affairs. Olearius reported a tale of the Persian sultan "Mahomet Casain" who drank coffee to such excess that "he had an inconceivable aversion for women," was unable to beget an heir, and therefore was cuckolded by a humble but virile baker. One might also recall the accounts of George Sandys and George Manwaring of coffeehouses in Turkey and Persia which kept male prostitutes to attract customers. Here, coffee was associated not so much with impotency per se, but with what was generally regarded as wasteful, nonprocreative, not to mention sinful, sex. These stories remained current and were reprinted throughout the seventeenth century and yet they appeared, interestingly enough, in texts which were on the whole favorable to the consumption of coffee.[32] It seems that the licentiousness of the oriental coffeehouses was seen by the English as quite distinct from the medical virtues and sobering qualities of the coffee drink itself, for the English coffeehouses were never blamed for harboring the sin of sodomy, perhaps because sodomy was often viewed as a vice to which the Turks were particularly prone. This distinction between eastern and western mores did not hold as fast when Englishmen turned to the issue of the putative association of coffeehouses with political subversion. John Evelyn commented on Thomas Smith's account in the *Philosophical Transactions* of the Turkish sultan's reported desire to shut down the coffeehouses of Constantinople, because the discourse there tended to "sedition" by writing: "Coffe-hou[ses are] impolite, permissive, even among us, for the same reason, as I have always thought."[33]

For some, coffee's anti-venereal reputation was considered to be yet another commendable quality of a new drink that virtuously "preserves chastity" and thus "restrains inordinate venery," as one work proclaimed. But it was the enemies of coffee consumption, and even more so the enemies of the coffeehouses in which the drink was consumed, who seized upon this supposed side effect with the greatest vigor. A series of late seventeenth-century satirical pamphlets purported to present the complaints of English women against the growing fashion for coffee consumption. One was entitled "The Women's Petition Against Coffee" which represented "to publick consideration the grand inconveniencies accruing to their sex from the excessive use of that drying, enfeebling liquor." The petition claimed to be "presented to the right honorable the keepers of the liberty of Venus," and proceeds to detail the unfortunate consequences faced by those wives abandoned by their husbands who frequent the coffeehouses and have consequently lost their masculine sexual vigor. Coffee drinkers were thus likely to be "cuckol'd by dildo's." Another contemporaneous pamphlet purported to be "the women's complaint against tobacco," and lodged a similar grievance: "that tobacco is the only enemy to pleasure and procreation."[34] These works may be understood as cases of the well-established genre of inversion literature in which the world was portrayed as it might appear "turned upside down" to contemporaries. Like the Civil War–era pamphlets which ridiculed "the ridiculous fashions of these distracted times," or posited the unthinkable prospect of a "Parliament of women," the women's petitions against coffee sought to reveal to contemporaries the disastrous consequences that might entail should the men of England relinquish their patriarchal obligations to maintain proper order in state and society. Indeed, these fears could only be heightened in the years following the Restoration, when the memories of actual women petitioning, in support of the Levellers no less, was still fresh in the mind of the (male) political nation.[35] And like the lascivious verse satires on the rising popularity of the French dildo among the ladies of the English court, the pamphlets drew a clear parallel between the loss of masculine sexual vigor and the decline of the state of the English polity.[36] For the opponents of the coffeehouses in the later seventeenth century, those establishments threatened the social and political order by potentially gathering together men of various social estates to share a common table, and what was worse, perhaps even common discourse over matters of state; the pamphleteers suggested that this was an inversion of the way things ought to be every bit as frightening as the prospect of women sitting in Parliament or of men abandoning their wives to foreign sex toys.

But it was the very jocularity of these texts that prevented the development of any serious opposition to the consumption of coffee or similar beverages. By self-consciously exaggerating the sober warnings of contemporary medical opinion, the texts actually deflated the gravity of those concerns. If the worst that one could say about coffee was that it restrained one's lust — as when the "wandering whore" complained in one pamphlet that "the coffee-houses have dried up all our customers like sponges," so that "lust and leachery were never in lesse repute than since that liquor came up" — then it was hard to mount a concerted moral campaign against the consumption of the drink. In an age which saw serious rioting aimed at brothels favored by courtiers, followed by persistent attacks on the court as dominated by popery, debauchery, and whoredom by both elites and commoners, the defense of lechery was never an easy task.[37]

Not all of the new exotic hot drinks of the seventeenth century were necessarily associated with a lack of sexual vigor, however. Chocolate, which was often served in coffeehouses and was consistently considered alongside coffee and tea in both medical and popular discussions of the drinks, was in fact widely understood to be an aphrodisiac. This reputation began with the earliest accounts of the Spanish conquistadors with the Meso-American substance, and it was perpetuated by English medical writers like Henry Stubbe as well as popular playwrights and pamphleteers. Unlike "hot" coffee, chocolate was thought to be cold and dry, and prone to provoking the blood flow, all of which were conducive to the stimulation of sexual ardor in Galenic physiology.[38]

Chocolate never attained the popularity of coffee in the seventeenth century, perhaps because its advocates were open to charges of "tending to sensuality, and upholding carnal lusts and desires," as Henry Stubbe noted. The best possible means to counter such accusations was to argue that chocolate, like all other drugs, must not be abused, and that the Galenic "spermatic economy" warned against the unhealthy consequences of the constant retention of seminal fluids. Thus "the use of venery is as natural, as for a man to blow his nose," Stubbe remarked, while hastening to add "though [it is] not so lawfull every way." Although the Galenic physiology of sex was a part of early modern medical orthodoxy, Stubbe and the partisans of chocolate put a rather more positive spin on the value of venereal indulgence than did most other physicians, both classical and modern, who were far more concerned over the consequences of excessive sexual activity.[39] Just as the chocolate drink was understood to be an aphrodisiac, so were the distinctive "chocolate-houses" of post-Restoration London understood by contemporaries to be centers for "gallantry, pleasure, and entertainment" — an identification made famous in Richard Steele's *Tatler* papers which regularly opined on such matters under the rubric of White's Chocolate-House, perhaps the most fashionable of such establishments in early eighteenth-century London.[40]

Despite these associations, chocolate and chocolate-houses were never linked to sexual immorality in the severe ways in which many of the other unsuccessful exotics considered here were considered. Rather than seeing it as "coffee's opposite," early modern consumers found chocolate to be a pleasant complement to related exotic hot drinks such as coffee and tea. Samuel Pepys and Anthony Wood, two of England's earliest *devotés* of the new drinks, consumed coffee, tea, and chocolate with equal relish, and often at a coffeehouse, although coffee tended to be the drink of preference for both men.[41] These hot drinks were often taken with sugar added, and the coffeehouses they were often consumed in were also convenient and accepted places to smoke tobacco.[42] Taken as a whole, the complex of these relatively new and exotic consumer "luxuries" formed an interlocking complement of consumption habits. The success of one aided the progress of the others in establishing themselves as English consumer habits.

Just as important for the reception of the coffee commodity was its reputation for promoting the virtue of sobriety. From the very beginning of its introduction into England, coffee had been identified as a "sober" drink. James Howell's published letter to Walter Rumsey in 1657 praised the benefits of coffee as a sober substitute for alcohol. He claimed that "whereas formerly apprentices and clerks with others, used to take their mornings draught in ale, beer, or wine, which by the dizziness they cause in the brain, make many unfit for businesse, they use now to play the good-fellows in this wakefull and civill drink." The truth of this statement as an accurate social observation was doubtful, but the rhetorical purpose was clear: coffee was suited for clear thought and efficient work, and as such it was a preferable alternative social beverage to alcohol. Edward Chamberlayne's survey of the state of England in 1671 could claim that "there is generally less excess in drinking especially about London, since the use of coffee." In a similar text, Guy Miège also contrasted coffee and tea with those "strong liquors" which "are apt to disorder the brain," while the former "settle and compose it, which makes it so much used by men of learning and business, who know best the virtue of 'em."[43]

Business transactions were indeed commonly conducted in public houses such as inns, taverns, and later coffeehouses, but the latter profited greatly from coffee's association with sobriety.[44] A 1673 tract in defense of coffee noted that it was

> almost a general custome amongst us [English], that no bargain can be drove, or business concluded between man and man, but it must be transacted at some publick house, this to persons much concerned in the world must needs be very injurious, should they always run to taverns or ale-houses, where continual sippings, though never so warily would be apt to fly into their brains, and render them drowsie and indisposed for business; whereas having now the opportunity of a coffee-house, they repair thither . . . and so dispatching their business, go out more sprightly about their affairs than before.

While alcohol was never entirely displaced from the rituals of commercial sociability, drunkenness was hard to reconcile with the demands of respectability and good conduct that were the foundation for a merchant's reputation. After concluding a deal in Durham over a bottle, the Newcastle merchant Michael Blackett later chastised his partners in a letter to his uncle: "the shame take them all for with filling there gutts with all sorts of wine. They made me sick for 2 dayes after." Although alcohol remained the social beverage par excellence, the consequences of drunkenness were generally lamented in numerous jeremiads against the overconsumption of alcohol as the cause of wasted time, illness, and unnecessary quarrels.[45] Likewise, the social spaces in which alcoholic beverages were publicly consumed — the tavern and above all the alehouse — remained inextricably associated with drunken disorder.

The Restoration-era notes of advice given to a Cambridgeshire justice of the peace document clearly the continuing anxiety caused by the presence of public tippling houses to those entrusted with preventing licentious behavior and maintaining social order. The author's concerns were manifold:

> You are to certify what tavernes, inns, alehouses, and tipling houses there are with in every severall parishes who keep the same, how long they have kept them, and where of those alehouses are licenst and which are not and whether they sell there ale and beare according to the assises or not; which of these inns intertaine neighbours; and alehouses [serving patrons] who have been *drunk* within the said parish since the last assises and in what inn or ale house the same hath happened and who hath maintained any unlawfull games there, and whether the numbers of any innes or alehouses in any one parish bee burthensome and more then in convenient and which of them may bee best spared and whether there houses stand in inconvenient places; whereof [if any of] them bee scituate in hookes, or by lanes, . . . and [are likely] to bee dangerouse to the people in respect of intertainment, and shelter of theeves robbers and other lewd company.[46]

Despite its centrality to the rituals of social interaction in early modern Britain, the consumption of alcohol was tainted by the perceived and actual threat to the ideal of social order posed by drunkenness.

Coffee offered a way out of this routine: it was like alcoholic drinks in that it could be consumed in a public house and could thus be used as a means to facilitate the social interaction, the collegiality, and the mutual trust that was crucial to the success of an early modern businessman, but it did not intoxicate. Coffee was thus "a drink at once to make us sober and merry," while the patrons of a coffeehouse were thought to include mainly "the sober and ingenious, that come not so much to ingurgitate vast quantities of stupifying liquors, as to enjoy society and good discourse." Coffee's reputation as a "sober drink" was as much a construct of the promotional rhetoric surrounding it as a clear-cut understanding of the real effects of the drink. Seventeenth-century perceptions ran far ahead of physiological realities, for coffee's sobering qualities were thought to be so strong that it could make a drunk man sober.[47] Coffee's reputation for promoting sobriety was due more to the ways in which it was conceived of as the inverse of alcoholic beverages than to any real effects of the new drink.

This is worth remembering, since it is often asserted that caffeinated drinks such as coffee and tea filled the growing social "need" of modernizing European economies for sober and alert laborers. The problem with these arguments is that they often assume rather than demonstrate the existence of their proposed social needs, such as sobriety. Furthermore, it is far from clear that the economy of seventeenth-century Britain was in any greater need of a sober workforce than, say, the sixteenth-century economy. There is no reason to believe that the seventeenth century saw any actual increase in workers' sobriety; indeed, if we were to believe the jeremiads of the clergy and social reformers, one might well conclude that alcoholic intoxication was in fact on the rise throughout the century. Matthew Scrivener thought that the "disease of drinking" had been introduced to England by soldiers returning from service in the Netherlands after the wars with Spain in the 1590s, while Daniel Defoe attributed a rise in drunkenness to the cavaliers' custom of drinking to the health of the king after the restoration of Charles II.[48]

The post-Restoration era did witness the emergence of a rather new and positive value attached to the benefits of inebriation for the stock-type character of the loyalist cavalier drunkard, who would "lay aside plotting and thinking" in order to drink another health to the king, or as one popular ballad put it: "the loyal subject (as it is reason) drinks good sack and is free from treason." "The honest drunken curr," another pamphlet suggested, "is one of the quietest subjects his majesty has, and most submissive to a monarchyal government. He would not be without a king, if it were no other reason than meerly drinking his health." Of course, the loyal sot "hates coffee as Mahomatizm." But even these apologia for inebriation had their tongues planted as firmly in their cheeks as that of the author of the "Tavern Huff," who began his verse with the lines "Drink wine and be wise."[49] Whig-leaning writers such as John Phillips could easily counter these mock praises of the loyal but sottish cavalier by sternly declaring "that loyalty does not consist in drinking tavern healths," and thus "the peek is not between loyalty and disloyalty, but between huzzah-loyalty, ranting, rouring, damming, swearing loyalty, and sober, serious, solid, and temperate loyalty." On the whole, then, temperance and sobriety were neither more nor less virtuous in the seventeenth century than they had been for the previous or the succeeding generations. But coffee did benefit from its association with sober conduct, and this association would allow coffee, tea, and chocolate to be understood as thoroughly "respectable" drinks in the eighteenth and nineteenth centuries.[50]

Coffee, the Medical Marketplace, and the English Consumer

Most societies cannot distinguish clearly between their pharmacopoeia and their diet.
— Ivan Illich

Coffee not only avoided the negative taints of illicit sexuality and drunken intoxication that plagued other exotic commodities; it also rapidly gained a positive reputation for promoting a plethora of salubrious effects. Coffee, tea, and chocolate were received by English consumers both as medicines and as recreational drugs. They were sold by apothecaries as a medicine, by quack doctors as an instant remedy, and by tobacconists, coffeehouse-keepers, and retail grocers as a commercial foodstuff (Figure 3).[51] The sale of coffee beans, tea leaves, and the like for domestic use was not monopolized or regulated in any way, and thus its distribution was adopted by a variety of agents within the medical marketplace of seventeenth-century Britain. By contrast, the structure of medicine in early modern France remained much more firmly under the control of the privileged medical monopolists. The seal of approval of the Faculty of Medicine at Paris remained a crucial element behind the success of new drugs or similar medical commodities in France. The variegated and highly competitive nature of the English medical market meant that it was particularly receptive to assimilating new drugs and new remedies into its pharmacopaeia.[52] Most of these remedies failed to become popular consumer items, however, because they were not so readily exploitable by such a wide variety of different commercial interests.

It was not for want of trying that many new and exotic drugs, remedies, and nostrums did not succeed in becoming popular items of everyday consumption. The ubiquitous medical entrepreneurs known as "quacks" were constantly trying to foist new medical products on the English public, particularly in the metropolis of London. The standard repertoire of a quack was thought to include "some East-India rarities and curiosities . . . and the skeletons of several strange beasts and insects, with which he amuses the ignorant" (Figure 4). Some even tried their hand at promoting exotic substances from the East Indies, such as one Mr. Brook, who called to the attention of curious Londoners the "Nature, Vertues, Use, and Excellency of INDIAN CATTEE," or *catechu,* an chewable East Indian wood product, which was reputed to be effective

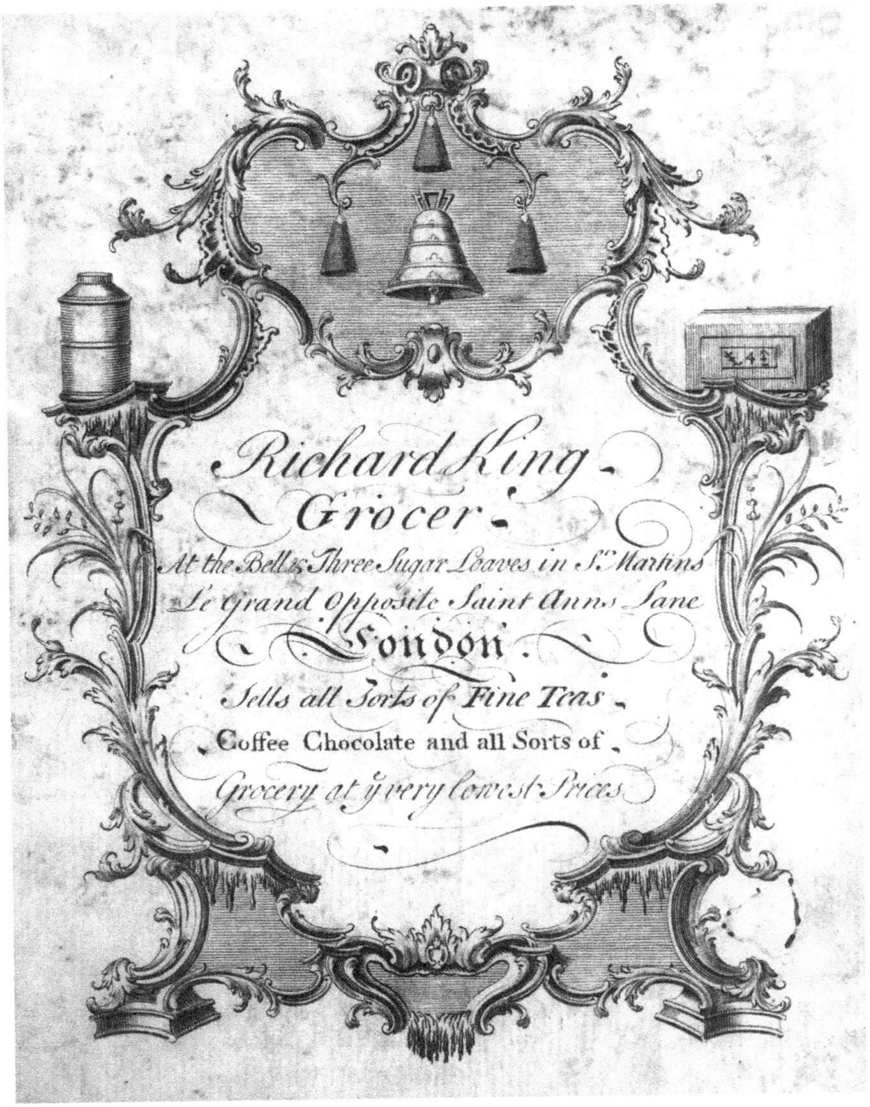

Figure 3. Trade card of Richard King, grocer [mid-eighteenth century]. Huntington Library Print Box 345 (E-J), English Trade Cards Seventeenth to Nineteenth Centuries, 345/24. Courtesy of the Huntington Library, San Marino, California.

"against a stinking breath; a sovereign medicine for the teeth, and fastening the gums," and not least, "very good against the scurvey." The product had been mentioned by Linschoten in his famous account of his travels in the Indies, and Brook did not fail to mention Linschoten's authority in his handbill used to promote the sale of his supplies of catechu at most of the "principal coffeehouses" in the Holborn area. As with so many other quack remedies, however, Brook's catechu never caught on with the wider consumer public. Neither did the remedy purveyed by Doctor Ketch near Hyde Park Corner. For thirteen and a half pence, Londoners could avail themselves of *cannabis sativa,* which Ketch promised his customers "infallibly cures all sorts of distempers whatsoever in half an hours time at farthest."[53] But, again, the drug did not capture the fancy of English consumers, at least not in the seventeenth century.

The correspondence between the nostrums hawked by the quacks and the objects of virtuoso curiosity is striking. The only thing that distinguished the quacks' medicines from those of the virtuosi was a lack of social cachet. This crucial credibility gap may well explain why the quacks desperately sought to cloak themselves in the approbation of the virtuosi.

At first glance, the appearance of coffee, tea, and chocolate in the mid-seventeenth-century medical marketplace looked a lot like the quack advertisements for their strange cures and exotic nostrums. One of the earliest handbills promoting the use of coffee, issued by Pasqua Rosée in 1652, claimed that it was a useful cure for headaches, consumption and coughs, dropsy, gout, scurvy, scrofula, and miscarriages, and was, no less, "a most excellent remedy against the spleen, hypocondriack winds, or the like." Thomas Garraway's advertisements for tea made much the same sort of claims for that drink when the self-described tobacconist and retailer of tea and coffee began to promote his trade in 1660. Some "patent" remedies sold by quacks were recommended as a complement to coffee drinking.[54] But unlike most quack medicines, they were not patented or distributed in limited supplies; indeed, the drinks were available at the very coffeehouses where many of the quack doctors soon learned to best ply their trade (Figure 5).

Of course it was helpful that physicians of the highest reputation recommended the use of coffee for medicinal purposes. The eminent physician Thomas Willis often prescribed coffee as a cure for nervous disorders and even declared that he preferred "to send the sick to the coffee houses sooner than to the apothecaries shops." Samuel Pepys's wife began to make tea for herself at home after learning from her apothecary that it might be an effective remedy for her "cold and defluxions," and Henry More recommended the use of coffee to Anne Conway as a means of curing her headaches. When the plague

Figure 4. E. Kirkall, "Dr. Silvester Partridge's Predictions," engraving (1700): Silvester Partridge was a satirical invention of the Grub Street wit Thomas Brown, who satirized the pretensions of quack doctors and astrologers (among many others), but the figure was based on real astrologers such as John Silvester and John Partridge.

descended upon England in 1665, the physician Gideon Harvey recommended coffee as an effective means of warding off the dreaded disease. Recipes for how to prepare coffee and chocolate were included in seventeenth-century commonplace books along with other cures and remedies for health complaints.[55] Some apothecaries stocked coffee and tea alongside the rest of their materia medica. The apothecary John Houghton, FRS, was perhaps the

Figure 5. Will's Best Coffee Powder (c. 1700), woodcut engraving. The coffeehouse was a key venue for the promotion of coffee as a desirable new commodity, as demonstrated by this late seventeenth-century ad for the retail sale of coffee at Mawaring's Coffeehouse. Bodleian Library, University of Oxford, Douce adds 138 (84). Courtesy of the Bodleian Library, Oxford, England.

most famous retailer of coffee along with other medicines, although it seems that most apothecaries did not regularly stock coffee or any other exotic drinks for general sale.[56] Recommendations from the medical elite certainly helped garner new customers for the emergent trade in hot drinks.

Although the salubrious effects of coffee, tea, and chocolate were reputed to be wide-ranging, actual claims that these drinks might constitute some sort of panacea, or a universal medicine that would be efficacious against all ailments, were very few. Unlike the reception of tobacco in the later sixteenth and the earlier seventeenth centuries, coffee and its ilk were not seriously considered as candidates for a universal medicine. By the later seventeenth century, the orthodox medical establishment had soured on the notion that such a remedy could exist. "The true *panacea* is nowhere but in the mouths of mountebanks," declared the Montpellier physician Daniel Duncan in a tract which was translated for English readers. Had it been widely accepted as a universal medicine, it is unlikely that coffee would have been able to reach a broader market, for the use of medicines of such potency had been traditionally limited by their cost and prestige to social elites.[57] Coffee may have been an exotic drug, but it was not a particularly expensive one. The coffeehouses famously boasted that anyone could have their fill at a coffeehouse for just a penny at the door, but a quack remedy might cost as much as a shilling — roughly the cost of twelve pints of ale or one day's wages for a laborer — for one dose, and the fees of a regular medical practitioner might be far more than that.[58] Drinking coffee thus allowed non-elites to begin to share a pharmacopoeia once restricted to the privileged.

Coffee drinking also appealed as a remedy because it offered an agreeable cure that could be easily self-administered. As such, it was well suited for a society that was accustomed to "the self-dosing habit" — in which each individual chose his or her own preferred repertoire of drugs, cures, and health-care regime. As both pleasant drink and efficacious drug, coffee occupied a sort of middle ground between diet and medicine. It was as adaptable to the still resilient Renaissance (Galenic) medical orthodoxy that stressed the importance of diet and consistent regulation of the humors as it was to the emerging faith in the "power of the pill" that Roy Porter identified as a distinctive characteristic of the more substantially commercialized eighteenth-century medical imagination.[59]

Although the medicinal virtues of coffee were touted initially as the primary reason why one should begin drinking it, these claims could quickly slide into an admission that coffee drinking could also be simply a harmless and "divertive amusement," as one early eighteenth-century tract stated. Indeed, over the course of the eighteenth century it gradually came to be viewed primarily as a pleasant social beverage rather than as a truly effective cure for one's ailments. The coterminous understandings of coffee as both drug and luxury foodstuff are probably best indicated by the various ways in which the commodity was handled by the revenue officers of the crown. When coffee was still quite novel and relatively unfamiliar to English palates in the 1660s, the farmers of the customs were inclined to consider coffee as just another exotic drug, and they refrained from charging customs duties on coffee at the exotic drug rate only in response to the lobbying efforts of the East India Company.[60] Coffee, tea, and chocolate were very quickly considered to be excisable commodities, on par with alcoholic beverages such as beers, wines, and "other outlandish drinks," as one commentator put it. The first Restoration excise statutes of 1660 added these drinks to the traditional alcoholic excise that had been established by the Long Parliament during the Civil War.[61]

Some medical writers of the later seventeenth century followed suit and began to warn against the dangers of excess consumption of luxury goods such as coffee and tea. The radical Pythagorean mystic and vegetarian activist Thomas Tryon cautioned his readers not "to drink more than need and Nature requires," even "if it be coffee or tea," for "if a man be not wary, the use of it shall enslave him, so that he shall not know how to be without, and from drinking it moderately, he shall by degrees, and as it were insensibly slip into excess." Tryon was uncharacteristically in line with the medical mainstream on this matter, as even the most sanguine supporters of coffee warned against the abuse, or the excessive consumption, of the drink. While DuFour recommended coffee as a medicine, he frowned upon taking it as a "dainty dish." As drugs, the exotic new hot drinks were welcomed, but as luxury drinks, they became subject to the same sumptuary anxieties (as well as sumptuary taxation) that governed indulgence in alcoholic drinks or tobacco. Coffee entered the consumer world of seventeenth-century Britain as a particularly promising new addition to the nation's pharmacopoeia, but by the end of the century, it had been accepted as an agreeable element of everyday life by a large number of consumers. As Roger North put it, "custome hath prevailed so farr as to make" coffee, once considered to be "ordinaryly superfluous," now was commonly regarded as "necessary to a general wellfare," and we might add, a valuable source of additional revenue for the growing fiscal demands of the British state.[62]

Why Was Coffee Special?

The market success of coffee, tea, and chocolate was by no means certain. It was not determined by any socioeconomic requirements for a sober workforce, nor was there a proven track record for the success of similar commodities. Tobacco was the only substantial precedent, and the paths taken by the new drinks were quite similar to the one paved by tobacco earlier in the century. The political economies behind the various new commodities varied widely, of course. Crucial to the progress of tobacco consumption was the success of the Virginia/Chesapeake colonies, while coffee and tea were dependent upon the support of the monopolist merchants of the Levant and East India Companies, as we shall see in the next chapter.[63] But these divergent political economies would have come to naught had they not been in some way responsive to the evolving vicissitudes of domestic consumer demand during the course of the seventeenth century. Those changes were shaped by the attitudes about sexuality, bodily health, and sobriety that congealed around these new commodities in ways which allowed for them to succeed where so many other foreign drugs, spices, and luxury goods had failed before them.

To be sure, what one might call the "real" psychotropic effects of coffee, tea, and chocolate cannot be entirely ignored as factors which were conducive to their reception by English consumers. They were indeed quite dissimilar from those of some of the other drugs discussed here. Coffee does not intoxicate to the same extent, or even in the same way, as opium, and this undoubtedly allowed for coffee to be troped as a "sober" drug in a way that was impossible for opium. But the physiological discourses surrounding these drugs extended into areas far beyond the "natural" — that is to say, the ahistorical and the noncultural — mechanics of brain and body chemistry. Exotic drugs were often attributed mind-altering or body-affecting qualities that had no basis in biological fact. The putative anti-aphrodisiac effects of coffee are perhaps the most salient case in point.

Coffee and its ilk successfully found a market outside of the rarified circles of the virtuosi because the stories told about these commodities were unusually positive for drugs of their kind. Thus they were able to escape much of the skepticism and the scorn that had been heaped upon other Asian or exotic goods. But they also owed their success to the ease by which they were adapted to the interests, both material and intellectual, of a broad-based assembly of actors in the seventeenth-century marketplace. Doctors and patients, apothecaries and customers, overseas traders and London retailers, and of course coffeehouse-keepers and their patrons were all able to find both profit and pleasure in buying and supplying the new commodities. In so doing, they took a curious item from the cabinets and travelogues of the virtuosi and made it into a routine part of the English urban marketplace.

3

From Mocha to Java

The virtuosi who played such an important role in discovering and promoting the virtues of coffee drinking in the seventeenth century were not ultimately the agents of its commercial success. This required the intervention of the profit-seeking overseas merchants who had the capital and the wherewithal to begin trading in coffee abroad and thus supply the English market with the new commodity. One of the ironies of the early commercial history of coffee is that the merchants who ultimately stood to profit most handsomely from the growing popularity of the drink were much more hesitant in recognizing its potential as a commodity in the home market. Whereas the utopian projecting of virtuoso culture was vigorously inquisitive and willing to encourage consideration of what at first seemed to be unimportant, perhaps even frivolous, novelties for the sake of what they believed was the advancement of learning, the business culture of overseas trade was entrepreneurially conservative.

Although many of the travelers who first encountered coffee were in the service of the overseas merchant community, the ostensible purpose of their travels was not to find new products to bring back for sale to the English domestic market, but rather to find new markets for English goods abroad. The already existing business of overseas trade in markets for established exotic goods such as pepper or spices was profitable enough for overseas traders, and they had no great need to investigate potential new markets at home. The initial markets for exotic imports in the early seventeenth century were small and inelastic, so there was little incentive to explore new markets for untried commodities such as coffee.[1] The exploitation of the commercial potential of coffee occurred, to paraphrase Sir John Seeley's famous characterization of the acquisition of Britain's imperial possessions, in a fit absence of mind. Coffee was not immediately introduced into the domestic marketplace upon its discovery by English merchants abroad. It was only slowly and rather fitfully brought back home for sale to English consumers over the course of the seventeenth century.

When it was discovered by English travelers, coffee was grown and cultivated in a very restricted part of the globe. Large supplies of coffee for sale were found only in the markets around the Arabian peninsula, in southern Yemen, and a few areas in Ethiopia. The chief wholesale coffee market in the world was the port city of Mocha (Al Mukha), located to the west of the port of Aden and at the point where the Red Sea opens into the Arabian Sea (Figure 6). Coffee could reach a domestic market in the British Isles only through the efforts of overseas traders who sought to bring it back to Britain for sale. The introduction of coffee into the merchant culture of seventeenth-century Britain offers an instructive case study into the workings of the overall expansion of overseas trade that historians often call a commercial revolution. The story of coffee's assimilation into the trading world of the British Isles can also help us understand how mercantilism worked in practice.[2] As an item of international trade carried primarily by large monopoly trading organizations such as the Levant or the East India companies, coffee was deeply ensconced in the trading practices of early modern mercantilism. Yet as coffee was a nonnative commodity that could be bought only abroad with bullion, the growth of the coffee trade would be viewed with great suspicion by the mercantilist mind. This chapter details the gradual triumph of the profit potential of coffee over the initial reservations of the English overseas trading community.

Coffee and Mercantilism: The East India Company's Discovery of Coffee

English contacts with the major coffee markets of the Levant and Red Sea areas began almost as soon as major trading ventures to the Ottoman Empire and the East Indies were organized around the turn of the sixteenth century. The founding of the Levant Company in 1585 and the East India Company in 1600 instituted two large cooperative merchant ventures dedicated to the advancement of English trade with the Ottoman Empire and the Asian markets east of the Turks.[3] As early as 1608, Sir Edward Michelborne

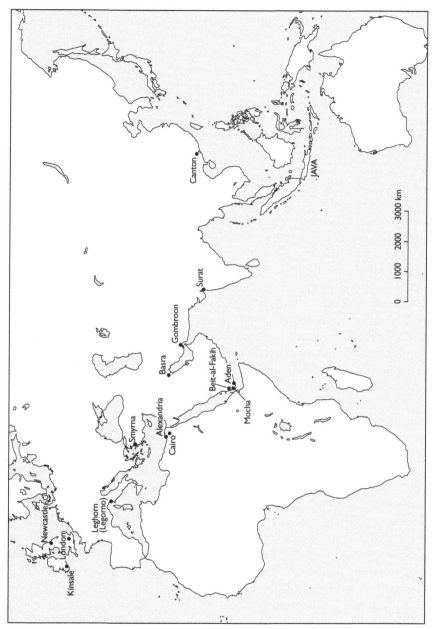

Figure 6. The major entrepôts in the international coffee trade (c. 1600–1720). Map courtesy of Bill Nelson.

was recommending that the English East India Company consider establishing a trading outpost at the Red Sea port city of Mocha. It had the advantage of access to the Red Sea and Indian Ocean trades, but was more hospitable to hosting foreign traders than the nearby port of Aden, which was also a garrison town. Aden was subject to regular naval patrol by Portuguese ships in the service of their Estado da India; Mocha, by contrast, being "governed by merchants only," was "a place of special trade" and had "a good harbour and water" as well. It was by the far the main commercial center of Yemen.[4] Michelborne's advice was heeded and the East India Company's fourth voyage, which set out for the East Indies in March 1608, put a visit to the Red Sea and Mocha on its agenda.

When the fourth voyage reached the Arabian peninsula in the spring of 1609, they encountered the great coffee markets of Yemen that supplied the Ottoman Empire and the Indian Ocean territories. Not long after setting forth for Mocha from Aden on a small expedition by land while his ship sailed for the port by sea, the East India merchant John Jourdain came across an Arabian coffeehouse on the desert route. Within the next week, he had seen the mountains upon which Arabian coffee was cultivated. He noted that the villages of the area sold coffee and fruit. "The seeds of this cohoo is a great merchandize, for it is carried to the Grand Cairo and all other places of Turkey, and to the Indias. And, as it is reported, this seede will growe at noe other place but neere this mountaine [Sumâra], which is one of the highest mountaines in Arabia."[5] Reports of the difficulty of cultivating coffee outside of the Arabian peninsula were deliberately encouraged by the native vendors as a means of maintaining their lock on the international market. Despite this introduction to the Arabian coffee trade, Jourdain and his fellow East India merchants took no interest in engaging in the trade themselves.

The East India Company's ill-fated sixth voyage under Sir Henry Middleton called into the port of Mocha in the spring of 1610, but again Middleton paid no heed to the coffee trade in the region during his visit. Middleton's visit to Mocha was entirely unsuccessful and resulted in his temporary imprisonment by the Ottoman authorities there. The resultant damage to diplomatic relations between the Turks and the rest of the English merchant community took years to repair, and the East India Company ultimately paid out £900 as a "free gift" to the Levant Company in acknowledgment of their fault in the mismanagement of Middleton's Mocha affair.[6]

Attempts to revive an English trading presence in the Red Sea were put on hold in the immediate aftermath of the sixth voyage, but it was not long before they resumed again. By late 1617, Sir Thomas Roe was recommending that a ship be sent to Mocha. The coffee trade was not the focus of this continuing interest in Mocha and the Red Sea trade; rather, it was the strategic importance of the port as a wintering place for English ships en route further east and its key role in the trading world of the Indian Ocean that kept Mocha on the East India Company's agenda. Coral, rather than coffee, made Mocha important in the early seventeenth century. In 1618 and 1619, the company made a number of supplications to the Turkish governor of Mocha asking him to grant it the privilege of establishing a trading factory at the port. The request was favorably received and Roe soon held "excellent hopes for trade" in Mocha, although the governors of Surat were much less enthusiastic about the prospect of English encroachment on a trade which had hitherto been the preserve of Gujarati merchants.[7]

As the East India Company became drawn into the economy of the Indian Ocean, its factors abroad gradually came to recognize the commercial potential of coffee. The company's factory at Surat became the chief English trading station in the Indian Ocean, and its president, Thomas Kerridge, soon got word from merchants in the area that Mocha coffee was in much demand in Safavid Persia and Mughal India. In March 1619, he told his factors in Mocha that they should begin to buy coffee there so that the company could profit from supplying the existing Asian markets. The English entry into the coffee market would remain limited to the intra-Asian "country trade" for many decades. Although Kerridge and his fellow factors at Surat had initially considered sending some coffee back to England after the first shipment had arrived from Mocha in November 1619, they decided against the notion, as they esteemed coffee to be "worth more heere in Suratt then your advice valueth it there" in England. By October 1621, company factors in the Surat region had established warehouses to store the coffee imported from Mocha to serve the country trade.[8]

From the 1620s through the 1650s, the East India Company took an active interest in supplying coffee to markets in Persia and in the Indian subcontinent. The profits from this trade could be substantial. President Kerridge reported back to the company's court of directors in London that he was able to sell Mocha coffee at a markup of 33 percent. The company bought both the "seed," coffee beans, and the husks from the coffee berry, "both which are usefull in making the drinke, though the one be better and dearer then the other," he told the directors. In January 1628, he sent samples of the coffee beans as well as the husks to London. This shipment may well have carried the first coffee to reach England. The company's venture into the Asian coffee trade met with success and was gradually expanded over time. In December 1630, the new president at Surat, Thomas Rastel, regretted that the coffee trade had been "so much neglected," and resolved that in "the future we intend to goe still augmenting as wee finde incouragement thereunto." In 1632, company factors in Persia were informing the president and his council at Surat that coffee "can at all times be sold to good profit" in Persian markets. By 1636, the Surat factors recommended to the company directors that a regular ship be dispatched from London to Mocha en route to Surat; such an action would facilitate the coffee trade while also protecting the company's fleet from the threat of piracy in the Red Sea region.[9] Piracy would remain a persistent danger for Mocha merchants throughout the century.

New opportunities in the coffee trade emerged as a result of the collapse of Turkish rule over Yemen in 1636. Ottoman control of Yemen, always tenuous, had been slipping drastically since the outbreak of a revolt against the sultan in the 1620s. Word reached Surat in August 1636 that the local Arabs had revolted against Ottoman rule in Yemen and had established their own self-rule. The prospect was enticing, for it was rumored that they intended to lower the customs dues on trading in Mocha and Aden.[10] The new imam of Mocha welcomed the arrival of English traders and the company was soon back in the business of supplying Persia and western India with coffee.[11] Henceforth European traders in Mocha would deal directly with the local imam rather than with Ottoman administrators.

Of course the English entry into a lucrative new trade did not remain unnoticed by its competitors in the Indian Ocean market. Although the focus of Dutch trading efforts in the East Indies was placed on the profitable spice trade of Indonesia, the Dutch East India Company had taken as keen an interest in the Red Sea trade as the English had, and Dutch ships also began to call in at Mocha in the late 1610s and early 1620s. Soon thereafter, the Dutch too had engaged themselves in the inter-Asian coffee trade. French traders were also suspected of wanting to intervene in the Red Sea markets. In November 1647, English company agents noted the presence of a French pirate ship operating in the Persian Gulf which had seized the coffee cargo from a small vessel which had been bound for the port of Basra.[12]

Although the country trade profits from the English East India Company's involvement in the coffee trade were encouraging, it took nearly thirty years after the arrival of President Kerridge's coffee samples in London for the company to recognize that there might be a domestic market for coffee consumption. Five years after the foundation of the first coffeehouse in London, a company committee decided in December 1657 to order their Surat factors to send ten tons of coffee back to England for domestic sale. Until this point, the coffee supplied to England must have come in smaller quantities from Levant or other Mediterranean merchants. About a year later, another order was placed for twice as much coffee, twenty tons. Perhaps the success of the London coffeehouses had finally encouraged the company to jump into the long-distance coffee trade. Dutch merchants noted this move carefully, and by 1660 the Dutch East India Company had also ordered a shipment of coffee to be sent from Persia, noting that the popularity of coffee drinking was on the rise in Europe generally but especially in England.[13]

Some of the English company's factors in India proposed establishing a permanent factory in Yemen if a regular coffee import trade were to be undertaken. The company's Rajapur agents suggested that "if England will vend a considerable quantity [of coffee], its worth setling a factory att Bettlefucky [Beit-al-Fakih], which lyes higher up then Mocho; and then you may sell your goods better [than] that you send from Surat, and buy what quantitie of coho seed you please, which seles for good profitt in Bussora [Basra] and Persia." The proposal was not heeded, for earlier attempts in the 1640s and 1650s to establish a permanent trading factory had proven unprofitable. Continued attempts to maintain a factory at Mocha even after the assumption of regular coffee imports in the 1660s would not succeed. For the rest of the seventeenth century, the Mocha coffee trade would fall under the jurisdiction of the Surat presidency in western India.[14]

Matching supply with the nascent consumer demand for coffee in Britain was not an easy task. The company declined to make an additional request for coffee in its February 1660 directions to the Surat factory, as it thought that the previous year's supply of twenty tons would be more than sufficient for the time being. These directions arrived too late, however, and a fresh supply of coffee was sent back to London from Surat in December 1661. Demand for the new coffee supplies seems to have been strong after its debut on the London market, and the company continued to submit orders for new coffee supplies on a regular basis. As Mocha coffee made it to London, the months of transit time took their toll as supplies often arrived spoiled or damaged. The shipment of "black and rotten" coffee was a perennial hazard of the trade, and the company often found itself obliged to offer refunds to merchants who had inadvertently purchased such goods. As a means of loss control, the company would nevertheless put up its damaged coffee for sale along with the quality supplies at its regular auction sales. Quality control remained a large issue for the international coffee trade, and the company remained concerned that consumers were beginning to think that the coffee supplied by the Levant Company was of a higher quality than its Mocha coffee.[15]

Even as the London market for coffee was opening up, the English East India Company remained engaged in the Asian country trade in the later seventeenth century, although it seems that Mocha coffee was increasingly sent back home to London rather than sold in Persian and Indian markets. The success of the company in opening up new domestic markets for previously unknown commodities such as coffee also seems to have encouraged its merchants to engage in bolder entrepreneurial activity. The company began to import tea in small amounts in the 1660s and much larger quantities in the 1670s; the first appearance of tea at a company auction sale occurred on 21 September 1669. The company also began to consider ways by which it might seize control of the means of production of its imports. An attempt was made to take nutmeg seeds from Bantam in Indonesia back to England, where an "experiment" might be made with growing the seeds in other English plantations abroad. Nothing came of this project, but the will to experiment with product innovation was now clearly present in the company's correspondence with its factors abroad. In its September 1682 instructions to Edward Halford, a company factor on a ship bound for Mocha, the company told him that once he arrived at the port, he should be on the lookout for "all manner of commodities" brought there. "You may gain so much knowledge in all kind of India commodities as to know which of them is most proper for Europe," they added. "The more variety you can meet with and buy for us at Mocha the better we shall esteem your service." The company sent similar instructions to the Surat factors: "Provide and send us as much and as great variety of all sorts of new commodities . . . for such is now the humour not only of our own nation but of France, Holland &c. that every new thing takes, especially if it be lightsome or gawdy, so that a new commodity hardly ever fails to turn us exceeding well to account."[16] The success of coffee may not have been the sole cause of the East India Company's new entrepreneurial spirit, but it must have given encouragement for the prospect of even more profits from opening up new markets for new commodities.

The East India Company's success with coffee also bred imitators. The Levant Company was also deeply involved in the late seventeenth-century coffee trade through its connections with Mediterranean ports such as Leghorn, Smyrna, and especially Cairo, an Egyptian port which received Mocha coffee through the Red Sea trade via the port of Suez. The Turkey merchants were hindered, however, by occasional prohibitions imposed by Ottoman authorities preventing the exportation of coffee by Christians out of the Grand Seigneur's dominions. One way of getting around this difficulty was to cut out the middlemen and open up a direct trading route to Mocha. In the early 1680s, the Levant Company's jealousy of the East India Company's profits and its discontent with the India Company's restricted joint-stock organization encouraged it to go through with the plan, and a ship named the *Arcana Merchant* was launched on a trading mission to Mocha.[17] This maneuver risked the ire of the East India Company by encroaching upon its stated monopoly of trade with the East Indies, an area traditionally defined as the lands east of the Cape of Good Hope. The Levant merchants tried to circumvent this argument by claiming that they too had a right to engage in the Red Sea trade by virtue of their own royal charter granting them the right to trade with the Ottoman Empire. Mocha thus fell within the purview of two claims to monopoly trade.

When the *Arcana Merchant* returned to London in March 1681, the conflict between the two chartered monopolies came to a head. The East India Company wanted the ship to be declared an illegal interloper and to seize the goods imported from Mocha. The Levant Company wanted an affirmation of its right to participate in the Red Sea trade, and it used the question to launch a propaganda campaign against the East India Company as a closed and corrupt monopoly. The Levant Company's ultimate goal was not merely the recognition of its right to trade at Mocha, but to open the East India joint stock to investment from the rest of the London merchant community. Although the case proceeded in the court of admiralty, the real contest was for the favor of King Charles II. Both the East India and the Levant Company petitioned the king for a royal resolution to the dispute, although the India merchants sweetened their supplication with a gift of one thousand guineas.[18] Deliberations continued at repeated meetings of the privy council in the latter half of 1681, and the king ultimately decided against the Levant Company. Not only did the Turkey merchants fail to secure the wholesale revocation of the monopoly privileges of the East India Company that they had hoped for, but they were not able to recoup their losses from the seizure of the *Arcana Merchant*'s cargo, which was sold off on 29 December. The East India Company's monopoly remained secure and the Turkey merchants did not attempt any further incursions into the Mocha trade, even if they continued to challenge the legitimacy of the East India monopoly.[19]

Further attempts at interloping voyages to Mocha from other parties continued, however. By the 1690s, the coffee trade was lucrative enough to attract independent merchant ventures from entrepreneurs who were prepared to take the risk of defying the East India Company's monopoly. The problem of piracy and interloping in the last decades of the seventeenth century was so serious that doubts began to circulate about the continued viability of the East India Company. Legal challenges to interloping were not always successful or viable options for the company, and interlopers sometimes succeeded in unloading and selling their East India goods in London and especially the outports of the British Isles in the 1680s and 1690s. This new situation forced the company to adapt its business strategies accordingly. Upon advice in February

1692 that an English interloper had succeeded in buying coffee at Mocha, the company advised its factors at Surat that they should refrain from any large purchases of coffee, while adding that company ships in the area should attack the interlopers using "what other means you can as we did formerly to ruinate their voyages, according to the powers granted to us by our charters." They did not succeed in intercepting the pirates, and the *Mary* arrived in Kinsale, Ireland, in December 1692 with a cargo full of Mocha coffee. In July 1693, the *Success* also arrived safely in Newcastle with 252 bales of coffee on board. Later that year another interloper's coffee supplies were sold in London without any legal problems and such sales became a regular part of the wholesale coffee market for the rest of the decade.[20]

Along with the new supplies from interlopers and continuing competition from the Turkey merchants, another new source of coffee in the 1690s came from the cargo of French ships captured as the prizes of war. This intense competition for the coffee market caused prices to drop, and buyers were reluctant to take on the risk of purchasing large quantities of coffee for domestic sale. East India Company merchants frequently complained about the cheapness of coffee in the 1690s and lamented its slim profit margins compared to those obtained from other Indian commodities such as myrrh or olibanum. Company voyages to Mocha seemed designed to discourage the arrival of interlopers and to repair the damaged reputation of the company with the Indian merchant community after Sir Josiah Child's disastrous war against the Mughal emperor in 1687–88 as much as they were to procure coffee for the British market. With the foundation of a New East India Company by parliamentary legislation in 1698, the competition for the coffee trade continued to increase as the new company also sent ships out to Mocha to buy coffee.[21]

Despite these difficulties, the old East India Company remained engaged with the coffee trade in the first years of the eighteenth century, and its directors noted in 1708 that "coffee continues to be greatly in demand." The perspective became rather rosier as the threats of interlopers and piracy receded and a merger with the New Company reduced the competition in the trade. The dispatch of company supercargoes bound direct for Mocha was authorized in 1705 and they continued on a regular basis in the years following.[22] Prices for coffee increased substantially in the later years of Queen Anne's reign at both the wholesale rates abroad and the retail levels in Britain. Daniel Defoe complained in 1711 that the coffeehouses were obliged to raise their prices from a penny to three half-pence per dish of coffee.[23] With such favorable trading conditions, the East India Company began to make moves to consolidate its commanding position in the coffee trade. In March 1712, the company's court of directors authorized an annual voyage direct to Mocha to obtain coffee; in August 1714, they formed a committee to consider once again the viability of setting up a permanent factory at Mocha. This time the plans for a factory proved successful, despite the protests of the supercargoes for the regular voyages who were put out of work by the assignment of a permanent trading station. By establishing their Mocha factory, the court of directors thought they might be able to purchase coffee of better quality and at cheaper rates as well as to free themselves from dependence on Indian Surat merchants. By 1718–19, company factors had obtained the favor of the local governors at Mocha and had set up their factory. The Mocha factory would survive, save for a short period of closure from 1726–28, through the rest of the eighteenth century and remained active in the early years of the nineteenth.[24]

The East India Company's encounters with coffee in the trading world of Asia from its first voyage to Mocha in 1609 to its establishment of a permanent trading factory there in the second decade of the eighteenth century offers an instructive example of the commercial reception of coffee. What began as a minor curiosity of little note and no commercial interest was slowly incorporated into the structure of the company's trade. Beginning with the Asian country trade in the 1620s, the company's engagement with the coffee trade grew slowly but surely. By the time that domestic interest in the virtues of coffee had been spurred by virtuoso discourse and writing on the topic, the company was well positioned to exploit its knowledge of the trade and its access to the main Arabian markets of supply in the later seventeenth century. Although the company never achieved a monopoly over the coffee trade, it did retain a commanding presence and it managed to outwit and survive competition from various quarters at every turn. Coffee was never the most profitable commodity sold by the East India Company, but its relative importance grew steadily over time. Coffee never accounted for more than 2 percent of the value of the company's total imports during the first two decades of its regular auction sales of coffee (1664–84). But by the 1710s and 1720s, the company's coffee revenue was more than 2 percent of the total value of its imports, and in certain years (1718, 1724) coffee was worth as much as 17 and 22 percent of the total, respectively (Chart 1).

Although the East India Company was the classic "mercantilist" corporation—aspiring as it did to a monopolistic position in the East India trade both at home and abroad, and reliant as it was on the state for its legitimacy and on military force for its competitive viability in overseas trade—it was hardly the ossified, conservative, and inefficient business imagined by its critics. The successful assimilation of coffee into the business operations of the East India

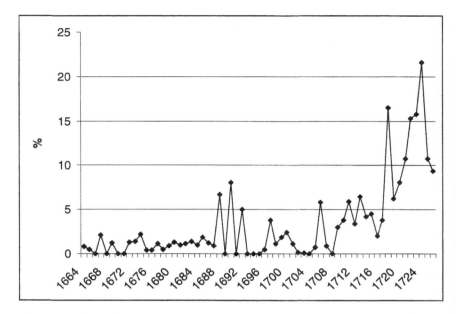

Chart 1. Value of East India Company Coffee Imports as a Percentage of Total Company Imports, 1664–1724
Source: Chaudhuri, *Trading World of Asia,* 521.

Company demonstrates how flexible mercantilism could be in practice. The initial entrepreneurial conservativism of the company eventually became entrepreneurial dynamism as the profit potential of new commodities such as coffee began to be recognized and developed by the company's factors abroad and its directors in London.[25] The East India Company did not set out to forge a new market for coffee in the Red Sea and Indian Ocean when it began its trading enterprises in the early seventeenth century, but it did succeed in making itself an indispensable agent in the growth of the British coffee trade over the course of the next century.

Home and Dry: The British Coffee Market

Although the East India Company did not become the major supplier of coffee in Britain until the 1710s, it did conduct a number of substantial sales on a regular basis. A careful study of the structure of the company's coffee sales can help us understand the ways in which coffee was assimilated into the domestic economy for new exotic goods. The records of the company's court of general sales are the only detailed record of wholesale coffee sales in London during the period in which coffee was introduced to the metropolitan market. As was the case for the discovery of the coffee market abroad, it seems that merchants entered the domestic market with trepidation. What began as a rather open market without any clear dominant presence soon became the preserve of a select few merchants who sought to make themselves the major players in the coffee trade.

The first sale of East Indian coffee by auction took place at the company's court of general sales on 1 August 1660. Here ten bales of coffee seed were sold to a merchant named John Johnson, while another bale of "damaged" coffee was sold to Thomas Short along with three extra bags of coffee. Neither Johnson nor Short was a particularly large dealer in other East India goods at the time, and their reasons for jumping into the coffee business at this date are now unclear. Johnson's experience in selling this new commodity must have been successful, as he returned the next year when another thirty-five bales of coffee were put up for sale at the company auction on 20 March 1661. Although Johnson bought up about one quarter of the supplies on offer, he was joined this time by a much more substantial East India dealer, a merchant named James Brome, who bought more than half of the coffee at the sale. While Johnson appears to have stuck to his coffee purchases, Brome bought considerable quantities of East India goods besides coffee at the company's sales, including more traditional commodities such as pepper, saltpeter, and indigo. Later company sales also saw the arrival of larger merchant dealers into the coffee trade. Thomas King, a major dealer in East India goods such as pepper, cassia lignum, china roots, sugar, and saltpeter, also bought nine bales of coffee at the company's October 1661 sale.[26]

It difficult to identify further information about the merchants who began to buy coffee at the East India Company's auction sales beyond the information left by the records of the court of general sales. Most coffee buyers must have been substantial domestic merchants, for they needed a large supply of ready capital and working credit to make purchases at company sales, and many probably had a substantial interest in the grocery trades, given the proclivity of early modern merchants to specialize in their trading. None of the company's coffee buyers was a coffeehouse keeper, but some may have sold portions of their stock directly to larger coffeehouses. The coffee merchant Thomas D'Aeth, who operated primarily through his Italian Levant connections, spoke of being prevailed upon by the "coffy men" to buy more coffee in the perilous market of the late 1690s. D'Aeth profited through his Italian associates, but few merchants who bought coffee at the East India sales were of foreign extraction. Overseas merchants with an interest in coffee, such as D'Aeth, may have preferred to take advantage of their international networks to purchase coffee at cheaper rates abroad in the hope that they could import the coffee to Britain at a lower transaction cost than that burdened by the East India Company. Merchants such as Moses Francia, or Symon Jacob and Francis Lusto, both of whom bought the company's coffee at its 30 October 1667 sale, may have been of Jewish or Levantine origin, but these traders were not substantial or frequent coffee purchasers. Despite contemporary impressions that Jews were overrepresented in East India commodity trading, the surnames of most of the company's coffee buyers appear decidedly English.[27] Names such as Johnson, Short, Brome, King, Winter, Barker, and Stevens recur frequently. Francis Lascoe, Mr. Legendre, and Mr. Dubois may have been Huguenots, as was Henry Gambier, who carried on a substantial coffee trade in the 1710s and 1720s. Only two purchasers, Sir John Lethullier and Sir Thomas Rawlinson, were identified as gentlemen. One of the most prominent coffee merchants of the 1680s and 1690s, Nathan Long, identified himself as a ship's captain.[28]

It seems that the coffee market at auction gradually came to be dominated by a few key dealers. Robert Wooley, who began purchasing coffee at the company's auctions in September 1669 and continued to do so into the 1680s, established himself as the first major dealer in East India coffee. Wooley's purchases account for more than 15 percent of the total coffee sold by the company between 1660 and 1677. This was substantially more than the second largest purchaser in the same period, Humphrey Brome, who bought a bit more than 3 percent of the total, and all of that in the early years between 1662 and 1664. Just as Wooley's reign as chief coffee merchant came to an end, a new contender, of Captain Nathan Long, arose to take his place. Long began to buy coffee in September 1680, and by the 1690s he was the dominant coffee merchant at the company sales, sometimes buying all or the vast majority of the stocks on offer at an auction. Although Wooley and Long became a commanding presence in the coffee trade, neither of them restricted his purchases exclusively to coffee. Both invested substantially in a variety of East India goods such as pepper and textiles, and both were quick to establish themselves as tea dealers as well. By the late 1680s, Wooley had stopped purchasing coffee and devoted his resources instead to purchasing tea.[29]

The "sale by inch of candle" was the preferred means by which the company sold its imported goods, such sales were highly anticipated by the London merchant community and were newsworthy events (Figure 7). Restoration-era newswriters seem to have taken a particular interest in the sale of coffee at company auctions. The company did its best to publicize its sales by circulating in advance handbills detailing the commodities which would be exposed to sale.[30] The auction was an efficient means of selling imported coffee quickly

Figure 7. Thomas Rowlandson, "The India House Sale Room" (1 December 1808), in Ackermann, *Microcosm of London* (1808–1810), plate 45. Beinecke shelfmark ByzL 080, vol. 2. Courtesy of the Beinecke Rare Book and Manuscript Library, Yale University.

and efficiently, assuming that the successful bidders expeditiously paid for and removed their purchases from the company's warehouses. Many buyers were not so conscientious. In March 1704 the company finally resolved to forbid buyers who did not promptly claim and pay for their goods from attending future candle sales. While the auction sale worked well in markets with substantial numbers of purchasers with a great demand for the commodity, it appeared to be less attractive as the coffee market became less crowded in the 1680s and 1690s. Another disadvantage to the auction sale for the company was that advance notice of a large sale of coffee inevitably drove down its price in the open market.[31]

The company attempted to maintain a higher price for coffee through a number of stratagems. The first was simply to set a base level price. Beginning in June 1681, the court of committees established price guidelines for the coffee sold at company auctions and began to arrange private sales of coffee to individual merchants at a prearranged price. By October, just such a deal had been struck by the merchant John Flavell, who contracted to purchase the hefty quantity of 283 bales of coffee from the company at the price of £8 17s 5d per pound. Fixed price selling was not new to the company; it had been the practice for East Indian spices in the early seventeenth century. Flavell's contract did signal a new stage in the development of the East Indian coffee trade, however. Flavell indicated his faith in the quality and the marketability of the company's coffee by offering to put up £1,000 as a down payment on his purchase, the largest in the history of the company's coffee sales. At the same time, the company showed its preference for dealing with a single large wholesaler at a fixed price rather than a larger group of dealers at varied prices. Flavell's contract obliged him not to hoard his coffee supply or to use his now commanding position in the domestic market to set an exorbitant price: he agreed to sell half of his stock to any other coffee dealers in London at a fixed profit margin of 2 percent.[32] By the 1680s, the domestic coffee market had become a safe bet for the wholesale traders in East India imports. The court of committees continued to set price guidelines for its coffee, and coffee continued to be sold by individual contracts as well as through the auctions at the general court of sales. After arranging a sale of one hundred bags of coffee at the rate of £10 per hundredweight to Robert Wooley in February 1687, the court of committees concluded that private contracts should be preferred to public sales of coffee. This resolution was swiftly approved by the company's court of directors.[33]

Although private contracts may have been a more convenient means of selling East India Company coffee, some lesser merchants, who lacked either the connections or the means to finance such sales, were chagrined at the increasing popularity of private sales and complained that these arrangements were "not customary." There was little these prospective buyers could do, however, and the practice of private sales of coffee only further encouraged the consolidation of the London coffee market into the hands of a select few. Both Robert Wooley and Nathan Long eagerly took advantage of private coffee sales. Big buyers such as Wooley and Long were able to extract favorable terms from the company regarding the return of coffee supplies later discovered to be "damaged" or below an accepted standard quality; they also secured an agreement from the company not to compete with their own sales by putting up more coffee from its warehouses on sale. Often the damaged coffee returned to the company would be put up for resale at auction, so these preferred purchasers were effectively given an opportunity to pick only the top quality coffee imported from the East Indies. Indeed, it seems that coffee merchants such as Wooley and Long benefited more than the company from these private sale arrangements. In January 1691, the company agreed to a private sale not to garner a higher price for coffee but because its stocks were already substantial and, they reckoned, "not likely to find vend at the generall sales in any reasonable time." Hence the court of committee was authorized to sell off those stocks at the best price possible. Long was quick to agree and he soon arranged to buy up all the coffee in the company's warehouses.[34]

As the Mocha trade was regularized in the first decades of the eighteenth century, the company began to experiment with newer means of selling its coffee. In September 1706, the court of committees resolved to fix the sale prices for coffee and tea sold by the company. By December, the Company resolved to forbear from any coffee sales until the next March and ordered that this notice be published on the Royal Exchange, the main gathering place for overseas merchants in London. The purpose behind these moves was presumably to inflate the market price for coffee. The practice of restricting company coffee sales to select occasions continued in the years to follow. In August 1711, the company's court of directors considered abolishing the practice of auction sales by candle for all of its goods, but the motion was rejected and the practice continued for the rest of the century. In a further attempt to maintain the price of coffee, the company resolved in March 1714 to restrict its coffee auctions to an annual sale and had the resolution published on the Royal Exchange. This practice seems to have met with general approval and it was later extended in response to a petition from several coffee dealers who complained about the inconveniences they experienced through the company's continued resort to private contracts for coffee sales. In September 1716, the court of directors decided not to hold any sales of damaged coffee or private coffee sales before its annual coffee auction.[35]

The detail provided by the East India Company's sales records could be misleading. It would be wrong to confuse the company's sales with the British coffee market as a whole. Many buyers at the company's sales may well have intended to reexport their coffee for ultimate consumption outside Britain. Similarly, some British coffee supplies may have been obtained from markets abroad, especially in Holland. Sales of Dutch East India Company imports were international events, and the commodities sold in Amsterdam made their way throughout a much wider European marketplace. The fortunes of the Dutch East India market, carefully watched by merchants in London, had a direct impact on prices obtained by the English India Company. A tight supply of imports in the Netherlands could lead to higher prices on the London market and vice versa.[36]

Just as important, the East India Company was not the only supplier of coffee in Great Britain. Indeed, before the company began to make regular voyages to Mocha in the early eighteenth century, the bulk of the coffee imported into Britain came from Levant and Mediterranean merchants. Along with Mocha, Cairo was a major transit center for the international coffee trade in the seventeenth and early eighteenth centuries. Approximately half of the coffee imported into Egypt from Yemen in 1697 was sent on to Istanbul and other parts of the Ottoman Empire. The remaining half was most likely bought by European Levant merchants eager to supply their own domestic markets. A majority of the coffee imported into the Netherlands in the early eighteenth century was Levantine, and not East Indian, in origin.[37]

The same was true in Britain. Precise figures for the origins of coffee imported into the British Isles are not available until the commencement of regular customs ledgers in 1697–98, but it is clear that Levant merchants were responsible for substantial imports of coffee by the 1660s at the latest. They maintained this dominance into the early eighteenth century. The customs records reveal that the majority of the coffee imported into England in the first decade of the eighteenth century came from Levant merchants operating out of either Turkish or Italian ports (Table 1). Although in individual years East Indian coffee imports could be substantial, such as in 1699 when they comprised 69 percent of the total, they were most often overshadowed by Mediterranean imports until the 1710s. With the commencement of annual voyages to Mocha however, the East India Company was soon able to dominate the coffee market by 1720. The quantities imported by the company in the 1710s were so great as to make Mocha coffee imports equivalent to almost two-thirds of the aggregate total of coffee imported in the first two decades of the eighteenth century. Even after Mocha coffee came to dominate the market, the "Turkey" coffee imported from the Levant retained a reputation for being of higher quality than the East Indian imports, perhaps because Levantine coffee did not have to make the long trip around the Cape of Good Hope and thus did not remain exposed to potential contamination from water or other goods shipped along with the coffee.[38]

The Dutch contribution to the British coffee market was negligible by the early eighteenth century. Coffee imports from Holland never amounted to even 1 percent of the total in any year between 1697 and 1720, an input that was even exceeded by Iberian merchants operating in Spain and the Straits of Gibraltar. The same cannot be said for the coffee export trade, however. Here the Dutch staplemarket was the top destination for British coffee reexports (Table 2). Much of the coffee exported to the Netherlands was destined for European consumption well beyond the United Provinces, but the Dutch ports remained the major entrepôt for the delivery of such goods from the British metropole. Coffee exports to the Dutch staplemarket were far more significant than the colonial trade to British territories in Ireland, North America, and the

Table 1. Source of British Coffee Imports, 1700–1720

	1700	1710	1720	1697–1720
East India	22%	41%	95%	65%
Holland	0	0	0	0
Italy	66	56	5	22
Turkey	12	1	0	12
Spain	0	1	0	0
Straits of Gibraltar	0	1	0	0
Total	100	100	100	99

Source: PRO, Cust. 3/1–22.

West Indies. By the 1720s, British coffee exports were increasingly shipped directly to their principal markets for consumption in German central Europe rather than through the Dutch staplemarket, but the dominance of these European markets for coffee was never challenged by British colonial markets in Ireland or North America.[39]

The early eighteenth century also saw a structural change in the nature of the British overseas coffee trade. At the beginning of the century, most of the coffee imported into the country was retained for home consumption. By the 1710s and 1720s, increasingly substantial amounts of the coffee brought to Britain was being reexported to other markets abroad. Often less than half of the coffee brought to British ports was retained for domestic consumption in the 1720s. It is impossible to measure these values precisely as there was a wide discrepancy between the import valuations and the reexport valuations of coffee; the former tended to be too low, while the latter were rather over-rated and included insurance and freight costs as part of their total valuation.[40] Nevertheless, the general trend is clear. As the East India Company came to dominate the supply of coffee to the London metropolitan market, that market itself was becoming an entrepôt for an international coffee trade that stretched from mainland Europe to the British colonial territories across the Atlantic. Domestic British consumers figured less and less prominently in this trade over the course of the eighteenth century.

None of the existing aggregate trade statistics for the British coffee imports and exports accounts for the clandestine coffee trade. The practice of coffee smuggling was clearly on the rise in the early eighteenth century. The introduction of customs duties on coffee by Parliament in 1689 provided an incentive to smuggle coffee into Britain undeclared. The problem was grave enough to force Parliament to reconsider its rates, which were halved in 1692 in recognition

Table 2. Destination of British Coffee Exports, 1700–1720

	1700	1710	1720
North America	1%	2%	0%
West Indies	1	3	0
Germany	8	6	9
Holland	85	72	88
Ireland	4	17	3
Total	100	100	100

Source: PRO, Cust. 3/1–22.

that very little of the coffee imported had been declared to the customs officers. As the war with France continued to drag on, additional coffee duties were imposed as a means of funding the costs of war and reconquest in Ireland. During Queen Anne's reign, the duties were again raised and continued, and they were ultimately made a permanent part of the state revenue. A system of bonded warehouses was authorized in 1711 in which duties were paid only when coffee was released from the warehouses for domestic consumption. Although the bonded warehouses were initially designed to prevent merchants from making excessive and fraudulent claims for their drawback payments, another result of this new fiscal policy, as David Ormrod has argued, was to further encourage the diversion of coffee away from the home market and on to the Dutch staplemarket.[41]

The new warehousing system may have made the business of the East India Company easier, but it did not end the practice of coffee smuggling. Although it had been granted a preferential 4.5 percent reduction on the duties it paid for its coffee imports, the company remained at a competitive disadvantage in relation to clandestine coffee dealers who imported and sold their supplies duty free. The company formed a committee in 1717 to research the problem of coffee smuggling. They determined that the clandestine trade focused on running undeclared coffee through landings in the west country, but suggested no clear solution to the problem. Customs officials also complained that the clandestine coffee trade was substantial and a great loss to the national revenue, but they too were at a loss for proposing a remedy. The mainland standing army became the front line in the mercantilist state's war against smugglers, and the enforcement of the customs revenue laws became an increasingly important part of the army's domestic duty over the course of the eighteenth century.[42]

The Decline of British Coffee

Although the discovery of coffee in the seventeenth century blazed a trail for the introduction of other new exotic commodities such as tea and chocolate, Britain has not been commonly known as a coffee-drinking nation. Tea, of course, ultimately supplanted coffee as the national hot drink of choice in the 1700s. This transition took place in the second decade of the eighteenth century, as the quantities of tea imported began to increase dramatically. Around 1700, it has been estimated that coffee consumption per capita was about ten times as great as that of tea. This would soon change. By the 1720s, the value of the teas imported into Britain was substantially higher than the value of the imported coffee (Table 3). These tea supplies were also directed at a domestic market and not for re-export abroad, as was increasingly the case for the coffee imported to Britain (Table 4). This situation would persist for the rest of the eighteenth century.[43]

What accounts for this relative shift from coffee to tea drinking in the early eighteenth century? The change is best explained by a new fiscal system which made coffee relatively more expensive and tea relatively cheaper. Simon Smith has demonstrated that a growing price differential between the two hot drinks encouraged the growth in tea consumption at the expense of coffee drinking. As the price of tea went down, it became an increasingly popular drink throughout the British Isles.[44]

By 1713, the East India Company had secured the right of access to the great Chinese port of Canton and was therefore able to begin regular shipments of tea directly from China beginning in 1717.[45] From this point onward, tea supplies would be regularly available on the British wholesale market. Supply

Table 3. Relative Values of Coffee and Tea Imported into Britain, 1715–23

	Coffee	Tea
1715–16	62%	38%
1716–17	50	50
1717–18	47	53
1718–19	45	55
1719–20	31	69
1720–21	33	67
1721–22	21	79
1722–23	12	88

Note: Percentage by value in pounds.
Source: BL, Additional MS 38330.

Table 4. Coffee and Tea Imports Retained for Home Consumption, 1701–21

	Coffee	Tea
1701	91%	31%
1711	39	85
1721	29	73

Source: Schumpeter, *Overseas English Trade Statistics,* 60.

would no longer impede the development of a tea market in Britain, but this alone cannot account for the growing preference for tea in early eighteenth-century Britain. The same period saw the growing exploitation by the East India Company of the opportunities for coffee supply through its Mocha factory. A full explanation for the relative decline of coffee must also take into consideration the changing position of coffee in the global political economy of the eighteenth century. Coffee shifted from being a specialty product of the Red Sea region to a colonial plantation crop, harvested primarily by slave labor. The rise of colonial coffee completely transformed the global coffee market, and here again the British position was unique.

Although it aggressively pursued a dominant position in the Mocha coffee trade, the English East India Company did not imitate the actions of the Dutch East India Company and encourage the development of new coffee plantations outside of the Red Sea region. The Arab merchants of Yemen had jealously guarded the secrets of coffee cultivation in the seventeenth century as worldwide demand for the drink began to grow dramatically, but they were not able to maintain their monopoly over coffee cultivation in the eighteenth century. The directors of the Dutch East India Company made a concentrated effort to encourage the transplant of coffee plants to their plantations on the Indonesian island of Java. The first plants arrived there in 1696, but the crop was destroyed in a great flood in 1699. A re-plantation was undertaken in 1704, but the first Javanese coffee shipment was not made until 1711. From this point onward, however, the structure of the international coffee market had been changed forever. Coffee would now soon join sugar and tobacco as one of the major colonial crops harvested by European plantation owners in both the East and the West Indies. By 1712, the coffee plant had been transferred to Surinam, and Dutch planters were soon growing the crop in the New World as well as in Asia. The French too began to cultivate coffee on the islands of Réunion and Bourbon in 1715 and later extended their coffee plantation enterprises to Martinique, Guadeloupe, and St. Domingue (present-day Haiti). These new supplies of Indonesian and Caribbean coffee would soon find their way back to the Asian trading worlds that first nurtured the coffee market in its infancy, and by the later eighteenth century, European colonial powers such as the Netherlands and France were net exporters, rather than importers, of coffee to Asia.[46]

The British West Indies were much less eager to exploit these new possibilities. Coffee cultivation began on the islands of Jamaica and Montserrat in 1728, but coffee never supplanted sugar and tobacco as the main cash crops of the British West Indies. As Simon Smith has shown, coffee remained "sugar's poor relation" in the plantation economy of the British West Indies. There was little official support for the promotion of coffee cultivation in the British West Indies. Sugar planters tended to outbid coffee planters for the best land on which to grow their crops, and above all, the colonial tariff system consistently favored sugar production. Coffee remained decidedly a second-choice crop resorted to only by the poorer planters. West Indian coffee never amounted to more than 5 percent of British coffee imports even by the 1750s, and metropolitan consumers consistently regarded it as a poor substitute for Arabian coffee.[47]

As a result of this situation, British tea developed an increasingly significant price advantage over coffee in the eighteenth century. By the end of the century, tea was cheap enough to be regularly drunk by the working classes as well as the rest of society. Coffee was not exorbitantly expensive, but it had clearly been displaced by tea as the caffeinated drink of choice in the British Isles. Whereas the French *sans-culottes* of the 1790s thought of coffee as a necessity along the same lines as their daily bread, and they used the lack of affordable coffee as a legitimate cause for food rioting, such a situation was inconceivable in Britain. In 1807, William Young observed that in Germany, coffee was considered to be "the drink of all, to the very porters and postillions." He could not have said the same about Britain, for tea had clearly captured the popular palate. Tea drinking was so popular among the working classes by the latter part of the century that Dr. Richard Price could complain that "the lower ranks of people" have come to think of "tea, wheaten bread and other delicacies" as "necessaries which were formerly unknown to them." Coffee and tea were widely available to people of all classes throughout the British Isles by the later eighteenth century: Samuel Johnson was surprised to find both being served in Hebridean homes during his tour of the western islands of Scotland in 1773. Dr. Johnson famously drank prodigious quantities of tea, but coffee he indulged in only irregularly.[48] By this time coffee was clearly tea's second cousin.

PART II

Inventing the Coffeehouse

It should be easy to identify what a coffeehouse was at the dawn of the eighteenth century: a place where people gathered together to drink coffee, learn about the news of the day, and perhaps to meet with other local residents and discuss matters of mutual concern. Yet beyond this simple rubric lay a wide variety of places. The coffeehouse was an innovative new institution that emerged in the mid-seventeenth century, but it was built on a number of familiar templates. The coffeehouse was a public house much like the ale-houses, inns, and taverns that had long formed a part of the British urban landscape. The term "public house" captures nicely the paradoxical juxtaposition of the domestic and the public spheres found inside these places, and the term was increasingly being used to refer to homes open to customers for rest and refreshment in the post-Restoration era.[1]

Coffeehouses did not look much different from taverns or alehouses on the outside, or even on the inside (Figures 8 and 9). They were all rather ephemeral structures. The surviving images of the coffeehouses suggest that the interiors at least were decorated almost entirely in wood, which would have made the places extremely vulnerable to fire as well as damage from heavy rains and the changing temperatures from season to season. Few of the original buildings seem to have survived past the late nineteenth century. Most coffeehouses were in fact hardly distinguishable from the rest of the building around them.

Coffeehouse proprietors tended to live on the premises with the rest of their family, and the "coffeehouse" proper was really little more than a room within the larger domicile. Some of the larger and more prosperous coffeehouses may have offered several rooms to their various customers, perhaps even private rooms, but the standard coffeehouse model seems to have been one large room with one or more tables laid out to accommodate customers. Anthony Sambach's coffeehouse had five tables; Samuel North's coffeehouse had nine tables in his "great coffee room." Some coffeehouses had benches; others had chairs for their customers (Figures 10 and 11). Like most early modern households, each coffeehouse had a number of servants, usually younger boys, who served coffee and attended to the needs of the customers. Other boys working as shoe-shiners or porters for hire also plied their trade on the premises.[2] Many eighteenth-century images of coffeehouses include household pets such as birds, but especially dogs (Figures 12 and 13). Coffeehouse-keepers were also heads of their households, and as such they were usually men, widows, or occasionally unmarried single women. One could usually find the keeper of a coffeehouse located behind a bar at the head of the room. This was where the drinks and other goods on offer were prepared for customers, although the coffee itself was usually prepared in a vat over a large fire. Here the ground coffee beans and the water would be boiled together to brew the freshest coffee. Extra coffee might be kept warm in metal pots by the hearth.[3]

The coffee served was much weaker than the coffee we normally drink today. There was no early modern "espresso." Seventeenth-century estimates of the ratio of coffee to water used by coffeehouse-keepers range from one ounce of grounds per quart of water to two ounces per pint and a half of water. The coffee was unfiltered, but it was often mixed with milk to make "milk coffee" or with sugar, a habit that was increasingly common by the last two decades of the seventeenth century. There was some debate as to whether spring water or "river water" from the Thames made for better coffee, but it seems that river water was used most commonly as it was much easier to obtain.[4] Although coffeehouses were of course best known for serving coffee, they quickly became known as places where one might find a wide variety of exotic drinks. Tea and chocolate were commonly served alongside coffee. The chocolate drinks served in the coffeehouses were much thicker and richer than the coffee and tea: along with the chocolate grounds, a substantial number of eggs, some sugar, milk, and even "a thin slice of white bread" could be added to the mix. Other possible chocolate additives included flour for "breakfast" chocolate or wine for an alcoholic chocolate drink.[5] More exotic concoctions served at some coffeehouses included: sage tea; a drink called "content" which consisted primarily of milk and eggs; and ratesia, a drink fortified with brandy.

Figure 8. Joseph Highmore, attributed (previously attributed to William Hogarth), "Figures in a Tavern or a Coffeehouse" (1720s), oil on panel (19.7 × 46.4 cm); BAC, Paul Mellon Collection, B2001.2.86. Courtesy of the British Art Center, Yale University. The interior of the public house depicted here would suit either a tavern or a coffeehouse and it is not clear whether coffee or alcoholic drinks are being served. Certainly the table, pipes, papers, and servant staff would be appropriate for either a tavern or a coffeehouse.

GARRAWAY'S COFFEE-HOUSE.   *(From a Sketch taken shortly before its Demolition.)*

Figure 9. William Henry Prior, Garraway's Coffeehouse (from a sketch taken shortly before its demolition), (London, 1878 or later), hand-colored wood engraving from a sketch by William Henry Prior and originally produced for the part-work *Old and New London* (London, 1873–1878), (10.5 × 14.5 cm). Courtesy of the author. The outward appearance of the early modern coffeehouse was nondescript. They were commonly located on the ground floor of a larger building.

Sometimes other alcoholic liquors such as mum, mead, metheglin, cider, perry, usquebaugh, brandy, aqua vitae, strong-waters, beer, and ale were sold in the coffeehouses.[6] While coffeehouses offered many drinks in addition to coffee, it seems that coffee was not sold in other drinking establishments, such as taverns, ordinaries, or alehouses.

Along with its drinks, the coffeehouses offered a place to smoke tobacco, another exotic drug whose consumption was becoming increasingly popular over the course of the seventeenth century. Judging by the presence of pipes in nearly every representation of the early coffeehouses, smoking was a natural complement to drinking coffee. By the turn of the century, snuff tobacco was also popular in the more fashionable coffeehouses. It was this combination of a variety of different exotic consumption options that made the coffeehouse distinctive among early modern public houses. Although one could smoke just

Figure 10. W. Dickinson, "The Coffeehouse Patriots; or news, from St Eustatia" (London, 15 October 1781), stipple; no. 12 of a series (11 3/4 ×14 in.). BM Sat., 5923; HL, Print 216/4. Courtesy of the Huntington Library, San Marino, California. The booths, animals, and food served at table are all characteristic of the later eighteenth-century coffeehouse. The public reading of the news, and the satiric denigration of the practice, were both commonplace in the early modern coffeehouse.

about anywhere, and one could find wine, ales, or beers on offer at most taverns or alehouses, a coffeehouse might offer any of this plus the newly fashionable hot drinks such as coffee, chocolate, or tea. In this way, the coffeehouse became an important new venue for the introduction of innovative consumption habits.

Some coffeehouses were quite modest, with just enough supplies to cater to a handful of customers, but others could be very large indeed. It was not unusual to find more than forty or fifty men together in a coffeehouse at the

Figure 11. James Gillray, "Un Diplomatique, settling affairs at Stevens's [Coffee-house]" (9 June 1797); etching with hand coloring (30.1 × 22.2 cm), BM Sat., no. 9067. LWL, 797.6.9.1. Courtesy of the Lewis Walpole Library, Yale University. The print probably refers to Stevens's Coffeehouse and Hotel on Bond Street, London, which flourished in the 1790s and the first decades of the nineteenth century.

same time. The coffeeman Samuel North's stock in trade included enough coffee dishes, mugs, and glasses to serve ninety customers, although it is un-likely that he ever had occasion to use all of them at once. Coffeehouses catered to their customers day and night: candles were always on hand to provide illumination when natural sunlight was not available through the

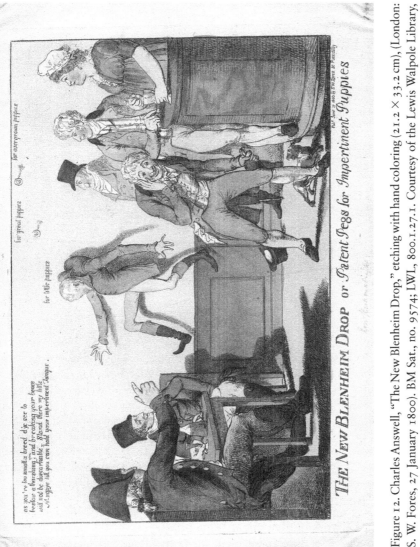

Figure 12. Charles Answell, "The New Blenheim Drop," etching with hand coloring (21.2 × 33.2 cm), (London: S. W. Fores, 27 January 1800). BM Sat., no. 9574; LWL, 800.1.27.1. Courtesy of the Lewis Walpole Library, Yale University. The anxieties about impertinent coffeehouse talk and behavior documented for the seventeenth and early eighteenth centuries in this study did not abate in the ensuing years, as this print attests.

THE SILENT MEETING.

Publish'd 11 May 1794 by LAURIE & WHITTLE, 53 Fleet Street, London

Figure 13. Isaac Cruickshank, "The Silent Meeting," etching and engraving with hand coloring (16.5 ×23.1 cm), (London: Laurie & Whittle, 12 May 1794); LWL, 794.5.12.53. Courtesy of the Lewis Walpole Library, Yale University. By the later eighteenth century, quiet reading and relaxed sociability had become an important coffeehouse ideal and coffeehouses assumed a rather genteel aura. The Russian Karamzin recorded in 1790: "I have dropped into a number of coffeehouses only to find twenty or thirty men sitting around in deep silence, reading newspapers, and drinking port. You are lucky if, in the course of ten minutes, you hear three words. And what are they? 'Your health, gentlemen!' " See also Figure 32 below.

windows. The working day might begin around six in the morning and a continuing parade of different clientele might find their way in and out of the coffeehouse over the course of the day. Some might stop in briefly to catch the latest news or to look for a friend; others might spend hours at the coffeehouse "either to transact affairs or to enjoy conversation."[7] Coffeehouses that stayed open too late, usually past nine or ten at night, were suspicious. Both royal and civic proclamations often enjoined that public houses close their doors at nine or ten in the evening, although these demands could never be fully enforced. These late-hour coffeehouses catered to a nighttime demimonde and their attractions probably resided as much in the alcoholic drink and the free-spirited company on offer there. One paid the reckoning at the end of one's stay. The coffeehouses were famous as inexpensive "penny universities," and Joseph Addison's Mr. Spectator frequently remarks upon how he paid his "penny at the bar" of the coffeehouse before leaving the premises. Humphrey Kidney, the waiter at St. James's coffeehouse, kept a book of debts for the regular customers, noting carefully those patrons who left the premises without paying.[8]

While the coffeehouse is rightly associated primarily with print and scribal publications because it was an increasingly important venue for the reading and distribution of such materials, the coffeehouses were also important sites for the display of visual images as well. Many early eighteenth-century images of coffeehouses represent them with at least one, and often several, pictures hanging framed on the walls (see Figures 36 and 37). These artworks were not likely to be the products of imported grand masters such as Rembrandt, Titian, or Poussin, but they may well have been more representative of a native English taste for portraits and landscapes. Along with painted pictures, the walls of coffeehouses were often also filled with cheaper prints such as broadsides and woodcuts. In this, they were not much different from the walls of contemporary alehouses, which were also filled with cheap prints. Both highbrow connoisseurship and low-brow popular print culture flourished in the early coffeehouse milieu.[9]

The early coffeehouses were most notable as centers for news culture. The coffeehouses bundled news and coffee together as a means of attracting their customers. News could be consumed in a variety of different forms: in print, both licensed and unlicensed; in manuscript; and aloud, as gossip, hearsay, and word of mouth. Why did coffeehouses, of all places, become such important news centers in post-Restoration Britain? Any attempt to link sober coffee drinking with serious consideration of important matters would fail to explain the often playful and unserious nature of early coffeehouse sociability and newsmongering. There was no necessary functional association between the coffeehouse and news culture — the link had to be invented. The chapters in this section offer one important source for the construction of this link between news and the coffeehouse: the virtuoso culture of curiosity that had also nurtured the initial interest in coffee itself. Chapter 4 locates the origins of the coffeehouse as a novel social institution in the social world of the English virtuosi. Unsurprisingly, given their interest in the coffee drink itself, the virtuosi were among the first to patronize the earliest British coffeehouses, and their interests and their social codes and conventions set the template upon which the coffeehouse milieu developed. The virtuoso fascination with novelty and the penchant of the virtuosi for wide-ranging discourse on multifarious topics set the tone for later expectations of what a coffeehouse would be. But the coffeehouse, being of course a "public" house, was soon exposed to influences well beyond the initial virtuoso culture out of which it emerged. This interaction between elite virtuosity and the popular and commercial cultures of the early modern city in the London coffeehouses is the subject of Chapter 5. Virtuoso culture gave birth to the coffeehouse phenomenon of post-Restoration Britain, but in doing so it was itself transformed into a much more diverse and open set of interests and individuals.

4

Penny Universities?

Because England's virtuosi were the most vocal proponents of coffee consumption as well as the earliest and most enthusiastic patrons of the coffeehouses, their interests, attitudes, and modes of sociability were bound to influence the culture of the coffeehouse. Indeed, the peculiarly "virtuosic" emphases on civility, curiosity, cosmopolitanism, and learned discourse made the coffeehouse such a distinctive space in the social world of early modern London. But virtuoso culture itself was transformed by its increasingly close relationship with the commercialized and urban elements of the coffeehouse milieu. We must pay close attention to this reciprocal relationship between the community of the curious and the commercial institutions they patronized if we are to understand how the coffeehouse etched out its place as a distinctive and novel social institution in later seventeenth-century Britain.

When "virtuosity" was made more accessible to the patrons of the coffeehouses after the Restoration, it became less and less the exclusive preserve of a tightly knit gentlemanly elite, as it had been during the first half of the seventeenth century. The English virtuoso thus came into direct contact with the preexisting forms of "bourgeois" sociability whose "social and cultural associations mainly revolved around the countless inns, taverns and alehouses of the towns."[1] This was a process of "bourgeoisification" also insofar as it brought virtuoso culture into direct contact with the commercial world of metropolitan London. The precious icons of a virtuoso's erudition and prestige, such as rare works of art or natural curiosities, were now freely bought and sold in the public houses of London; even the less material markers of virtuosic status, such as knowledge of foreign lands and cultures or a familiarity with the codes of elite civility, could now be acquired for the price of a dish of coffee by any patron with a penchant to learn about such matters. Such a broadening of the accessibility of gentlemanly prestige was not an entirely welcome prospect to those virtuosi, such as John Evelyn, who had acquired their cultural capital through much more arduous and costly means, and did not wish to see the distinctiveness of their virtuosity diminished by its contact with the less discriminate, more commercialized, and vulgar public of metropolitan London.

From Oxford to London: The Invention of the British Coffeehouse

The first coffeehouse in Britain was established in Oxford in 1650 by a Jewish entrepreneur named Jacob who opened a coffeehouse at the Angel. Oxford remained an important early center for the creation of a distinctive coffeehouse culture throughout the 1650s. By late 1654, another Oxford coffeehouse had been established by one "Cirques Jobson, a Jew and Jacobite," who added chocolate to the drinks on offer.[2] By Jacobite, Wood was referring to the Monophysite Christians from Syria. Presumably, Wood's use of "Jew" in this context was to identify Jobson as an ethnic Semite, rather than a practicing Jew. The coffeehouse trade began like the coffee commodity itself, an exotic transplant into English society.

But this situation did not last for long. In 1656 Anthony Wood recalled that Arthur Tillyard, an "apothecary and great royallist," also joined the trade as he began to sell "coffey publickly in his house against All-Soul's College. He was encouraged so to do by some royallists, now living in Oxon, and by others who esteem'd themselves either *virtuosi* or *wits*." These early coffeehouse virtuosi included the young Christopher Wren, Peter Pett, Thomas Millington, Timothy Baldwin, Georg Castle, William Bull, John Lamphire, as well as Matthew and Thomas Wren, the sons of Dr. Matthew Wren, the bishop of Ely. According to Wood, "this coffey house continued till his majestie's returne and after; and then they became more frequent."[3] We have already seen how the 1650s Oxford milieu was particularly conducive to the development of the new coffeehouses because that decade saw a peculiar conjunction of orientalist scholarship at the university and a vibrant new scientific community in the town. It was these same Interregnum virtuosi of Oxford, and later in London as well, who established a distinctive style of coffeehouse sociability that became a sort of template upon which the later, and much more numerous, coffeehouses of the Restoration era modeled themselves.

Little is known about the coffeehouses of Oxford in the 1650s save what Anthony Wood and John Evelyn recorded in their memoirs. Yet it seems clear from Wood's occasional jottings that these coffeehouses catered more to a select clientele rather than to the general public. Indeed, they were much more like private clubs than public houses. The earliest coffeehouses were characterized by an air of exclusivity and aloofness that remained at odds with their supposed openness as commercial drinking places. "At Tilliard's," Wood recalled with a barely concealed twinge of bitterness, "a club was erected . . . where many pretended wits would meet and deride at others."[4] In the early 1660s, Peter Staehl of Strasbourg the chemist, Rosicrucian, and "great hater of women," began to offer instruction in chemistry to a select group of Oxford virtuosi at Tilliard's coffeehouse. The chemistry club included a number of hangers-on from the original Tilliard's clique, including Christopher Wren and Thomas Millington; they were joined by Dr. John Wallis, Nathaniel Crew, Thomas Branker, Dr. Ralph Bathurst, Dr. Henry Yerbury, Dr. Thomas Janes, Richard Lower, Richard Griffith, and several others. John Locke was among the participants in an earlier chemistry club with Staehl. Wallis, Wren, Bathurst, Lower, and Locke would later become important Fellows of the Royal Society.[5]

Later in the 1660s, a group of young men from Christ Church donated books for a library to be set up in the study at Short's coffeehouse. Wood noted that the holdings consisted of works of "Rabelais, poems, plaies, etc."[6] In these formative years in which a novel social space for the coffeehouse was constructed, we find the distinctive imprint of virtuosic social forms and preferences. The coffeehouse was a place for like-minded scholars to congregate, to read, as well as to learn from and to debate with each other, but it was emphatically *not* a university institution, and the discourse there was of a far different order than any university tutorial. The coffeehouse thus occupied a social space distinct from those older centers of learning which were constrained by their dependence on church or state patronage as well as their stubborn "scholastic" refusal to accept the methods and supplements offered by Bacon's "new learning," which were so dear to the virtuosi. By contrast, the coffeehouse offered an alternative space for the promotion of virtuosic interests.

The relationship between the new coffeehouse and the established university was not necessarily an antagonistic one. While some virtuoso projectors strongly lobbied for the creation of continental-style "academies" for the promotion of the new learning as well as the requisite gentlemanly social graces such as "riding the great horse . . . dancing, fencing, singing, playing on musical instruments, mathematics and the like," others saw no need for such institutions due to the emergence of coffeehouse learning as a useful supplement to the traditional university curriculum. The eminent Oxford professor of geometry, John Wallis (1616–1703) — who had been a member of Peter Staehl's chemistry club at Tillyard's coffeehouse — expressed this view forcefully in his animadversions on Lewis Maidwell's proposal to erect a London academy in 1700.[7] He praised those extra-university clubs that met "by voluntary agreement and consociation, for particular parts of usefull knowledge in our universities." A prime example of these associations, he thought, was indeed the Tillyard coffeehouse clique:

> It is now near fifty years ago, that Mr. Staal (a skillfull *Chymist*) came to *Oxford*, (being invited hither for that purpose) and made it his business here, to instruct such as desire it, in the practice of *chymistry* (a piece of knowledge not misbecoming a gentleman:) that is, when 6, 8, or more (of the better rank amongst us) agreed together for that purpose; he did, with them (in a convenient place for that affaire) go through a whole *course of chymistry.*
>
> And the like practise hath been pursued ever since by Dr. *Plott*, Mr. *White* and others successively to this time.

Wallis also thought it entirely unnecessary to provide instruction in the more fashionable, but less scholarly, aspects of genteel culture. Where would it end, he asked: shall the young now need instruction "to drink wine, ale, coffee, tea, chocolat, &c."?[8] Wallis's sharp wit focused on the uneasy cohabitation of intellectual achievement and social cachet, or between learning and fashionability, in virtuoso circles that was both a singular characteristic of the new coffeehouse social scene, and yet also a source of much anxiety for many of the more earnest citizens of the later Stuart republic of letters.

Anthony Wood was certainly one of them. Although he was an early aficionado of the Oxford coffeehouse scene, Wood gradually came to resent their impact on the state of learning in the town and the university. As early as 1674, Wood included among a series of general laments on the debased mores of his times the specific complaint that "the decay of study, and consequently of learning," was due to "coffy houses, to which most scholars retire and spend much of the day in hearing and speaking of news, [and] in speaking vily of their superiors." For Wood, coffeehouse discourse reflected a general decline in late seventeenth-century English intellectual life: "Since the king was restored it was looked upon as a piece of pedantry to produce a Latin sentence in discours . . . to dispute theologically at the table at meales, to be earnest or zealous in any one thing. But all, forsooth, must be gentile [i.e., genteel] and neat — no paines taken." This was to his mind little more than "bantring," and it was to be lamented as much as was the popular taste for "playes, poems, and drollery" in books, rather than more serious works of practical divinity. Wood also complained about this bantering "in public places and coffey houses," which he found to be "fluently romantick nonsense, unintelligible gibberish, florishing lyes and nonsense."[9] Instead of providing a space for enhancing the intellectual life of the university, Wood found that the coffeehouses of Oxford were most often used to avoid study in frivolous chat, or perhaps even worse to the mind of an embittered scholar: self-interested lobbying for preferment. Furthermore, Wood found that the coffeehouses of post-Restoration Oxford were not like the cozy and cliquish clubs he had enjoyed in the 1650s: the later coffeehouses were much more open to all sorts of patrons he considered undesirables, such as papists, Members of Parliament, and local townsmen. Wood's pessimistic view of the rise of the public coffeehouse as a sign of the decline of scholarly standards was shared by many of his contemporaries, such as Roger North and Thomas Tenison. These complaints reflect a growing division in academic taste between the prolix Latinate "erudites" and the witty, vernacular *mondains* whose tastes were to remain ascendant through most of the eighteenth century.[10] Much to the lament of scholars like Wood, North, and Tenison, the character of the coffeehouse would adapt to the times, and it would become much more so a venue for fashionable wit than a center for serious scholarly study.

For this reason, the university authorities also viewed the rise of the coffeehouse in their towns with great suspicion. By the later seventeenth and eighteenth centuries, both Oxford and Cambridge universities had devised statutes and regulations to control the coffeehouse attendance of their students. In 1663, the vice chancellor of Cambridge University licensed coffeehouses only if they agreed that the keepers "suffer no scholars of this University, under the degree of Masters of Arts, to drinke coffee, chocolate, sherbett, or tea . . . except their tutors be with them."[11]

But not all virtuosi were as melancholic about the role of coffeehouses in the republic of letters as Anthony Wood. John Aubrey wrote to Wood in praise of the great boon the coffeehouses had been to his own biographical scholarship. He noted that he had gathered up enough material for another sixteen "lives" based on anecdotes and stories he had picked up in coffeehouse chat. "Before coffee-houses," Aubrey gushed, "men could not be so well acquainted with one another. They were afrayd and stared at all those that were not of their own sodalities." In January 1681, Aubrey also expressed his concern with "what the academiques say at the coffee-houses about [his biography of] Mr. Hobbes's life," and he seemed to regret that its reception there might be overshadowed by the growing political crisis over the succession to the crown. Aubrey was one of the earliest English virtuosi to take advantage of the novel coffeehouses in ways which aided his own scholarship and advanced his personal reputation among his peers, although Aubrey's "coffeehousing" with his fellow virtuosi could just as well present more opportunities for personal embarrassment, and indeed some found the eccentric antiquarian to be "as mad as anyone in the University of Bedlam."[12]

The Oxford milieu of the 1650s was crucial to shaping English expectations of what sort of place the new institution called a coffeehouse was supposed to be. Although they were clearly understood to be public houses for the retailing of beverages, from the very beginning they were invested with a distinctive brand of learned, but not at all pedantic, sociability that was far from the well-established association of alehouses and taverns with a wide variety of vices, such as drunkenness, criminality, and public disorder. The coffeehouse was a place for "virtuosi" and "wits," rather than for the plebes or *roués* who were commonly portrayed as typical patrons of the alcoholic drinking houses. A social stereotype for coffeehouse society was established in its Oxford origins, but it was in metropolitan London where this model was most fully developed.

The first coffeehouse in London was established by one Pasqua Rosée, a Greek servant to a Levant Company merchant named Daniel Edwards, in 1652 (Figure 14).[13] There is no reason to suspect that the opening of this first coffeehouse was related to the lapse of the licensing acts of September 1651, for the early coffeehouses had not yet developed the close association with news culture that would develop after the Restoration. The summer of 1652 did see a "period of relative independence in the press," but it is not clear that this was a direct result of the lapse in licensing. Rosée's establishment was succeeded by a handful of other coffeehouses, but there is very little evidence from the 1650s that the coffeehouses initially attracted a very large clientele. John Houghton recalled that the early coffeehouse keepers faced opposition from the "ale-sellers" who complained to the Lord Mayor that the new coffeemen were not freemen of the City, and thus ineligible to retail drinks there. In 1657, the coffeehouse-keeper and barber James Farr was presented before the wardmote of St. Dunstan's in the West "for making and selling a drinke called coffee, whereby in making the same he annoyeth his neighbors." They claimed that his constant fires had presented a great fire hazard, which brought "great danger and affrightment" to his neighbors. It was not until November 1659 that Thomas Rugge noted "att this time a Turkishe drink to bee sould, almost in every street, called coffee and another kind of drink called tee, and also a drink called chacolate, which was a very harty drink."[14] Apparently it took many years before the new coffeehouses became an accepted part of the Lon-

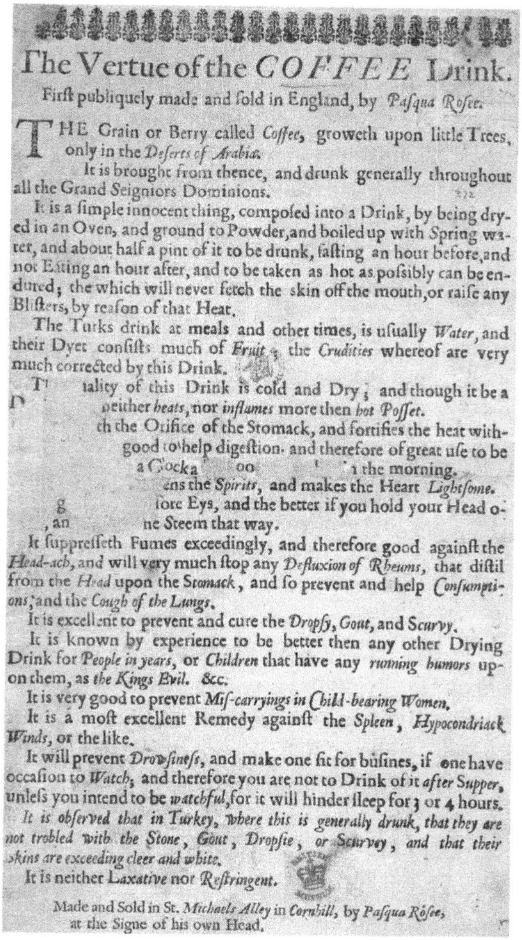

The Vertue of the *COFFEE* Drink.

First publiquely made and fold in England, by *Pasqua Rosee.*

THE Grain or Berry called *Coffee*, groweth upon little Trees, only in the *Deferts of Arabia.*

It is brought from thence, and drunk generally throughout all the Grand Seigniors Dominions.

It is a fimple innocent thing, compofed into a Drink, by being dryed in an Oven, and ground to Powder, and boiled up with Spring water, and about half a pint of it to be drunk, fafting an hour before, and not Eating an hour after, and to be taken as hot as pofsibly can be endured; the which will never fetch the skin off the mouth, or raife any Blifters, by reafon of that Heat.

The Turks drink at meals and other times, is ufually *Water*, and their Dyet confifts much of *Fruit*, the *Crudities* whereof are very much corrected by this Drink.

T[h]e [qu]ality of this Drink is cold and Dry; and though it be a [Drink,] [it is] neither *heats*, nor *inflames* more then hot *Poffet.*

[It clofe]th the Orifice of the Stomack, and fortifies the heat with[in,] good to help digeftion. and therefore of great ufe to be [had] a Clock [in the aftern]oo[n, as well as in] the morning.

[It much quick]ens the *Spirits*, and makes the Heart *Lightfome.*

[It is good a]gaine [f]ore Eys, and the better if you hold your Head o[ver it, and take in] the Steem that way.

It fupprefeth Fumes exceedingly, and therefore good againft the *Head-ach*, and will very much ftop any *Defluxion of Rheums*, that diftil from the *Head* upon the *Stomack*, and fo prevent and help *Confumptions*, and the *Cough of the Lungs.*

It is excellent to prevent and cure the *Dropfy, Gout*, and *Scurvy.*

It is known by experience to be better then any other Drying Drink for *People in years*, or *Children* that have any *running humors* upon them, as *the Kings Evil.* &c.

It is very good to prevent *Mif-carryings in Child-bearing Women.*

It is a moft excellent Remedy againft the *Spleen*, *Hypocondriack Winds*, or the like.

It will prevent *Drowfinefs*, and make one fit for bufines, if one have occafion to *Watch*; and therefore you are not to Drink of it *after Supper*, unlefs you intend to be *watchful*, for it will hinder fleep for 3 or 4 hours.

It is obferved that in Turkey, where this is generally drunk, that they are not trobled with the Stone, Gout, Dropfie, or Scurvy, and that their skins are exceeding cleer and white.

It is neither *Laxative* nor *Reftringent.*

Made and Sold in St. *Michaels Alley* in *Cornhill*, by *Pasqua Rosee,* at the Signe of his own Head.

Figure 14. Pasqua Rosée's handbill advertisement for his coffee drink (1652). BL shelfmark C.20.f.2 (372). Courtesy of the British Library, London.

don social landscape. As late as the mid-1660s, coffee sellers were still trying to carve out a niche in the London retail market. The proprietor of the Turk's Head coffeehouse in Exchange Alley offered free coffee on New Year's Day 1663 to all "gentlemen" willing to give the new drink a try, and promised to continue doing so until "the worlds end," and the proprietor of the Grecian coffeehouse offered to teach his patrons how to prepare coffee for themselves "gratis."[15]

Perhaps it was a coincidence that Rugge began to pay attention to the

growing popularity of coffee in London at the very time that James Harrington established what was to become one of the most famous coffeehouse
clubs of the century: the Rota club, which met at Miles's Coffeehouse in the
New Palace Yard. James Harrington, along with his friend and fellow traveler
in republican politics, Henry Neville, were both early aficionados of the new
coffeehouses and they quickly saw the new institution as a suitable venue for
the propagation and discussion of their ideas and their politics. John Aubrey
recalled that after the publication of the *Oceana* in 1656, they would speak
"dayly at coffee-houses," and their "smart discourses and inculcations . . .
made many proselytes." In the summer of 1659, Harrington and his friends
had instituted a "Commonwealth club" which met at a tavern owned by John
Wildman on Bow Street in Covent Garden, the purpose of which was apparently to draw up petitions for constitutional reform which they presented to
the restored Rump Parliament.[16] Whether these proposals were "quite seriously intended," or were rather "essaying a politics of absurdity or being
merely facetious," the actions of these outspoken "well-wishers to a republic"
were taken seriously enough by the informants to Henry Hyde's royalist intelligence network. The proposals would be brought up again as proof of Harrington's disloyalty to the crown in formal accusations at his interrogation
after his arrest in December 1661. The Rota club quickly succeeded the short-
lived Bow Street group: it began meeting at Miles's Coffeehouse in October
1659 and continued until the end of February or early March 1660, by which
time the restoration of Charles II had been well assured. On 20 February
1660, Pepys wrote, "the [Rota] club broke off very poorly, and I do not think
they will meet any more."[17]

   The Rota club was established for the primary purpose of allowing Harrington's "disciples and the virtuosi" to debate matters of politics and philosophy, and it gathered quite some notoriety despite its brief existence. John
Aubrey had been present at the meetings, and he recalled that "the discourses
. . . [there] were the most ingeniouse, and smart, that ever I heard, or expect to
heare, and bandyed with great eagernesse. . . . The roome was every evening
[as] full as it could be crammed." The Rota was clearly something more than a
Harringtonian clique, as the earlier Bow Street club had been, for it attracted
many interested observers who were not necessarily committed to maintaining
or reestablishing a republic, but it was not entirely the "free and open academy
unto all comers" that the club's own rhetoric proclaimed it to be. There was an
admission fee: Samuel Pepys paid the not inconsiderable sum of 18 d. to
become a member of the club; and just as important were the informal means
of exclusion which obtained — the Rota was not an open public house, but
a club for self-styled "virtuosi," who were by their nature a very rarified and

self-selected breed. Michael Hunter points out that "few can have afforded as much time for endless talk" as the virtuosi.[18]

The proceedings at the Rota were by all accounts well organized, and they proceeded according to Harrington's notions of how to govern an ideal commonwealth. The organizing principles were that all decisions should be resolved by casting votes by ballot, and that all offices should rotate among the members. Whether or not the Rota was merely "a coffee-house academy, and not a political pressure group," like the Bow Street club, has been a matter of some historical debate, but the point was made moot by the restoration of the monarchy.[19] During his 1661 interrogation, Harrington disavowed any practical political purpose to his Rota activities in 1659, claiming that they were only abstract exercises in philosophy, and he chided his accusers thus: "Did Alexander hang up Aristotle; did he molest him?" But this is of course the only response one would expect from him under such forbidding circumstances. The newly restored monarchy took the Rota-men seriously, so much so that Derek Hirst has concluded that royalist polemic of 1659–60 took great care to counter what they perceived to be "the brainsickness on which the Rota fed."[20]

What is clear is that for its brief lifespan, the Rota was *the* place in London for the English virtuosi to assemble for discourse. The aspiring young virtuoso Samuel Pepys attended the Rota meetings primarily to hear the "admirable discourse," and "exceeding good argument," on matters of political philosophy, and to rub shoulders with the Earl of Dorset and another nobleman. While William Petty, who had already earned his stripes as a respected virtuoso in Samuel Hartlib's circle, showed up to trouble "Harrington with his arithmeticall proportions, reducing politie to numbers." Debate—contentious but still civil, and learned but not didactic—was the Rota's real raison d'être. The club's published "model of a free state" suggested that such an ideal government should provide accommodations for an open academy of virtuosi, and "that this academy be governed according to the rules of good breeding or civil conversation"—a concept that had been promulgated for over a century in English-language gentlemanly courtesy literature, and for even longer among the Italian virtuosi, who in many ways provided a model for their English cousins.[21] This discursive ideal provided a model for coffeehouse conversation for the rest of the Stuart era.

Other members of the Rota included the ubiquitous John Aubrey; Cyriac Skinner, a friend and assistant to John Milton; gentlemen such as Sir John Penruddock, the earl of Tyrconnel; Sir William Poulteny; and a number of future Fellows of the Royal Society, including Sir John Hoskins and Sir Philip Carteret. This significant correspondence between the erstwhile Rota-men and the future Royal Society has led some scholars to conclude that

Harrington's club offered a political and organizational model for the new scientific academy. Michael Hunter has estimated that eleven out of twenty-seven, or nearly 40 percent, of the identifiable Rota-men went on to become Royal Society Fellows.[22] Certainly there were some formal and informal correspondences between the organization of the Rota and that of the Royal Society, particularly in the use of balloting and in the emphasis of both on allowing for free and open debate which was nevertheless constrained by a formalized means of procedure.[23] But contemporaries such as the Rev. John Ward, who heard that Charles II had founded the Royal Society in opposition to the Rota club, "not thinking fitt to putt down the [Rota] by open contradiction," were able to clearly distinguish between Harrington's republicanism and the overt monarchical loyalism of the Royal Society.[24] What made this rumor so plausible to men like Ward was the way in which both the Rota and the Royal Society were fishing for the same punters, as it were. The curiosity of those virtuosi who attended Harrington's late-night sessions in order to partake in the debates there might well have had their attention diverted by the emergence of a rival society.

The Rota also resembled the Royal Society in its remarkable capacity to provoke the ridicule of the cheap-print wits.[25] Indeed, some authors focused their satire on both targets. Samuel Butler derided the "Rota-men" as too "full of . . . politicks" for their own good, and he similarly sneered at the experimental virtuosi as "those wholesale criticks, that in coffee-house, cry down all philosophy." In Henry Stubbe's squib *The Rota or, news from the commonwealths-mens club,* a Rota-man is called "a learned asse," and the discourse derided as both impudent and frivolous: "A question here, although nere so rude, / Is so belaboured, and so tewd, / And into sundry pieces hewd."[26] Stubbe would later vent his wrath upon the Royal Society in a series of polemic tracts, an act which would ironically cause him to be labeled a "Rota-man" by John Evelyn. Years later, Thomas St. Serfe would also scoff at the erstwhile "politick speculists of the round-table" by calling them "ballating projectors" who foolishly debated "whether the hen or the egge was first . . . and heav'n knows . . . what havock they made of Bodin, Machiavel, & Plato." The ridicule heaped upon the Rota seemed to have as much to do with the "dilettante air" which surrounded their proceedings as it did with Harrington's republicanism. In this respect, the Rota was just the first butt of a long-running series of jokes aimed at the virtuosi throughout the Augustan era.[27]

Despite its short lifespan, the memory of the Rota died hard for the chattering classes of late seventeenth-century England. While the specter of a resurgent republicanism gave the Rota the same fearful currency that animated the persistent tales (most often perpetuated by fervent royalists and tories) of the meetings of "Calves-Head Clubs" who celebrated the execution of Charles

I every January 30, the image of the Rota was also maintained by its association with the coffeehouse culture that began to flourish after the Restoration. When John Dryden's enemies wished to deride his play *The Conquest of Granada* (1673), they did so by invoking the memory of the Rota, which by then was remembered not so much as a cabal of subversive republicans but rather as a group of "Athenian virtuosi in the Coffe-Academy instituted by Apollo for the advancement of Gazett Philosophy, Mercury's, Diurnalls, &c." Invoking the memory of the Rota in this context probably had more to do with satirizing Dryden's role as a "coffeehouse wit" than to tar his work with the taint of republicanism.[28] The example set by the Rota remained fresh in the mental world of the Restoration wits not only because it provided a telling example of the ludicrous failure of arm-chair republicanism but also because it had created a workable and enduringly successful model for coffeehouse sociability.

The coffeehouse retained its reputation as a center for informal learning and debate among the virtuosi well after the Restoration. According to Randall Caudill, "the coffee-houses catered for the entire range of 'gentlemanly arts' prescribed by contemporary courtesy literature and projected in the curricula of the gentlemen's training academies." One could take lessons in the French, Italian, or Latin languages; it was possible to sign up for instruction in dancing, fencing, or equestrian skills, or take in lectures in poetry, mathematics, or astronomy — all in the coffeehouses of late seventeenth- and early eighteenth-century London.[29] At the turn of the century, John Houghton published his effusive assessments of the contributions that the coffeehouses had made to the advancement of learning since their introduction both in the Royal Society's *Philosophical Transactions* as well as in his own financial weekly, *A Collection for the Improvement of Husbandry and Trade*. He thought that:

> Coffee-houses make all sorts of people sociable, the rich and the poor meet together, as also do the learned and unlearned. It improves arts, merchandize, and all other knowledge; for here an inquisitive man, that aims at good learning, may get more in an evening than he shall by books in a month: he may find out such coffee-houses, where men frequent, who are studious in such matters as his enquiry tends to, and he may in short space gain the pith and marrow of the others reading and studies. I have heard a worthy friend of mine . . . who was of good learning . . . say, that he did think, that coffee-houses had improved useful knowledge, as much as [the universities] have, and spake in no way of slight to them neither.[30]

By the eighteenth century, the coffeehouse had become a widely accepted part of urban social life, and its character as a serious center for practical learning had been well established. The virtuoso ideal was now, in principle, available to everyone, regardless of their wealth, status, or education.

The relative openness of coffeehouse learning to all comers, however, made the new institution vulnerable to charges that a site so indiscriminate could hardly promote the advancement of learning, but it was instead quite likely to debase learning through its association with the vulgar, dilettantism, and the plain inept. Although critical and satirical works recognized the distinctiveness of the *claims* to erudition by the patrons of coffeehouses, these critics were quick to burst the pretensions and shortcomings of coffeehouse discourse. A 1661 tract complained that since coffeehouse conversation proceeded with "neither moderators, nor rules" it was like "a school . . . without a master." "Education is . . . [in the coffeehouse] taught without discipline. Learning (if it be possible) is here insinuated without method." Another scoffed at the coffeehouse as "a new erected Grecian Academy" that harbored only drunken gallants who refused to pay their reckonings, while Richard Leigh derided the coffeehouses as "tattling universities." These criticisms were echoed by a pamphlet published in 1662, which claimed to be "printed and . . . sold at the Latine coffee house near the stocks [market]" in Cornhill, and offered its readers an account in doggerel verse of a coffeehouse duel of wit and scholarly acumen. The coffeehouse here is portrayed as a place "where doctors and schollars assemble / [and] where the folk do speak, nought but Latin and Greek," although the author advises: "But did you but hear, their Latin I fear / You'd laugh till you'd burst your breeches."[31] The pamphlet proceeds to scoff at the indiscriminacy and dilettantism of coffeehouse discourse, which ranged from debates on the relative merits of Calvinist and Arminian theologies to problems in mathematics or much more mundane matters: "the one talks of news, the other of stews / and a third of pick-pockets and bears, / A fourth doth always curse masques, balls and plays." Another broadside published several years later continued to ridicule the supposed erudition of coffeehouse patrons. How could the coffeehouse compare to a university, it suggested, if at a coffeehouse "you may a schoolar be / for spending of a penny." Similarly, Thomas St. Serfe's play *Tarugo's Wiles* scoffed at the coffeehouse scientists who awed at spectacles such as the early Royal Society trials at blood transfusion, or those "journey-man" virtuosi who pompously discussed the aesthetic merits of paintings but could not distinguish a crude Dutch genre piece from the work of an Italian master.[32]

These criticisms did not go unanswered, but they were a part of a consistent refrain in the ongoing debates about the role of the coffeehouse in English society for the rest of the seventeenth century.[33] What is most remarkable about such satires is the way in which they mirrored the anxieties that the virtuosi themselves harbored about their relationship to the coffeehouse and the metropolitan milieu with which they were associated. Did the coffeehouse offer an exciting new venue for the sharing of useful new knowledge? Or was it rather the lamentable site for the replacement of real learning with superficial, merely fashionable, social display? While the majority of the virtuosi welcomed the coming of the coffeehouse, a vocal minority persisted in voicing their worries that the new institution presented a hindrance to the advancement of learning.

From Great House to Coffeehouse: Virtuoso Sociability After the Restoration

Recent studies of the role of the coffeehouse in Restoration society have noticed that its emergence was the subject of a great deal of contentious polemic, and that it is indeed "hard to find kind words for the coffeehouse during the Restoration period." Steve Pincus has argued that much of the animus toward the coffeehouses came specifically from the camp of the "Anglican Royalists" — and even more particularly, the "new High-Church movement" of the 1670s — who were most insistent in their desire to turn back the clock on the dramatic Civil War and Interregnum transformations in the English church and state. For Lawrence Klein, the Restoration-era anxieties about the proprieties observed in coffeehouse society were part of a more generalized ethos which sought to "reassert authority over discourse and culture." I will return to these important arguments on the politics of coffeehouse society in Chapter 7, but we should note at this stage that one important reason for the resilience of coffeehouse sociability, even when it came under the most serious criticism from both high Anglican royalists and Grub Street wits, was its initial and persistent claim to "civility" — a term I invoke to suggest a peculiarly *urban* brand of social interaction which valued sober and reasoned debate on matters of great import, be they scientific, aesthetic, or political. This was not the courtly civility made famous by Norbert Elias; it was rather a sense of propriety which guided the actions of those who laid claim to the identity of a "gentleman."[34]

This was precisely the ideal promulgated by the virtuosi of Harrington's Rota, and it was only further elaborated in the decades after 1660. Although the civil ideal was by no means an exclusive preserve of the virtuosi, such manners were crucial in maintaining the bonds which held the community of the curious together, and it was primarily by means of its initial virtuoso patrons that the coffeehouse came to be associated with polite society. Although the genealogy of this "civility" may be traced back to the manners and social forms prescribed by courtly courtesy literature, in late seventeenth- and eighteenth-century Britain, it took a distinctively urban, and indeed *metropolitan* form.[35] Coffeehouse "civility" did not have to await the Glorious Revolution and the appearance of the *Tatler* and *Spectator* papers in order to receive vindication; it had been present from the very first gatherings of virtuosi in the coffeehouses of Interregnum Oxford.

What made the coffeehouse such an attractive locale for the social life of England's virtuosi? First and foremost was the convenience of visiting a coffeehouse, an advantage which became only more pronounced as London became the unchallenged focal point for virtuoso culture after the Restoration. Whereas the virtuosi of the early seventeenth century had centered their activities and social interactions in aristocratic "great houses" such as Thomas Howard's Arundel House, those of the latter half of the century increasingly migrated to London and found common ground in the public houses of the metropolis.[36] In their migration from country to the town, the virtuosi were merely following a much larger, slower, and more profound transformation in the modes of gentry sociability which saw the rise of the London "season" and its national marriage market, the residential development of London's West End, and the privatization of the social ideal of good hospitality.[37]

Unlike the formal social interactions prescribed by a visit to the great house, coffeehouse visits were more spontaneous and less rigidly ritualized. The protocols of recognizing rank and precedence were abandoned within the coffeehouse, a convenient social fiction which was celebrated in a broadside which proclaimed the "Rules and Orders of the Coffee-House": "First Gentry, tradesmen, all are welcome hither, / And may without affront sit down together: / Pre-eminence of place, none here should mind, / But take the next fit seat that he can find: / Nor need any, if finer persons come, rise up to assigne to them his room" (Figure 15). This convention was not meant to promote social "leveling," as many of the early detractors and modern historians of the coffeehouses have assumed, but it was rather a means by which the genteel manners of the new metropolitan "Town" were to be distinguished from what were perceived to be the excessive and stifling formalities of the past.[38]

Similar moves to promote a social fiction of equality may be found in late seventeenth- and eighteenth-century scholarly academies that refused to make social distinctions between their members, as well as in the extracourtly world of the French salons, in which it was thought that "the pleasure of talk derives precisely from a collective effort to create the illusion of a world where hierarchy does not exist." By the early eighteenth century, this sort of polite complaisance would be celebrated by the *Spectator* as one of the superiorities of

Figure 15. "The Rules and Orders of the Coffee-House." *Brief Description of the Excellent Vertues of that sober and wholesome drink, called coffee;* BL shelfmark C.20.f.2. (377). Courtesy of the British Library, London.

urban gentility to that of the country. Previously, Addison thought, "conversation, like the Romish religion, was so encumbered with show and ceremony, that it stood in need of a Reformation to retrench its superfluities, and restore it to its natural good sense and beauty. At present therefore an unconstrained carriage, and a certain openness of behaviour are the height of good breeding. The fashionable world is grown free and easie; our manners, sit more loose upon us: Nothing is so modish as an agreeable negligence."[39]

This transformation in the manners of England's social elite was mirrored in the changing modes of virtuoso sociability after the Restoration. While they were not entirely abandoned by 1700, social visits to the private cabinets of virtuoso gentlemen were no longer the primary means by which a gentleman's status among the community of the curious was affirmed and maintained. This function was now supplemented by the emergence after the Restoration of two important new institutions, the first being the formal honor-bestowing places, patronage, and publications of the Royal Society, while the second was the informal collegiality which prevailed in the London coffeehouses. The informality of English intellectual sociability stood in stark contrast to the more formalized French manner for the Huguenot refugee Abel Boyer: "The English have no settled *Academies de Beaux-Esprits,* as we have in Paris, but instead of such assemblies, the most ingenious persons of their nation, meet either in places of promiscuous company, as coffee-houses, or in private clubs, in taverns."[40]

A major advantage to coffeehouse sociability was its relative ease, cheapness, and frequency. One could visit a coffeehouse, or several of them, either daily as part of a regularized routine or spontaneously without much forethought or effort. In contrast, a formal visit required a proper introduction, a prior appointment on the part of the visitor, and the responsibilities of hospitality on the part of the host.[41] The visit was a personalized ritual which was conducted on the private property of the host. The visit was also part and parcel of the traditional social economy of patronage and clientage; it was therefore also a powerful means of reinforcing the status differentials between the visitor and the host. Coffeehousing, by contrast, was conducted on neutral ground. Taking place in public space, the social intercourse of the coffeehouse allowed for, and indeed encouraged, the social fiction of equal status between patrons. While some gentlemen virtuosi such as John Evelyn clearly continued to prefer the visit as a means to display their virtuosity, others — especially the less well-off among the community of the curious — found coffeehouse society the perfect means to learn from, and show off in front of, one's peers. Although the private hospitality of the visit remained a vital social institution throughout the seventeenth century and beyond, it could now be complemented by the equally civil, but less formal and more egalitarian, sociability found in the coffeehouse.

It had to be the distinctive and novel institution known as the coffeehouse which opened up this new opportunity for virtuosic socializing. The other alternatives offered by London's rapidly expanding commercial hospitality industry — the traditional taverns, inns, and alehouses — were all burdened by their various associations with harboring drunkards, prostitutes, common tradesmen, or plebeians. Although such places were not considered off-limits to a gentleman or an aspiring virtuoso, they were nevertheless tainted by an unmistakable patina of low status. This is not to say, as Peter Clark once claimed, that the alehouse milieu constituted an "alternative society," or a haven for a popular culture that existed in stark opposition to the social world of the more genteel elites or even the respectable middling sort, for it is now clear that the alehouse "constituted a rival pole to the respectable, establishment meeting place of the church" only in the minds of the overzealous godly.[42] Although they were hardly cordoned off from the social world of the "better sort," public drinking houses were commonly thought to be places conducive to misbehavior. And if many found this to be part of their allure, few people wished to be known as one who made a regular practice out of frequenting taverns or alehouses.

Coffeehouses, by contrast, were a virtual tabula rasa whose social character was open to being cast with a more genteel and polite tone, and thus they came to be generally understood as places "too civil for a debaucht humour." An early defense of the coffeehouse explicitly invoked its civility: "In brief 'tis undenyable that as you have here [in the coffeehouses] the most civil . . . [and] the most intelligent society, the frequenting whose converse, and observing their discourses and deportment cannot but civilize our manner, inlarge our understandings, refine our language, teach us a generous confidence and handsome mode of address, and brush off that *Pudor Subrusticus* (as I remember Tully somewhere calls it) that clownish kind of modesty, frequently incident to the best natures, which renders them sheepish and ridiculous in company." Of course, coffeehouses were not necessarily in practice more civil and sober locales than taverns or alehouses, but by and large they were perceived to be so by contemporaries.[43] And that made all the difference.

Robert Hooke (1635 – 1703) probably offers the most enthusiastic example of a virtuoso habitué of the London coffeehouses. He mentions visiting at least sixty-four London coffeehouses between 1672 and 1680 in his first diary, and rarely a day went by when he did not stop into at least one, and sometimes as many as three, even when he was ill and the weather was bad. Both Robert Iliffe and Adrian Johns have recently shown how Hooke used such opportunities to draw on the knowledge of a wide variety of individuals, from servants and skilled laborers to aristocrats, as well as to share and display novel scientific instruments. Hooke also used the coffeehouse as a venue to discuss and adjudicate philosophical and personal conflicts, and even to form his own cliques or "clubs" of like-minded virtuosi.[44] Hooke viewed the coffeehouse as a place for serious work, and he complained when there was "little philosophical" work accomplished there; it was indeed the premier locale in which Hooke could "fulfill his own view of himself as a virtuoso, as a man of business, [and] as a man at the center of intellectual life in the city." Although there is little evidence that scientific experiments were actually conducted at a coffeehouse, it is clear that they were an important complement to the laboratory as a public space where experimental facts could be discussed and debated. Hooke himself used Garraway's coffeehouse as the venue in which he accused John Flamsteed of not knowing how to use his own telescopes properly. Coffeehouse conversation and debate offered an important face-to-face complement to the often unruly world of print publication and the formal meetings of the Royal Society in the social world of the virtuosi. The coffeehouse offered a space in which arguments could be conducted in an immediate and relatively unconstrained manner; for this reason, it was also an important place for the construction, or the diminution, of intellectual reputations among the virtuosi.[45]

Hooke's virtuoso interests extended beyond the well-documented world of the new science, and again it was in the coffeehouses that he found the most convenient means to explore those interests. He could cultivate his connoisseurship of art by viewing prints, pictures, as well as other sorts of "raritys" or by purchasing them at auction, as well as discoursing with painters in a coffeehouse. He sometimes engaged in long discourses about foreign lands, such as the East Indies, and the exotic creatures in these places at Garraway's Coffeehouse. It was also at Garraway's that Hooke could inspect newly published books, presumably in the company of his learned peers. Even Hooke's coffeehouse newspaper reading could serve to reinforce his immersion in virtuoso culture: he read one "high Dutch gazet" in which "mention is made of certaine men walkin[g] the water."[46] Nuggets of curious information such as this were the common currency of virtuoso conversation.

Only slightly less ardent in his devotion to coffeehouse society was Samuel Pepys (1633–1703), whose diary from the 1660s includes around eighty visits to coffeehouses, mostly to those located near the Navy Office in Cornhill (where he worked) and the Royal Exchange, although he was an occasional patron of several coffeehouses in Covent Garden as well. For Pepys, the coffeehouse was less a venue to display his own virtuosity, which was in the 1660s only in its formative stages, than it was a place where he might learn from others. After attending the Rota meetings, Pepys continued to converse with other former members of the club such as William Petty, of whom Pepys thought was "in discourse . . . one of the most rational men that ever I heard speak with a tongue, having all his notions the most distinct and clear." Petty and Pepys chatted at various times on topics as various as contemporary literature, music, "the Universall Character" (an attempt to produce a system of characters or symbols which could represent the words from any language), the art of memory, the notorious forger Abraham Gowrie Granger's method of counterfeiting signatures, the Cartesian dream argument, "and other most excellent discourses."[47]

Before he became a fellow himself, Pepys eagerly listened to coffeehouse tales of the experiments that were being performed by the virtuosi of the Royal Society at Gresham College as well as their general proceedings. He also found an occasion to meet with fellows of the society, including Henry Oldenburg, "the Secretary of the Virtuosi of Gresham College" (i.e., the Royal Society), in a coffeehouse by the Royal Exchange. In November 1663, Pepys dropped by a coffeehouse near the Navy Office and there he listened to "a long and most passionate discourse between two Doctors of Physique . . . and a couple of Apothecarys" in which the relative merits of Galenic physic and Paracelsian iatrochemistry were debated. Pepys's reflections on the exchange are telling: "The truth is," he thought "one of the Apothecaries, whom they charged most, did speak very prettily; that is, his language and sense good, though perhaps he might not be so knowing a physician as to offer a contest with them. At last they came to some cooler term and broke up."[48] This sort of coffeehouse discourse must not have been uncommon, and it seems to have been conducted according to a mutually recognized, if not explicitly expressed, code of civil conduct. Persuasion was to be achieved through mellifluous ("pretty") rhetoric which combined a show of learning with good reason. In this respect, it might resemble the formal disputations of the universities, but coffeehouse debates were different in their spontaneity, their more casual tone, and their open-ended nature: when the conversation "cooled," it could end just as quickly as it had begun. Although the topics of conversation could be quite serious, the milieu in which they were set encouraged a rather relaxed tone to the proceedings — the purpose of coffeehouse chat was entertainment and relaxation as much as edification, hence the common expression by Pepys and other coffeehouse habitués of their delight at the "excellent discourse" that they enjoyed at a coffeehouse.

Pepys also engaged in his own speculative discourse on matters as wide-ranging as biology and natural history (such as whether insects were produced by spontaneous generation), new mechanical inventions, and strange natural phenomena, as well as medicine and chemistry.[49] His interest in virtuoso culture was, like Robert Hooke's, hardly limited to scientific matters, and he used his coffeehouse socializing to acquaint himself with painters or composers, or to discuss theories of political economy or the history of the Roman Empire.[50] In February 1664, Pepys popped into Will Urwin's coffeehouse on Bow Street in Covent Garden, where he found the poet John Dryden and "all the wits of the town" engaged in their "very witty and pleasant discourse." His interest in the "history of trades"—a favorite virtuoso project that was high on the agenda of the early Royal Society—could be cultivated in discourse with merchants or artisans. Another favorite topic of coffeehouse conversation was tales of foreign countries and cultures. In a Cornhill coffeehouse, Pepys listened to "Lieutenant Collonell Baron tell very good stories of his travels over the high hills in Asia above the cloudes." While on another occasion Pepys chanced to meet with Sir Henry Blount, one of the first Englishmen to drink coffee during his travels in the Levant, who regaled him with stories of "Ægypt and other things."[51] The coffeehouse thus provided a new venue for the retailing of the traveler's tales that were central to virtuoso culture.

Pepys's coffeehouse conversations were of course not always devoted to virtuosic inquiries into the arts and sciences, although the preponderance of such instances is quite remarkable. He certainly engaged in much idle chatter or "common discourse," conversation about his professional concerns with the business of the Navy Office, as well as a great deal of rumor mongering and spreading social or political gossip. Coffeehouse socializing might also present opportunities for embarrassment as well as edification or entertainment: on one occasion, Pepys found himself "shamed" in front of the "whole house" at a Covent Garden coffeehouse, when one of the patrons ridiculed his recent speech before Parliament.[52]

Aside from the conversations and social interactions, Pepys also used the coffeehouse as a means of accessing the world of print. Some coffeehouses were closely associated with booksellers and offered their stock for sale on the premises. In this manner, Pepys was able to purchase a book on architecture at a coffeehouse in Exchange Alley, although he regretted having done so after reading it, judging it to be "not worth a turd." Although he was a frequent consumer of the newly licensed newsbooks of the early Restoration, in his diary Pepys never specifically mentions reading a coffeehouse newspaper; perhaps he preferred to read in private, and to listen and discuss the news in the more public setting of a coffeehouse.[53]

The centrality of the coffeehouse to virtuoso sociability did not wane after its initial introduction. By the 1690s, the coffeehouses of London were well established and they offered a quite diverse variety of venues for urban social life. James Brydges (1674–1744), FRS (elected 30 November 1694), and the future first duke of Chandos (1719), was perhaps the last great virtuoso of the long seventeenth century, and his conjoint searches for preferment and further erudition as a young man led him straight to the coffeehouses of London.[54] He kept a journal of his London activities in the later 1690s which documents some 280 visits to various coffeehouses between 8 February 1697 and 12 December 1702. This count does not include visits to more than one coffeehouse in a single day, and on some days Brydges might visit three or more. Brydges visited about 65 coffeehouses, chocolate-houses, and taverns during his stay in London.[55]

Brydges's use of the coffeehouse as a social institution was quite straightforward: he knew which houses were likely to attract interesting company and potential patrons, so he made it a point to become a regular customer at those institutions. Brydges was a regular at such fashionable chocolate houses as Ozinda's and White's as well as the more businesslike coffeehouses such as Garraway's, Man's, or the Grecian. Most often he was successful in finding some worthy company at these places, but if he found "no gentleman coming there," then he felt free to leave and move on in search of a more congenial locale.[56]

By the 1690s, the chocolate house had taken a complementary place alongside the coffeehouse in the social round of the London elite, and indeed the chocolate houses tended to cultivate an air of even greater distinction than did the much more "democratic" coffeehouses. Although the chocolate houses were established primarily to cater to the social rounds of the leisured class to which Brydges belonged, the discourse which took place there was not entirely devoted to the light-hearted matters of "gallantry and pleasure" that Richard Steele thought were most characteristic of places such as White's and that William Congreve epitomized in the first act of *The Way of the World* (1700). It was at White's Chocolate House where Brydges disputed with one Mr. Barber "concerning the right of the people originally in government," and he also discussed more topical matters, such as the prospects for a peace and the question of the Spanish succession. He also polished his virtuoso credentials there, by discussing the contents of the earl of Sunderland's library with the Lord Derwentwater and the son of John Lake, the non-juring bishop of Chichester. At Tom's Coffeehouse, Brydges was able to meet with the owner of some ancient manuscripts, and thus arranged a more formal visit to see them before moving on to discuss the art of painting with another interested virtuoso.[57]

As Pepys had done decades earlier, Brydges maintained his valuable contacts with the fellows of the Royal Society through his coffeehouse socializing. He often met with Dr. Hans Sloane at the Temple Coffeehouse, where they discussed matters of curiosity such as the ways to navigate the bogs of Ireland; on other occasions, Brydges took the opportunity to get some free medical consultation from Dr. Sloane about his back pain, or his "rheumatick pains." At Pontack's tavern, Brydges was a frequent dining companion with the Royal

Society men before heading off to Gresham College, and these occasions were often punctuated by a visit to Garraway's for a dish of coffee. It was at one of these dinners that Brydges made the acquaintance of the diplomat and art connoisseur William Aglionby, FRS.[58]

Although the coffeehouse was key to furthering his social aspirations in his early life, Brydges seems to have had less time for such activities after he was appointed paymaster of the armies abroad in 1705.[59] By 1710, he had become weary of the often very heated debates and discourses of the coffeehouses, and he confided privately to his friend John Drummond his hope that "some method can be found to quiet people['s] tempers and passions, which rage beyond expression at present (for your Gazettes can never treat some people half so ill, as they are in some coffee houses here all day long by word of mouth)."[60] When he began to accumulate his vast collection of rare books and art, Brydges chose to use purchasing agents and dealers resident abroad rather than to attend the auctions held in the London coffeehouses.[61] In this respect, Brydges's increasingly distant relationship to the world of coffeehouse sociability reflected his newly secure status as a prominent virtuoso patron of the arts and sciences. He no longer needed to curry favor with potential patrons at White's, nor was it necessary for him to work hard to establish his reputation among the virtuosi of Gresham College. By the early eighteenth century, Brydges was a powerful patron in his own right, and his standing as a virtuoso was now to be secured through the advantages of his position as a landed magnate, in particular the prestige of his collection at his country estate, Cannons, and as the host of visits to that collection.[62]

In this respect, James Brydges the landed peer had moved from a youthful social world akin to that of Samuel Pepys to one more like that preferred by John Evelyn. Even Pepys dramatically reduced the extent of his public house socializing as he grew older. Although the virtuosi played a central role in shaping the development of the coffeehouse milieu, especially in its early stages, the coffeehouse was never entirely accepted by the whole community of the virtuosi. Evelyn, in particular, remained wary of the institution, and indeed never mentions setting foot in a coffeehouse at any point in his diaries. When he did speak of coffeehouses, he was apt to be dismissive at best, or derisive at worst. Although he occasionally referred to the men of the Royal Society in jest as "the learned Coffee-Club," in a more serious vein he approved of Thomas Tenison's complaints that the young clerics of his parish spent little time with their books and far too much time "frequenting taverns or coffè-houses." Evelyn revealed his true opinion of the new coffeehouses in his marginal annotations to his copies of the Royal Society's *Philosophical Transactions*. Upon reading Thomas Smith's article on his travels to Constantinople, where the authorities had considered suppressing the coffee-houses because of their tendency to promote seditious assemblies, Evelyn averred that "Coffe-hou[ses are] impolite, permissive, even among us, for the same reason, as I have always thought."[63]

For Evelyn, the coffeehouse was an inappropriate venue for the learned discourse that was the common currency of virtuosity. It was too modish, too open to all comers, and too informal to maintain the elitist character that Evelyn thought socially appropriate for polite conversation. In this respect, Evelyn struggled valiantly against the dominant discourse of politeness in his day, which rendered the boundaries of class more permeable. Unlike Robert Hooke, Evelyn could never be comfortable in the company of lowly artisans and other such "mechanical and capricious persons," even when he thought there might be something to be gained from their practical knowledge. This genteel aversion to the manners of commoners was a major reason for his failure to make progress on the much vaunted "history of trades" for the Royal Society, and it kept Evelyn on the margins of the burgeoning coffee-house milieu of metropolitan London. Evelyn's attitude to London itself was of course a vexed one for the author of *Fumifugium* (1661), a work which was at once a panegyric for the capital city and a strident complaint against the smoke and filth found there. As early as the 1650s, Evelyn was publicly derid-ing the metropolis as "a very ugly town" that was indeed "a resemblance of hell upon earth," and he inveighed privately "against the iniquities of [the] Mad City" to his cousin.[64] The fashionability of coffeehouse society made it seem all the more repugnant to the culturally abstemious Evelyn. For a disciple of the earl of Arundel, the advancement of learning could hardly be achieved in a place which was devoted to worldly leisure and the conspicuous consump-tion of luxurious novelties.

Robert Boyle, another gentleman virtuoso with a well-established social status, also seems to have maintained a certain aloofness from the London coffeehouses, although he was less vehement in his dislike for the institutions than Evelyn was, and he certainly retained an interest in the medical properties of coffee itself. William Nicolson (1655–1727), the Bishop of Carlisle during the reign of Queen Anne, seems to have preferred to make personal visits to the homes of his fellow virtuosi rather than to meet them in the coffeehouses. Although Nicolson apparently did not frequent the coffeehouses, he did occa-sionally stop in at a tavern and he could not resist examining some of the natural curiosities on display in the public houses. The Irish intellectual Wil-liam Molyneux, FRS, told his friend John Locke that he thought "coffee-houses and publick tables are not proper places for serious discourses relating to the most important truths." This comment was made in the course of chastising their mutual acquaintance, John Toland, for his indiscreet religious discourse in public houses, a practice which drew the shock of many of his contemporaries.[65] Toland himself later disavowed the practice of "railing in coffeehouses" and told the third earl of Shaftesbury that he was no longer prone to "sauntering . . . in coffeehouses, nor keeping so much tattling company" as he had formerly. The same reserved distaste for coffeehouse society was expressed by Shaftesbury himself, who associated the coffeehouse with "the world" — the English equivalent of the French *le monde* — and saw it as harboring little more than frivolity, gossip, sycophancy, and imposture. Shaftesbury recommended instead that his fellow virtuosi take advantage of "the liberty of *the club,* and of that sort of freedom which is taken amongst gentlemen and friends who know one another perfectly well," rather than to mingle "in mixed company, and places where men are met promiscuously on account of diversion or affairs" — precisely the locales in which Robert Hooke and the young Samuel Pepys moved so effortlessly.[66]

It is perhaps ironic that some of Britain's greatest virtuosi of the seventeenth and early eighteenth centuries remained aloof from the social and commercial transformations that their fellow travelers so eagerly embraced, but these anxieties were not entirely idiosyncratic. Indeed, they reveal some of the major strains within British virtuoso culture itself. The coffeehouse became the primary site for the newer, more public, more commercialized, and urbanized modes of virtuoso sociability in the later seventeenth and early eighteenth centuries, but these changes were not entirely welcomed by those virtuosi who still held on to the more circumscribed, private, and personal social forms that were the preserve of the landed gentleman and his great house. It should not be thought that the older ideal grew stagnant and was gradually replaced by the vibrant new world of the metropolitan coffeehouses. Some virtuosos, like James Brydges, found it possible to operate comfortably in both worlds at various times. The Virginian gentleman and fellow traveler amongst the virtuosi William Byrd, FRS (1674–1744), spent most of his London social life in the coffeehouses, and was also privileged enough to visit the collection of Lord Islay.[67]

The coffeehouse did not supplant the great house as the central focus of virtuoso social life, but it did supplement it in a way that was not entirely comfortable for those who had invested a great deal of their cultural and financial capital in mastering the more venerable means of establishing one's learned reputation. For those aspiring virtuosi of lesser means, however, who could not afford to go on grand tours or amass great collections in their country houses, the coffeehouses opened up a hitherto restricted or severely regulated world of information and social access.

5

Exotic Fantasies and Commercial Anxieties

It wasn't every day that one could see a rhinoceros in seventeenth-century London. On 22 October 1684, John Evelyn got lucky. He went with the ex-ambassador to Spain, Sir William Godolphin, to see what was most likely the first rhinoceros — or was it a unicorn, he wondered — that was ever brought to England. "Twas certainly a very wonderful creature," he remarked, though he thought it most "particular & extraordinary" that her eyes were placed "in the very center of her cheekes & head, her eares [were] in her neck." Her teeth were "most dreadfull," and her horn "was but newly Sprowting, & hardly shaped to any considerable point." He supposed that it "more ressembled a huge enormous Swine, than any other Beast amongst us." Evelyn had no idea how large she might grow, but he speculated that "if she grow proportionable to her present age, she will be a Mountaine." As an aside, he noted in his diary that "she belonged to Certaine E[ast] *Indian Merchants,* & was sold for (as I remember) above two-thousand pounds."[1]

In fact, she was sold at an auction for precisely £2,320. Unfortunately (for the merchants at least), the original bidder, John Langley, never came up with the money, and she failed to attract another offer at a second auction. The rhino was therefore put to work as a standing curiosity at the Belle Savage Inn on Ludgate Hill. The Belle Savage was particularly well suited for holding a rhinoceros, for it had two courtyards, including a rather large inner yard with stables.[2] Anyone could have a look at her for "twelve pence apiece." Those who wanted a ride on the beast had to shell out two more shillings, or for the whole day, a full fifteen pounds. And within three months after it made its debut appearance at the Belle Savage, Londoners could purchase a picture of the rhino "curiously engraven in *mezzo tinto*" and "printed upon a large sheet of paper" as a sort of souvenir of their experience meeting the strange beast.[3]

Evelyn's encounter with the rhinoceros in London encapsulates much of the peculiar combination of circumstances with which this chapter is concerned, and it is therefore an instructive entrée into the social milieu that shaped the development of the early English coffeehouses. John Evelyn was one of the best known and most respected virtuosos of seventeenth-century England, and his interest in the strange appearance, as well as the natural history, of an exotic beast was characteristic of the virtuosic enthusiasm for such things. It combined an aesthetic appreciation for a "wonderful creature" with a scientific interest in the workings of the natural world. For the seventeenth-century virtuosi, art and nature were closely intertwined and equally worthy objects of inquiry.[4] Yet Evelyn was only one among many paying customers who thought the sight of a large, horned animal from the East Indies was worth the cost of admission. Furthermore, the rhino had been brought to London through the profiteering motive of some overseas merchants, and had been sold by auction. The mezzotint prints of the rhino were probably bought mostly by virtuoso collectors such as Evelyn or Samuel Pepys, but they too were commodities to be sold for a profit in the rapidly expanding art market of post-Restoration London. During the latter half of the seventeenth century, the exotic subjects of virtuosic curiosity were progressively assimilated into London's commercial culture, and the social space in which much of this fusion took place was provided by the public houses, and especially the coffeehouses, of the metropolis, whose social character had been so decisively shaped by the virtuosi themselves.

The relationship between the social world of England's virtuosi and the metropolitan coffeehouses was a reciprocal one. Until this point, I have emphasized the important formative influence of the virtuosi on the development of the social character, as it were, of the new coffeehouses. But the habits and values of the virtuosi were themselves transformed by their contact with the coffeehouse milieu. In particular, the coffeehouses brought the virtuosi quite literally face to face with the commercial, and the consumer, cultures of a city that was rapidly becoming the center of a global trading network. This chapter explores the commercialization of virtuoso culture by looking at the ways in which the exotic interests of the virtuosi were made available to a wider urban consumer market. I will then look more carefully at the emergence and reception of auction sales in the coffeehouses of early modern London. Auctions of books and works of art catered primarily to the interests of virtuoso collectors and were held, for the most part, in the coffeehouses. The history of sales by auction offers therefore an excellent means to explore the effect of metropolitan commercial culture on the social life of the virtuosi.

Buying Exotic: Orientalism and the Commercialization of Virtuosity

The early English coffeehouses did not try to hide their oriental origins; instead, they downplayed the predominantly negative images of the heathen Turk by emphasizing the innocence of the coffeehouse experience. The coffeemen claimed that coffee was merely a pleasant diversion, a "harmless and healing Liquor," "a Drink at once to make us Sober and Merry." Its taste, although initially unappealing, when "familiariz'd by a little use will become pleasant and delightful." But coffee was consistently associated with things oriental, even by the drink's most fervent advocates. "Through the happy Arabia [*Arabia Felix,* or contemporary Yemen], Nature's spicery prodigally furnishes the voluptuous world with all kind of aromaticks and divers other rarities," gushed one encomium for the coffeehouses. The popularity of coffee drinking in the east was seen as yet another reason why English consumers should give it a try: "any that are but moderately acquainted with shashes and turbants can witness . . . this innocent and wholesome drink that is so generally used by so many mighty nations, and those too celebrated for the most witty and sagacious." No less than thirty-seven London coffeehouses adopted the name "Turk's Head" and many of them used a symbol of a turbaned Turk on their identifying sign or on their trade tokens. Others were titled the "Sultan's Head" or "Sultaness' Head," or took the names of famous Ottoman rulers such as Murad the Great. Nor was the practice limited to London, as Oxford coffeehouses also took the name "Turk's Head."[5] Some coffeehouses went quite far in order to cultivate an attractive yet inoffensive oriental mystique, by either serving Turkish sherbets or even offering Turkish baths, called bagnios or hummums, along with their drinks. This phenomenon was hardly confined to England: no London establishment could rival the Parisian café of Francesco Procopio Coltelli, who opened an opulent coffeehouse in 1676 where waiters in eastern garb served various exotic liquors, spices, and foods. In Paris, it was claimed, "every coffee-house is an illuminated palace."[6] The exotic nature of the coffee drink and the exotic distinctiveness of the coffeehouse became part of the attraction of both the drink and the drinking house to seventeenth-century British consumers.

This use of exotic cultures for commercial purposes constituted something we might call "consumer orientalism." Since the publication of Edward Said's *Orientalism* (1978), it has become commonplace to discuss western attitudes toward Asian states and societies under the oft-times monolithic rubric of "orientalism." Whether this is entirely justified—especially with reference to the seventeenth century, when the imperial and neo-imperial institutions and discourses which are the main concern of Said's study were either nonexistent or only in their formative stages, and when the balance of power between European and Asian states was by no means entirely in favor of the former—is very much open to question.[7] Nevertheless, there was an "orientalism" of the seventeenth century, even if it was not the hegemonic imperialist discourse that is the subject of *Orientalism,* and its influence extended far beyond the scholarly circles of Oxbridge and the curiosity cabinets of the virtuosi. To say that early modern orientalism was not imperialist is not to deny that it was invested with assertions of occidental supremacy; it is merely to point out that the imperial hierarchies of the modern age had not yet been established.[8] The coffeehouses of post-Restoration Britain brought a sort of orientalism to anyone willing to step in and try a dish of the exotic new drink and thus participate in a social ritual previously adhered to by only select circles of virtuosi and their fellow travelers. In so doing, the coffeehouses managed to transform virtuoso culture itself.

The approbation of the virtuosi was crucial to establishing the legitimacy of both the medical value of coffee as well as the propriety of the coffeehouse as a social institution, but the exotic appeal of the new coffeehouses also tapped into a longstanding "popular" fascination with things marvelous, strange, and foreign that was commonly associated with the spectacles of Bartholomew Fair and the impromptu promotional shows of quack doctors and mountebanks.[9] In so doing, they provided yet another point of potential contact between the culture of the patricians and that of the plebes. This was especially true given the explicit appeals to openness, informality, and accessibility by the proponents of coffeehouse sociability. Far from providing their elite patrons with a secluded refuge from contact with the vulgar masses, the coffeehouses, much like the works of cheap print that were often read within them, brought both the genteel and the plebeian together to indulge their taste for exotic drinks and curious spectacles.[10]

The most striking example of the success of the consumer orientalism of the coffeehouses was the welcome accorded to those establishments that set up Turkish baths on their premises. These "bagnios" or hummums were virtually unprecedented in English social life. Public baths in England and throughout

Europe had been closed in the late Middle Ages in response to fears that they were responsible for spreading disease (the plague and syphilis) and fostering prostitution. But by the early seventeenth century, medical writers began to rehabilitate the reputation of the hot bath as an important therapeutic practice, primarily by insisting on the importance of balneology in Greco-Roman as well as Turkish medicine. Travel writers who had ventured to the east made note of the use of public baths in the Ottoman Empire, and some virtuosi advocated the hygienic benefits of hot baths.[11] While the medical entrepreneur Peter Chamberlen failed to make much progress with his Parliamentary patent for a Turkish steam bath in the 1640s, a commercial bagnio was eventually and successfully introduced to London consumers in 1679.[12]

The London bagnios were unabashed in their adoption of the Turkish custom. The champions of the Royal Bagnio on Newgate Street noted that "the Grand Seignior (whose government is founded on notable maxims of policy) thought it would be convenient for to have them erected throughout his dominions, not only for pleasure and delight, but also for the preservation of his subjects," and they dismissed the thought that English constitutions could not benefit from a "Turkish invention." "It is as near the Turkish fashion as may be." A German visitor to London, Zacharias Conrad von Uffenbach, visited the Royal Bagnio in 1710 because he heard that it was "supposed to be the most elegeant and . . . commended as being the best and arranged entirely in Turkish fashion" (Figure 16). Brook's bathhouse called itself the "China Hummum" and offered "sweating and bathing both at once, after the China manner."[13] So much attention has been devoted to the great opprobrium heaped upon "luxury" by early modern moralists that the idea that luxury could also be appealing to many early modern consumers often seems to be forgotten. Indeed, the moralists' warnings would have had little purchase if their sumptuary anxieties were shared by their contemporaries. The bagnios invoked an image of oriental hedonism as a sort of sales pitch. Not all bagnios adopted a strictly oriental mystique. Some proprietors, such as John Evans, claimed to practice in the "New German manner," or Charles Peter, whose bagnio followed the "Italian manner," but in each case the appeals were still to foreign techniques hitherto unknown to England.[14]

The bagnios provided more than just baths for their patrons, as they were staffed by "rubbers" (masseuses), barbers, and "cuppers" who offered therapeutic bleeding treatments. Of course, coffee and other hot drinks were offered. Like the coffeehouses, certain bagnios became known as resorts for clubs of wits and critics. The Royal Bagnio hosted lectures and sermons on its premises, received the duke of Monmouth and his entourage for a visit, and was the site for an auction of pictures in 1687.[15] Both women and men were

Figure 16. "The Turk's Head," the card of Wilcox the cupper (c. 1702), from Thompson, *Quacks of Old London* (1928), 268.

welcomed by the bagnios and given "the same reception and entertainment," although the proprietors were careful to keep the sexes segregated in order to avoid any taint of promoting bawdry. The most scrupulous establishments remained closed on Sundays. The Royal Bagnio proved to be so successful that the owners soon opened a second, smaller bath adjoining to the main one. The smaller bath was offered at 3s., while the main one cost 5s., 6d. The charge "for the whole house" was later dropped to a flat rate of 4s.[16]

Although they worked hard to avoid any association with prostitution, it seems that so many bagnios were in fact fronts for bawdy houses that the word

itself soon came to be a synonym for brothel. Moralists urged the city government to monitor these "hot-houses" for the presence of "strumpets or women
of ill-fame." Londoners of a more lusty disposition found them a convenient
place to consummate affairs with mistresses and city bawds; William Byrd
seems to have used London's bagnios exclusively for such purposes. The pre-
existing stereotypes of libidinous orientals and decadent Romans who overin-
dulged their appetites in public baths were perhaps too powerful to prevent
these connections from adhering to the bagnios, and it is likely that many of
their proprietors were aware of this commercial appeal of the orient and
exploited it for their own profit. James Boswell's ruminations on the appeal of
the bath were not uncommon: "How great must have been the luxury of the
Romans, who solaced thus their entire bodies [in the public baths]. . . . A warm
bath is, I confess, a most agreeable kind of luxury, but luxury is very dangerous. . . . Above all things a young man should guard against effeminacy."[17]

These establishments also trivialized their orientalism in order to make it
safe for English consumption. The coffeehouses and bagnios of London encouraged their customers to believe that they could experience the orient
through sharing the same consumption patterns, such as drinking coffee or
taking a hot bath, and that this could be done without making any further
effort to understand or even to accept oriental cultures.[18] "Going Turk" in this
way offered a brief, perhaps even exciting, escape from the banalities of urban
life by providing an opportunity to transcend ethnic difference and to explore
a new drink culture, but do so in a way that did not fundamentally challenge
England's presumed cultural supremacy.

In this respect, the patrons of coffeehouses and bagnios were participating
in a newly commercialized form of status inversion in which pre-existing
status boundaries are reaffirmed through a controlled and limited reversal of
the established social hierarchy.[19] Although coffeehousing involved only the
imaginative subversion of traditional English consumption practices to the
exotic, Turkish "culinary Other," it was precisely this transgression that made
the coffeehouse so alluring. The consumer orientalism of the coffeehouse milieu had its origins in the old regime of carnival and the licensed liberties of the
fairs, but it was also the first apparition of a new capitalist mode in which
inversion occurred not as the result of an established and seasonal ritual, but
rather at the behest of the paying public. The consumer culture exemplified by
the coffeehouse was both traditional and modern at the same time. Coffeehouse orientalism offered much the same sort of traditional pleasures offered
by the seasonal experience of ritualized inversions of the normal social order,
but it was now on offer throughout the year and the pleasures were thoroughly
commercialized.

Without succumbing to the simple but false allure of a strict dichotomy between traditional ritualized consumption and modern egoistic consumerism, we may still recognize the important novelty of the way in which the coffeehouses allowed consumers to immerse themselves in the exotic fantasy of going Turk on their own initiative and not at any one carefully prescribed time of year. The commercial escapism first espoused by the seventeenth-century coffeehouses and bagnios would take the form of the masquerade in the early eighteenth century, the rise of the department store in the nineteenth, and the emergence of the "ethnic" restaurant in the twentieth century. The coffeehouses created a precedent for a recognizably modern type of consumer culture which valorizes fantasy and ephemerality over permanence and the fixing of social boundaries. And it is significant that in each of these cases, the consumer's fantasies have been troped as "oriental."[20]

The bagnios, like the coffeehouses with which they were closely associated, were entirely new commercial institutions in post-Restoration Britain. Their success was dependent upon finding a niche that was distinct and yet not so utterly unfamiliar that their services would be ignored, or deemed unnecessary for Englishmen. The coffeehouses and the bagnios both promised their patrons a pleasant combination of healthy care for the body along with a relaxed environment in which their customers could experience a fantasy of hedonistic indulgence through imbibing exotic liquors, or bathing like Turks. This extravagance was made legitimate through the appeal to the medicinal properties of coffee and the therapeutic benefits of hot bathing. By combining innocent leisure with medical claims, the coffeehouses provided an important new social space in which novel consumer demands were sanctioned. The commercial success of the coffeehouses in post-Restoration Britain was founded to a large degree on their customers' misrecognition of the ways in which the coffeehouses licensed demands which might otherwise have been considered luxurious or even immoral. Long before the economic theorist Nicholas Barbon controversially announced in 1690 that consumption should be indifferent to moral concerns and that "the wants of the mind are infinite," Londoners had been expanding their imagined desires in the coffeehouse milieu.[21]

Monsters in the Barbershop

The closest forerunner to the coffeehouse or the bagnio in early modern Britain was not the alehouse, but rather the barbershop, which often served as an important center for the care of the body and personal hygiene, as well as providing "places of resort for men, offering music, drink, gaming, conversation, and news." Medical advice and medicinal products, such as tobacco, could also be purchased there. The early tobacconists' shops also provided a similar setting and services.[22] Barbershops were also significantly known on occasion to provide collections of curiosities on display for the entertainment and edification of their patrons (Figure 17). In this respect they aped the cabinet collections of the most esteemed virtuosi, and made such curiosities accessible to a much wider audience (Figure 18).

The most famous barbershop collection of curiosities was held by one James Salter, whose shop also doubled as a coffeehouse. Salter offered the usual barber's services — shaving, bleeding, and tooth pulling — and he entertained his customers with his fiddle playing.[23] Salter, who had been a servant of Sir Hans Sloane, took the Spanish nom de plume "Don Saltero" and his collection of rarities assembled at his coffeehouse in Chelsea remained a major attraction for virtuosi and the curious public alike throughout the eighteenth century. In 1729, he published the first of many catalogues of the contents of Don Saltero's collection. His preface, addressed to "all my kind customers," both "gentlemen and ladies," stated: "I have endeavoured for several years, to gather and preserve curiosities, for the delight of the publick, and have met with such success, by the assistance of several noble benefactors (a list of whose names I have, as a specimen of my gratitude, set down) that I can now venture to say the most curious may be entertained in speculation." Saltero's collection included items which may be considered relics, such as the "painted ribbands from Jerusalem with the pillar, to which our saviour was tied when scourged, with a motto on each" and the "saint's bone"; others were natural curiosities such as "an embrio of a seal" and a block of "amber with insects in it." Other attractions included items of historical interest, such as "Queen Elizabeth's strawberry dish" and "King James the IId's coronation shoes." Exotica such as "a Chinese idol" and "Indian tammahacks" were also on display.[24]

Saltero and his curiosities soon became the target of the satirical jests of the London wits. His coffeehouse was dubbed the "Chelsea Knack," short for the knackatory, or house of trifles; and Saltero himself was derided as "Gimcrack Salter" or the "Grubstreet Dabler." Most famously, in the *Tatler* he drew the censure of Richard Steele's Isaac Bickerstaff, who recounted his visit to Saltero's and his judgment upon the collection therein to his reading public: "When I came into the Coffee-house, I had not time to salute the company, before my eye was diverted by ten thousand gimcracks round the room and on the sieling. . . . I cannot allow a liberty he takes of imposing several names (without my licence) on the collections he has made, to the abuse of the good people of England . . . this is really nothing, but under the specious pretence of learning and antiquity, to impose upon the world." Saltero's collection was probably an easy target for Bickerstaff's ridicule, composed as it was of the

Figure 17. The barbershop satirized: W. H. Toms, after Egbert van Heemskerck the younger (c. 1730), etching and engraving (25.7 cm × 23.8 cm). BM Sat., no. 1859; published by John Bowles, c. 1766; LWL 766.0.5. Courtesy of the Lewis Walpole Library, Yale University. Alternative text at the bottom reads: "A Barber's Shop adorn'd we see, / With Monsters, News, and Poverty: / Whilst some are shaving, others bleed, / And those that wait the papers read. / The Master full of Whigg or Tory / Combs out your wig and tells a story / Then palms your cole & scraping smiles / And gives a bill to cure the piles."

castoffs and duplicates from the more renowned collection of Sir Hans Sloane, and because of the vulgarity of Saltero's trade as a common barber. "Whence should it proceed," Bickerstaff mused sarcastically, "that of all the lower order, barbers should go further in hitting the ridiculous, than any other set of men. . . . Why must a barber be forever a politician, a musician, an anatomist, a poet, and a physician." But the polite critic denied that his disapproval resulted from a snobbish disdain for the sorry attempts of a common artisan to imitate the interests of his more genteel superiors. "It is my way," he reminded his readers, "to consider men as they stand in merit, and not according to their figure." Bickerstaff's gibes at Saltero seem tame indeed when compared to his satires on the frivolous gentleman virtuosi "who are wholly employed in gathering together the refuse of nature . . . and hoarding up in their chests and cabinets such creatures as others industriously avoid the sight of."[25] Perhaps Addison and Steele disapproved of Saltero's pretensions because they saw him as encouraging an already lamentable enthusiasm for things trifling and bizarre among the genteel virtuosi rather than because they thought he aspired to rise above his station.

The more earnest among the virtuosi themselves were kinder in their appraisal of Saltero's collection. The German Zacharias von Uffenbach, who on other occasions disapproved of the lack of respect for scholarly civilities in the English virtuoso community, seemed to think well of Don Saltero's coffeehouse: "It looks more like a museum of art and natural curiosities than a coffee-house. For both standing round the walls and hanging from the ceiling are all manner of exotic beasts, such as crocodiles and turtles, as well as Indian and other strange costumes and weapons. It is a pity that these things, of which many are truly curious, should hang there in the tobacco smoke and become spoilt." A similar vote of approval was voiced by the accomplished Yorkshire antiquary, Ralph Thoresby, FRS, upon his visit to Don Saltero's in May 1723. "Mr. Salter's collection of curiosities . . . is really very surprising considering his circumstances as a coffee-man," he reported, but then hastened to add, "several persons of distinction have been benefactors." Indeed, Saltero's first catalogue of his rarities included the names of sixty-eight benefactors to his collection, of whom eight were peers.[26] The compilation and publication of the catalogue itself signaled Saltero's arrival among the higher echelons of the virtuoso community, as it opened to public inspection the contents of his collection and served as a testament to the generosity of his many benefactors. The compilation of a proper catalogue of a renowned collection of rarities, or a famous library, was a scholarly undertaking of major importance to the early modern republic of letters, and its contents were viewed as a reflection of the honor and learning of its owner or patrons. For

Figure 18. The virtuoso cabinet of curiosities. Engraved plate, Ferrante Imperato, *Dell'historia Naturale* (Naples: C. Vitale, [1599]); Beinecke shelfmark 016 040. Courtesy of the Beinecke Rare Book and Manuscript Library, Yale University. The virtuoso cabinet, like the coffeehouse and the barbershop, was designed to facilitate conversation and social interaction, but unlike the public houses,

this reason Narcissus Marsh wished to conceal the publication of the contents of the late Archbishop James Ussher's library, for he thought that it "comes very short of its and its owners fame; it might have been thought a good library for another man, but not for that learned Prelate." New editions of Don Saltero's catalogue, however, were proudly printed well into the later eighteenth century, and long after the death of Salter himself.[27]

Well before the *Tatler* focused its satire on Salter's coffeehouse, Thomas Faulkner's *Antiquities of Middlesex* had called it one of the primary attractions of the Chelsea neighborhood. Faulkner considered Salter's establishment to be one of "the pleasures of the city," where "many honourable worthy inhabitants, being not more remarkable for their titles, estates, or abilities than for their kind and facetious tempers . . . have a general meeting every day" at the coffeehouse, which was already "well known for the pretty collection of rarities in nature and art, some of which are very curious." The coffeehouse remained a major London attraction throughout the eighteenth century; it was recommended as a place where "many genteel people go" in Fanny Burney's *Evelina* (1778), and it piqued the curiosity of the young Ben Franklin. Although the contents of the collection were finally sold by auction in 1799, Don Saltero's continued to do business as a coffeehouse and tavern until the mid-nineteenth century.[28]

James Salter was not alone in providing his patrons with curiosities for their edification and their entertainment. As early as the 1670s, Robert Hooke was inspecting the coffeehouses for their "raritys," while at other times he might inspect and comment on the prints of his fellow virtuosi. An issue of the *Athenian Mercury* in late 1691 recommended to its readers that they visit the newly opened collection of curiosities owned by one Mr. John Conyers, an apothecary in "Shooe-Lane" who also happened to be a Fellow of the Royal Society and an antiquary who "made it his chief business to make curious observations, and to collect such antiquities as were daily found in and about London." At Conyers's shop and cabinet of curiosity, the public were encouraged to view such things as exotic animals and vegetables, various antiquities of "Egyptian, Jewish, Grecian, Roman, British, Saxon, [and] Danish" provenance, ancient books and manuscripts in the "Latin, Chinese, Saxon, Islandish, Muscovite, French and English languages," as well as "his outlandish garments, weapons, his pictures, prints and a vast many other things." In 1698, some entrepreneur in the curiosity market opened "a Monster-shop, where every thing that is ugly, or strange, proves a very vendible commodity," near the London Stocks-Market.[29] For a price, the once private cabinet of curiosities was made accessible to all interested comers in the new and commercial milieu of London's public houses.

Along with taverns, inns, and especially the fairgrounds, coffeehouses offered a space for the display of exotic spectacles such as the rhino inspected by John Evelyn. Exotic animals were a particularly favored exhibition. Sir James Simeon believed that exposure to the exotic animals on display in London "would enlarge [his son's] knowledge in what the Lord & nature doth produce."[30] Before the rhinoceros of 1684, an Asian elephant had been brought to London in 1675. After being sold at an auction at Garraway's Coffeehouse, it was exhibited to the public for the price of three shillings for each showing. Admission to this event was carefully guarded, as a young apprentice learned when he was stabbed by a guard who caught him trying to sneak a peek at the elephant without paying. The elephant provoked not only the curiosity of the virtuosi, but also the imagination of the town's wits and pamphleteers (Figure 19).[31] Elephant exhibitions had long captured the attention of both learned and popular audiences. While in Rotterdam, Evelyn saw an elephant "so extreamly well disciplin'd and obedient, that" he claimed he "did never wonder at any thing more." An elephant was even brought to Longleat House in Wiltshire for the private entertainment of the Thynne family. Performances of trained monkeys were a common attraction at Bartholomew Fair and Southwark Fair, and the exhibition of a tiger could attract the attention of "all persons of quality and character." Although the virtuosi found such shows too curious to resist, their indiscriminate appeal also caused some consternation. Whilst watching the monkeys at Bartholomew Fair, Samuel Pepys complained that "it troubled me to sit among such nasty company," and even when accompanied by his wife he found the monkey show "such dirty sport that I was not pleased with it." Ned Ward's appraisal of the crowd at May-Fair was even less equivocal: "I never in my life saw such a number of lazy, lousie-look'd rascals, and so hateful a throng of beggarly, sluttish strumpets." Public curiosity displays could even on occasion be considered nuisances subject to regulation by civic authorities, as John Gill and Mr. Lasker discovered in 1685 when they were presented at a Farringdon wardmote "for keeping a crocodile, and . . . for shewing a hairy woman which caused a great concourse of people to the great disorder and trouble of all the neighbours."[32]

The confluence of popular and patrician interest in the spectacles of the fairs and public houses does not mean that the curiosity shows were indiscriminately pleasing to all classes; in fact, they may have provided different sorts of pleasures to the different sorts of classes. Virtuosi such as Pepys and Evelyn went to the fairs to see the curiosities on offer, but they were uncomfortable doing so when this required them to join a "nasty" crowd of commoners. The author of *Essay in Defence of the Female Sex* (1696) seized on this uncomfortable confluence of interest between the virtuosi and the masses in its satirical

Figure 19. Title page, *True and Perfect Description of the Strange and Wonderful Elephant* (London: J. Conniers, [1675]); Houghton Library, Harvard University, shelfmark *EO65 A100 675t. Courtesy of the Houghton Library, Harvard University.

character of a virtuoso. Here, the visit to a virtuosic cabinet of curiosities is ridiculed as little more than an eccentric gentleman's *"Raree Show; the particulars of which he repeats [to his visitors] in a whining tone,"* the marvels of "his Philosophical *Toy Shop*."[33]

Perhaps as a means of countering such criticisms, the virtuosi themselves did not accept the spectacles at the fairs and coffeehouses uncritically. Although akin to the wonderful displays on offer in the curiosity cabinets of their esteemed fellows, the public shows were clearly considered by the virtuosi to be of a distinctly lower order. Perhaps the line between respectable curiosity and dubious entertainment was too fuzzy in these locales. While one could rest assured that one's curiosity was legitimate in the private company of a fellow virtuoso gentleman, a visit to the fair often required sharing the show with commoners or indeed, with women, whose interest was presumably not considered to be on par with that of the virtuosi. Women were invited into the virtuoso cabinets of curiosity, or meetings of the Royal Society, only on very rare occasions, but the fairs — considered to be sites of entertainment rather than learning — were open to all.[34]

Hence virtuoso fairgoers were always on the lookout for impostures and cheats, and they certainly did not believe that they were on the same level as the common dupes who fell for the fraudulent curiosities found all too often at the fairs or other commercial arenas. When John Verney went to an inn in Smithfield to see a boy who was reputed to speak several languages, but was told that the prodigy was asleep, he concluded that he had been lured by "nothing but a gull to draw people to the house," an impression reinforced by his discovery that most places at the inn were taken up with "company a-drinking." Martin Lister expressed his surprise at "the impudence of a booth" at the Saint Germain fair in Paris that advertised four exotic animals, but actually offered only two, "and those very ordinary ones," in his estimation: a raccoon and a leopard. Lister's response was ferocious: "I ask'd the Fellow, why he deceived the people, and whether he did not fear cudgelling in the end." Lister mercifully refrained from attacking the booth owner.[35]

Nevertheless the virtuosi and similar gentlemen and ladies of quality often ventured to see the curiosity shows at the fairs. The displays were frequently similar to those found in the much praised *Kunst- und Wunderkammern* of the virtuosi. Aside from exotic animals, perennial favorites included human freaks of nature, such as the two-bodied man, giants and dwarves, a bearded lady, a child with three penises, and a woman with three breasts. Such human monstrosities were eagerly sought out by the gentlemen of the Royal Society, believing as they did in Bacon's dictum that "a compilation, or particular natural history, must be made of all monsters and prodigious births of nature; of everything, in short, which is new, rare, and unusual in nature."[36] Reports of monstrous births and natural curiosities were regularly reported in the Royal Society's prestigious *Philosophical Transactions* as well as in John Dunton's less lofty but much more accessible periodical, the *Athenian Mercury*. This sort of scientific interest could make the spectacle only more interesting to the general public. A notice advertising the appearance of a boy covered with bristly hairs announced with obvious pride that "the learned part of mankind" have taken such an interest in the boy that his case was published in the *Philosophical Transactions*.[37]

Sometimes, however, just a very foreign person would do (Figure 20). One handbill announced that one could see at the Golden Lyon in Smithfield "the tall *Black,* called the *Indian-KING,* who was betrayed on board of an English interloper, and barbarously abused on board of that ship . . . from thence carried to *Jamaica* and sold there for a slave, and now redeem'd by a merchant in London." He remained there dressed "in his *Indian* garb."[38] For a price, one presumes that this escaped prince would tell his amazing tale at length to anyone who cared to listen.

The literary critic Dennis Todd has argued that the English fascination with these bizarre spectacles was provoked by the way in which the "blurring of boundaries and collapsing of identities . . . is at the heart of the experience of monstrosity." The shows presented people and animals that were just familiar enough to be recognizable and thus be the recipients of the spectator's sympathy. Freaks and Indian princes may have been unusual, but they were nevertheless human beings just like their spectators. A rhino may have been big and fearsome, but it still looked something like a large pig, or perhaps an ugly unicorn. "It is not the merely monstrous that draws the viewers," Todd notes, but "rather it is the *frisson* that comes with seeing how closely the monstrous verges on the normal, the human, the everyday." Joseph Addison disagreed. In his famous *Spectator* essay on the "pleasures of the imagination," he claimed that the appeal of the monstrous (and by extension, the exotic) came from the variety and diversion from the ordinary that such things provided: "Whatever is *new* or *uncommon* . . . serves us for a kind of refreshment, and takes off from that satiety we are apt to complain of in our usual and ordinary entertainments. It is that that bestows charms on a monster, and makes even the imperfections of nature please us."[39] Perhaps there is some truth to both explanations, but neither can account for the changing tastes in exotica and freakery during the early modern era (and indeed the modern as well).

Although human monstrosities had been on display since at least the mid-sixteenth century, what was new to the spectacles of the seventeenth century was the appearance of so many more creatures and people from the East and

Figure 20. The "Little Black Man" at the May Fair (c. 1700s). BL shelfmark N.Tab.2026/25 (37). Courtesy of the British Library, London.

West Indies. By the mid-eighteenth century the Indies would no longer seem so strange and their place would be taken by exotica from the more recently discovered lands in the South Pacific and Africa. It is often forgotten by commentators on the monstrosities and exotic beasts of seventeenth-century London that these people and these creatures were commodities. They were bought and sold by entertainment impresarios in order to titillate the taste for curiosities and novel pleasures of the London populace — a point that was not lost on Richard Steele, who noted that the queen's suppression of the shows at May-Fair "has quite sunk the price of this noble creature [the elephant] as well as many other curiosities of nature."⁴⁰ And as with the coffee commodity itself, the prestigious patina of virtuoso interest in these matters provided an important reason for making these tastes appear more legitimate among the general public.

Not everyone approved of the consumer orientalism that flourished in the coffeehouse milieu. To many commentators, the coffeehouses' consciously constructed Turkish aura raised the specter of a growing degeneracy in English mores which was signaled by the popularity of such a luxurious, debauched, and effeminate oriental custom as frequenting coffeehouses. There was a long-standing apprehension against merchants who "go amongst the Moors, Turks and Pagans" in order to bring exotic "trifles" into England. Readers of Livy and other Roman historians would have recognized that the introduction of Asian habits of luxurious consumption often signaled the beginning of the end for a hitherto vigorous and masculine polity. Thus John Evelyn lectured the Countess of Sunderland to take heed of the "fatal experience" of the Romans "after their Asiatic conquests: the lux and softness of those nations, effeminated the most glorious empire under heaven."⁴¹ Coffee's early reputation as an anti-aphrodisiac only helped to buttress these anxieties over the effeminizing consequences of coffeehouse culture. The men who frequented coffeehouses could be viewed as neglectful of their domestic duties as heads of households who instead spent their time gossiping like women, and a taste for novel, foreign, and exotic drinks could be likened to the common trope of a feminine appetite for the latest fashion.⁴²

Perhaps the most extreme example of the xenophobia provoked by the coffeehouses was John Tatham's *Knavery in All Trades: Or, the Coffee-House: A Comedy* (1664). The protagonist, a coffeehouse proprietor who was portrayed as a Turkish immigrant named Mahoone, speaks a pidgin English-French with a Dutch accent and manages to swear constantly in at least as many languages. Mahoone is a greedy, cuckolded fool who constantly boasts of the health-affirming qualities of the watered-down wares he prepares in his chamber pots. A roughly contemporary satirical poem also combines scatology with anti-Turkish xenophobia. It opens with this memorable stanza:

> For Men and Christians to turn Turks, and think
> T'excuse the Crime because 'tis in their drink,
> Is more then Magick, and does plainly tell
> Coffee's extraction has its heats from Hell.

It then proceeds to offer a simile between excrement and coffee. Other poems likened coffee to "The Sweat of Negroes" and the "Blood of Moores" and claimed that

When Coffee once was vended here,
The Alc'ron shortly did appear:
For (our Reformers were such Widgeons,)
New Liquors brought in new Religions.[43]

All of these refutations strenuously deny that drinking coffee is nothing more than mere consumption. They refuse to admit that drinking is an "innocent" thing, divorced from its cultural origins. One of the earliest anti-coffeehouse pamphlets fulminated: "Like Apes, the English imitate all other people in their ridiculous Fashions. As Slaves, they submit to the Customes even of Turky and India. . . . With the Barbarous Indian he smoaks Tobacco. With the Turk he drinks Coffee." Another derided the coffeehouse-keeper as a "Stygian-Puddle-Seller . . . that ap'd a turbant, and in conjunction with his Antichristian face, made him appear a perfect Turk." This notion of identity between foreign cultures and foreign commodities is well expressed in a picture which depicts two respectable Englishmen sandwiched between an Amerindian and a Turk (Figure 21).[44] The four men are brought together in the act of consumption; the implication is that an Englishman becomes a heathen by participating in his consumption preferences.

The extreme xenophobic strains in the anti-coffeehouse literature did not last long, however. As coffeehouses became more familiar and more fully assimilated into the daily life of British cities, it became more difficult to portray the coffeehouse as a dangerous and threatening foreign institution. By the 1690s, Ned Ward was virtually alone in his attempts to perpetuate the anti-orientalist trope against coffee in his *London Spy* satires.[45] The strange had by this time become quite familiar, and the exoticness of the coffeehouse had been thoroughly domesticated.

Pricing the Priceless:
The Anxiety of Auctions in the Early Coffeehouse Milieu

Along with their embrace of the exotic, the early coffeehouses of the Restoration era quickly established themselves as centers of commerce. The much vaunted achievements of Lloyd's coffeehouse, the forerunner to the modern insurance firm Lloyd's of London, and the early stock exchanges conducted at Garraway's and Jonathan's coffeehouses in Exchange Alley have long been recognized for their role in the English "financial revolution" of the 1690s and the eighteenth century. These functions will be discussed at further length in the next chapter. But one of the earliest and most common commercial uses of the coffeehouse was as an auction sales room. Coffeehouse auc-

Figure 21. Engraved plate, *Two Broad-Sides Against Tobacco* (London: John Hancock, 1672), 63; Beinecke shelfmark Ih J231 604Cb. Courtesy of the Beinecke Rare Book and Manuscript Library, Yale University.

tions were used to sell a wide variety of goods, from prize ships and bulk goods such as cloth and draperies and even whale oil.[46] They were best known, however, for the numerous auctions of books and artworks that began to be held in the late 1670s and soon became a regular fixture of the social life of both the virtuosi and the metropolitan elite. Even more so than the curiosity shows, the coffeehouse auctions brought the virtuosi out of their private cabinets and into close contact with the wider world of London society. For this reason the auction offers an excellent example of the transformations in virtuoso sociability that resulted from their embrace of the coffeehouse world of metropolitan London.

The coffeehouse became one of the premier sites for the emergence of the English auction. Overseas merchants commonly used "sales by candle" to sell their imports quickly on the London wholesale market by at least the early seventeenth century, and the practice appeared occasionally in Italy and the Netherlands as a means to sell off used books. But it was not until 1674 that artworks were sold by auction, and in 1676 the first auction of books was held in London.[47] A sales medium that had originated as a convenience for mercantile wholesaling was enthusiastically embraced by collectors of books, artworks, and similar "curiosities" in the post-Restoration era, and their preferred venue for these sales was the London coffeehouse.

Indeed the book and art auctions so favored by the virtuosi soon came to dominate the auction markets of Restoration London. A systematic study of auctions advertised in the periodical press for the last four decades of the seventeenth century reveals that 88 percent of all auctions held at the time were sales of books or artworks, while wholesale auctions comprised a mere 5 percent of the total. The English auction market was also clearly centered on the metropolis. London auctions accounted for approximately 92 percent of all English auctions. While the provincial auctions might be held at a private residence or a marketplace, the London auctions were overwhelmingly located in coffeehouses or taverns, such as Tom's Coffeehouse and the Barbados Coffeehouse in Cornhill, or Will's Coffeehouse in Westminster. The latter became so deeply associated with the auction business that it changed its name to the Auction House in 1691.[48] These coffeehouses held regular art auctions on their premises for several years.

Beyond the clear predominance of London coffeehouse auctions, the geographical distribution of provincial auctions was also strikingly linked to other centers of scholarly and aristocratic sociability. The university towns of Oxford and Cambridge were, not surprisingly, popular sites for book auctions, while elite leisure centers such as Tunbridge Wells, Epsom, and Bath hosted auctions of art, especially during the summer when many gentry families departed from the metropolis for these fashionable spa resort towns. It is also remarkable that auctions in foreign cities such as Brussels and Leiden were advertised in the English press. Such auctions clearly catered to the most eager of the virtuosi, for whom a journey to the Netherlands was no obstacle in their quest for rare oriental manuscripts, or a cabinet of curiosities containing "an exceeding great quantity of divers curious pieces both of the Indies, Africa, China, and other remote countries." The English virtuosi closely watched the Dutch auction market for books, art, and curiosities, and they were frequent participants at the sales in the Netherlands.[49]

Just as the aesthetic and social predilections of the virtuosi played a crucial formative role in the introduction of the coffee commodity and the coffee-house into English society, so were these virtuosi again decisive in shaping the early formation of London's auction market. The virtuosi flocked to the early auctions of books, pictures, and virtually any other rarities that could be put up for sale. The language used to promote the auction sales was taken directly from the vocabulary of the virtuosi: virtually every auctioneer promised his customers a "curious collection" of "rarities," works by learned authors, or pictures painted by the "most famous masters" both "ancient" and "modern." This was a direct appeal to, and emulation of, the sensibilities of the virtuosi, for whom the highest praise one could give to an item was to call it "curious" or "rare." The wide-ranging aesthetic of rarity was perhaps the common de-nominator that held Britain's virtuoso community together.

It is clear that some auctions catered directly to the virtuoso market. An auction in Soho in 1688 advertised the sale of "an excellent collection of paintings, drawings, and prints, with a vast collection of rare Indian shells and insects, and other natural rarities, in a cabinet consisting of two and forty drawers . . . to be managed with all candour imaginable." An earlier sale promised a chance to obtain that most precious item no virtuoso collector could go without—a unicorn horn.[50] Just as virtuosi tried to surround them-selves with curiosities of all sorts, some auctions offered a wide variety of valuable collectibles: pictures could be sold along with rare books, manu-scripts and relics of antiquity at an auction. A sale at the Black Swan in Ludgate advertised "several curious volumes of statues, Roman and Greek antiquities, geography, architecture, emblems, &c." in May 1689. Another auction at the Outroper's office in June 1692 even offered "a very large male cammel" along with a collection of paintings.[51]

The auction therefore quickly became an established aspect of virtuosic sociability in the city: it is no wonder then that the sales were held in coffee-houses where the virtuosi were already frequent customers. Robert Hooke was as avid an aficionado of the early auction scene as he was of the coffee-houses. He would read auction catalogues as soon as they were published in anticipation of a sale. During the height of the auction boom, Hooke might visit as many as four auctions in a day. Although he occasionally made a purchase—and could still complain that the books were "all too dear by half"—he was also careful to observe what was on offer and who successfully bid for the items up for sale. He noted in his diary the prices paid by others for various books of interest to him. Hooke did not go to auctions simply to purchase books or curiosities, but they also became part of his social round. He often accompanied his friends to the auctions, or he might meet them there. Given Hooke's notorious irascibility, this might mean that he could take the opportunity to scold them as well. Hooke's auction-going also allowed him to provide services, such as making purchases, for friends and patrons like Sir John Long.[52]

Hooke was not alone in making the auction a central part of his social life. For many virtuosi, the auction presented an opportunity not only to buy up a good number of items for their collections but also to do so in a uniquely public setting. The auction became a public medium by which putatively "priceless" curiosities were indeed priced by those consumers who most avidly desired to acquire them. The virtuosi may have consistently deployed a rhetoric of "sparing no cost" when they wrote about the practice of collecting rarities, but they were nevertheless acutely aware of their participation in a commercial market for their curiosities. Thus they annotated their auction sales catalogues carefully with the prices at which the goods were sold. They were also not shy about complaining when they thought prices got too high, usually as the result of the high bidding of upstart or over-eager collectors. Humfrey Wanley, an accomplished antiquarian as well as the library-keeper and purchasing agent for Robert and Edward Harley, the first and second earls of Oxford, breathed a sigh of relief upon the death of Charles Spencer, the bibliophilic third earl of Sunderland. "I believe that by reason of his decease," Wanley wrote, "some benefit may accrue to [the Harleian] library . . . by his raising the price of books no higher now; so that, in probability, this commodity may fall in the market; and any gentleman be permitted to buy an uncommon old book for less than fourty or fifty pounds."[53]

Competition through conspicuous bidding was part of the thrill of the auction. Roger North recalled in his autobiography how "one would have thought bread was exposed in a famine" at the 1688 sale of Peter Lely's prints and drawings that he managed. The art dealer Sonnius was commissioned to bid and purchase for Johan van der Does, Lord Berkesteyn of the Netherlands, at the sale, and got involved in a furious bidding war when a sheet of Raphael's drawings came up. While the price "was pushed up by the stubborn and opinionated Virtuosi," Sonnius was determined to win the lot, even when faced with an equally determined and "quarrelsome lord," and succeeded with a bid of £100. According to North, "the lord held up his eyes and hands to heaven, and prayed to God he might never eat bread cheaper." Sonnius's victory was a Pyrrhic one, however, for even two years after the sale, Berkesteyn was still fuming over being obliged to pay such an exorbitant sum for a drawing.[54]

Although the virtuosi were not the only customers who attended the auctions of late seventeenth-century London, it was their language, their tastes, and their social preferences that set the tone for the ways in which auctions were conducted in the metropolis. The virtuosi may indeed have been the victims of their own success as the auction market began to expand in the years after the Glorious Revolution. For in the midst of all of these sales, it became imperative for any one with a claim to good taste to distinguish between a worthy sale of valuable curiosities and an auction of worthless junk, forgeries, or copies. Even a confident connoisseur such as William III's personal secretary, Constantijn Huygens, often went to an auction only to be disappointed in finding nothing good for sale.[55]

The best way, of course, was to hold out for sales of known worth, such as those after death of renowned scholars, divines, or other great gentlemen of quality. Aside from providing a certain "name brand" stamp of approval on the collections, such sales also offered purchasers a chance to gain a little of the prestige of the deceased for themselves. The collections of Benjamin Worsley, of the Digbys, Kenelm and George, and the late Earl of Bristol, for example, were all put up for sale by auction. Each was eagerly picked over by virtuosi in search of quality purchases.[56] Some auctions were advertised in Latin or French, presumably as a means of touting the scholarly importance of the works for sale as well as excluding customers who were familiar only with the vernacular.[57] Other advertisements were more explicit, such as Edward Millington's preface to his catalogue for an auction of prints and drawings held on 12 November 1690: "Whereas many auctions have been kept for the more indifferent judgements, we thought fit for the benefit of the *Virtuoso's,* and more understanding gentry, to select out of vast numbers, such as for their fairness and rarity of their blackness will doubtless be admired by all that see them, such persons onely are desired to come. Those which are slight or defaced being reserved for other time and place, and another sort of people." In order to deter the wrong sort of people from attending, some elite auctions may have gone unadvertised, or were advertised strategically, by the select distribution of handbills or catalogues rather than through a public notice in the periodical press: both Robert Hooke and Constantijn Huygens seem to have attended such auctions. The auction of the earl of Melfort's pictures at the Whitehall Banqueting House on 21 June 1693 went unadvertised. There, John Evelyn observed, "divers more of the great lords" spent scores of pounds on "some very excellent [works] of Vandyke, Rubens, and Bassan." Even if undesirables could not be wholly excluded from an elite auction, there were other means to maintain status distinctions at a sale. Constantijn Huygens observed that a bench was reserved for aristocrats at the Tollemache sale he attended on 24 March 1695, and Hooke noted that a group of Dutch ambassadors "made a splendid entry" into an auction held in 1689.[58]

Aside from distinctions by class or status, gender also loomed large as a concern for the organizers of auctions. Edward Millington provided separate accommodations for prospective female purchasers when he conducted his sales at the Barbados Coffeehouse in Cornhill: "Conveniency of galleries" at the coffeehouse, he noted, "is set apart for ladies and gentlewomen," while adding that "attendance is given for viewing."[59] It was at the art auction, rather than the book or wholesale goods sales, that women were most prominent. Women had been among the earliest patrons of art auctions, and their attendance at the sales was regularly courted by the auctioneers.

The auction thus provided a convenient and public entrée for many people into the previously circumscribed culture of virtuoso connoisseurship. Auction-going extended well beyond the restricted circles of gentlemanly collectors. Just as the coffeehouse itself opened up virtuoso social conventions and cultural preferences to a much wider audience, so too did the coffeehouse auction allow the curious icons of a respected virtuosic collection to be bought up by anyone willing and wealthy enough to outbid his rivals.

Of course, the commercialization of virtuoso culture exemplified by the rise of the auction was not accepted without reservation: it was a process fraught with anxiety. Almost as quickly as they became an accepted part of the fashionable social life of London, the auction and the auctioneer became the targets of satires on the vices of the urban social and commercial scene. Because the auction provided a medium whereby putatively priceless objects were put up for sale, it became an almost irresistible conceit for satirists who wished to lambaste the venality of their enemies.

Thus the splenetic animosities of late seventeenth-century politics were quick to find their vent in the form of a series of auction satires. Here critics of the court of Charles II during the third Anglo-Dutch war circulated widely a manuscript which imagined "a publicke sale by an intch of candle at the Royall Coffy house," where one could make a bid for the duchess of Cleveland's honesty, Nell Gwynn's virginity, or the duke of Buckingham's religion.[60] Similarly, tory satirists in the wake of the exclusion crisis got a great kick out of the thought of an auction at the "Amsterdamnable-Coffee-House," in which "votes pipeing hot from the house of Commons," or "narrative sham plots" were put up for sale. Such political satires did not go out of fashion after the Glorious Revolution, and they continued to be directed at targets such as whig churchmen and the duke of Marlborough for several years. One such satire produced during the height of the controversy over the prosecution of Henry

Figure 22. Engraved plate, *Auction of State Pictures* (London, 1710); Newberry shelfmark Case J.54555.058. Courtesy of the Newberry Library, Chicago.

Sacheverell proposed an auction of portraits of those prelates and peers responsible for conducting the trial (Figure 22). The prices for pictures of these unnamed miscreants are absurdly low, some are unable to be sold at all, and must be given away to a nonconformist or a Quaker.[61] The joke here is that the pictures are worthless and unwanted, like the politicians they represent, and an auction is seen as the perfect public venue for the exposure of their true worth. The auction is thus used as a conceit for the revelation of public opinion, expressed in monetary terms.

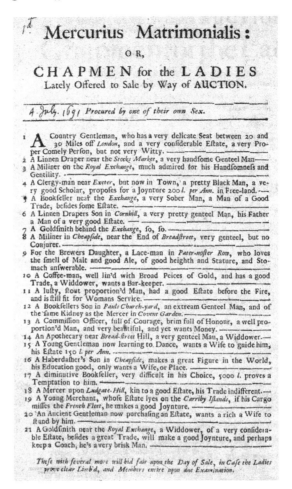

Figure 23. An auction of bachelors (c. 1702): *Mercurius matrimonialis: or, chapmen for the ladies lately offered to sale by way of auction. Procured by one of their own sex,* Newberry Case 6A 162 no. 1 [London, 1702?]. Courtesy of the Newberry Library, Chicago.

Almost as popular as the political auction satire was the imaginary "auction of women" or the sales "catalogue of batchelors" (Figure 23). These pamphlets took the notion of a marriage market to its extreme.[62] They raised the specter of a wholesale commercialization of even the family formation process. If an auction could set a price on a priceless work of art, why should it not be able to do the same for a potential spouse? The humor behind these mock sales catalogues was found in the way in which they laid bare the mercenary considerations already present in the marriage market, and indeed the joke became a reality among the popular classes, who were beginning at this time to invent the ritual of public "wife sales" as means of effecting a de facto divorce. It is worth noting that these marriage market satires were not reprinted much in the eighteenth century: perhaps the jests were no longer funny when one knew that the real thing could and did take place.[63]

Indeed the joke was not well taken even at the time of the pamphlets' publication, owing to some confusion as to their sincerity. John Dunton's periodical, the *Athenian Mercury,* received several letters inquiring whether or not the sales were legitimate or a hoax. While Dunton and company seemed assured that the pamphlets were disingenuous, they did not hesitate to chastise the Grub Street wits who published the catalogues, declaring, "Tis a teaguish sort of witticism to dispose of what's another bodies, without their consent." In other words, they were not amused "by such impertinent and reflective disingenuity." These auction satires may have been particularly galling because they also resembled another flourishing genre of late seventeenth-century cheap print: the catalogue of whores, complete with names, prices, and whereabouts.[64] An auction of women (or of men, for that matter) sounded a bit too much like outright prostitution, and that was no laughing matter, especially to such a fervent supporter of the Societies for the Reformation of Manners as John Dunton and his ilk.[65]

The satirists did not fail to skewer the real auctions as well. One print, entitled the "Compleat Auctioner" (Figure 24), aimed precisely at the pretensions to learning harbored by both the auctioneers and their many customers. It depicts a group of men and women, all gullibly perusing the contents of a book auctioneer's stacks, said to be from "the library of the late unborn Doctor" and containing a true hodgepodge of works which were both universally esteemed (Peter Heylyn's *Cosmographie*) as well as works of a rather more dubious reputation (such as the popular sex manual *Aristotle's Masterpiece* and the pornographic "Play of Sodom"). The text at the bottom reads:

> Come Sirs, and view this famous library,
> 'Tis pity learning shou'd discourag'd be:
> Here's bookes (that is, if they were but well sold)
> I'll maintain't are worth their weight in gold
> Then bid apace, and break me out of hand:
> Ne'er cry you don't the subject understand:
> For this I'll say — howe'er the case may hit,
> Whoever buys of me, — I teach 'em wit.

Figure 24. Sutton Nichols, engraving, "The Compleat Auctioner" (c. 1700?), (6.88 in. × 9.63 in.), BM Sat., no. 1415; BL shelfmark Harley 5947 (1). Courtesy of the British Museum, London. This print may refer to and satirize John Partridge, the almanac maker and astrologer ridiculed by Richard Steele, Jonathan Swift, and Tom Brown. Compare Figure 4.

The auction was a prominent target of satire because it offered such a public display of the buying and selling of precious objects that were thought to be outside the gritty realm of commerce. One simply could not "buy" wit, and that was precisely the specter raised by the auction sale. Of course, the obverse of this problem was the fear that in a marketplace of letters, cheap but bad taste would drive out the more costly, but inestimably more worthy, works of art. Perhaps Gresham's Law was as valid in the marketplace of ideas as it was for the fiscal state, and this prospect horrified the literati of Augustan England.[66]

Making the wrong choice at auction could be a source of particular embarrassment, especially for someone who esteemed himself to be a great collector. Banbrigg Buckeridge advised Sir Robert Child that "numerous collections of pictures injudiciously made, are the sport and contempt of the spectator, and a reflection on the owner." The same strictures applied to book collections. After purchasing some works at a sale, Henry Hyde, the second earl of Clarendon, confessed to the erudite divine Thomas Smith that "a more learned man would have bought books of more important subjects, but these were for my fancy." The contradictions between the individual freedom to buy what one pleased at auction and the restrictions placed on that freedom by the public strictures of "good taste" were aptly expressed by the third earl of Shaftesbury: "They who by pains and industry have acquired a real taste in arts, rejoice in their advantage over others, who either have none at all or such as renders them ridiculous. At an auction of books or pictures, you shall hear these gentlemen persuading every one 'to bid for what he fancies.' But at the same time they would be soundly mortified themselves if, by such as they esteemed good judges, they should be found to have purchased by a wrong fancy or ill taste."[67] This was the contradiction at the heart of the auction sale. It pitted the caprice of individual fancy against the communal values that dictated what constitutes good taste, or valuable learning.

Given his apprehensions about the coffeehouses themselves, it should come as no surprise that auctions also deeply troubled England's leading virtuoso, John Evelyn. Reflecting upon his estate at Sayes Court in Deptford, Kent, at the age of seventy-two, he told his brother George that he would not "willingly expose" his household effects there "at an *auction* (as the manner is)" now commonly practiced. He admitted to one John Harwood, a burgeoning virtuoso, Fellow of the Royal Society, and Doctor of Common Law, that he had never been to an auction of collectible prints. Evelyn was even less guarded when speaking to his daughter Susanna of an expected auction of pictures for the beau monde gathered at Tunbridge Wells: "What can there be but trash!" he averred.[68] He also lamented in a letter to Samuel Pepys "the sad dispersions many noble libraries and cabinets have suffered in these late times." The newly fashionable practice of auctioning these collections was, he thought, inappropriately named after the Latin *auctio,* or "an increase," which was meant to describe the bidding process. Instead he proposed to Pepys to "call it diminution" because "one auction . . . of a day or two, [can scatter] what has been gathering many years."[69]

For Evelyn, an auction was at best a frivolous waste of time, if there was nothing of worth to be had there, or at worst — if truly valuable curiosities were exposed to sale — it was a sad event in which the hard work of a lifetime came "to be dispersed amongst brokers and upholsterers, who expose them to the streets in every dirty and infamous corner" to anyone willing to bid for the items. Yet auctions had so quickly become established in virtuoso culture that even Evelyn could not entirely disavow them. He did, after all, allow his daughter to go to the Tunbridge auction and advised her to make some purchases, if she found "any faire paints worth having." He even attended an auction himself: the sale of the earl of Melfort's pictures at the Whitehall Banqueting House on 21 June 1693. And he applauded the efforts of Pepys and others to build their own collections out of the remains of those that were dissipated at sales. He recognized that, at an auction, "more [collectibles] may happly be procur'd at once, and at tolerable price, than one shall be able to find, and get together in many years, by collecting them one by one."[70]

This was both the crux of the problem and the lure of the auction to Britain's virtuosi collectors: auctions were public markets, where putatively "priceless" books, curiosities, and artworks were priced by, and sold to, the highest bidder. As such, they were an indignant end to the noble act of collecting that was the sine qua non of a virtuoso's reputation. Yet at the same time, an auction held an enormous appeal to those aspiring collectors who wished to assemble a respectable cabinet with little effort — it offered a chance to get rich quick in the virtuosic currency of curiosities. In pursuit of those books and artistic curiosities, the virtuosi were enticed into adopting a social and economic practice that had hitherto been used exclusively by London's merchant community.

Evelyn's anxieties about the auction paralleled those harbored with respect to the coffeehouses: they were public affairs and hence open to the participation of all sorts of undesirables; furthermore, they were fashionable and overtly commercial. All of this was unsettling to one whose virtuosity was private, erudite, and thought to be well above the dirty work of commerce. But despite all of his grumbling, Evelyn could do little to reverse the transformations in virtuoso sociability that were effected by its contact with the commercial world of the coffeehouse milieu.

This chapter has considered the coffeehouse's relationship to a whole host of related institutions, such as the inn, the barbershop, the bagnio, and the auction house. As we have seen, and shall see again, the distinctions among these various sorts of places were not always clear: often a coffeehouse could serve a dual function as a different sort of establishment. But all of these places shared a common relationship to the virtuosic culture of curiosity, and they all became a recognizable part of London urban life by the end of the seventeenth century. As such, they can be considered as participating in what I have called the "coffeehouse milieu."

The coffeehouse was clearly at the center of this new social world. Coffeehouses had become so successful and so numerous by the end of the century that many had differentiated into a variety of specialist institutions. To add the qualifier "coffeehouse" to the name of a new public house was to almost instantly identify that place with the new urban civility that was first associated with the original haunts of the mid-seventeenth-century virtuosi.

By the end of the seventeenth century, however, the culture of curiosity had been quite transformed by its close affiliation with the metropolitan coffeehouse milieu. The process of commercialization provoked several important changes in the social world of the virtuosi — all of them noteworthy for the ways in which they introduced monetary considerations, rather than social status *tout court,* as a social mediator. First, access to the coffeehouse milieu was controlled not by a process of honorary selection but rather as a matter of interest and willingness to pay the price of entry. Second, the collectible icons of curiosity themselves were now put up for sale in the coffeehouse auction market. The consequence of these changes was a substantial blurring of the hitherto carefully policed boundaries between the genteel and the popular that had been such an important element of virtuoso self-identity. This is why the rise of the coffeehouses caused Evelyn such great consternation; but even he found the rhinoceros an irresistible attraction.

PART III

Civilizing the Coffeehouses

The coffeehouse was a different sort of place than other public houses in early modern Britain. Unlike the tavern, the alehouse, or the inn, it was a novel institution. As such, it was treated differently from the more familiar forms of watering holes. Although the coffeehouse carried an air of distinct gentility that set it apart from other common victuallers and public-house keepers, the trade also faced a unique image problem as a result of its association with the dissemination of seditious rumors or "false news" among the general populace, along with meetings of persons disaffected to the established government. Attempts to suppress or to regulate the coffeehouses of the three kingdoms of England, Scotland, and Ireland were a regular feature of late seventeenth- and early eighteenth-century British political culture. Why did the coffeehouses provoke such hostility? And how did they survive and flourish in the face of determined opposition from the crown and many other authority figures?

Such questions have been argued over almost from the very inception of the coffeehouse phenomenon. Many high-flying royalists and subsequent tory historians defended attempts to regulate or even eradicate the coffeehouses as a necessary measure, and they continued to reiterate these views long after the survival of the coffeehouses was a foregone conclusion. Even in the early eighteenth century, Roger North lamented the failure of Charles II to suppress the coffeehouses such that "now," he thought, "the mischief is arrived to perfection, and not only sedition and treason, but atheism, heresy, and blasphemy are publicly taught in diverse of the celebrated coffee-houses . . . and it is as unseemly for a reasonable, conformable person to come there, as for a clergyman to frequent a bawdy house."[1]

More common has been the celebration of the survival of the coffeehouses after the Restoration as an indicator of the progress of English liberties. The rise of the coffeehouse, along with Parliament and party politics, has played an important role in the construction of a whig view of the transition from later Stuart England to early Hanoverian Britain. The failure of the crown to wipe out the people's coffeehouses has been seen as an early indicator that England could not be ruled in an arbitrary, despotic manner by its monarchs. This view has its origins in some of the earliest whig histories of the Stuart era, which also saw the coffeehouses as a necessary outlet for the English people's natural aversion to "the growth of Popery and the French power." For David Hume, the rise of the coffeehouse was proof of the "genius of the English government" and a sign of the "liberty of the constitution." Other whiggish historians have been even more forthright in their estimation of the constitutional significance of the triumph of the coffeehouses. Hume's contemporary and anti-Walpolean polemicist James Ralph thought that the desire to suppress the coffeehouses indicated a desire by the Restoration regime to "extinguish the light of reason" and to "subdue the power of reflection" among its subjects. When Henry Hallam wrote his *Constitutional History of England* in the early nineteenth century, he saw the Restoration-era proclamations against the coffeehouses as another example of royal "encroachments on the legislative supremacy of parliament, and on the personal rights of the subject." For Thomas Babington Macaulay, the coffeehouses of Restoration England were "the chief organs through which the public opinion of the metropolis vented itself," and soon became a veritable "fourth Estate of the realm," a phrase which he had coined himself in his review of Hallam's *Constitutional History* two decades earlier. The failure of the court to eradicate this new fourth estate was yet another confirmation of the triumphant historical progress of English liberties that was the subject of Macaulay's grand narrative.[2] In the twentieth century, the survival of the coffeehouses was seen by many historians as a victory against "a dictatorial challenge to freedom of speech and individual liberty" and a key step toward the establishment of the freedom of the press.[3] The rise of the coffeehouse was inevitable, according to this historical worldview, because it was simply an indicator of the inexorable progress of British politics away from royalist absolutism and its modern counterpart totalitarian dictatorship and toward a liberal parliamentary democracy. Although partisan capital-W "Whigs" such as White Kennett, Thomas Macaulay, and Henry

Hallam tended to be the most vociferous articulators of this triumphalist and teleological narrative, the self-congratulatory reassurance of a story of consistent progress toward constitutional government has been persuasive enough to capture the historical imaginations of even critics of partisan whiggery such as James Ralph and David Hume.[4]

While this unreconstructed sort of whiggish view of Stuart political history has long been out of fashion, it has been repackaged for recent audiences under the more fashionable guise of the concept of the emergence of a "public sphere." First adumbrated by Jürgen Habermas as a means of capturing an historical example of what he would later go on to call an "ideal-speech situation," the public-sphere rubric has been seized upon with vigor by early modern historians in recent years, especially since the translation of Habermas's 1962 text into French in 1978 and English in 1989. For Habermas, the coffeehouse exemplified his public sphere: it was open to all comers (except women); it was an urban and a commercial venue (hence it was "bourgeois"); and most important, it was a place in which rational debates on diverse matters, ranging from literary worth to high politics, could be carried out in a sober and rational way among equals. It was a place where right reason, and not social rank, was supposed to determine who won and who lost in debate.[5]

Few historians have taken Habermas's rosy view of the Augustan coffeehouse at face value, but many have endorsed the central and innovative role of the coffeehouse in the political culture of the period. For Steven Pincus as well as C. John Sommerville, the emergence of the coffeehouse as a center for political debate in the Restoration era signaled a decisive break with the elitist and religiously driven politics of the first half of the seventeenth century. It forged the way for a more inclusive and more secular political culture. Robert Bucholz's study of the court of Queen Anne argues that the rise of the coffeehouse, along with the world of commercialized leisure of which it was a part, offered the social elite of early eighteenth-century England an alternative venue for social and political advancement and hence it hastened the decline of the court as a center of elite sociability in the early eighteenth century. John Brewer pushes this supposed contrast between court and coffeehouse even further in portraying the later Stuart coffeehouses as outright "centres of opposition to the crown." For Lawrence Klein, the emergence of the coffeehouse is integrally related to the development of a post-Restoration political "culture of politeness," an urbane and secular world which must be clearly distinguished from the courtly and clerical political culture of the early Stuarts. Margaret Jacob's reading of Habermas's public sphere rubric, and the importance of the coffeehouse within it, is perhaps the most unapologetically celebratory. Coffeehouse politics, she argues, "set one of the preconditions for the emergence of modern democratic society in the West."[6] Accounts such as these have a whiggish tendency to explain the rise of the coffeehouse in terms of the ways in which it was new, or indeed modern. The survival of the coffeehouse is explained as the result of a gradual acceptance of this modern world of politics in the public sphere.

Historians of the post-Restoration period who have adopted a more revisionist bent have tended to ignore the political role of the coffeehouse in their work, preferring instead to emphasize the persistence of more traditional modes of political persuasion, such as royal charisma and court preferment along with the continuing prominence of the pulpit in Britain's old regime. The implication in these works is that the rise of the coffeehouse is at best an inconvenient, and perhaps ultimately irrelevant, fact in the revisionist understanding of post-Restoration political culture. But it need not be so. There remains room for an account of the rise of the coffeehouse in which it can be understood to have emerged organically out of the seventeenth-century political and social order.[7] The chapters in this section provide just such an account.

Both the older whig histories and the newer Habermasian explanations distinguish clearly between an old-fashioned state, epitomized by the court, and a new, vibrant and rising civil society, epitomized by the coffeehouses. In the whig view, this opposition often takes the form of a narrative of conflict between crown and people. For Habermas, it is described as the erosion of an older, "display-oriented" public sphere (*repräsentative Öffentlichkeit*) through the emergence of a new "discourse-oriented" and bourgeois public sphere (*bürgerliche Öffentlichkeit*). While recognizing that there were significant conflicts of interest and principle at stake in the debates over the legitimacy of the coffeehouse in post-Restoration Britain, the chapters in this final section suggest that these conflicts need not be understood in terms of a straightforward opposition between the state and civil society.

The "state" did make strong efforts to regulate coffeehouses in the British Isles, but the state was not simply the crown. The state was itself a part of the early modern social order; it included the local office holders and magistrates who were in fact more involved in the practical day-to-day regulation of the coffeehouses in their particular jurisdictions.[8] So too were the coffeehouses legitimized primarily through their relationship to the early modern political orders of the British Isles. State power actually played a crucial role in enabling the rise of the coffeehouses.[9] Chapter 6 details the ways in which the coffeehouses of the kingdoms were deeply integrated into the early modern urban social order and shows how their presence in the cities of the realm was crucially legitimated through the practice of public house licensing. Chapter 7 offers a narrative account of the various and persistent attempts by each of the post-Restoration regimes to keep a lid on coffeehouse politics. Chapter 8 turns from state politics to other informal, but just as influential, means of social regulation of coffeehouse society. The moral concerns voiced about the propriety of the various activities of both men and women in the coffeehouses exerted a powerful means of controlling the behavior within them. This chapter is particularly concerned with the ways in which gendered expectations of proper behavior for men and for women affected their different experiences of coffeehouse society. Rather than understanding the rise of the coffeehouse as an example of a growing opposition between the post-Restoration state and an increasingly resilient civil society, the accounts offered in the following chapters provide a useful case study in both the limitations and the flexibility of early modern governance. The coffeehouse emerges in this perspective as an important new site in which the negotiation of early modern power took place.

6

Before Bureaucracy

On the evening of 11 May 1703, Nicholas Blundell, a Catholic gentleman from Lancashire, paid a visit to Will's Coffeehouse on Bow Street in Covent Garden. Will's was at the time the center of London's literary life, and it had been made famous as the favorite haunt of John Dryden. Dryden was no longer alive by the time Blundell had ventured into Will's for the first time, but Blundell must have had great expectations for the evening. He did not meet any of the London wits who were trying to succeed Dryden as the doyen of the English literati, such as William Congreve, William Wycherley, or John Dennis. Instead, Blundell sat down to hear one Mr. Lawson lecture him on astrology.[1] Perhaps it was a slow day at Will's. Blundell did not remark upon whether he found Lawson's discourse to be pleasing, and we do not know if Blundell was disappointed that he did not meet any of the London wits at Will's that day. But it is striking that Blundell thought it worth his while to go there at all. Why was this northern Catholic gentleman walking into what was commonly regarded as the heart of London's intellectual world?

Blundell was a tourist at Will's, and by venturing into the famous coffeehouse he hoped to get a whiff of some of the excitement that he might have heard about the place, either in conversation with others or in one of the many pamphlets that associated Will's with the London wits. The London coffeehouse, and especially Will's place, had by the end of the seventeenth century become a synecdoche for metropolitan living. London was known throughout Europe for its famous coffeehouses, and they were thoroughly integrated into the daily life of Londoners. If one wanted to find out what London life was like, the easiest way was to step into one of its numerous coffeehouses. That is precisely what Nicholas Blundell was up to when he walked into Will's for the first time. On later trips to the metropolis, Blundell visited other London coffeehouses, along with a couple of return visits to Will's. This social pattern would persist through the rest of the eighteenth century. When James Boswell arrived in London in his early twenties, the young Scotsman quickly ensconced himself in the city's coffeehouses, and he took particular pride in drinking coffee at the venerable Will's, for he knew that this was the place "so often mentioned in the *Spectator*" and was mentioned so fondly by his hero, Dr. Johnson.[2]

This chapter explores the relationship between the coffeehouse and the early modern urban social order. Coffee consumption and coffeehouses were both decidedly urban phenomena in early modern Britain, and no urban center was more distinctive in this respect than London.[3] English coffeehouses were, above all, a metropolitan phenomenon, and the London environment decisively shaped their social character. London's various coffeehouses were understood to make the city a special and distinctive place, and it is only within this metropolitan context that we may fully understand the social and political significance of the English coffeehouse. London's immense size in terms of population, along with its prominence as the commercial, as well as the political, capital of the British Isles, meant that it could support a wide variety of public houses. The coffeehouses of London reflected the diversity of the metropolis itself. There was no one "ideal type" of London coffeehouse: there were rather a dazzling array of different establishments, each with its own particular character. Taken as a whole, however, the coffeehouses of London set the social template for what an English coffeehouse was supposed to be. Even outside of London, a metropolitan ideal still tended to influence the ways in which the coffeehouse was imagined.

The evidence presented here suggests that the coffeehouses were able to successfully integrate themselves into the urban social order, and for this reason they were able to secure a remarkable degree of social and political legitimacy, despite their novelty. Not long after their introduction, the coffeehouses became an integral part of neighborhood sociability in English towns and cities. The regulation of the coffeehouse became a matter of local concern, primarily at the parish and county levels. The chapter therefore concludes with a careful examination of the primary means by which coffeehouses were regulated at the local level, the system of public house licensing that was also used for alehouses, inns, and taverns. The practice of licensing demonstrates the ways in which the new coffeehouse society was able to negotiate a cautious sense of legitimacy and thus fit within the wider early modern social order.

Coffeehouse-Keeping and Urban Society

English towns outside London had their coffeehouses, and indeed Oxford was the first city to have a coffeehouse; but there were far more coffeehouses in London than in any other English city. Most English towns could support only a handful of coffeehouses in the later seventeenth century, or perhaps only one, but London abounded with them. Although four coffeehouses were founded in Oxford between 1650 and 1680, this number was not exceeded until the 1730s. The city of York, for example, had three coffeehouses as early as the mid-1660s, but probably no more than thirty by the late eighteenth century. The same pattern seems to have obtained in other provincial cities such as Birmingham, Bristol, Ipswich, Newcastle, Northampton, and Norwich, where the usual number seems to have been two to six coffeehouses even at the height of the Georgian provincial "urban renaissance." Nor were coffeehouses particularly numerous in the major Scots and Irish cities of Edinburgh, Glasgow, and Dublin. By contrast, as early as 1663 there were eighty-two coffeehouses in the City of London alone.[4] By the end of the seventeenth century, metropolitan London had at least several hundred coffeehouses, and perhaps more than one thousand. Estimates of the precise number are conflicting, and range from near three hundred to one thousand to two or even three thousand. The London Directories of 1734 provide the earliest source of precise data, and reveal 551 official London coffeehouses, a figure that neglects all unlicensed coffeehouses, of which there were a substantial number. Unfortunately, precise totals for the numbers of London coffeehouses do not exist. The treasury board ordered a survey of all of the coffeehouses in the kingdom at the end of 1689, but the survey was either never completed or did not survive.[5] There are, however, several useful guides to the proportionate relationship between the coffeehouses of the metropolis and those of the rest of the country.

It is likely that coffee was consumed in much greater quantities in the metropolis than in the rest of the British Isles. In 1725, 96 percent of the City of London probate inventories contained utensils for hot drinks, while only 15 percent of those in inventories from the rest of the country listed similar items.[6] A survey of the number of dealers in coffee and tea during the fiscal year 1737–38 reveals that nearly 70 percent of them were based in London (Table 5).[7] It is probable that London's share of the total was even greater in the seventeenth century than it was in the early eighteenth century. By that time, coffee consumption was known throughout the country, although coffee

Table 5. Number of Dealers in Coffee and Tea in England and Wales, 1736–37

Collections	Dealers	Percentage of Total
Barnstaple	3	0.06
Bedford	42	0.86
Bristol	74	1.51
Bucks	31	0.63
Cambridge	44	0.90
Canterbury	43	0.88
Chester	12	0.25
Cornwall	0	0.00
Cumberland	22	0.45
Derby	31	0.63
Dorset	3	0.06
Durham	58	1.19
Essex	92	1.88
Exon	15	0.31
Gloucester	18	0.37
Grantham	37	0.76
Hantshire	20	0.41
Hertford	36	0.74
Hereford	11	0.22
Lancaster	32	0.65
Lichfield	27	0.55
Lincoln	26	0.53
Lynn	119	2.43
Isle of Wight	0	0.00
Marlborough	20	0.41
Northampton	33	0.67
Northumberland	9	0.18
Norwich	106	2.17
Leeds	12	0.25
Oxford	31	0.63
Reading	30	0.61
Richmond	6	0.12
Rochester	134	2.74
Salisbury	22	0.45
Salop	13	0.27
Sheffield	19	0.39
Suffolk	123	2.51
Surrey	32	0.65
Sussex	3	0.06

Table 5. Continued

Collections	Dealers	Percentage of Total
Taunton	10	0.20
Tiverton	1	0.02
Wales East	8	0.16
Wales Middle	11	0.22
Wales North	6	0.12
Wales West	5	0.10
Warwick	19	0.39
Westmoreland	1	0.02
Worcester	16	0.33
York	11	0.22
London	3,415	69.81
Total	4,892	100.00

Note: The excise collections were grouped loosely around major cities, and did not correspond directly to the county boundaries.
Source: PRO, CUST 48/13 (1733–45), 206. Compare the table based on the same source in John Chartres, "Food Consumption and Internal Trade," 176.

drinking was still considered a "treat" even among the gentry. John Chartres has concluded that throughout much of the seventeenth and eighteenth centuries, consumption patterns in the metropolis differed "radically . . . from that of the rest of England," perhaps two or three times greater.[8]

London's significance is magnified even more when we take into consideration the role of the capital as the principal entrepôt for imported goods which gradually made their way throughout the rest of the country. The nearly thirty-five hundred coffee and tea dealers of the 1730s not only supplied the residents of the metropolis, but they also catered to visiting customers or even provincial clients who preferred to buy their coffee or tea from a reputable London merchant. Nicholas Blundell apparently bought all his coffee in London, or had his friends deliver it to him in Lancashire upon return from their visits to the capital. Even when coffee was not consumed in London, then, it still retained an aura of metropolitan urbanity. The same might be said of provincial coffeehouses: they tried to imitate an ideal set by the more famous coffeehouses of London.[9]

Where were coffeehouses to be found within the metropolis? A lack of sufficient source material makes it difficult to determine the precise social topography of London's coffeehouses, but enough documentation exists for the state of affairs within the walls of the City of London to hazard some guesses with regard to the area as a whole.

The first is a survey of the coffeehouses of the City of London conducted in 1663 (Figure 25). The reasons why this survey was undertaken are unclear, and it may have understated the actual number of coffeehouses, for unlicensed and occasional coffee sellers were presumably not included. The list may have been drawn up for the City's quarter sessions, where licenses for coffee retailing were issued. The survey reveals that City coffeehouses were not entirely concentrated in the most populous wards.[10] Although Farringdon Within and Farringdon Without were densely populated, the high concentration of coffeehouses in Broad Street, Cheap, Coleman Street, and Cornhill Wards demonstrates that the earliest London coffeehouses arose in the heart of London's mercantile sector. These wards included Gresham College, the Royal Exchange, and the booksellers' district in Cornhill. The rest of the City's coffeehouses were fairly evenly, and rather sparsely, distributed.

Almost from the very beginning, then, we might speculate that two quite different types of coffeehouses developed in metropolitan society. The first are best characterized by the famous coffeehouses clustered around the Royal Exchange and its environs; they are also significantly located in or near some of the wealthiest sections of the City. These institutions specialized quite quickly and developed to serve the business and social needs of London's merchant and governing elite. Such grand coffeehouses offered the functional equivalent of office space for early modern businessmen and professionals. Although they were not included in the 1663 survey, we might also include in this category the numerous coffeehouses around Covent Garden and in Westminster which catered to the resident gentry and courtiers of London's West End. By the later eighteenth century, this concept of the principal coffeehouses of the City was codified in the London directories which listed their names and addresses. The 1796 directory classified eighty-five coffeehouses in this way.[11] The second type of coffeehouse was much more modest and mundane. These were located in less fashionable areas of the city and did not develop in clusters. These were the "local" coffeehouses whose customers were primarily neighborhood residents. They provided refreshment, newspapers, and various other sundry services to their locals, but they were unlikely to attract tourists such as Nicholas Blundell.

It seems that the basic distribution of coffeehouses in the City had not changed much between the Restoration and the end of the seventeenth century. As a means of financing the wars against France, the Williamite regime instituted a poll tax in 1692.[12] Studies of London poll tax data from the 1690s

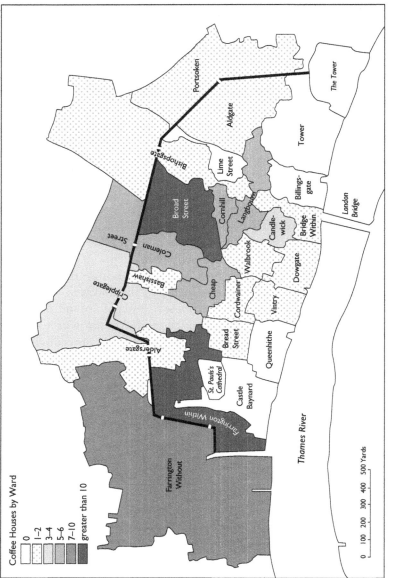

Figure 25. The distribution of coffeehouses in the City of London, by ward. Map courtesy of Bill Nelson, after John Stow, *Survey of London*, Charles L. Kingsford, ed. (Oxford: Oxford University Press, 2000).

show roughly the same concentration of coffeehouses at the heart of the City's mercantile district in Cornhill, Cheap, and Broad Street wards. This data may also be compared to the totals accumulated from the returns of licensed victuallers for the year 1701 (Table 6). Although these incomplete sets of data are unable to provide us with a total of the coffeehouses in the City, they indicate that the number in London had continued to expand in the thirty years after the first survey. Cornhill, most notably, had nearly tripled its coffeehouses, as it went from six in 1663 to seventeen in 1698 and eighteen in 1701. Some wards, such as Bridge Within, seemed to have lost their coffeehouses entirely, although it is not clear whether these were real losses or rather the function of the exclusion of minor coffeehouse-keepers from the poll tax assessments. Certain people were exempt from the tax, most notably those in receipt of poor relief or those who were too poor to contribute to their parish poor rates, and these exempt individuals were not listed in the returns. The children of low income workers were also exempt.[13] Such exemptions probably account for the low numbers of alehouse-keepers reported in the returns. It seems likely that a fair number of impoverished coffeehouse-keepers were similarly exempted from the tax or simply overlooked by the collectors. The coffeehouses of Aldgate may have been all rather small enterprises, for it is unlikely that the nine coffeehouse-keepers licensed in 1701 had sprung up within the course of a few years after the poll tax returns.

The poll tax data also reveal the relationships between coffeehousing and general victualling in the City. There was very little correlation between the numbers of victuallers and coffeemen in any given ward. Those wards with high numbers of victuallers, such as Bishopsgate, often had few coffeehouses, while those with a substantial concentration of coffeehouses, such as Cornhill, actually had fewer victuallers than coffeehouses — a rare occurrence for most of the City. This suggests that the two sorts of establishments catered to different clienteles and served rather different functions. The occupation of "victualler" was an extensive one throughout the City. The three categories of food retailers, victuallers, and innkeepers made up more than 17 percent of all householders identified in the poll tax. Coffeehouse-keeping, by contrast, seems to have employed only about one-fifth as many people. The predominance of traditional forms of commercialized urban hospitality, such as ordinaries, taverns, inns, and alehouses, went unchallenged by the rise of the coffeehouse in the late seventeenth century. The alcoholic drink trade, in particular, continued to thrive and indeed remained the single largest source of employment in the City. Overall, there was at least one alcohol-serving watering hole per thirteen households in the City. The coffeehouses never approached that level of density, and such figures reveal the hyperbole behind contemporary

Table 6. London Coffeehouses and Victuallers by Wards, c. 1692–98, 1701

	Coffeehouses c. 1692–1698	Victuallers c. 1692–1698	Coffeehouses 1701
Aldersgate	6	27	N/A
Aldgate	0	17	9
Bassishaw	*	*	N/A
Billingsgate	*	*	3
Bishopsgate	4	71	N/A
Bread Street	6	11	5
Bridge Within	0	1	N/A
Broad Street	*	*	7
Candlewick	3	13	1
Castle Baynard	*	*	11
Cheap	11	21	N/A
Coleman Street	*	*	N/A
Cordwainer	*	*	2
Cornhill	17	14	18
Cripplegate	*	*	N/A
Cripplegate Without	0	33	N/A
Dowgate	*	*	2
Farringdon Within	15	83	1
Farringdon Without	13	92	N/A
Langborne	15	36	11
Lime Street	*	*	N/A
Portsoken	*	*	N/A
Queenhithe	0	30	0
Tower	*	*	9
Vintry	*	*	N/A
Walbrook	*	*	0
Total	90	449	79

Note: Poll tax assessment documentation for many wards does not exist; and many wards neglected to distinguish between the different types of victuallers licensed. Missing data is indicated by an asterisk. The 1692–98 poll tax coffeehouse totals include one chocolate house; victualling totals include ordinaries; alehouses; vintners and brandy-shops.

Sources: Data for 1692–98: P. E. Jones, "Index to Trades, 1690s," in the CLRO search room, based on a survey of the CLRO Assessment Boxes for the poll taxes of 1692–94, and 1698. Data for 1701: CLRO, LV (B), 1701, no. 2a, Aldgate Ward (22 Oct. 1701), no. 2b, Aldgate Ward (6 Nov. 1701); no. 3, Billingsgate Ward (1701); no. 5a, Breadstreet Ward (1701); no. 7a–c, Broadstreet Ward; no. 8a–b, Candlewick Ward; no. 11a–b, Coleman Street Ward; no. 12, Cordwainer Ward; no. 13a–b, Cornhill Ward; no. 16a–b, Dowgate Ward; no. 17, Farringdon Within; no. 24, Langbourne Ward; no. 28; no. 27a–b, Queenhithe.

claims that the rise of the coffee habit was driving alewives out of work or increasing the general sobriety of the English nation by luring customers away from the alehouse.[14] It seems that the coffeehouses filled a social need that the traditional public houses could not. In doing so, they created a distinctively new social space in metropolitan society.

Who were the coffeehouse-keepers? Were they substantial retailers who made up the industrious members of the middle station along with other tradesmen and merchants as Daniel Defoe and other contemporaries assumed them to be? Or should they be rather understood to be part of the struggling poor, one step below the artisanate and one step above the paupers on the parish rate? The author of a 1729 pamphlet had little doubt about the social status of coffeehouse-keepers. They were, he claimed, "the very servilest and most contemptible of that part of mankind which pretends to subsist by trade." Aside from the assortment of "cast-off valets, discarded footmen," or "broken tradesmen," the rest of the coffeehouse-keepers were primarily "the children of destitute people, who at first are taken . . . for the meanest purposes . . . till, by a supple and tractable behaviour, they are promoted to the dignity of waiters, and in process of time, scraping together a little money by vails, and the bounty of their master's customers, and joining themselves to a helpmate of the same quality . . . by the kind assistance of a believing distiller, and benevolent druggist, set up for themselves."[15] Who are we to believe?

The poll tax data of the 1690s can once again illuminate this issue, and they reveal that coffeehouse-keepers occupied a sort of socioeconomic middle ground in the hierarchy of the London victualling trades (Table 7). While the rental value of their premises was not nearly as great as that of innholders or vintners, the coffeehouses were valued more than the premises held by alehouse-keepers, strongwater-men, or even regular victuallers. Many substantial coffeehouses may have felt a need to obtain choice property in fashionable areas, and indeed some of the greater coffeehouses were taxed at quite high rents: Jonathan's and Garraway's coffeehouses, the two centers of the early London stock market, were both taxed at the considerable value of £150. Lloyd's Coffeehouse was taxed at the lesser but still substantial sum of £75. The value of the coffeemen's stock, however, which was in effect a measure of one's net wealth since debts owed were subtracted from the assessed total, was the lowest of all the victualling trades. This may reflect the high costs and low returns of the coffeehouse trade. Aside from the rental costs of keeping a room fit for customers, a coffeehouse-keeper had to maintain a ready supply of coffee, tea, and chocolate and perhaps alcoholic drinks as well. Nearly two-thirds of the coffeehouses identified in the poll tax assessments possessed liquor licenses.[16] Along with the costs of maintaining

Table 7. Relative Wealth in the London Victualling Trades, 1692–93

Trade	Individuals	Householders	Mean Rent	Mean Stock
Victuallers	773	768	£21	£26
Coffeemen and Women	137	135	30	20
Vintners	131	123	80	149
Innholders or Keepers	91	91	80	74
Tapsters	23	3	—	—
Alehouse-keepers	10	10	21	25
Strongwater-men	10	10	16	42
Total	1,175	1,140		

Source: Alexander, "Economic and Social Structure of the City of London," Table 5.08, 135.

the drink and victualling supplies, the expense of providing newspapers and other reading materials could be considerable.

Nevertheless, some coffeehouse-keepers did quite well (Table 8). An examination of a few surviving probate inventories for coffeemen reveals a great disparity in wealth between the substantial coffee merchants such as Edward Haines (d. 1722) and Joseph Webb (d. 1726), who may have made their livings by supplying the lesser coffeehouse-keepers with their coffee rather than actually running a business themselves, and the more modest estates of the others. None of these individuals, it should be said, was extremely wealthy, although Haines must have been a substantial merchant and indeed his trade extended well beyond the usual stock of coffee and tea. The two wealthiest of the full-time coffeehouse-keepers, John Rowley (d. 1729) and Joseph Waggett (d. 1697), died with a fortune that put them in league with the average apothecary, a rather well-remunerated trade in post-Restoration Britain, and just above the £1,000 of capital worth that Peter Earle has deemed sufficient to qualify as a member of "the middling sort."[17] One suspects, however, that more humble men such as Anthony Sambach (d. 1672), Samuel North (d. 1693), and Edward Jack (d. 1696) were more representative of the average coffeeman's state. With a net worth at death of around £100–200, such individuals must have found it hard enough just to pay the rent on their coffee-house from year to year. Finally, mention should be made of the exceptional "gentleman" coffeehouse-keeper, William Peart (d. 1682) of Lincoln, whose meager wealth contrasts strikingly with his claim to gentility and perhaps indicates his reasons for taking to the coffee trade. Peart must have been exceptional in many respects. He seems to have been the only coffeeman in

Table 8. Fortune at Death of Selected Coffeemen, 1672–1729

Date		Total Value of Estate
1722	*Haines, Edward	£3,084.88
1726	*Webb, Joseph	1,550.18
1729	Rowley, John	1,180.38
1697	Waggett, Joseph	1,001.69
1721	*Sorrell, Henry	758.71
1720	*Iveson, Daniel	392.00
1716	*Montague, Thomas	322.10
1729	Branch, Isaac	311.79
1691	Howing, David	306.00
1672	Sambach, Anthony	188.08
1693	North, Samuel	168.75
1682	Peart, William, Gent.	157.76
1696	Jack, Edward	122.46

Note: Asterisks indicate individuals who may have been only coffee merchants rather than true coffeehouse-keepers. Values in pounds, shillings, and pence have been converted into a decimal fraction of a pound.

Sources: CLRO, Orphans Ct. 2240 (CS Bk. vol. 5, fol. 13); CLRO, Orphans Ct. 2211 (CS Bk. vol. 4, fol. 317); CLRO, Orphans Ct. 813 (CS Bk. vol. 2, fol. 299b); PRO, PROB 4/7592; CLRO, Orphans Ct. 3297 (CS Bk. vol. 6, fol. 127b); CLRO, Orphans Ct. 3080 (CS Bk. vol. 6, fol. 48b); CLRO, Orphans Ct. 3091 (CS Bk. vol. 6, fol. 53); CLRO, Orphans Ct. 3112 (CS Bk. vol. 6, fol. 59b); PRO, PROB 4/8534; CLRO, Orphans Ct. 3315 (CS Bk. vol. 6, fol. 134b); CLRO, Orphans Ct., 3237 (CS Bk. vol. 6, fol. 102b); CLRO, Orphans Ct. 3124 (CS Bk. vol. 6, fol. 63); *Probate Inventories of Lincoln Citizens, 1661–1714* 79–81.

seventeenth-century Lincoln, and it may be that coffeehouse-keeping was not seen as so demeaning to an impoverished country squire. After all, it meant that he could provide hospitality to his neighbors (albeit now for a price), and he would remain at the center of the action of the town by collecting local gossip and serving as the main source of news from London for his fellow citizens.

It is impossible to know whether these few selected probate inventories are by any means representative of the men involved in the Augustan retail coffee trade. The selection offered here is by no means a random sample of coffee-house inventories. By their very nature, probate inventories are biased in favor of those who owned substantial property at death. Given that coffeehousing was often a profession of last resort, taken up by widows or poor families (not to mention cast-off valets), it is likely that many coffeehouse-keepers died destitute and thus with little to report to the probate clerks. Probate inventories also capture a person's net worth at a point when it is usually at its greatest, after a lifetime of accumulation. Other inventories of coffeehouse-keepers that were not taken at decease, but at other stages of life, reveal a meager existence indeed. One coffeeman's goods were valued at £11.65 in 1670; John Wood's worth was placed at £26.15 in 1671. Francis Devonshire was assessed at less than £39, and another coffeehouse-keeper was valued at £91.46 in 1682.[18]

Despite the great costs and the many risks involved in the coffeehouse business, some benefits to the trade set the coffeehouse-keeper above the average victualler. Running a coffeehouse, and thus providing a space for sober conversation and newsreading, carried a greater social cachet than that offered by the mere purveyance of food and drink. Some coffeehouse-keepers could develop ties to men of wealth and power who frequented their establishment. In a fundamentally credit-based economy, these connections could be useful in times of financial need. Samuel Booth benefited from the patronage of Sir Roger L'Estrange for keeping Sam's Coffeehouse as a redoubt for tory propaganda efforts in the early 1680s. On the other side of the political divide, Daniel Button, who had been a servant of Joseph Addison, was set up by Addison as the proprietor of Button's Coffeehouse in Covent Garden around the year 1712 in order to host regular assemblies of the whig literati. Button thought his ties to the whig establishment would stand him in good stead for his retirement after the Hanoverian accession, and he duly petitioned the Treasury Commission for recognition of his years of service in providing a place "for the resort of gentlemen who distinguished themselves by their unshaken zeal for the Protestant Succession when most in danger." Whether Button's petition met with a positive reception is not known, but it is unlikely that he could have done worse than Timothy Harris, an erstwhile keeper of a coffeehouse on Ormond Street that attracted the virtuosi surrounding Sir Hans Sloane. Harris was subsequently jailed for debt at the King's Bench Prison; his only hope for escape, it seems, was to rely on the patronage of Doctor Sloane, but there is no record of any response from the doctor to Harris's pleas for help. Even the composition of an ode to Sloane's deceased wife and the promise to publish an "Indian Pastorall Eclogue" failed to move the doctor to act beneficently. Harris proudly noted, "I am a piece of a schollar, and my birth [is] not too obscure and mean." But these pretensions did not save him from debtor's prison. His fate captures the dilemma faced by the coffeehouse-keepers of London: they had reason to be proud of their occupation, for they provided "the grand magazines of intelligence" to the men of the Town, but it was difficult to make a comfortable living as a coffeeman or woman.[19]

Even the some of the great coffeemen could suffer from the fragility of the coffeehouse trade. Will Urwin, the founder of Will's Coffeehouse in Covent Garden and perhaps the most renowned coffeeman in England, prospered as his place gained fame for being the favored resort for the London literati. Although his coffeehouse may have been established as early as 1664, he did not become a full paying member of the parish poor rate in St. Paul's Covent Garden until 1675. In the 1680s, he could afford to pay £55 per year to the excise collectors for his coffee sales, but the charge was onerous enough that he thought it worth petitioning directly to the excise commissioners for relief.[20] By 1693, Urwin was paying a full pound to the poor rate, a sure sign that he had attained a secure standing within the parish, but when he died in 1695, his widow was unable to maintain the payments, and she soon passed away as well. Will's Coffeehouse, however, continued to flourish long after the passing of the Urwins. No one knows who took Urwin's place behind the bar at Will's, but even in the mid-eighteenth century Samuel Johnson could still recall Dryden's favorite chair by the fire there.[21]

Coffeehousing allowed a claim to gentility that the other victualling trades lacked. Even the coffee-boys, the house servants who served coffee to the customers, were thought to take on genteel airs "in imitation of the real gentlemen." Indeed, visual representations of coffee-boys do present them as rather well dressed for household servants (Figure 26). John Macky recorded his surprise upon visiting the town of Shrewsbury and discovering there "the most coffee-houses round it that ever I saw in any town: but when you come into them, they are but alehouses, only they think that the name of coffee-house gives a better air."[22]

Coffeehouse-keeping may have been work often associated with civil and sober conversation on important affairs of state and trade, but the pay from the trade itself was meager. Some great coffeehouse-keepers may have made additional profits through other business activities. Work in the news trade was a logical and common accompaniment to coffeehouse-keeping as we shall see. Jonathan Miles, who ran Jonathan's Coffeehouse and hosted the stock-jobbers, may have profited greatly from his close associations with the brokers who plied their trade at his establishment. Edward Lloyd, founder of Lloyd's Coffeehouse, held auctions of ships, sold insurance, and eventually published his own financial paper, *Lloyd's News,* from his coffeehouse. By the later eighteenth century, Lloyd's Coffeehouse charged the insurance merchants working on the premises a subscription fee of ten guineas per year for the privilege. Francis White's famous and fashionable chocolate house charged a sixpence cover fee for entry, and White undoubtedly profited from the gaming and gambling that he permitted in his house, for he left an estate valued at a substantial £2,500 in his will. White's wife, Elizabeth, also sold tickets to

Figure 26. Part of a coffeehouse tile panel inscribed "Dish of Coffee-Boy" (early eighteenth century). Courtesy of the Museum of London. The buttoned jacket and fashionable long hair of the coffee-boy identify him as a well-heeled servant.

operas, masquerades, and ridottos at the chocolate house. Tom King and his wife, Moll, earned their fame and fortune even less salubriously, by offering a convenient venue for late-night rakish carousing and prostitution (Figures 27 and 28). King's profits from this trade allowed him to purchase an estate near Hampstead.[23]

There was clearly a great deal of variance in the coffeehouse trade of early

Figure 27. Tom King's Coffeehouse, interior. *Tom K — g's: or the Paphian Grove* (1738), plate engraving facing p. 44, Beinecke Library shelfmark 1979 108. Courtesy of the Beinecke Rare Book and Manuscript Library, Yale University.

modern Britain. The famous London coffeehouses of lore may have prospered through their connections to the good, the great, and the merely wealthy in an age of commercial, consumer and financial revolutions, but many more keepers struggled to simply earn a living. Coffeehouse-keeping was a trade as varied as the urban society in which it thrived.

Figure 28. Moll King, perhaps the most notorious coffee-woman of eighteenth-century London. Huntington, Bull Granger collection; James Granger, *Biographical History of England* (1769), engraving. Courtesy of the Huntington Library, San Marino, California.

Coffeehouses and the Metropolis

Why did the coffeehouses thrive in London in particular? First and foremost, the London coffeehouses were able to offer a diverse array of services and cater to different political, professional, and social groups. The coffeehouses of the provinces had nothing to match the famous Will's and Grecian coffeehouses for the wits, Garraway's and Jonathan's coffeehouses for the stock-jobbers, or the Marine and Lloyd's coffeehouses for maritime affairs and insurance sales. It was well known that certain London coffeehouses had distinctive "characters" defined by the clientele that they attracted. A Swiss visitor to London, Cesar de Saussure, remarked in the 1720s that "some coffee-houses are a resort for learned scholars and for wits; others are the resort of dandies or of politicians, or again of professional newsmongers; and many others are temples of Venus." Different coffeehouses developed for distinct purposes. The coffeehouses created a social space that was defined in terms of personal affiliation, or "lifestyle."[24] With so many coffeehouses to choose from, Londoners could pick the place whose social or political tenor they found most agreeable. In this way, they began to carve out self-selected and distinct communities within metropolitan society.

Regional affiliations brought men of like backgrounds to the same coffeehouse, for the county feasts held in London by and for provincials were organized at specific coffeehouses. The British Coffeehouse near Charing Cross served as a social center for Scots resident in London beginning in Queen Anne's reign, and it continued to thrive well into the nineteenth century. It was later joined by establishments such as the Caledonian Coffeehouse, which took the place of Button's, and the Edinburgh Coffeehouse. The existence of other coffeehouses bearing names with regional affiliations, such as the Essex, the Gloucester, the Kentish, the Lancaster, the Northumberland, the Norwich, the Oxford, the Salopian, and the Sussex testify to the strength of regional identity within the metropolitan social context. International affiliations could also be maintained in the London coffeehouses. When the German visitor Zacharias Conrad von Uffenbach visited London in 1710, he found only one coffeehouse to his liking, the Paris Coffeehouse, where the host was a Frenchman but most of the customers were German.[25]

Different coffeehouses also arose to cater to the socialization and business needs of various professional and economic groups in the metropolis. By the early decades of the eighteenth century, a number of separated coffeehouses around the Exchange had taken to catering to the business needs of merchants specializing in distinct trades, such as the New England, the Virginia, the Carolina, the Jamaica, and the East India coffeehouses. Child's Coffeehouse, located conveniently near the College of Physicians, was much favored by physicians and clergymen. Because such affiliations were well known, entry into one of these specialized coffeehouses offered an introduction into the professional society found therein. A correspondent to the *Spectator* joked that "a young divine, after his first degree in the university, usually comes [to London] only to show himself; and on that occasion is apt to think he is but half equipp'd with a gown and cassock for his publick appearance, if he hath not the additional ornament of a scarf of the first magnitude to intitle him to the appellation of doctor from his landlady and the boy at Child's." While poking fun at the foppish pretensions of a young cleric, the writer also makes clear the importance that personal recognition still held in an urban, but still credit- and patronage-based, social order. Notoriety in the right coffeehouse cliques could be the key to professional success. One Dr. Hannes, an aspiring physician in late seventeenth-century London, sought to promote his professional reputation by hiring a footman to go to the most fashionable coffeehouses and pretend to be calling for Hannes at the bequest of some noble patients. When the footman reached Garraway's Coffeehouse, and the table of the prominent physician John Radcliffe and his circle, the servant received a dry rebuke: "No, no, friend you are mistaken; the doctor wants those lords."[26] Professional reputations were increasingly made or ruined in the coffeehouse milieu.

The divisiveness of the various political identities in the long eighteenth century most prominently distinguished many metropolitan coffeehouses from one another. Almost as soon as the labels "whig" and "tory" became identifiers of political identity in the early 1680s, there arose coffeehouses associated with each affiliation. The Amsterdam Coffeehouse, kept by the dissenter Peter Kidd, was closely associated with Titus Oates and whig opposition politics in the 1680s, while Sam's Coffeehouse was the base from which Roger L'Estrange directed his loyalist propaganda campaign to discredit the whigs. After the revolution of 1688, a number of Jacobite coffeehouses were identifiable in London, while the whigs and tories continued to patronize their own distinct coffeehouses. Whigs favored Richard's Coffeehouse in the 1690s and later establishments such as Jenny Man's, St. James's, and Button's coffeehouses in Queen Anne's reign.[27] Tory politics found a welcome home at the Cocoa Tree Chocolate House and Ozinda's Coffeehouse. These rivalries were most intense in the metropolitan cockpit of political conflict. While John Macky remarked in the 1720s that "a Whig will no more go to the Cocoa Tree or Osinda's, than a Tory will be seen at the coffeehouse of St. James's," he also noted that these distinctions mattered less outside of London. In the coffeehouses of the fashionable spa town of Epsom, he noted, "a Tory does not stare when a Whig comes in, nor a Whig look sour and whisper at the sight of a Tory. These distinctions are laid by with the winter suit at London, and a gayer easier habit worn in the country."[28]

Despite the political divisions and disparate identities which were supported and fostered by the numerous metropolitan coffeehouses, it is remarkable how well aware the patrons of the different places were of the actions and the discourses that took place in the other coffeehouses. Roger L'Estrange made it a key part of his political strategy to report on the inopportune slips of the tongue made by his political opponents in the London coffeehouses in the pages of his journal the *Observator*. The same tactic was also adopted by the loyalist newswriter Nathaniel Thompson. A correspondent to the *Spectator* noted in 1712 how an untruthful remark made in one morning would fly through the coffeehouses of the city throughout the course of the day. In the evening, the writer regaled his friends with "an account of what censure it had at Will's in Covent Garden, how dangerous it was believed to be at Child's, and what inference they drew from it with relation to stocks at Jonathan's." The widespread currency of such "common knowledge" of the political talk of the town belies the contemporary obsession with the presumed pervasiveness of behind closed doors caballing and seditious plotting. Far from being the fragmented and mutually exclusive world of private cliques and subversive clubs that haunted the Augustan social imaginary, the coffeehouse system of post-Restoration London seems to have been one in which its various constituent parts were constantly communicating with each other, through gossip as well as the circulation of texts in both print and manuscript.[29]

The numerous coffeehouses of the metropolis were greater than the sum of their parts; they formed an interactive system in which information was socialized and made sense of by the various constituencies of the city.[30] Although a rudimentary form of this sort of communication circuit existed in early modern England (and especially London) well before coffeehouses were introduced in places such as St. Paul's walk or the booksellers' shops of St. Paul's churchyard, the new coffeehouses quickly established themselves at the heart of the metropolitan circuitry by merging news reading, text circulation, and oral communication all into one institution. The coffeehouse was first and foremost the product of an increasingly complex urban and commercial society that required a means by which the flow of information might be properly channeled. London's dramatic population growth in the seventeenth century necessitated an increasingly "organic" solidarity dependent on a more complex division of labor, and especially the division of communicative labor, in metropolitan society.[31]

The coffeehouse arose to meet this need. Overseas merchants needed places to congregate to discuss the state of trade in the lands that they did business with; investors needed places to meet the brokers who could buy and sell their shares in the joint-stock companies that they were financing; and even the literary wits needed a place to discuss the relative merits or demerits of the latest plays on the stage. Notices of particular interest to the habitués of a particular coffeehouse were often posted in such places publicly. Lloyd's Coffeehouse was an important clearinghouse for the posting of official notices regarding overseas trade as well as private lost-and-found notices regarding personal property. Bridge's Coffeehouse in Pope's Head Alley near the Royal Exchange regularly posted the bills of entry provided by the Customs House. Advertisements in the form of cheap print, broadsides, and even large posted placards were ubiquitous. In 1702, the town council of Edinburgh tried to regulate the posting of placards in the city's coffeehouses and hand over the trade as a monopoly to the keeper of the Edinburgh exchange. They particularly wanted to maintain control over the posting of notices regarding the departures and arrivals of ships from the Scottish port of Leith.[32] Of course taverns or other important public spaces such as the Royal Exchange or St. Paul's walk might also serve such communicative purposes, but the coffeehouses were seen as particularly amenable to fostering metropolitan sociability because they were invested from their origins with a patina of sober respectability and genteel refinement.

Above all, the coffeehouse became the primary social space in which "news" was both produced and consumed. The association between coffeehouses and news culture began in the 1660s and surely accounts for the popularity of the institution beyond the virtuoso community after the Restoration. Restoration coffeehouses soon became known as places "dasht with diurnals and books of news." The news business was a key means by which many coffeehouse-keepers could supplement their income. Some coffeemen published newspapers of their own, or copied manuscript newsletters of material too sensitive to commit to a press. As early as 1664, a coffeeman on Bread Street was obtaining parliamentary news from a clerk of the House of Commons and selling access to it at his coffeehouse. A few years later, the Italian visitor Lorenzo Magalotti commented that English coffeehouses generally contain "various bodies or groups of journalists where one hears what is or is believed to be new, be it true or false." Manuscript newsletter writers began to turn coffeehouse gossip into news stories sent out to their subscribers.[33]

Although primarily metropolitan, coffeehouse newsmongering was not limited to London. Slater's Coffeehouse in Nottingham took in private intelligence derived from the Secretary of State's offices as did Simon Heath's Coffeehouse in Birmingham. Brunsden's Coffeehouse in Devizes, Wiltshire, as well as Hancock's Coffeehouse in Hereford both took in newsletters. Mrs. Davies's Coffeehouse and Fogg's Coffeehouse in Oxford each received scribal newsletters from London booksellers such as Thomas Guy and Francis "Elephant" Smith. Thomas Marshall in Norwich also received newsletters from the London-based scrivener William Mason. The Edinburgh postmaster Robert Mein supplemented his income by supplying the city's coffeehouses with copies of the newsletters he received in the post for the use of the town council; the scheme worked well until the council decided to cancel its payments to Mein in 1685 because of the practice. This sort of dual employment was not uncommon. Some suspected that a number of the king's messengers moonlighted as news suppliers or coffeehouse-keepers and used their position in the king's service for their own profit.[34]

Estimates of the actual profitability of the scribal news business varied widely. Marshall in Norwich paid £5 per year for his news in 1684, while Will Urwin was charging his London customers twice that much in 1679. William Cotton estimated the net income of his fellow coffeehouse newswriters varied from £16–20 to £100–150 per year in 1683. Ephraim Allen, another newswriter, told an investigating committee in the House of Lords in 1707 that he paid his coffeeman 18 d. per week for the intelligence he received from the coffeehouse. This would amount to less than £4 per year. Allen himself could not have earned more than £32 per year from his newswriting, as he pulled in no more than sixteen shillings per week from selling news to other coffeehouses, and that was only when Parliament was in session. No doubt the price one received for news supplied varied according to its quality and the level of popular demand for it. The newswriter Hancock, who had access to "greate intelligence both from court and councell," charged each of his customers £4–6 per year. Others specialized in supplying specialized markets: newswriters such as Cleypole, Gay, and Robinson sent their news primarily outside of London, while one Blackhall served London customers with news from Holland and Scotland. A great deal of news recycling took place in the scribal publication business: Cleypole and Reive paid Hancock and Robinson for the privilege of copying their news items, which they slightly reworded to suit their own clientele.[35]

No coffeehouse worth its name could refuse to supply its customers with a selection of newspapers. Nathaniel Thompson estimated in 1683 that each coffeehouse spent four or five shillings per paper per week to supply customers with the newspapers they so desired. At this rate, a coffeehouse would be obliged to pay £13 per year for each newspaper. This is clearly a very high estimate. The coffeehouse-keeper Isaac Branch paid £4 a year to Edmund Jones for supply of "French news." The growing diversity of the press in the late seventeenth and early eighteenth centuries meant that there was great pressure for a coffeehouse to take in a number of journals. Indeed, many felt the need to accept nearly anything Grub Street could put to press. In 1728, a coterie of coffeehouse-keepers complained that "when a news-paper is first set up, if it be good for any thing, the coffee-men are, in a manner, obliged to take it in. And a paper once received into a coffee-house, is not easily thrust out again," for "every paper in a coffee-house has its set of partizans, to whose humours and understandings it is better suited than the rest. And if a coffee-man turns a foolish rascally paper our of doors, 'tis ten to one but some or other of his customers follow it, and he sees no more of them." The cost for taking in such papers could run as high as £10 to £20 or more per year. Not all coffeehouses could afford to take in every paper published, of course, but many also supplied their customers with news published abroad. Papers from Paris, Amsterdam, Leiden, Rotterdam, and Haarlem were commonly delivered to many coffeehouses in early eighteenth-century London. The Scotch Coffeehouse in Bartholomew Lane boasted regular updates from Flanders on the course of the war in the 1690s. Along with newspapers, coffeehouses regularly purchased pamphlets and cheap prints for the use of their customers.[36]

Aside from the significant financial costs, coffeehouse newsmongering was a dangerous business that could provoke arrest by the authorities. Even a private party with a grudge could pose a threat. One coffeeman learned this the hard way when he encountered a gentleman who believed he had been "scandalized in his newes paper." The hapless newswriter was severely beaten in public, and town's judgment on the matter was far from sympathetic: "severall others waitt an opportunity to thresh his jackett in the same manner, which is the least could be expected by people who venture so far beyond their province in matters too which require so much niceness, penetration and judgement."[37] Although coffeehouse-keeping and news writing developed in tandem in the post-Restoration decades, they ultimately remained distinct professions. Most coffeehouses had to pay subscription fees to receive their news, even if some of them received payment in return for the news gathered on their premises.

This tension broke out into open conflict between the coffeemen and the newswriters in the 1720s. It began with the grumbling by many coffeehouse-keepers about the excessive cost of providing news to their customers. A proposal was vetted among the London coffeehouse-keepers in 1723 to enter into a collective boycott of all papers aside from those published "by authority." This proposed self-denying ordinance met fierce resistance from the periodical publishers and it was quickly dismissed but the grievances were vetted again in 1728 when several of the more prominent metropolitan coffeehouse-keepers attempted to band together to form their own exclusive news publishing business. They proposed to consolidate the news industry by establishing a collective system in which each of the subscribing coffeehouses would oversee the collection of newsworthy notices from their patrons and send them twice daily to a general compiler who would then redistribute the news thus gathered back to the coffeehouses. By cutting out the middlemen, the coffeemen hoped to augment their income by reducing their expenditure on newspapers and collecting the subscription and advertising fees themselves. Of course, the action simply invited the scorn of the professional newswriters, and it failed because both the coffeehouse and the news industries of the early eighteenth century were far too decentralized and freewheeling to admit the imposition of such a monopoly.[38]

Along with both scribal and printed news production, the association between the coffeehouses and print culture more generally was very strong. Even before his appointment as Surveyor of the Press in 1663, Roger L'Estrange warned that "the principall and professed dealers in [seditious libels] are observed to be some certain stationers and coffeemen and that a great part of their profit depends upon this kinde of trade." Booksellers and coffeehouses often lived cheek by jowl. James Farr, the keeper of the second coffeehouse to open in London, began his trade in the same building occupied by the stationer Daniel Pakeman. The bookseller Bernard Lintot lived next door to Nando's Coffeehouse on Fleet Street, and the high churchman Thomas Bennet published at the Half Moon Tavern and Coffeehouse on Cheapside near St. Paul's Churchyard. Some coffeemen entered into final and social bonds of credit and mutual obligation with London stationers. Tobie Collier, who ran a coffeehouse near Newgate, posted bail for the bookseller Richard Janeway when he was taken into custody for publishing seditious news in April 1682. Some coffeehouse-keepers were stationers themselves. Benjamin Harris, the publisher of several newspapers in the 1680s and 1690s, took up the coffee trade during his stay in Boston, where he published the first American newspaper. John Houghton, FRS, and founder of the financial journal *A Collection for Improvement of Husbandry and Trade* (1692–98), took up the trade of apothecary and coffee retailer when he retired from publishing; the bookseller John Southby also turned to coffeehousing in retirement.[39]

It is easy to overlook the other mundane but very useful services that coffeehouses provided to their patrons. Coffeehouses were often where one might deposit and receive one's mail. Will's Coffeehouse in Covent Garden took in the mail for customers like Lord Culpepper, who lived nearby. In the 1680s, the Penny Post used coffeehouses as both pick-up and delivery centers. Some coffeehouses offered a sort of surrogate penny post service themselves. Tobias Collier's Coffeehouse at Pye Corner regularly conveyed the letters deposited with the house to the general post office on collection nights; Collier later found himself the victim of an attempt by the penny post undertakers to smear his name when they desired to corner the business for themselves. He was accused of taking in letters and postage fees without following through on the delivery of his post. The penny post too came in for its share of criticism. Despite the post's pledge to deliver inter-London mail quickly and cheaply, the bookseller John Smith complained that a letter sent to him postage paid from Garraway's Coffeehouse did not arrive from the penny post until late the next day and was only delivered to him after he was entreated to tip the postman an additional two pence.[40]

Many correspondents used a coffeehouse as a convenient place to write their letters as well as to send them. Jonathan Swift seems to have used coffeehouses primarily for these purposes; he told his "Stella" that he "would never go" there but to look for her letters. He may have had an extra incentive in doing so quickly, as it seems that some coffeehouse patrons had no qualms about inspecting other people's mail. Robert Harley chided Swift over the handwriting of one letter which he observed "through the glass-case at the coffeehouse." Indeed, the practice of reading other people's mail seems to have been widespread. Private letters could be exposed publicly in coffeehouses. In 1690, the postmaster John Wildman had to print a pamphlet declaring emphatically that the government was not systematically engaged in reading and destroying correspondence related to the forthcoming parliamentary elections; he was, of course, carefully monitoring letters carried through the post for indications of Jacobite sedition. One of the many critics of the radical John Toland relied on the practice of reading other people's mail when he sent an incriminating letter, unsealed and anonymous, addressed for Toland at Nan's Coffeehouse. Predictably, the contents of the letter soon became public knowledge and Toland had to go to great lengths to defend his reputation from the smear.[41]

What did coffeehouse keepers get in return for this rudimentary postal service? Not much, it seems. Accepting and holding the mail for one's customers seems to have been a service that the proprietors provided gratis in order to encourage the custom of their neighbors, although they might hint to their infrequent customers that the service was intended only for regulars, as Jonathan Swift learned when he discovered that his local coffeehouse "will grudge to take in my letters," after he had stopped patronizing it. The coffeehouse remained an important postal center through the eighteenth and even well into the nineteenth centuries. With the introduction of regular mail coaches in the 1780s, the Gloucester Coffeehouse in Piccadilly accepted and received correspondence from the West Country as well as serving as a staging ground for coaches setting out westward (Figure 29).[42]

It was through providing services such as this that the coffeehouse was thoroughly integrated into the economy and society of London's various neighborhoods. "London society may be conceived of more fruitfully as a mosaic of neighbourhoods rather than as one single amorphous community," the urban historian Jeremy Boulton has suggested. The term "neighborhood" is rather difficult to pin down — founded as it was (and is) on the subjective mental worlds of urbanites rather than objective structures of city government — but it is a useful means of identifying the micro-societies that were forged by the daily rounds of urban living.[43] A neighborhood may be understood as an important subset of the parish society that is usually taken as the characteristic unit of analysis by urban historians.

Coffeehouses became an important aspect of the mental framework that constituted Londoners' understandings of their neighborhoods partly by offering an easily recognized and remembered landmark. In a time before the *London A-Z* and one in which city dwellers' local knowledge of their surroundings was forged primarily through perambulation, coffeehouse shop signs helped to remind Londoners of their orientation in the metropolis. Nearly every coffeehouse referred to its sign as a means by which prospective customers could identify the premises. The shop signs of Restoration London were regulated in size — they could extend no further than two and a half feet into the street and had to be raised at least nine feet above the ground to allow room for men on horseback to pass by — and the signs for coffeehouses often prominently displayed a recognizable symbol such as a Turk's head or a coffeepot. Saussure thought that one could locate a coffeehouse that harbored prostitutes if it had a sign of "a woman's arm or hand holding a coffee pot." The specific content of London signs could be also regulated, and one tavern was required to change its symbol because its existing sign was deemed to be "superstitious." The poor artistic quality and the execrable orthography of London signs were lamented in the *Tatler*, which complained that "many a man has lost his way and his dinner by this general want of skill."[44]

An even more fundamental way in which the coffeehouse became a part of neighborhood society was through the issue of token trade credits (Figures 30 and 31). These coffeehouse tokens were used as a substitute currency in the early years of the Restoration era. They were issued primarily in the denomination of halfpennies or farthings and could be redeemed at the coffeehouse of origin, or indeed at any local shop willing to accept them as valid tender.[45] Such tokens were a convenient means of solving the problem of insufficient

Figure 29. Charles Rosenberg after James Pollard (1828), "The West Country Mails at the Gloucester Coffee-House," hand-colored aquatint (62.5 × 79.4 cm), BAC, Paul Mellon Collection, B.1985.36.845. Courtesy of the Center for British Art, Yale University.

Figure 30. Coffeehouse trade tokens (obverse), seventeenth century. Museum of London, negative 20015. Courtesy of the Museum of London.

Figure 31. Coffeehouse trade tokens (reverse), seventeenth century. Museum of London, negative 20016. Courtesy of the Museum of London.

specie that often plagued early modern economies, and they offered neighborhood inhabitants an important mental and economic link to their local coffeehouse. As such, they provided instant advertising for the coffeehouse.

They were highly illegal as well. Such tokens infringed upon the carefully
guarded royal prerogative as the sole legitimate source of legal tender in the
kingdom, and their minting was denounced in a series of royal proclamations
in the early 1670s. The crown attempted to suppress, or at least actively
discourage, such activity, and many offenders found themselves called before
the king and his privy council to answer for their illegal "coyning of coffee
pence." The fact that such activity persisted despite this royal pressure demonstrates the way in which coffeehouses had quickly become central to the
micro-economics of daily life in Restoration London. The coining of trade
tokens persisted through the eighteenth century, although it seems that coffeehouses did not continue the practice for as long.[46]

Despite the lamentations of their contemporary opponents and the encomi-
ums of their modern champions, the coffeehouses should not be understood as
an institution that developed in complete opposition to the existing structures
of government. In most cases, the coffeehouses fit smoothly into the various
and overlapping layers of government in the early modern state. County quarter sessions, city wardmotes, parish vestries, and civic corporations throughout the British Isles found that the coffeehouse was a convenient place to
conduct their business. Beginning as early as 1672, the vestry meetings of the
London parish of St. Stephen Walbrook were held at various local coffeehouses.[47] The City ward of Cornhill, which was crawling with coffeehouses,
held its wardmote inquests at Farren's Coffeehouse beginning in 1674. The
town council of Edinburgh began to hold regular meetings at an Edinburgh
coffeehouse in 1707. Even judicial functions such as petty sessions could be
hosted by coffeehouses, as the Ship Coffeehouse on Mansell Street, near
Goodman's Fields, Whitechapel, did. Quarter sessions for Hertfordshire were
often held in local coffeehouses by the mid-eighteenth century.[48] The wardmote inquests for Vintry ward in London were often held at the Dogg Tavern
until 1717, when they were moved to Solford's Coffeehouse. The City of
London's committees for market regulation also met at a coffeehouse. Private
civic organizations such as the Tower Hamlets Society, a key agency behind
the Reformation of Manners movement, held meetings at coffeehouses such as
Hamlin's near the Royal Exchange.[49] Coffeehouses did not hold a monopoly
on this sort of business, of course, for such meetings had commonly been held
at other sorts of public houses, especially inns and taverns, but it is striking
how quickly and how fervently the new coffeehouses were welcomed as useful

Figure 32. William Hogarth, "Characters who frequented Button's Coffeehouse about the year 1730," aquatint engraving (1786), based on an original drawing by Hogarth in the collection of Samuel Ireland; BM, Dept. of Prints and Drawings. Courtesy of the British Museum, London.

meeting places by the numerous governmental and voluntary organizations of post-Restoration Britain.

Along with public hospitality for official functions, coffeehouses offered another option for the provision of private hospitality in an urban setting. The gentry resident in London had long preferred to situate their social dining, and sometimes their accommodations as well, in public houses, rather than at their town homes. Many coffeehouses offered meals as well as liquid refreshment, and thus the coffeehouse soon became a favored location for social dining. In this way, a well-equipped coffeehouse was little different from a tavern or an ordinary.[50] By the end of the eighteenth century, some of the most fashionable London coffeehouses were known as much for their fine food and drink as they were for the familiar coffee and newspapers that made them distinctive in the seventeenth century. Many were quite like modern restaurants with their private booths, tables, and well-dressed waiters. The private coffeehouse booth seems to have been an innovation of the earlier eighteenth century, as they begin to appear in images of coffeehouses around the 1730s (Figures 32 and 33).

Figure 33. C. Lamb after George Moutard Woodward, "A Sudden Thought" (London: S. W. Fores, 1 Jan. 1804), etching and stipple (25 × 35.5 cm), BM Sat. 10325.1; LWL, 804.1.1.7. Courtesy of the Lewis Walpole Library, Yale University.

The word "restaurant" was imported from the French in the nineteenth century, and even then the term was associated with French dining establishments. In the century before the Regency era, it was the coffeehouse or the tavern which first came to mind when one thought of eating out. The most famous dining establishment of early eighteenth-century London was Pontack's Tavern, a place which supplemented the usual coffeehouse fare of news and drinks with elaborate dinners. On his tour of the Midlands in 1798, John Byng began to wax nostalgically about the quality of food in the metropolitan coffeehouses: "A London gentleman steps into a coffeehouse, orders venison, and turtle, in the instant; and (if known) a delicious bottle of port or claret: upon a clean cloth, without form, he dines at the moment of his appetite and walks away at the moment, he is satisfied; neither opportuned by civilities, or harrass'd by freedoms; he labours not under obligation, he has not submitted to ridicule, or offended from a want of high breeding." The elegance and ease of a genteel coffeehouse meal in London was not to be found outside the

Figure 34. The metropolitan coffeehouse compared with the country alehouse. Isaac Cruickshank after George Moutard Woodward, "Caricature ornaments for screens, &c.," pl. 6 (S. W. Fores, 4 June 1800), etching with hand coloring, 42.7 × 31.7 cm; LWL, 800.6.4.1. Courtesy of the Lewis Walpole Library, Yale University.

metropolis, he thought.[51] Byng's contrast between polite London dining and the rustic appeal of the country was illustrated in a 1800 print by Isaac Cruickshank (Figure 34), which drew a contrast between a polite London coffeehouse, with its fashionable booths, elaborate dinners, and fine wines in elegant glassware, and a country alehouse with its simple décor, tankards of ale, and dancing patrons.

Some coffeehouses offered so many services beyond the basic provision of news and coffee that they were hardly distinguishable from inns. Tonsar's Coffeehouse in Epsom boasted accommodations for men, horses, and coaches, along with "as good wine (and at as cheap a rate) as can be had in London." It was not unusual for coffeehouses to take in lodgers in order to supplement their income. Many visitors to the capital city found it convenient to lodge at coffeehouses. During the war with France in the 1690s, some coffeehouses were impressed into service for quartering soldiers in accordance with the terms of the 1689 Mutiny Act, which obliged public-house keepers to billet traveling soldiers on their premises.[52]

An important adjunct to the coffeehouse's role as a victualling center was that it offered a convenient place in which candidates for Parliamentary election might dole out their obligatory pre-election largesse. Borough electioneering was a common function for urban victuallers, and the coffeehouses fit right into this system of ritual feasting. Coffeehouses also served as organizing centers through which partisan voters might find transport to the polls. Such was the function of the Rainbow Coffeehouse at Temple Gate, which conveyed tory voters to Guildford for the Surrey election in 1710. Far from being an "underground world," it seems that the coffeehouse had little difficulty fitting into the existing structures of society and government in post-Restoration Britain.[53] The nature of this fit becomes clear when we examine the primary legal means through which the development of coffeehouse society was regulated at the local level, the system of licensed drinking and victualling.

Licensing Hospitality

Coffeehouses were regulated through the same system of licensing used for public houses that specialized in the sale of alcoholic drinks, such as alehouses and taverns. The licensing of retail sales of coffee, tea, chocolate, and sherbet was enjoined by the 1663 excise reform act. Such retailers were required to obtain their licenses at the general sessions of the peace for their county or from the offices of the chief magistrate of whatever jurisdiction they lived in. The principal reason for this statute was to allow for the orderly collection of the excise revenue due to the crown on these goods, for no license was to be granted to anyone who could not show that he or she had paid their excise duties. Although complete records of coffeehouse licensing seem not to be kept in any jurisdiction in the country, it is clear that the statute was obeyed and licenses for coffeehousing were issued at quarter sessions as well as in other legal jurisdictions throughout England. The licensing of coffeehouses in Scotland also became a common practice administered by the borough governments of Glasgow and Edinburgh in the 1670s.[54]

The coffeehouse-keepers of metropolitan London applied for their licenses at the sessions for Middlesex county, or those held by the cities of Westminster and London. The lord mayor of the City of London issued licenses for coffee sales for eighteen-month periods, and so did the justices of the peace at the Westminster and Middlesex sessions. Often coffeehouse-keepers obtained their licenses in conjunction with the licensing of other victuallers, tipplers, or petty hawkers (badgers). Coffeehouse-keepers who did not obtain the proper license could face official inquiries and perhaps prosecutions at quarter sessions for their negligence. Concern for the proper administration of coffeehouse licensing in the metropolis seems to have been at its greatest during the 1670s, for there is little information in any of the London jurisdictions on the licensing of coffeehouses after 1680, nor do we find any record of coffeehouse-keepers finding themselves prosecuted at quarter sessions for running an unlicensed coffeehouse after that date. If the existing licensing system had fallen into abeyance, this may explain why a bill was introduced in the House of Commons in 1689 which would have introduced a new licensing system for all retailers of beer, ale, cider, mum, coffee, tea, and chocolate. In April 1692, the magistrates at the City of London quarter sessions became so concerned that the licensing system for coffeehouses was being ignored that they reminded their fellow citizens that it was still required, and they followed this up a few months later with a request that the beadles in each ward present a return of all of the coffeehouses and their keepers. The court of aldermen subsequently ruled that all unlicensed coffeehouses should be prosecuted at the next quarter sessions, but there are no records of any mass prosecution at the time. Unlicensed coffeemen in the City of London were occasionally presented before their wardmote inquests, which suggests that the process of issuing licenses remained in force even if care was not taken to document the licensing process. By the eighteenth century, however, coffeehouses were licensed along with all other victualling licenses.[55]

The regulation of coffeehouses was not solely a metropolitan phenomenon, although documentation for the licensing of coffeehouses beyond London is quite scarce. Oddly enough, it seems that magistrates outside the metropolis were more concerned with maintaining the system of coffeehouse licensing that had fallen into abeyance in the metropolis. William Pearce's Coffeehouse in Warminster was suppressed at the Wiltshire quarter sessions in January 1681 because he "made it his dayly practice to expose to the view of the inhabitants divers seditious pamphlets and libells against the government now established in both Church and State." Nevertheless Pearce was able to renew his license within half a year. The justices of the peace in Lancashire licensed the coffeehouse run by Richard Hilton, a barber-surgeon living in Lancaster in 1688. In the city of Cambridge, the office of the university vice chancellor was charged with the issue of coffeehouse licenses and he continued to do so with diligence until at least 1699. The vice chancellor also added stipulations to his licenses that they take care to observe the sabbath and to prohibit unlawful gaming on the premises, but most notably that the younger scholars of the university be prohibited from frequenting the coffeehouses without their tutors. Cambridgeshire justices were also aware of the coffee licensing laws, and they may have issued licenses of their own at quarter sessions.[56]

Coffeehouse licensing was supposed to serve the dual purposes of ensuring that the crown received its due from the excise duties on the exotic drinks purveyed in the houses and of serving as a means of social discipline. It was generally agreed by the authorities at every level that the number of all public houses should be kept to a bare minimum: licensing was the means by which these numbers could be kept down. The lord mayor of London and the City of London's political elite saw all public houses, be they alehouses, taverns, or coffeehouses, as public nuisances in need of close observation and careful municipal regulation. A license could be denied to anyone who had a reputation for disorderly conduct or disaffection to the government or the established church by local magistrates. City wardmotes also revoked licenses for running a disorderly house within their jurisdiction. Those who spoke ill of the government — or worse, of the local magistrates who issued the licenses — risked having their houses suppressed at quarter sessions. Royal proclamations and the orders of the local magistrates made this clear: no coffeehouse-keeper or tippler should be licensed unless he or she could demonstrate his or her reputation as a loyal subject. In 1662, Roger L'Estrange was already recommending that a condition be added to all coffeehouse licenses enjoining the keeper from allowing manuscript libels to be read on their premises, and such a clause was ultimately added as a compromise after the failure of the December 1675 proclamation suppressing the coffeehouses.[57]

The best index of one's loyalty was taken to be regular attendance at the parish church. Both Roman Catholic and dissenting recusants were clearly judged to be unfit to run a public house because such places would naturally become the haunts of seditious cabals and centers of political unrest. During the political crisis surrounding the anxieties over the Catholic duke of York's potential succession to the throne in the early 1680s, the high constables of each parish were enjoined to issue certificates of conformity to their local tipplers and coffeehouse-keepers.[58] Peter Kidd, the master of the notorious Amsterdam Coffeehouse, in which Titus Oates regularly held forth, ran afoul of this stipulation and was arrested and tried at court several times for his nonconformist recusancy. John Thomas, another dissenting coffeehouse-keeper on Aldersgate Street, was served with a royal writ of *excommunicato capiendo* and imprisoned by a church court for his recusancy.[59] Even a show of loyalty through proper voting could be required of prospective license holders. In late 1682, a moment of supreme confidence, the king informed the lord mayor of London that he should require every alehouse and coffeehouse-keeper in the City to attend their wardmote meetings and "there to vote for such men as are right to the King and government," if "they shall expect licenses for the year ensuing." The crown's attempt to purge suspected whigs from the London City government reached as far down as attempts such as this to impose a religio-political litmus test upon drinking-house licenses. The tory stalwart Roger L'Estrange defended this practice as a matter of "civil and politicall consideration," in which the state had an interest in denying potential troublemakers the opportunity to foment discontent with the government.[60]

The imposition of such litmus tests on the issuance of licenses persisted into the eighteenth century, although the primary victims had changed. Rather than aiming primarily at whigs and dissenters, the targets of licensing discrimination after the Glorious Revolution were primarily Jacobites and Catholics. The magistrates at the Middlesex quarter sessions declared in December 1716 that licenses should be denied to all "papists, non-jurors, and other persons disaffected to his majesty's person and government" by administering the oaths of abjuration, allegiance, and supremacy to both the licensee and his or her security. Much discretion in this matter depended upon the prejudices of local magistrates. In 1702, a Barnstaple justice refused to license a coffee-woman in his jurisdiction unless she promised him that she would refuse to supply John Tutchin's virulently whig paper the *Observator* on her premises. This was thought to be an unwarranted abuse of authority, and Tutchin urged the woman to hire an attorney to press her case at the next quarter sessions.[61]

If the public houses of Stuart and Hanoverian Britain were representative of an increasingly dense and influential "fourth estate" of public opinion, as they certainly were, they were also consistently regulated by the structures of national and local government and these structures were based upon the assumption that some members of society, namely loyal subjects of the crown and the established church, were more fit than others to be privileged guardians of that fourth estate. The persistence of aspirations to, if never the complete achievement of, a confessional state shaped the development of the political structures through which public opinion could be expressed in post-Restoration England. This confessional state was not adamantine, of course: dissenters such as Peter Kidd and John Thomas could slip through the cracks and receive licenses even if they were not supposed to do so in theory. It is likely that other, more quiescent, dissenting coffeehouse-keepers were able to go about their business without being troubled by local or national authorities. But the use of religious and political tests to determine the worthiness of a potential coffee-house license-holder demonstrates just how powerful and how deeply entrenched into the structure of local as well as national politics was the notion that only participation in the national church as established by law qualified one to be a full participant in the body politic.

License-holding mattered greatly to the struggling men and women of the middling sort who comprised the coffeehouse-keeping trade. The possession of a license could provide a degree of security and legal recognition to those who possessed them. Although the coffeemen of England did not attempt to form a guild or a corporate identity as the café proprietors (*limonadiers*) of seventeenth-century Paris did, it seems that they viewed their licenses as a sort of privilege. The founder of the first coffeehouse in Glasgow and indeed all of Scotland, Col. Walter Whytfoord, petitioned the Glasgow authorities in 1673 not only for a license of nineteen years' duration, but also a monopoly right to the sale of coffee within the city for the same amount of time.[62]

All coffeehouse-keepers guarded their privileges jealously, and were not afraid to assert their right to practice their trade unhindered by virtue of their licenses. In 1672, no less than 140 coffeehouse-keepers signed a remarkable petition to the lord high treasurer of England in which they complained of their harassment by agents of the crown despite their possession of licenses obtained in good faith and by virtue of statutory authority. The petition included the names of some of the most prominent coffeehouse-keepers of London, including William Urwin of Will's Coffeehouse, Thomas Garraway of Garraway's, and James Farr, who had opened one of the first coffeehouses in London in the late 1650s. The petition was an implicit challenge to the prerogative power of the crown to regulate economic affairs as it saw fit, and similar arguments were raised in response to Charles II's efforts to eradicate the coffeehouse phenomenon. The implication here was that a license granted by parliamentary statute could not be revoked by royal whim. Of course, dedicated royalists would have none of this, and it was their belief that King Charles was entirely within his rights to revoke these licenses should he wish to. Although the crown never backed down from this position, the king never succeeded in pushing through a wholesale revocation of the coffeehouse licensing system. The keepers of public houses often complained of unjust treatment or arbitrary suppression by their local magistrates, and they used their licenses, especially the contribution to the revenue of the crown signified by those licenses, as a defense against such assaults on their livelihoods.[63]

Licensing was not, however, the only means by which the coffeehouses were regulated. Like all other traders, coffeehouse-keepers within the jurisdiction of chartered civic corporations such as the City of London or the Burgh of Edinburgh were required to possess the freedom of the City before practicing their trade. City of London coffeemen were more likely to be presented before their wardmotes for trading without the freedom than they were to be questioned about the state of their license or excise certificate. The monopoly rights of freemen of the City to trade within its jurisdiction continued to be jealously guarded well into the eighteenth century, and citizens were unafraid to challenge their neighbors to show proof of their freedom if they were suspected of interloping.[64]

Coffeehouse-keepers were also subject to the discipline of parish government. Although the parishes did not have a judicial branch, they could present and fine members of the parish for misconduct. Parish assessments could be made of house-keepers who maintained disorderly houses, or of local customers who were drunk, swore, drank on a Sunday, or otherwise disturbed the peace. Of course, these offenses could be prosecuted only irregularly, but fines in some parishes were meted out. The Westminster parish of St. Paul's Covent Garden was particularly vigilant in this regard, most likely to the great chagrin of local coffeehouse-keepers, who were occasionally fined for offenses on their premises. Other London parishes, such as St. Dunstan's and St. Alphage's, took care to present local coffeehouses for moral offenses in the wake of the Restoration, although their attention to such concerns seems to have waned by the end of the seventeenth century.[65]

Local magistrates also occasionally tried to prosecute sabbath violators. In December 1679, the lord mayor of London proclaimed that a series of fines would to be levied on public houses that opened their doors on Sunday. During the 1690s and the early eighteenth century, the Societies for the Reformation of Manners provoked a heightened vigilance against public houses that remained open on the sabbath or that condoned "lewdness" or other sorts of "wickednes, swearing and unseemly talk" on their premises. To some reformers, the very raison d'être of keeping a public house was to profit from "the sins of others," and they sought to keep up the regulatory pressure on such places.[66] Coffeehouses were not exempt from these anxieties, and authorities at all levels responded to the call from reformers to more closely monitor and prosecute sabbath-breaking or disorderly coffeehouses. Vigilance against sabbath violations by coffeehouses was particularly strong in Scotland after the Glorious Revolution from both the official magistracy as well as the private efforts of the active Edinburgh chapter of the Society for the Reformation of Manners. Well into the eighteenth century, the town council of Edinburgh sought to keep a close eye on the moral tenor of Scottish coffeehouse society. In April 1704, the council banned all game-playing such as cards or dice in local coffeehouses because such gaming was seen as an incitement to moral depravity (Figure 35).[67] Similar moves

Figure 35. Coffeehouse Gambling: Brown, *Works of Mr. Thomas Brown*, 4 vols. (London: Al. Wilde, 1760), engraved plate facing 3:261; Beinecke shelfmark Ij B815 C707k. Courtesy of the Beinecke Rare Book and Manuscript Library, Yale University. Gambling remained a popular recreation at establishments such as White's Chocolate House and Young Man's Coffeehouse, although foreign visitors thought it was not quite as common as in continental coffeehouses.

against gaming houses were made by London area magistrates after the Hanoverian accession, although notorious but fashionable gambling dens such as White's chocolate house survived the century without running into any trouble from the local magistrates. As one of the favored watering holes for the grandees of the whig aristocracy, White's had little to fear.[68]

Despite the varied layers of governance in which the coffeehouses were enmeshed, to many this was not enough. Amidst the fury of projecting that took hold of the English fiscal imagination in the decades of war with France after the Glorious Revolution, the coffeehouses were a perennial target for new fundraising schemes and projects. Projectors seeking to collect money for the relief of widows of sailors killed in naval combat or lost at sea quickly turned to new coffeehouse excises as an easily milkable cash cow. Nehemiah Grew thought that three-quarters of the public houses, coffeehouses not excepted, in London were superfluous because "they are a continuall temptation to all sorts of working people, as well as others, to loose their time." The most common recommendation as to what to do about these public nuisances, however, was not outright suppression, but social control through selective taxation. An increase in excise duties along with a more vigorous system of tax collection, it was argued, might simultaneously rid the kingdom of its excessive coffeehouses as well as increase the revenue to the crown.[69] "It has been observed in all ages, men will have their pleasures, let the price be what it will," observed Thomas Fox when drawing up a proposal to increase the excises on coffeehouses in 1692. He thought it was socially responsible as well as fiscally prudent to make sinners pay more for their vices. A reform of the collection of coffee excises would have been well advised, given the extensive problems with embezzlement and maladministration among coffee excise commissioners, but these projects appear to have gone nowhere. Responsibility for the collection of coffee duties was ultimately shifted from the excise to the customs administration. Concern for the contribution of coffee and coffeehouses to funding the fiscal-military state gradually diminished over the course of the eighteenth century as the dramatic rise in tea consumption, and tea smuggling, made the revenues derived from coffee seem miniscule. If the consumption of coffee "will be allowed to decrease as that of tea increases," as John Oxenford thought it would, then the financiers of the British state's sinews of power saw no need to devote any special efforts toward exploiting this revenue potential.[70] Coffee and the coffeehouses never became the sources of revenue that the projectors dreamed of in the age of financial revolutions.

Coffeehouses thrived because they offered a social space in which the various parts of urban society could communicate with one another through media as various as speech, manuscript, print, and of course, money and credit. The coffeehouse became an important micro-vector through which disparate information from abroad might be obtained on an individual basis.[71] An increasingly complex, but still very personalized, political and social order required a place like the coffeehouse in which likeminded individuals might find one another in order to transact their business. The London coffeehouse milieu was diversified as a whole, and yet each particular coffeehouse maintained a distinctly intimate atmosphere. Coffeehouse patrons could continue to meet one another and conduct business face-to-face in a traditional manner, but they did so in the context of an increasingly specialized set of opportunities within which they might make those interactions. Hence the rise of the financial coffeehouses such as Jonathan's and Garraway's, the mercantile coffeehouses such as Lloyd's, Bridge's, and the Marine, political party and propaganda headquarters such as Sam's, the Cocoa Tree, or the Amsterdam, as well as the famous literary centers at Will's and Button's. But this was an intermediate stage in the growing division of urban labor. Although many of the early coffeehouses fulfilled the functional equivalent of what we would today call office space, they were not bureaucratic institutions. Indeed, they were hardly institutions at all. They kept no records, appointed no officers, and had no formal means of replacing lost members.[72] They remained informal spaces wholly dependent on the voluntary activities and the continued patronage of their customers. In this way, the coffeehouse fit the requirements of the post-Restoration social and economic order. They were conveniently located in an urban setting and they offered a suitable neutral and dignified locale in which coffeehouse patrons might interact. The coffeehouse was perhaps the most important social space in which civil society began to flourish, in the century before Enlightenment writers such as David Hume and Adam Ferguson gave it a name and theorized its significance.

Because the coffeehouse emerged amidst the commercial, consumer, and financial revolutions that were transforming the nature of British social and economic life in the later seventeenth and early eighteenth centuries, the coffeehouse was taken by many contemporaries to epitomize the best and worst of these revolutions. At their best, the genteel respectability of the coffeehouse traders at Garraway's, Jonathan's, and Lloyd's near the Exchange represented the growing prosperity of a metropolitan-centered "gentlemanly capitalism." Similarly, the clever witticisms of the literati at Will's and Button's in Covent Garden, carefully recorded for posterity by coffeehouse journals such as the *Tatler,* the *Spectator,* and their many imitators, demonstrated the growing importance of English culture to the rest of Europe and indeed the world. At their worst, however, the volatile world of stock-jobbing at the City coffeehouses could easily be understood as a symptom of the unholy ascendancy of a speculative, self-interested, and often foreign "monied interest." For their part, too, the Covent Garden wits could be ridiculed as artificial pretenders to true literary talent.[73] For this reason the coffeehouse and the activities that took place within them remained controversial. The next two chapters explore the ongoing debates about the proper role of the coffeehouse in post-Restoration Britain.

7

Policing the Coffeehouse

The preceding chapter has discussed at length the various ways in which the coffeehouses of post-Restoration Britain became ensconced within the social and political order. Rather than viewing the coffeehouses as natural and habitual centers of opposition to the status quo, it has been suggested that they are better understood as having developed according to the prevailing customs, conventions, and indeed the legal regulations of early modern society. Yet the new coffeehouses remained controversial throughout the late seventeenth and early eighteenth centuries. If coffeehouses were so well integrated into the social order, one might well want to ask why they continued to provoke such intense anxieties. The answer lies not in the fundamental nature of the coffeehouses themselves but rather in the torturous vicissitudes of later Stuart and early Hanoverian political conflict. The rise of the coffeehouse coincided with what has often been called "the rage of party," a partisan conflict that shaped the perception of coffeehouse politics. This period saw a number of dramatic upheavals in British politics as the restored Stuart dynasty fought hard for its survival against enemies both domestic and foreign and was ultimately replaced in 1688–89 by a new Protestant line of succession heralded by King William III and Queen Mary II. These high political revolutions had to affect the regulation of the coffeehouses; each regime faced a different set of political problems and each responded with specific tactics to control their coffeehouses. This chapter offers a narrative history of these reactions to coffeehouse politics by the successive British regimes in the six decades follow- ing the Restoration of the monarchy. Although the particular challenges posed by coffeehouse politics changed along with the political configurations in the state, the continuity of the anxieties about coffeehouse politics is striking. The monarchical state and its several managers only gradually and grudgingly learned to accept that the coffeehouses of the British Isles could not be sup- pressed, and the authorities never ceased to try to monitor and regulate the political activities that took place within them.

The Restoration and Coffeehouse Politics (1660–75)

The Restoration state was caught in a bind with regards to its policies toward the new world of the coffeehouses. On the one hand, a vital part of the fiscal basis of the restoration settlement was the award to the crown of the revenues based on coffee excise taxes, and yet from their very inception, the coffeehouses were viewed by Charles II and his brother James as potentially dangerous centers for subversive activity. Charles II and the earl of Clarendon were well aware that James Harrington's republican Rota Club was meeting at Miles's Coffeehouse in London even after the restoration of the monarchy had been well assured in early 1660. Some contemporaries thought that dissenters, in particular, were "great frequenters of coffeehouses." None of this could have endeared Charles II to the coffeehouses, but it was their role as centers for political debate and news circulation that most frightened the managers of the restoration regime.[1] As we have seen, coffeehouses became the prime sites in which news was consumed and often produced soon after the restoration of the monarchy. It is no wonder, then, that from its beginning the Restoration regime thought it wise to monitor the activities that took place in the coffee- houses. The job was entrusted to men like Henry Muddiman and then Roger L'Estrange, both of whom held monopolies on the publication of licensed news and had an interest in seeing that their prerogatives were not infringed upon.[2] For an anxious monarch newly restored to his throne, however, this was not enough, and Charles II was determined to eradicate the coffeehouses from his kingdom.

In late 1666, Charles II conferred with his high chancellor, the earl of Clar- endon, to discuss the possibility of suppressing the coffeehouses outright. Clarendon agreed with the king that this was desirable, given that the coffee- houses allowed "the foulest imputations [to be] laid upon the government," and that "people generally believed that those houses had a charter of privilege to speak what they would, without being in danger to be called into question."

He proposed banning the coffeehouses by royal proclamation as well as the skillful use of spies to record the conversations of those who persisted in deriding the government so publicly. Charles agreed with the suggestion and asked Clarendon to propose a suppression of the coffeehouses in a meeting of the privy council. The proposal was shot down by secretary of state William Coventry, who argued that the excise duties on coffee were valuable to the crown, and that such a total ban might stir up even greater resentment against the monarch. Besides, he added, "the king's friends had used more liberty of speech in [coffeehouses] than they durst do in any other." The king was swayed, and the matter was dismissed for the moment.[3] This brief clash of wills between Clarendon and Coventry in 1666 established the subsequent terms of debate on the question of managing the coffeehouses. Were coffeehouses such a threat to the monarchy that they must be suppressed? Or might they be seen as a valuable new venue through which loyalist sentiment might be cultivated? Although the latter argument prevailed in 1666 and continued to do so at every challenge, many governors persisted in pursuing the dream that they might finally quell the potentially seditious chatter that filled the coffeehouses of their kingdoms.

Instead of prosecuting the coffeehouses directly, the privy council issued an order banning the sale of printed works to the hawkers who sold libels and pamphlets in the coffeehouses. It was not long after Clarendon's ill-fated proposal that the crown again began to consider taking further action against the coffeehouses themselves. By February 1671, the king was again openly querying his privy council whether there might be a legal and effective means of suppressing the coffeehouses. Although nothing was done at the time, later that year the secretary of state Joseph Williamson put on his agenda the notion that "nothing can be more to the establishment of the government" than pulling down the coffeehouses in London. By early 1672, the king had referred the question of the legality of outlawing the coffeehouses to the lord keeper Orlando Bridgeman and a committee of judges for their consideration.[4]

It seems that their judgment was not favorable to the plan, for rather than pursue an outright suppression of the coffeehouses, Charles II resolved at this point to chastise the seditious behavior he saw taking place there. In May 1672, the king ordered his attorney general, Sir Heneage Finch, to prepare a draft for a proclamation against coffeehouse rumor-mongering, and in June, he duly issued a royal proclamation to "command all his loveing subjects of what[ever] state or condition soe they may be, from the highest to the lowest, that they [shall not] utter or publish any false newes or reports or . . . intermeddle with the affaires of state and government, or with the persons of any of his Majesties counsellors or ministers in their common and ordinary discourses."

Coffeehouses in particular were singled out for royal scorn, and anyone who even heard such political discourse in a coffeehouse was enjoined to report the speaker to the authorities. The proclamation was reiterated and republished in Edinburgh and in Dublin for Charles's Scottish and Irish subjects as well.[5]

Official disgust with the venting of criticism aimed at the regime picked up steam in the 1670s. On 2 May 1674, the king issued yet another proclamation declaiming against the practice of spreading false news and "licentious talking of matters of state and government" in public. It had as little effect as its predecessor, and secretary of state Henry Coventry continued to complain about the "making publick of such scurrilous language" in political discussions. Anti-court libels were attached to the king's statue at Charing Cross after the prorogation of Parliament in November 1675. Soon afterward, the controversial pamphlet *A Letter from a Person of Quality to His Friend in the Country* (1675) appeared in the coffeehouses. This work accused the court of falling prey to a cabal of high churchmen and cavaliers who wished to introduce popery in religion and an absolutist state into the kingdom. The House of Lords ordered it to be burned, and that the identities of the author, printers, and distributors of the work should be revealed. They started by searching the coffeehouses of London, and the hawkers who frequented them, but the ultimate source of the tract, the earl of Shaftesbury and his circle, went unpunished. Banning the pamphlet only made it a more desirable read, and clandestine booksellers immediately more than doubled the price for it.[6] In the face of this very public criticism in the coffeehouses, the king was ready again to try to eliminate the coffeehouses by the end of 1675.

This time Charles's privy council was prepared to support him. Steve Pincus has shown how the temporary ascendancy of high church royalists at court in late 1675 provided the necessary political capital to push through a proclamation suppressing the coffeehouses. Thus on 29 December 1675, the king declared that after 10 January 1676 it would be forbidden to sell by retail "any coffee, chocolet, sherbet, or tea." All justices of the peace were enjoined to revoke the licenses for such sales and to refrain from granting any more such licenses in the future. The proclamation was duly recorded by the privy council and the court of common council of the City of London and it was published as a broadside as well as in the official *London Gazette* and manuscript newsletters. The proclamation was accompanied by another on 29 December encouraging the more vigorous prosecution of people who circulated libels and offered a £50 reward for their discovery.[7]

Resistance to the king's uncompromising fiat was immediate, but for a time, it seemed to some that the ban might actually work. Richard Langhorne noted that London was "now in a mutinous condition . . . upon the account of coffee-howses." He thought that "the suppression of them will prove a tryall of skill. All wytts are at worke to elude the proclamation," but he was "doubt-full they will doe it. If soe then the advice was ill, and if the Government shew itselfe to feare the people, I suspect the people will hardly feare the Government." After the ban had been announced, the stakes in the crown's contest with the coffeehouses had been raised considerably. The credibility of the monarchical will was now on the line along with the fate of the English coffee trade and the livelihoods of the coffeehouse-keepers.

Skeptics were quick to doubt that the proclamation could achieve its desired effect. "I doe not beleeve the putting downe coffy houses will hinder peoples speeches and discourses," mused Edmund Verney upon hearing news of the suppression. His son Ralph was even more cynical; he declared: "Noe English-man will long endure to bee forbid meeting together, soe long as they doe nothing contrary to law. I beleeve the meetings will bee as greate, and as constant as ever, and . . . they will rather drink sage, betony, and rosemary drinkes rather then tea, or coffee, because those native commodities pay nei-ther excize, nor customes, soe the crowne will bee the only looser by this new needlesse prohibition. Nay they will meet though they take nothing but to-bacco there."[8]

The most serious opposition to the proclamation came from the coffeehouse-keepers themselves. They of course had the most to lose in the affair, so a large number of them banded together to present a petition to the king. Some ob-servers saw this move as a carefully coordinated attack on lord treasurer Danby. The coffeemen were received at Whitehall on 6 January 1676, where they argued before the king that the proclamation was most unjust and that it would ruin the livelihoods of everyone who followed their trade. They noted that many coffeehouse-keepers had already invested much in their trade, in-cluding not only large stocks of coffee, tea, and other liquors but other signifi-cant obligations such as property leases and the hiring of servants and appren-tices.[9] After receiving this petition for leniency, Charles met with his privy council and an assembly of legal experts to debate the matter further.

The next day, the council considered in earnest the legality of the king's actions. The chief issue was the question of licensing. Could the crown legit-imately revoke licenses to retail liquors that were granted legally and by statu-tory authority? For the county of Middlesex, the question was moot: all of the licenses had expired, and the judges agreed to request that magistrates refuse to renew any licenses. But many coffeehouse licenses in the City of London remained valid, and here the crown was on much shakier legal ground. Even Charles's friendly advisors were at odds on this point. One of those present, chief justice Francis North, recalled that "wee did not agree in opinion, but returned at length that there remained some doubts, and differences of opin-ions amongst us, whereupon his Majestie pressed us no further."[10] This impasse seems to have provoked the king to reconsider, and the council was soon deeply involved in figuring out a face-saving way of rescinding the proclamation while retaining its original intent of chastising the seditious activities that were thought to take place in the coffeehouses.

The lord chief baron proposed that it might be legal to allow coffeehouse-keepers to retail their coffee "as the shops do," meaning "for people to buy and go away, but to sit there and drink it, forty or fifty in a room, may be a nuisance, and for that reason a license may be refused." North agreed. He thought that "retailing coffee might be an innocent trade, as it might be exercised but as it is used at present in the nature of common assemblys to discuss matters of state news and great persons, as they are nurserys of idleness, and pragmaticallness and hindered the expence of the native provisions, they might be thought a common nuisance." This left the problem of the outstanding licenses as well as the apparent cruelty implied by depriving several hundred householders of their livelihoods with only a few days' notice. Thus Charles resolved to grant a six-month reprieve. Another proclamation was duly issued stating that the coffeehouses could remain open until 24 June 1676, the intent being that all current coffeehouse-keepers should endeavor to sell off their existing stocks. In the meantime, all coffeehouse-keepers were enjoined to enter into a recognizance by which they would not accept any "scandalous papers, books or libels" into their houses, nor to permit "any false or scandalous reports against the government or its ministers," and to inform the authorities should anyone do so. By the next midsummer, however, it was reiterated that the coffee trade would be extinguished. This additional proclamation was duly published and announced throughout the kingdom.[11]

At this point it was still not clear whether the coffeehouses might ultimately endure royal scrutiny. "If coffy houses must enter into recognizances to betray their guests," Edmund Verney opined, "it is a better way to put them downe then by a proclamation." This is worth remembering since the additional proclamation is sometimes represented as a dramatic and embarrassing about-face for the crown. Embarrassing it was—Verney thought "it a very imprudent and inconsiderate contrivance" and the city wits soon began to ridicule the fiasco in libelous verse—but it was not intended to be a wholesale revocation of the initial proclamation. The king's aspiration to suppress the discussion of politically sensitive matters in the coffeehouses did not abate in the new year. Just days after backing down from the initial ban on the coffeehouses, several persons, including the coffeehouse-keeper William Peate, were taken into custody on suspicion of promulgating "seditious discourses, and spreading false and seditious news" in an attempt to put the fear of royal wrath into the coffeehouses.[12]

Party Politics (1676–85)

Attempts to regulate the coffeehouses persisted long after the failure to push through a royal ban on the coffeehouses in January 1676. King Charles ultimately did not reinstate his demand that the coffeehouses be fully suppressed in midsummer 1676, when the extension granted in January was due to expire, but even at this point he refused to relinquish the right to reconsider his leniency. On 21 July 1676, the king granted the coffeehouse-keepers another six-month extension on their licenses.[13]

The pretended reformation of the coffeehouses did not last long. Business continued more or less as usual after the king's failure to achieve outright suppression. Few coffeehouse-keepers felt compelled to inform on their customers, although Thomas Garraway did cooperate with Joseph Williamson when questioned about the behavior of George Villiers, the second duke of Buckingham, after the duke had reportedly called for a general health to be drunk to "a new Parliament, and to all those honest gentlemen of it that would give the king no money" at Garraway's Coffeehouse. Even in the face of persecution by local magistrates, some provincial coffeehouse-keepers thought they could survive by reemerging as alehouse-keepers. Perhaps most infuriating to the court was that they knew quite well that the earl of Shaftesbury continued to rail against the regime and to prepare his oppositional politics in John's Coffeehouse, and yet the only solution that the king could think of was to try to suggest to Shaftesbury that it was best to leave London and give up on political entanglements altogether.[14]

Other offending coffeehouses with less powerful patrons, however, did not fail to escape the royal wrath. The "greate liberty some take to suffer the coffee houses with newes" was understood by many, and not just the king, to be a grievous breach of national security. In October 1676, a plan to engage in a naval expedition against the pirates of Algiers was scuppered because the news had been leaked to the London coffeehouses and it was feared that word would get back to the pirates, who were presumed to have "very good spies" there. Samuel Pepys reported the leak to the king. So once again a number of offending coffeehouse-keepers were brought before the king and his privy council, warned not to take in any newspapers, and interrogated as to the source of the story of the Algiers expedition. By November, secretary of state Williamson had learned that the leak came from his own office. Two clerks working for him had been supplying sensitive information about foreign affairs to the coffeehouse newsletter writers.[15]

The issue of allowing the continued licensing of coffeehouses in general therefore came up again when the king's second six-month extension expired in January 1677. After the fiasco over the Algiers leak, the king was not inclined to be as gracious as he had been in the past year. A group of leading coffeemen and women petitioned his majesty once more to allow them to continue practicing their trade. The king accepted their petition, but he added an important proviso: "If at any time hereafter . . . the petitioners or any of them have misbehaved themselves, or not punctually observed their . . . promise and engagement" not to accept libels or scandalous discourse, he warned that he might rescind "this gracious favour and indulgence to them."[16] It seems that by this point a tenuous compromise on the coffeehouse question had been reached. While the king refrained from pushing through an immediate revocation of coffeehouse licensing, he reserved the right to do so in the future. The threat of yet another royal proclamation suppressing the coffeehouses remained a real possibility.

Joseph Williamson continued to keep a watch on coffeehouse discourse, and he took care to interview both the servants and the patrons of London area coffeehouses. Peter Kidd, the proprietor of the Amsterdam Coffeehouse, was called before the king in June 1677 in order to receive a royal scolding in person for allowing a libel entitled "The Spanish Memorial" to be read on his premises.[17] Several months later, on 12 September 1677, the king called some twenty to thirty London coffeehouse-keepers before the privy council in order to publicly chastise them and to order that their licenses must not be renewed after they had expired. This time no attempt was made to revoke their licenses outright: Charles had tacitly recognized that there was a limit to his royal prerogative in this respect. Nevertheless, word soon got out to the town gossips that the crown had once again showed its resolve to punish those coffeehouse-keepers the court viewed as "sordid mechanic wretches who to gaine a little mony, had the impudence and folly to prostitute affaires of state indifferently to the view of those that frequent such houses, some of whome are of lewd principles and some of mean birth and education." The immediate cause for this royal scourging was the distribution of the "Spanish Memorial" libel, but it is not surprising that the targets of the court's displeasure were notorious offenders, all of whom were well known to secretary Williamson, such as the now notorious Peter Kidd; a servant of Thomas Garraway at Garraway's Coffeehouse; and Rebecca Weedon, who allowed the circulation and copying of manuscript newsletters at her coffeehouse.[18]

By prosecuting these coffeehouses for the crime of spreading "false news," the court was taking the opportunity to prosecute certain coffeehouses that it thought to be particularly dangerous for an offense that appeared to be in the public interest and not simply a fit of personal malice. The libel circulating in these coffeehouses offered a false report about an imminent conflict with

Spain. It was in everyone's interest that news reports be truthful and reliable, especially those merchants who relied on them to conduct their affairs, and thus this was a perfect chance to settle some longstanding scores. A less cynical interpretation of this event might emphasize that the regime also had a legitimate interest in preventing writers from spreading false news that might disrupt overseas trade, or that might cause unwanted diplomatic interference in matters of state foreign policy. In any event, the court continued to prosecute offending coffeehouses on an individual basis. Later that year, the Scottish privy council ordered the Edinburgh magistrates to suppress a coffeehouse run by a cabal of notorious dissenters.[19]

Despite these efforts, the coffeehouses continued to serve as centers for political discourse. Even the supposedly suppressed Amsterdam Coffeehouse as well as Weedon's and Garraway's continued to flourish. In February 1678, secretary of state Williamson drew up a list of thirteen coffeehouse-keepers he thought were "still offenders" despite the last order of the privy council and the direct intervention of the king. Some of these coffeemen were clearly chastened by their personal encounter with the king. Peter Kidd of the Amsterdam felt compelled to send his servant to the offices of secretary of state Henry Coventry to inform on some of his customers who hazarded speculations on the prospect of another war with the Dutch. The servant took care to plead to Coventry that "if any public arrest or trial . . . may happen, Mr. Kid may not be concerned, for he was not in the room at the time." Kidd obviously wanted to keep his nose out of trouble for the time being. Likewise, Thomas Garraway was sufficiently frightened by the affair to take special care to mend his ways. He asked Edward Sing, a notorious Roman Catholic newswriter, to "forbear sending any sort of news [to Garraway's Coffeehouse] in manuscript, lest what you designed for my satisfaction should through my servant's error bring me under his Majesty's displeasure. It is my advice to you as a friend not to correspond with any town coffeehouse whatever for fear of rebuke." Garraway nevertheless lamented, "my case is somewhat hard, since almost all the coffeehouses about me have the confidence to take in all sorts of papers and especially those persons who by order of Council ought to have been bound to the contrary." He blamed the lord mayor's reluctance to obey the crown in demanding a security deposit from licensed coffeehouses as a major reason for the continued proliferation of the unlicensed news trade in London's coffeehouses.[20]

Coffeehouse politicking was hardly eradicated by such stopgap measures, especially in the wake of the controversies surrounding the suspected "popish plot" in late 1678, so the king returned to consider another attempt to suppress the coffeehouses. In December 1679 — amidst the mass petitioning campaigns calling for the exclusion of the duke of York from the succession — the proposal was once again floated in the privy council. It seemed that the old debates of late 1675 and 1676 would be rehearsed once more, and indeed the same lobbying effort by the coffeemen of London was mobilized. They attended the meeting of the council with petitions in hand, and they argued strenuously that such a ban would ruin great numbers of honest men who had already invested in substantial stocks of perishable coffee beans.[21] The council caved in to this pressure again, and a general suppression was not proclaimed.

The king and his court were not alone in their disdain for the profusion of coffeehouse politics in the exclusion crisis. Even members of Parliament looked askance at the ways in which coffeehouse newsmongers exploited popular interest in affairs of state. The House of Commons forbade the publication or dissemination of its votes in the coffeehouses as Parliament began to investigate the possibility of a popish plot in October 1678. MPs were dismayed to learn of the circulation of parliamentary votes in the coffeehouses, for it was thought to be contrary to the "honour and conscience" of the institution. This sentiment would recur throughout the rest of the century. Parliament soon took to investigating seditious words spoken at coffeehouses. The MP Sir Robert Cann was deprived of his seat and sent to the Tower in October 1680 when he was convicted of denying that there was any popish plot afoot, but only a presbyterian one at a Bristol coffeehouse. At the same time, some MPs considered summoning up for punishment a number of Oxford scholars who were suspected of circulating seditious petitions in the coffeehouses around the university.[22]

Anxiety regarding the political role of coffeehouses in the wake of the popish plot hysteria and the political polarization over the duke of York's succession which followed was shared at all levels of government and by people of all political persuasions, both court and Parliament, whig and tory. The royal administration of Charles II took the lead in persecuting coffeehouse-keepers and coffeehouse news- and rumor-mongers, but the crown faced no principled objection to the regulation of coffeehouse politics per se. When it was phrased as an assault on the dissemination of "false news," nearly everyone could rally round the cause of regulating the coffeehouses. The difficulties arose when it came to determining which news was false and what was true, especially in an intense climate of fear of popish and/or nonconformist plots. The terms of the debate over the political role of the coffeehouse in the late 1670s and early 1680s were not framed as a conflict between an absolutist monarchy that sought to squelch all political opposition and a freedom-loving civil society ensconced in its coffeehouses. The debate was over which element of the polity was more dangerous to the established constitution in church and state, a potentially papist court or a potentially republican opposition. Insofar as coffeehouses figured in this debate, they appeared as dangerous vectors through which the seditious principles and the false news of one's political opponents were propagated. At best, they were a necessary evil through which the views of one's opponents must be countered.[23]

The goal of suppressing public political debate remained in sight. Beginning in late 1679, prosecutory pressure intensified against all of the newswriters, libelers, and hawkers who supplied the coffeehouses of the kingdom with their political news and propaganda. Information obtained from several coffeehouse-keepers allowed for the identification of several news and libel writers, along with one coffeehouse-keeper named Mason, all of whom were called before the privy council on 17 December 1679. Mason was later released on payment of £100 bail. In January 1680, the privy council ordered the arrest of two Bristol newswriters and the bookseller Francis Smith II was arrested for selling seditious libels to a coffeehouse. In the next month, Benjamin Harris, the publisher of the opposition newspaper *Domestick Intelligence,* was arrested for printing a seditious libel, a move which was widely seen as punishment for his news writing. The privy council consulted with several judges to consider the legality of using the royal prerogative to regulate the news and pamphlet trade. By May, a royal proclamation against the publication of news and news pamphlets had been issued.[24]

The regime also stepped up its campaign against the coffeehouses in Scotland. In January 1681, the Scottish privy council examined and imprisoned two Edinburgh coffeemen, John McClurg and Umphray Clerk, who had undertaken to publish a gazette. Not long thereafter, the privy council decided that the punishment of McClurg and Clerk was not enough. They declared that henceforth all coffeehouses or suchlike "houses of intelligence" were to refrain from the selling of any news, except that which had been cleared by the bishop of Edinburgh, a clerk of the privy council, or another responsible officer of state, upon penalty of a five-thousand-mark fine. The Scottish coffeemen were given forty-eight hours to comply. Word of this harsh decision soon reached the metropolitan press, and the English newspapers duly reported an exaggerated story that the court had ordered the suppression of all the coffeehouses in Edinburgh. In the meantime, McClurg was petitioning the Scottish privy council in the hope of having his license restored after he promised to mend his ways in the future.[25] It is not known whether his petition was successful or not, but the coffeehouses of Edinburgh continued to supply the city with news and information.

The authorities in London demonstrated the same degree of heightened government concern over the probity of the coffee trade. In September 1681, the court of London aldermen ordered an investigation into the qualifications and fitness of all persons keeping coffeehouses in every ward of the City, but this order did not spur another general persecution of the coffeehouse trade. Direct government intervention in the coffeehouse trade was again threatened in October 1681, when the magistrates at the Middlesex quarter sessions declared their intention to prosecute any "publick howeses . . . where factious persons meet to keep clubbs and consult together how to disturb the government" within the county.[26]

The preferred option for dealing with offending coffeehouses during the exclusion crisis was to encourage local authorities to prosecute them on a case-by-case basis. When word got out in September 1679 that a Bristol coffeehouse had become the forum for the reading out of newsletters in which peers such as the earl of Anglesey and the marquis of Worcester were implicated as conspirators in the popish plot, the privy council met to decide on a course of action. It appears that they referred the matter to the local authorities in Bristol. A few months later, John Kymbar's Coffeehouse, a notorious gathering place for Bristol dissenters, had been forced to relocate, although Kymbar remained in business and promised to accommodate all of his customers as he had previously. Sir Robert Cann, a justice of the peace for the city of Bristol who had already been expelled from Parliament for his own coffeehouse discourse, continued to investigate Kymbar's Coffeehouse and he prepared to prosecute. Cann reported to secretary of state Henry Coventry that Kymbar encouraged the meetings of a number of "insulting nonconformists of [Bristol]" and they were thought to "frequently spread their false scandalous newes" in his coffeehouse. Cann took depositions from the patrons and tried, albeit unsuccessfully, to get them to inform on each other. He recommended to Coventry that "if this coffee house were suddainly suppressed, it may be a meanes to prevent some evill." Cann's efforts were initially frustrated, but later in the year Kymbar's Coffeehouse was presented for prosecution at the Bristol quarter sessions, ostensibly on the grounds that "divers idle persons do in the time of divine service tipple and smoak tobacco therein."[27] The grand jury in Norwich took similar action against two offending coffeehouse-keepers at the same time. When the third exclusion Parliament met in Oxford in March 1681, the vice chancellor of the university expressly forbade the scholars there from frequenting any coffeehouses in the city in order to prevent the outbreak of disputes between members of Parliament and the university community.[28]

Nowhere was the pattern of official intimidation of coffeehouse society more intense than in metropolitan London. Patrons of notoriously seditious coffeehouses such as the Amsterdam or Richard's (Dick's) were interrogated and encouraged to inform on their friends and fellow patrons. Roger L'Estrange, serving in his capacity as a justice of the peace for Middlesex county, was able to secure information from one Thomas Adamson on anti-Yorkist chat and rumors of Monmouth's legitimacy which were circulating at Richard's Coffeehouse. Adamson also revealed that the Amsterdam Coffeehouse made the seditious pamphlet *A Full Relation of the Contents of the Black Box* (1681) available to its customers, even though he offered the convenient, common, and highly unlikely excuse that he simply found it underneath a table and never bothered to read it.[29] Informants kept a close eye on the most frequent patrons of the Amsterdam Coffeehouse and assessed the potential for sedition of other London coffeehouses, such as Captain Powell's and Jones's in Bartholomew Lane. The incessant ramblings of Titus Oates at the Amsterdam and the distribution of seditious literature there continued to be monitored when informants from the place could be located and interrogated. Combes's Coffeehouse, another well-known center for the production of manuscript newsletters, was searched when it was thought that he was harboring Don Lewis, an alleged party to the Rye House conspiracy.[30] The republican sentiments of a patron at Elford's Exchange Alley Coffeehouse were exposed by Mr. Army, a druggist in the company there. The coffeehouse-keeper Charles Kiftell was examined when an astrologer who styled himself a prophet and practiced his trade at Kiftell's Coffeehouse began to prognosticate future dangers to the king.[31]

Tory magistrates were accused of using legal obstruction to harass suspected "whig" coffeehouses. Richard Turvor, the proprietor of Dick's Coffeehouse, assumed that permission to repair his doorway had been hindered by the attorney general because he was suspected of running a "whig coffeehouse." Turvor had indeed been implicated in the trial of Stephen College as one of College's creditors. More confrontational harassment strategies could backfire on the persecutors, as a loyalist sea captain learned when he burst into the Amsterdam and tried to take away a copy of a petition to Parliament. The Amsterdam customers forced him to return their petition and then proceeded to present him before the lord mayor's court to be interrogated on suspicion of being a popish spy.[32]

As tory partisans grew increasingly impatient to expose and prosecute anyone with questionable allegiance to a Yorkist succession, they brought local coffeehouse disputes over such matters to the attention of the crown. Sir John Coventry, an MP for the borough of Weymouth, was prosecuted for allegedly calling the king a rogue and a traitor in the heat of a coffeehouse debate. John Robinson of Chichester informed on his neighbor Robert Haslen when the latter refused to drink to the health of the duke of York at a local coffeehouse. Thomas Hyde of Oxford informed the crown of two local coffeehouses that received "very fanaticall letters, full of sedition" on a weekly basis. Edward Whitacre was prosecuted at the court of King's Bench for arguing in a Bath coffeehouse that the parliamentary cause in the civil wars of the 1640s had been just and that King Charles I had not been murdered but punished after a fair trial. William Warde reported the discontented discourses he heard in a Warminster, Wiltshire, coffeehouse and elsewhere in the West Country in the summer of 1683. Seditious toasts drunk to the health of the duke of Monmouth and the imminent death of the king at a "phanaticall" Taunton coffeehouse were also reported to secretary of state Lionel Jenkins.[33]

Not all coffeehouses were dens of sedition and opposition politics. Some, such as Beake's Coffeehouse near Charing Cross, cooperated with the government, and Beake himself seems to have served in good faith as a royal messenger. Sam's Coffeehouse remained the famous home base for Roger L'Estrange and his crew, who gathered there regularly to manage their tory propaganda machine. In L'Estrange's words, it was a place "where a company of honest fellows meet to confound the lyes of a caball of shamming whigs that make the popish plot a stalking horse to get a shot at the king." The newswriters William Cragmile and Thomas Blackhorne sought explicit permission from the crown to vend their news to coffeehouses in London and the country in return for "promising not to meddle in base pamphlets or any seditious concern."[34]

Nor was tory coffeehouse activity entirely free from official harassment or even prosecution by whiggish magistrates or members of Parliament. When an anti-exclusionist cleric tried to scribble marginalia over copies of the votes of the House of Commons in the second exclusion Parliament in a London coffeehouse, he was taken into custody and chastised before Parliament. In December 1680, Edward Rollins, one of the cabal of tory writers of the propaganda journal *Heraclitus Ridens* (1681– 1682), was seized by a constable and brought before a magistrate for his discourse at a Fleet Street coffeehouse which was construed as "strange and seditious words against the government." The government in this case was the House of Commons, which was considering a bill for the toleration of dissenters that Rollins opposed. Roger L'Estrange found his own publisher Joanna Brome prosecuted for printing libels in his tory paper the *Observator,* and the London aldermen ordered the arrest of the tory writer Nathaniel Thompson for publishing what they thought was false and seditious news.[35] For writing the *Observator* L'Estrange himself nearly faced prosecution by Robert Stephens, a messenger of the press who harbored a grudge against L'Estrange. The loyal customers and Samuel Booth, the proprietor of Sam's Coffeehouse, soon found themselves forced into this tussle and were compelled to make depositions in defense of their patron. When a band of tory troublemakers led by Mr. Wine, the king's fishmonger, descended upon the Amsterdam Coffeehouse in order to intimidate the regulars there through threatening oaths and challenging them to deny that the popish plot had in fact been a presbyterian one, the proprietor Peter Kidd put a stop to the fracas by invoking his authority as a local constable. He had Wine seized and bound before a local magistrate, who committed Wine to Newgate prison. Wine was later convicted for the crime at the London sessions in September 1682. Roger L'Estrange ridiculed "Kidd the constable" in print and found his local office hard to reconcile with Kidd's notorious nonconformity.[36] Kidd too would face charges of his own two months later when he was accused of encouraging a brawl between his local watchmen and a regiment of the London-trained bands under the command of one Captain Bloomer. Peter Kidd's multiple roles as an Exchange Alley coffeehouse-keeper, a local constable, and a vehement friend to the cause of whig politics on the national level are instructive of the complicated place held by the coffeehouse in the social and political structures of English society after the Restoration. Although he was no friend to the court, Kidd was himself part of the "government" insofar as he held a recognizable place in his parish as a good neighbor, an honest businessman, and a local constable. It was this integration with the local structures of government, structures best conceived in terms of the "micro-politics of the parish" or even as an "unacknowledged republic" within the monarchical state, that allowed the coffeehouses to survive and flourish.[37] High political maneuvers designed to check the flourishing of coffeehouse politics were themselves countered by resistance from the micropolitical structures of local society of which the coffeehouses had become a part.

The climate of universal suspicion of popish and/or dissenting plots, along with the uncertainty of the direction in which the winds of politics were blowing in the early 1680s, had an effect on popular discourse in the coffeehouses. For the politically astute, circumspection became the order of the day. The dissenting London milliner Benjamin Clarke warned his friends to forbear discussion of matters of state in coffeehouses. Despite his professed caution, Clarke found himself under suspicion of spreading rumors of a design afoot to set up a popish and arbitrary government. When confronted with coffeehouse talk that turned to regicide, the ship's porter George Drake left his company quickly, being as he claimed "afraid of such dangerous discourse." Casual conversation about politics could land one in a sea of confusion, suspicion, and even incarceration by local officers. In the course of a coffeehouse debate, one Mr. Beresford's mention of his wide-ranging experience overseas and his fluency in the Portuguese language, deployed as he thought "the better to run down his opponent," was construed by his fellows at the table as a confession of his being a Jesuit. He was summarily seized and taken to Bridewell and later transferred by a judge to Newgate prison, where he awaited trial at the next sessions.[38]

In this climate of fear, few could escape suspicion. Even the loyalty of the king's messengers, those royal agents of the crown who were often entrusted with the dirty work of apprehending suspects, could be doubted. Mr. Needham, a Lambeth curate, watched the activities in the coffeehouses around Charing Cross with interest and concluded that a number of messengers were friendly with leading dissenters, including the bookseller Francis Smith and local newswriters. If these messengers "are necessitous, poor men, and not paid," Needham concluded, "then I humbly conceave it rational to suspect that there may be some such amongst them as may be tempted by gifts and bribes to betray his majesties business to his adversaries."[39]

By the latter part of 1682 and coincident with the onset of a tory reaction against the remnants of a whig opposition, local magistrates renewed their vigilant oversight of coffeehouse society. Justice Dolbin instructed the grand jury of Middlesex to present any coffeehouses discovered with seditious pamphlets allowed on the premises. In the spring of 1683, a number of grand juries in the counties took care to present the unlicensed and seditious coffeehouses within their jurisdictions. Their complaints were the usual ones. County magistrates feared that their coffeehouses were "places where false and seditious news are uttered and spread abroad to delude and poyson the people," or that they tend to "gather disaffected persons together, who then intermeddle with state affairs, reflect on their superiors and debauch the affections and loyalty of liege people." With the purge of suspected whigs from local office now nearly complete, it was felt at court that the campaign to suppress the circulation of news, libels, and cheap print in the coffeehouses could be reinstated. Francis North, lord keeper Guildford, expressed this opinion in a meeting with the lord mayor, the recorder, and an assembled committee of loyal London aldermen later that summer.[40]

Despite rumors that the London court of aldermen had banned entirely the common practice of hawking pamphlets and newspapers in the City coffeehouses, the London courts actually prosecuted the hawkers on a case-by-case basis. The Stationers' Company had been arguing for years that more strenuous efforts needed to be made by both the Lord Mayor and the county magistrates to suppress the hawkers of unlicensed pamphlets. At the January 1684 London sessions at the Guildhall, a female pamphlet hawker who served the Amsterdam Coffeehouse was fined for selling libels there, an action which could hardly have prevented the continuing flow of seditious literature from this redoubtable center of opposition politics.[41] The jurors at the sessions also took care to register their disapproval of the "great resort of persons to taverns and coffie houses especially in time of divine service," and they admonished the local officers to do their duty in policing the public houses of the metropolis. Refrains of such displeasure were commonplace by this time: a few months earlier, lord keeper Guildford had admonished the London court of aldermen for failing to suppress the circulation of libels and pamphlets in the City's coffeehouses.[42]

The Jacobite Succession Crisis (1685–1702)

Unsurprisingly, King James II proved to be no greater a friend to the coffeehouses after he ascended to the throne than his elder brother had been. During the meeting of James's new Parliament, the fervently royalist ex-army officer Jacob Bury urged the House of Commons to pass a statute barring "unlawful assemblies, or meetings in coffee-houses," but the proposal went nowhere. Nevertheless, the king himself continued to make efforts to restrain the character of coffeehouse discourse. Soon after his accession, James declared his intent to reestablish a thorough system of licensing and regulation of the press, and the Stationers' Company remained vigilant in its attempts to prosecute hawkers who frequented London coffeehouses. The king finally issued a proclamation that forbade the hawkers of cheap print from plying their trade. James's reign was further marked by a number of royal proclamations issued to admonish against voicing criticism of the crown or spreading information that might be prejudicial to the royal interest, the code phrase for which was "false news." In November 1685, the lords justices of Ireland officially denounced those "persons who speak or publish false news or reports or intermeddle with affairs of State and those who shall use any bold or unlawful speeches of this nature, or be present at any coffee house, or other public or private meeting where such speeches are used, without revealing the same in due time." This chastisement was no more efficacious than any previous efforts, and within but a few months time the earl of Clarendon, now lord lieutenant of Ireland, wrote to secretary of state Sunderland to complain of the delivery into Ireland of coffeehouse newsletters from London, filled "most commonly [with] very foolish stories told, and for the most part lies."[43]

Complaints against and prosecutions of individual coffeehouses continued in James's reign. Batson's Coffeehouse in London was prosecuted for taking in and selling "seditious and factious" newsletters. An international incident was almost provoked by the coffeehouse tirades of one Dr. Conquest in early 1687. Conquest had apparently publicly expressed some "very undecent scurrillous and reflecting words" regarding Prince William and Princess Mary of Orange in a London coffeehouse. The Dutch ambassador took offense and made a formal complaint at court; it appears that King James was not responsive to such importunities when the target of the offending libel was his dubiously loyal son-in-law, so Conquest remained unpunished for his expressions. The new king's relative leniency toward dissenters even allowed some nonconformist coffeehouses to survive. James pardoned the anabaptist coffeehouse-keeper Jones in 1686.[44]

As James came to terms with the consequences of his decisions to alienate loyalists to the Church of England, the coffeehouses were abuzz with speculation about activities at court and abroad. In May 1688, James ordered that no coffeehouses or any other public house should receive a license unless the proprietor first paid a security that he or she would refrain from allowing unlicensed books or papers on the premises. Local constables were at the same time enjoined to search all coffeehouses for seditious papers or libels, but it seems that the royal will was not translated into official policy this time. Rumors of an impending Dutch invasion led by William of Orange continued to flourish in the later months of 1688, leading one newswriter to observe: "Though there never was more occasion of enquiry for busy impertinent people that gad about all day long for coffee and newes, yet never was less certainty of what passes in the world, most people [affect] to disguise the truth and there being at present about this Citty many engines that are made use of to spray what most suites the humor of some party." This circumstance clearly did not suit an already unstable situation, and in early October 1688 the king ordered that all coffeehouses refuse to take in any newspapers other than the official *London Gazette*. Lord Jeffreys, the new lord chancellor, appeared before the justices of the Westminster and Middlesex sessions and demanded that they vigorously prosecute anyone who dared to speak publicly of "state affairs."[45]

On 26 October, James issued yet another a proclamation lamenting that "men have assumed to themselves a liberty, not only in coffee houses, but in other places and meetings, both public and private, to censure and defame the proceedings of state, by speaking evill of things they understand not," and he enjoined all of his subjects to cease such discourses and to inform on those who persisted to their local magistrates. The proclamation was duly printed in several editions. Now here was a futile endeavor if there ever was one, and the real reason for the proclamation was given away the next week when James specifically forbade propaganda distributed by the Prince of Orange.[46] Similar proclamations were issued twice by the Scottish privy council in Edinburgh and four times by Lord Tyrconnel's council in Dublin. In mid-November, the official *London Gazette* began to work overtime, publishing three issues a week "for the preventing of false news and reports," but with William firmly ensconced on the mainland, it was much too late for counterpropaganda.[47] The increasing frequency of these royal commands and propaganda efforts mirrored the rapidity of the collapse of King James's political position in the final months of 1688. The coffeehouse politicians did not cause the king's departure from the realm, but they did manage to outlast him. The crown would pass from James to William and Mary in 1689, but these new monarchs too would face the problem of managing their fourth estate in the coffeehouses of their new kingdoms.

Indeed, William's Glorious Revolution did not do much to change the attitude of the English state toward its coffeehouses. William's regime was no less concerned than those of the previous Stuart kings had been to ensure that the coffeehouses in his new kingdom did not become centers for political activity or discourse that took aim at the new order. Just as had been the case in the exclusion crisis, the House of Commons refused to authorize the printing of its votes in the first months of 1689 for fear that the debates therein would be discussed freely in the coffeehouses of the kingdom. Sir Joseph Tredenham thought that the circulation of parliamentary votes in the coffeehouses was "a great crime," and he and others urged that efforts be made to punish the clerks who supplied the coffeehouses with this information. Such action was sporadic, however, and parliamentary proceedings were in fact made public knowledge through the city's coffeehouses. In October, the House of Commons sanctioned the printing of its votes but prevented newspapers from reporting the results. Parliament continued to insist on its right to prosecute anyone in breach of this privilege until the famous printers' case of 1771 effectively guaranteed the freedom of the press to report on parliamentary proceedings. In defense of this parliamentary privilege, the House of Commons did not balk from taking coffeehouse newsmongers to task. In February 1696, Jeremiah Stokes, the new keeper of Garraway's Coffeehouse, and his news supplier Griffith Card, were called before the Commons and reprimanded for allowing the dissemination of the votes and proceedings of the House on their premises. The coffeemen managed to avoid further fines through apologizing for their indiscretions along with a show of due regret for their infraction.[48]

The parliaments of King William's reign occasionally entertained proposals to restrain the spread of news throughout the kingdom. Some members suggested restricting the franking privileges of MPs, as letters (sometimes forged) from Parliament were a major source of news. Others wished to go further and institute a whole new licensing system for the publication of printed newspapers. These fears only increased after the lapse of the general press Licensing Act in 1695 and Parliament's subsequent failure to replace it with any effective new legal means of prepublication censorship. Within months after the end of licensing, three new triweekly newspapers began publication, the *Post Boy, Flying Post,* and *Post Man;* by the end of William's reign, at least fourteen new newspapers had made their appearance at the coffeetables of the realm.[49] The proliferation of this sort of news culture was clearly unsettling to many at the helm of the Williamite state, and within a year of the Licensing Act's lapse, a bill had been introduced in Parliament that would have banned the publication of all newspapers save the official *London Gazette.* Although the bill failed to make it past a second reading, the issue remained on the legislative agenda. After the whiggish paper the *Flying Post* ventured to print its speculations on the valuation of Exchequer Bills by the government, the occasion arose to bring forward another bill in the Commons to prevent the publication of news without a license. This bill too failed to pass, but John Salisbury, the printer of the *Flying Post,* was prosecuted personally by the House for publishing false news. Not long before Salisbury's prosecution, pressure had been put upon other newspaper publishers, such as Edward Lloyd, the proprietor of Lloyd's Coffeehouse and publisher of *Lloyd's News,* a newspaper mostly concerned with mercantile affairs but which had also occasioned the ire of Parliament through reporting on its proceedings. Lloyd gave up his newswriting enterprise in the face of official displeasure and the threat of prosecution, and the last issue of *Lloyd's News* was printed on 23 February 1697.[50]

Efforts to outlaw or license the newspaper press were supported by lobbying from the Stationers' Company and especially the printers of the official *London Gazette,* as they would have protected their publications from extra competition. The restraint of newspaper sales also coincided with the Stationers' longstanding efforts to outlaw hawkers of papers and pamphlets from door to door, who consistently undersold the established booksellers. In February 1701, the Commons appointed a committee to consider the state of the laws regarding the circulation of false news, but their efforts did not result in legislation.[51] None of these bills or proposals to outlaw or even license the newspaper press was successfully enacted into law by Parliament, perhaps because of their unsavory connections with the monopolistic trade practices advocated by the Stationers, and partly due to the inability of the Lords and Commons to agree on suitable legislation. Nevertheless, the parliaments of William III's reign viewed the emergence of an unregulated public opinion in the press and the coffeehouses of the realm uneasily. The three estates of King, Lords, and Commons in Parliament did not welcome the entry of a fourth estate called public opinion onto the political stage, even if they were ineffective in halting its influence. It is telling that the term "fourth estate" was not generally applied to the press or public opinion before the early nineteenth century, and when it was used, the phrase was derisively to refer to upstart organizations or interests within the body politic.[52]

The Glorious Revolution did not usher in a new era of freedom for coffee-house politics. The political elite remained as concerned as ever about the destabilizing effect that the flow of unrestrained, and often false if not trea-sonous, information might have on a state that was now at war and threatened by both foreign and domestic enemies. What had changed after the revolution was a clear recognition by both crown and Parliament that the coffeehouses were too well entrenched within English society to be eliminated entirely. Neither King William nor Queen Anne after him made any attempts to sup-press the coffeehouses of their kingdoms outright, although both of these post-revolutionary regimes remained wary of the coffeehouses' potential to harbor seditious activity or to allow for the unrestrained venting of political senti-ments opposed to the current regime and its ministers.

Nothing was more menacing to the Williamite regime than the swift emer-gence of a Jacobite propaganda network after their accession to the throne; henceforth the new monarchs would be plagued by their own seditious libelers who made the metropolitan coffeehouses a primary venue for the venting of their disaffection. A network of Jacobite public houses developed in the 1690s that would persist well into the eighteenth century. Jacobite coffeehouses such as Ozinda's and Bromfield's were not clandestine operations: they were sur-prisingly well known and readily identified even by those who were loyal to the regime.[53] These Jacobite houses often served as the bases through which Jacobite political arguments were forged and disseminated throughout the metropolis and from there to the rest of the realm. The most common modus operandi for the Jacobite propagandists was a traditional combination of the surreptitious and the very public. Jacobite publicists would often disperse large numbers of libels to the streets and public houses of London in a clan-destine operation during the night so that the next morning would allow for the circulation of the papers while the authors and distributors remained comfortably anonymous. For maximum effect, the libels would be fixed to the doors of local magistrates or else sent via penny post directly to privy coun-cilors or members of Parliament.[54]

As a means of countering this threat, the new regime at Whitehall issued warrants to inspect coffeehouses where people disaffected to the new regime might "utter and maintain seditious words," and suspected Jacobites were arrested at the coffeehouses they were known to frequent. Some army officers who had served King James turned to keeping coffeehouses in their newfound retirement. Predictably, a careful watch was kept over those coffeehouses which might harbor potential discontent. In May 1689, a company of Dutch troops led by a royal messenger burst into a coffeehouse in Buckingham Court near Whitehall and arrested a suspect Irish man on the spot.[55] Servants of the crown did not refrain from searching the metropolitan coffeehouses for evidence of the circulation of Jacobite or opposition propaganda, and the keeper of a coffeehouse in which seditious works were found was liable to immediate arrest by a royal messenger. Parliament too undertook to investigate and prosecute reported cases of seditious discourse in the coffeehouses, one member declaring at the time that "people take great liberty in coffee-houses" and warned against showing a lack of resolve to punish such offenders. The justices of the peace and the lord mayor duly announced to the City of London in July 1689 that "many loose and disaffected persons by talking in coffeehouses and other places false newes and raising discourses against the government are a very great newsance and scandall to the same," a useful demonstration of their obedience to royal demands to be sure, but it was hardly effective in policing the behavior in the coffeehouses. Thus began what was to become a pattern of essentially futile complaints by the managers of the revolution settlement against the persistence of discontent with their government, opinions labeled by the regime as "false news," and exasperated attempts to goad local magistrates into doing something to stop the spread of this supposed false news.[56]

Foremost amongst the known opposition newswriters was the infamous John Dyer. Dyer followed in the footsteps of his Restoration-era predecessors by combining the occupations of coffeehouse-keeper and newswriter, and he managed to continue publishing manuscript newsletters well into the reign of Queen Anne. Based at his coffeehouse located on White Friars Street, Dyer began writing his manuscript newsletters with a strong high tory bias sometime prior to the Glorious Revolution, and for the next two decades he would remain a persistent thorn in the side of the new regime. Dyer's operation was a substantial one: he may have employed as many as fifty scribes to work for his news scriptorium and he was producing perhaps five hundred copies thrice weekly. His news circulated throughout the British Isles and on the European continent as well.[57]

Dyer seemed to take great pleasure in evading the numerous attempts by royal messengers of the press to apprehend him. As silencing Dyer through direct prosecution failed to stop his pen, alternative means of shutting him up were tried. Several coffeehouse-keepers who subscribed to Dyer's newsletter service were prosecuted at the Old Bailey sessions in September and again in October 1695. The prosecution in both cases was successful and on each occasion two of the coffeemen were fined. Later in the year Dyer himself was again apprehended, but he seems to have escaped once more and remained at large until April 1697, when he was taken once more into custody by the sergeant at arms for the House of Commons. Seemingly unperturbed by his travails, Dyer was yet again taken into custody in September 1699. Unfazed by this harassment, he continued to supply the coffeehouses with his newsletters during Queen Anne's reign despite continued attempts to suppress his news-writing generally and to prosecute him specifically. As late as 1716 — nearly twenty-eight years after Dyer began writing his newsletters and almost three years after the death of Dyer himself — Joseph Addison was still complaining that Dyer misled the public, especially those in the countryside. Dyer's readers, Addison thought, remained obstinately ignorant of the official news found in the printed newspapers since they still preferred to rely upon Dyer's handwrit-ten, and decidedly high tory, version of the news.[58] Dyer established a tradition of clandestine and opposition newsletter writing that survived his own death as well as the Hanoverian accession.

Despite these failures to silence opposition newswriters like John Dyer, the Williamite regime did not shirk from making other attempts to stamp out seditious discourse in the kingdom's coffeehouses. In March 1691, Queen Mary herself enjoined the lord mayor and the London City magistrates to discover and prosecute "several dangerous and disaffected persons to the Gov-ernment" who were said to "daily resort to coffeehouses within the City of London . . . on purpose to spread false and seditious reports." The crown took the initiative in policing the coffeehouses when it saw fit to do so. William's privy council took it upon themselves to exercise the royal prerogative to suppress Bromfield's Jacobite coffeehouse in Buckingham Court in 1689, and his secretaries of state remained vigilant in monitoring the diffusion of what they too regarded as "false and seditious news" in the coffeehouses. Secretary of state William Trumbull monitored reports of suspected Jacobitical activities at places like Bright's Coffeehouse in Bartholomew Lane, and he ordered searches of houses that were suspected of harboring plotters against the re-gime. Coffeehouse-keepers who were known to allow Jacobites on their prem-ises were prosecuted at the January 1693 quarter sessions. When the source of a false report that King William was dead in August 1695 was traced back to Pontack's posh London tavern, the proprietor was hauled before the lord mayor for chastisement. Not long afterward, a coffeeman named Spencely was also arrested and imprisoned for treasonous discourse against the king. He died in prison before he could be tried for his offenses.[59]

Individual convictions against people uttering "false news" in the course of coffeehouse conversation were rarer than the prosecution of the house-keepers themselves, but such prosecutions did take place, as one obstinate gentleman learned when he continued to insist in a City coffeehouse that the Turks had defeated the Imperial army in Hungary. Suspecting a Jacobite in their midst, his coffeehouse companions seized the man, who was asked to swear an oath of allegiance to the king and queen before a local magistrate. He refused and was fined the customary 40 shillings for the offense.

As rumors of a conspiracy to assassinate King William began to circulate in late 1695, and especially after the revelation of the real Fenwick plot to do so in February 1696, Jacobite coffeehouses were the first place to look for suspected conspirators. The privy council personally examined a group of ten suspects who were rounded up at a coffeehouse in Mitre Court on Fleet Street in March 1696, and the coffeehouse-keeper, a former captain in the former King James's army, was placed in the custody of a royal messenger. The widow of the Jacobite coffeeman Spencely was also arrested in connection with the assassination plot, and she was found to have a plethora of Jacobite propaganda on her premises.[60] In this climate of suspicion, public-house keepers were more eager to report on the suspicious discourse of their customers in order to avoid accusations being leveled against them of being soft on sedition. In July, the lords justices instructed local magistrates in Middlesex county to search all public houses for suspicious people, arms, and horses.[61] The Williamite settlement and the Protestant succession it entailed remained tenuous until the passage of the Act of Settlement, which secured the rights of the House of Hanover to the English throne in 1701, less than a year before the death of King William. In such a climate of dynastic instability, the coffeehouses of the realm remained suspect because their very presence provided a potential forum for the articulation of political dissent. As long as the range of the politically possible included a Jacobite reversal of the revolution settlement, the presence of the coffeehouses as a venue for the expression of the volatile and capricious opinions of the kingdom's fourth estate would remain a troubling prospect for those at the top who had staked their lives, their fortunes, and their careers on assuring that the revolution settlement would be a permanent one.

The Early Eighteenth-Century (1702–1720)

The accession of the Protestant and Stuart Queen Anne in March 1702 did not quell anxieties about the role of public opinion among the kingdom's political elite, but the early eighteenth-century state could afford a greater degree of complacency with regard to its coffeehouses than the more seriously embattled regimes of Charles II, James II, and William and Mary. Not long after her accession, Queen Anne issued a proclamation for "restraining the spreading false news, and printing and publishing of irreligious and seditious papers and libels," on 26 March 1702, but her declaration was not followed up with nearly the same prosecutory fervor against coffeehouse news mongering and propagandizing that had been characteristic of the 1690s. The House of Commons appointed a committee to consider how to suppress the circulation of libels and seditious works, but the best that they could come up with was a declaration against publishing any libels reflecting on parliamentary proceedings.[62]

Thomas Tenison, the archbishop of Canterbury, traced a rumor circulating in Croydon, Surrey, of the queen's death to its source in a London coffeehouse, but the matter was not deemed important enough to follow up. The grand jury at the City of London's quarter sessions continued to hear the old importunities to present those public houses that took in seditious libels, but there is little evidence that these harangues were taken to heart, as they had been previously. A few furtive attempts were made to silence the irrepressible John Dyer and other purveyors of "scandalous news," but not on the scale seen in the preceding decades. Even when occasional complaints were made to the earl of Nottingham, Anne's first secretary of state, of "so many Irish and Scotch colonels, majors, captains &c., all Papists, lately come over, [who] daily appear in herds in publique coffee-house[s] about Whitehall and St. James,' impudently bragging of their feats in France during the late war," very little effort was made by either the crown, Parliament, or local magistrates to suppress the coffeehouses or prosecute the suspected Jacobites that frequented them. The House of Commons did attempt to prosecute John Tutchin and the publishers of his rabidly whiggish *Observator* for misrepresenting the proceedings and votes of Parliament and presuming to distribute such false news in the London coffeehouses, but Tutchin's infractions did not inspire attempts to ban the publication of newspapers outright, as similar transgressions had in the 1690s. All that could be done at this point was to insist on the parliamentary privilege to be free of outside reports on its business. Tutchin was ultimately silenced not by government prosecution but by the hand of an assassin. He was murdered in September 1707, but his journal the *Observator* remained in print to press the case for staunch whig politics for another four and a half years.[63]

Of course, the news industry continued apace and newsletter writers continued to defy the law by supplying London coffeehouses with daily reports in manuscript of the proceedings of Parliament while it was in session. On the whole the practice was grudgingly tolerated, but the House of Lords began a serious investigation of the practice in February 1707 after one such newsletter misreported the details of a bill regarding church affairs. Five of the offenders — the newswriters William Rowley, John Creagh, Ephraim Allen, and another named Horton, along with the coffeeman William Bond — were brought into custody of the Lords, reprimanded on their knees before the bar of the House, fined, and finally discharged. This parliamentary scourging demonstrates the continued dangers that coffeehouse newsmongers faced in plying a trade of dubious legality. It certainly ruined the livelihood of William Bond, who lost the lease on his coffeehouse as a result of his imprisonment.[64] But the infrequency of such efforts also reveals the grudging acceptance that the coffeehouses had gained by this time. As long as they did not engage in sedition or irresponsible reporting, the coffeehouses were allowed to go about their business.

By the beginning of the eighteenth century, the English state had just about learned to live with the presence of the coffeehouse as a permanent fixture in the political landscape. Attacks on the coffeehouses per se were less frequent than they had been in the seventeenth century, and even the monitoring and prosecution of individual coffeehouses for seditious activities seems to have been much diminished, but acceptance of the social fact that the coffeehouse public was here to stay did not mean that the role of public opinion in shaping state policy was welcomed wholeheartedly by the policy makers. Robert Harley was perhaps the first head of state to attempt to actively manage, rather than to quell outright, the fourth estate during his ministry, but even Harley's tactics were designed to take the political bite out of public opinion. Harley's patronage and management of political propaganda during his ministry is now well known thanks to the research of Alan Downie. Harley recruited talented writers such as Daniel Defoe, whose periodical *Review* (1704–13) became the editorial voice of the government to its coffeehouse public, as well as Jonathan Swift, principal writer of the tory journal the *Examiner* (1710–14, first series). Despite this patronage of the newspaper press, the ministerial appeal to public opinion was a purely pragmatic one, and Harley's *Review* made a point of consistently criticizing the errors and excesses of fellow newswriters. It even went so far as to call for the suppression of all newspapers on several occasions. "Whether it be *Review, Rehearsal,* [or] *Observator,*" it was thought far better to "let the Parliament put limits to the pen, determine both what is fit to be wrote, and who is fit to write it."[65] With regard to the management of the kingdom's coffeehouses, Harley's agents in the secretary of state's office began to use their franking privileges to supply the London coffeehouses with newspapers approved by the government at a competitive rate. In the provinces, government agents like Defoe were hired to oversee the distribution of ministerial propaganda on circuit tours of the country, with key stops made at provincial coffeehouses. Defoe's visits to provincial coffeehouses allowed him not only to promote government policy but also to take in information about the sources of potential discontent. He noted from Newcastle that the Amsterdam and Hamlin's coffeehouses in London continued to serve as clearing grounds for the spread of "delusions" into the provinces, principally due to a number of dissenting ministers who dropped into those coffeehouses.[66]

Queen Anne's reign proved to be something more like a brief respite from official harassment rather than the beginning of a new age of laissez-faire for the coffeehouses of Great Britain. The unstable early years of George I's reign saw the return of longstanding anxieties about the place of the coffeehouses in the British body politic. The Hanoverian accession and the clear break with the hereditary right to succession that it entailed, along with the prospect of a resolutely whiggish regime to prop up the new king, raised the specter of serious Jacobite political resistance once more throughout the kingdom. The years following the crowing of George I in October 1714 saw a widespread and sustained pattern of political resistance to the new regime that ended only uncertainly with the military defeat of the Jacobite cause in November 1715.[67] In the face of widespread popular protest in England and outright armed rebellion in Scotland, it is unsurprising that the coffeehouses should once again come under scrutiny.

Many of the same tactics that had been used in the 1690s to police the opposition media were revived during the Hanoverian accession crisis. Both coffeehouse discourse and coffeehouse papers were carefully monitored for signs of sedition. When a Canterbury coffeewoman was caught voicing her discontent with the new regime in 1716, she soon found herself bound over and brought to London for interrogation and punishment, and the same happened again a year later to another woman who had kept a coffeehouse in Gravesend. Justices of the peace ordered the search of coffeehouses suspected of carrying suspect literature, such as Reverend Thomas Lewis's weekly journal the *Scourge*. The government began to put pressure on the revived tory periodical the *Examiner,* which began a new series in November 1714. Warrants were issued for the arrest of the publishers and the author of the paper, and by May 1715 the crackdown had reached the coffeehouses who supplied the *Examiner* to their customers. Along with the printed press, the government began to watch the revival of manuscript news circulation. Although John Dyer had died in September 1713, his place was soon filled by other opposition newswriters such as George Dormer. Dormer's manuscript letters carried on in Dyer's high tory vein, but in the political situation after the Hanoverian accession, they were seen as too dangerous to let pass without official scrutiny. Complaints were made to the postmasters, to members of

Parliament as well as to secretary of state Townshend about the seditious commentaries in Dormer's newsletters that circulated in the coffeehouses in the summer of 1715. By October 1715, Dormer had been arrested on suspicion of sedition and he was kept under careful watch.[68]

The newly ensconced Hanoverian state returned to the old policies of prosecution for spreading false news or for libel as a means of controlling their coffeehouse politicians. The treasury solicitor, Anthony Cracherode, recommended this choice of action in his confident October 1718 memoranda on the matter. He noted, "I don't doubt but that our journalists and other newswriters will quickly furnish us with matter for indictments, on which it will not be difficult to convict them." He was right. At the same time that Cracherode was writing his confident prediction, the opposition news publisher Nathaniel Mist was being examined on oath about his relationship with his newswriters. Mist would be constantly pursued for prosecution, as were his printers and booksellers. When he published a letter from "Sir Andrew Politick" (probably written by Daniel Defoe) in the 25 October 1718 issue of his *Weekly Journal* in which a strong criticism of government foreign policy was voiced, the government declared it to be treasonous and quickly moved for prosecution.[69] Mist and his business partners were investigated by royal messengers; his printing materials were temporarily seized; and Mist himself was apprehended at the Chapter Coffeehouse, his usual haunt. The *Weekly Journal* was presented as libelous at the next quarter sessions for Middlesex county as well as at the City of London's Old Bailey, but Mist was allowed to continue publishing his paper after making the appropriately deferential apologies and promising not to repeat the same mistake.[70]

The "Sir Andrew Politick" affair has been noticed primarily because the ensuing fracas blew Defoe's cover as a clandestine writer for Mist's *Weekly Journal,* but it also prompted the Stanhope/Sunderland regime into considering more draconian measures for cracking down on the spread of dissident opinion. A memorandum from then secretary of state Stanhope's office voiced concern over the damage that Mist's journal in particular was doing to the reputation of government among the "common people," and it offered an agenda for suppressing "newspapers of this nature." Along with prosecuting the authors, printers, and publishers of the paper for libel, it was suggested that the lord chamberlain should encourage the justices of the peace throughout the realm to prosecute all coffeehouses that accepted Mist's journal at quarter sessions. Furthermore, an intensive system of postpublication censorship of the press was proposed. Cracherode was suggested as a suitable person to be charged with reading all the newspapers of the kingdom as they came out and to immediately identify seditious issues so that action could be taken to swiftly search those coffeehouses or public houses, "particularly those where disaffected persons resort," so that the guilty parties could be caught, punished at sessions, and have their licenses revoked.

The Mist affair prompted further action against potential sources of opposition opinion. Warrants were issued for the arrest of other propagandists such as one Nye, a manuscript newswriter who supplied a Norwich coffeehouse, along with a London linen draper who also dealt in seditious libels and the keepers of non-juring meeting houses.[71] On the whole however, there was no wholesale scourging of the coffeehouses, nor was a new system of post-publication censorship put into place. Nevertheless, the ideas vetted in Lord Stanhope's office in the early years of the Hanoverian regime demonstrate the persistence of old habits of thought regarding the need to vigilantly police, and vigorously suppress if necessary, the expression of discontent in the public sphere. A regime that did not hesitate in passing the Riot Act (1715), in expanding the length of Parliaments from three to seven years through the Septennial Act (1716), and which wished to purge the universities as well as to fix the number of peers in the House of Lords was not one which can be called friendly to the free expression of public opinion. A politicized public sphere was no less welcome under the Hanoverian Whig ascendancy than it had been by the post-Restoration Stuart monarchs.

The desire to effect some sort of political regulation of the coffeehouses remained constant throughout the later seventeenth and earlier eighteenth centuries. This was not the prerogative of the crown alone: Parliament too showed its willingness to limit the spread of coffeehouse news as well as to punish individual offenders. In all cases, the effectiveness of this policing of the coffeehouses depended upon the willingness and the ability of local magistrates and officeholders to enforce the laws and instructions given to them by their superiors at court and in Parliament. Although local officers were not entirely ineffective in their efforts to regulate the coffeehouses, it proved impossible for them to entirely suppress the flow of news, rumor, and political propaganda.

A coffeehouse-centered fourth estate did develop as an increasingly powerful political force to be reckoned with, but its emergence was only grudgingly welcomed by the British body politic. Neither whigs nor tories were unqualified advocates of coffeehouse politics: Joseph Addison and Richard Steele in the reign of Queen Anne were just as critical as Roger L'Estrange had been in the reigns of Charles II and James II of the dangers of irresponsible popular meddling in high political affairs of state. As we shall see in the next chapter, the Addisonian whigs adopted different strategies for controlling coffeehouse politics than L'Estrange and his high tory allies, but the concern over unrestrained public opinion was shared by all shades of the early modern political spectrum. The debate as to what was permissible fodder for coffee-house conversation continued to rage well into the eighteenth century. As late as 1779, Lord North continued to deride the rights of "the populace, the readers of news-papers and coffee-house readers," to have access to information about the costs of military expenditures in the American War. By the age of the American Revolution, however, points could be scored in parliamentary debate by defending the rights of "coffee-house readers" to be informed on matters of state on the grounds that the public at large paid the taxes that supported the state that North and King George III led into war in North America.[72] Few such arguments can be found in the early eighteenth century. The grandees and magistrates of the old regime in Britain during the century following the Restoration would have preferred to see the kingdom's coffee-houses fade away as a political force to be reckoned with, even if they had in fact become too firmly ensconced in the social, economic, and cultural fabric of urban life for such dreams to ever become reality.

Learning to Live with Coffeehouses

How then did the British state come to terms with the existence of a permanent and volatile "fourth estate" that the coffeehouses represented in the later seventeenth century? The answer suggested here has been that it had little choice but to accept the coffeehouse phenomenon. The normative ideal of an organic state and society in which the interests and the opinions of the government and its subjects were one collided uncomfortably with the practical reality of a lively and diverse clash of interests and opinions expressed in coffeehouse debates and coffeehouse media.

This is why one must carefully distinguish between norms and practices when evaluating the ways in which the political culture of post-Restoration Britain learned to live with coffeehouses and the public opinion that was vented within them.[73] The practice of coffeehouse politics established itself quickly, almost from the inception of the new coffeehouse institution in the 1650s and 1660s. The sense that this was a legitimate and acceptable state of affairs developed much more slowly. British sovereigns, parliaments, and state servants were never comfortable with the emergence of coffeehouse politics, hence the repeated attempts by various parties detailed in this chapter to prevent royal subjects from using the coffeehouses as venues for political expression. The centralized power of the monarchy could cajole and command its subjects to behave themselves properly in the coffeehouses, but the strict enforcement of these orders was impossible without the complete cooperation of the press messengers, the parish officers, ward beadles, county magistrates, and city authorities that comprised the overlapping structures of government in early modern Britain. Cooperation there was — a defense of the right to speak "seditious libel" or to utter "false news" was not forthcoming from even the most tolerant of subjects — but it was fitful and hardly reliable in the last instance.

This was because the divisive politics of the period between the Restoration and the accession of George I made it increasingly difficult to reach an agreement as to who truly constituted a good subject of the realm, let alone what sort of discourse qualified as "libel" or "false news." The proclamations of Charles II and James II adhered to a tough line in which any political discourse in the coffeehouses was de facto illegitimate. Many of those faced with the practical realities of enforcing proclamations or other regulations of this nature were much more lenient. The City of London magistrates who initially issued the coffeehouse licenses to dissenters such as Peter Kidd and John Thomas obviously thought that they were citizens worthy of receiving such licenses, even if the magistrates were forced to revoke them later under the pressure of tory reaction. In Kidd's case, we see how a coffeehouse-keeper could participate in local government by taking on the office of constable. At the national level, the secretary of state Joseph Williamson may have sympathized with the royal desire to suppress the coffeehouses, yet clerks working within his own office were supplying coffeehouse newswriters with valuable political information and Williamson himself had for a time attempted to set up his own newsletter service to compete with that offered by the likes of Henry Muddiman.[74] There were many such cracks and fissures within the structure of the post-Restoration state. The normative values of the crown could not easily be translated into the political practice of the king's subjects.

Perhaps it is no coincidence that the state gave up on trying to suppress coffeehouse discourse outright at nearly the same time that the Toleration Act (1689) made Protestant dissent a legal form of religious expression. In neither case did toleration entail acceptance — to be "tolerable" was hardly the same as being welcomed. Dissent, and its hypocritical doppelganger " 'occasional conformity,' " remained the bugbears that animated the party fervor of high church tories well into the eighteenth century. By the same token, the fear that the coffeehouses could harbor false news or seditious political beliefs did not abate even after their existence was quite clearly necessary to the daily lives of most city dwellers. Both urban coffeehouses and dissenting conventicles tore apart at the mythic ideal of an inherent and total uniformity within the political and religious life of the English people.

Those of a high church disposition were most inclined to find this state of affairs intolerably disturbing. They hated coffeehouse politics as much as they did religious dissent. Tory observers of the late seventeenth- and early eighteenth-century political scene often thought that the whigs "are generally the greatest coffee-house mongers," even if this was hardly the case in terms of social fact. The grand jury of Middlesex set forth the case against conventicles in a 1682 general presentment: "Wee present as our opinion that conventicles are destructive to the interest of this kingdome. They publish our divisions to princes abroad, and consequently the weakness of the kingdome, and will inevitably perpetuate the unhappy separation which is amongst us, which every good man must deplore, and every wise man ought to use his endeavour to reconcile; wee esteem it our duty in the station wee now are, to make an essay towards union a part of our service." This was precisely the same complaint that was lodged against the coffeehouses. In 1681, the tory journal *Heraclitus Ridens* complained to its readers: "Conventicle and coffee-house, what's matter, there's no great difference, but that the law allows one and not the other, 'twill be all one a hundred years hence, they are both full of noise and phanaticks." It is a testament to the endurance of these fears that the work was reprinted by the same publisher, Benjamin Tooke, in 1713 long after the Toleration Act, the securing of the Protestant succession, and the publication of Addison and Steele's *Tatler* and *Spectator* papers in which the coffeehouse was foregrounded as the primary locus for the forging of a new urbane, polite, and whig consensus in the English polity.[75]

Although the specter of a divided society never ceased to haunt the political imagination of eighteenth-century England, it did nevertheless learn to live with the presence of both conventicles and coffeehouses in its midst. By 1713, Daniel Defoe could write in jest about matters which had so severely vexed the courts of the later seventeenth-century monarchs: "As to handing treasonable papers about in coffee houses, every body knows it was the original of the very thing call'd a coffeehouse, and that it is the very profession of a coffee man to do so, and it seems hard to punish him by it. . . . It being then so natural, nay so essential to our coffeehouse-keepers, to gratify their customers with a secret out of the bar, a bit of treason by the by; and that it was so in the beginning, is now, and always will be so."[76]

One man's treason, it seems, was another man's harmless entertainment. Accepting the social fact that coffeehouses and conventicles were here to stay, however, was a far cry from welcoming the social, political, and religious diversity that these institutions embodied. Some members of the political nation may have joined with Defoe in accepting the vigor and the fury of the political debate engendered by the coffeehouses, but for many it remained a force to be feared rather than embraced.

8

Civilizing Society

Consider these two images of the coffeehouse (Figures 36 and 37). One is sober and serene, the other chaotic and conflict-ridden. In the first image, the coffeehouse is portrayed as a site for polite conversation, the cultivation of connoisseurship in the arts — note the pictures on the walls and the conversation that they seem to provoke among the coffeehouse patrons — as well as the quiet contemplation of the daily news or the latest political pamphlet. In the second print, we find a mob scene. This "coffeehouse mob" is situated in a very similar setting — note the recurrence of the pictures, the prints and newspapers, as well as the coffee-boy and the matron at the bar — but the patrons are engaged in anything but civil conversation. The first scene presents the coffeehouse as it was imagined it should be, with everything in its proper order, while the second presents a vision of a world in disarray. It might be imagined that the first image champions the coffeehouse as a venue for polite sociability and civil society while the second ridicules the coffeehouse as little better than an alehouse or a boisterous outdoor gathering of the "mobile."[1]

On closer inspection, however, the differences between the two images are not as great as they might seem. The positive force of the first portrayal of coffeehouse society is called into question by the presence on the walls of a paper declaring "Here is right lyes" along with others which bear the names of Grub Street writers, one of whom can be identified as Thomas D'Urfey (1653–

Figure 36. Anon., "Interior of a Coffeehouse" (c. 1700), inscribed in brown ink: "A.S. 1668" (believed to be false) (147 × 220 cm); British Museum, Department of Prints and Drawings (Anon. English, dated c. 1705), body color 1931–6–13–2], British Roy PIIIa. Courtesy of the British Museum, London.

Figure 37. Engraving in [Edward Ward], *Fourth Part of Vulgus Brittanicus: or, the British Hudibras* (London: James Woodward, 1710), BL 11631.d, (3.75 × 5.75 in.). Courtesy of the British Library, London.

1723), the author of numerous popular songs and poems in the late seventeenth and early eighteenth centuries. The implication here is that the interests of the coffeehouse patrons are neither as serious nor as admirable as they appear at first glance. Both images offer anxious moralizing about the potential dangers inherent in coffeehouse society. Each suggests in its own way that beneath the veneer of gentlemanly decorum which was supposed to characterize the coffeehouse world at its best lay an unseemly underside. The dangers in the first are the lies, unfounded rumors, and frivolous time-wasting that might pass for polite coffeehouse conversation. The dangers in the second are more obvious: that the pretense of coffeehouse civility might easily dissolve into mob violence. These fears of civil society gone awry continued to haunt understandings of the role of the coffeehouse in English society from its inception until well into the eighteenth century.

They were also well-founded fears. The coffeehouses were indeed a primary venue for the distribution of false rumors, seditious libels, and political organizing. The coffeehouse violence portrayed in the second print was not a figment of the imagination of a hostile propagandist. Coffeehouse disputes frequently turned violent, especially during moments of intense political crisis, such as occurred in the late 1670s and early 1680s, during the post-revolutionary 1690s, and again in the 1710s. In the course of a heated debate in the Amsterdam Coffeehouse in 1683, the whig provocateur Titus Oates was struck several times over the head with a cane by one of his opponents. Being wedged in too close to the table, Oates could not retaliate in kind, and so he responded by throwing his dish of hot coffee in the eyes of his assailant.[2] Violent clashes of this sort were all too familiar in late seventeenth- and early eighteenth-century coffeehouses.

As with most aspects of the early modern social order, anxieties over the propriety of coffeehouse behavior were gendered. We should note that all the patrons in both of these images of the coffeehouse are men, and this is how coffeehouse society was supposed to be imagined. It was not that women were prohibited from entering any coffeehouse: such hard and fast rules did not exist, nor was there any need for them. Women were a vital part of coffeehouse society, as the presence of the women behind the coffee bar in both pictures suggests. Nevertheless, the activities commonly associated with coffeehouse society—especially debate on political or learned topics, business transactions, and the like—were considered to be traditionally masculine activities or responsibilities. Hence, the supposedly "real" business of coffeehouse life was thought to be distinct from the activities of the women and servants who made it possible. Richard Steele set forth the masculine coffeehouse ideal in the opening lines of his essay in the *Spectator:* "It is very natural for man who is not turned for mirthful meetings of men, or assemblies of the fair sex, to delight in that sort of conversation which we find in coffee-houses."[3] Here the coffeehouse was promoted as a venue for male sociability that complemented, but was separated from, mixed-sex meetings with ladies or those less serious gatherings among men that took place in clubs or at alehouses or taverns.

We have been trained to accept the polite ideal of a civil masculine coffeehouse society championed by writers like Richard Steele and Joseph Addison because it has been often reiterated by twentieth-century theorists such as Jürgen Habermas and Richard Sennett, who have seen in the rise of the coffeehouse a model for the emergence of a new sort of public life, one in which rational argument rather than other factors such as social rank or political power determined the course of debate on matters of general importance.[4] Coffeehouse public opinion could be trusted because it was rational. But this image of the coffeehouse as a paradigm for the emergence of an "enlightened" civil society always had to struggle against the more critical fears of coffeehouse incivility depicted in the two images highlighted here.

This chapter explores the development of different ideals of proper behavior for both men and women in the coffeehouses of post-Restoration London as these ideals tried to tame some of the less savory realities of the coffeehouse social world. British "civil society" did not emerge automatically and fully mature out of the coffeehouse milieu; it had to be constructed ideologically as well as practically out of a culture in which great suspicion still remained toward public associations not sanctioned by the established church and state. When Addison and Steele strove to present the coffeehouse as an important forum for polite masculine society in the early eighteenth century, they did so in opposition to much more widespread fears that coffeehouse society was decidedly uncivil and impolite.[5] The civilizing of the coffeehouse was therefore a slow, and ultimately an incomplete, process: it proceeded only hesitantly and in the face of significant opposition all along the way.

Fops, Newsmongers, and Coffeehouse Politicians

The coffeehouse was commonly thought to be a male preserve in the century after its inception. The peculiar notion of a "women's coffeehouse" is the exception which proves the masculine coffeehouse rule. Exceptional instances in which women gathered together in a public setting to consume coffee and discuss "politics, scandal, philosophy, and other subjects" were occasionally described as examples of a "women's coffeehouse."[6] Had women been considered a familiar part of the usual coffeehouse milieu, there would have been little point in remarking upon the existence of a special coffeehouse for the ladies. But just because coffeehouses were seen as exclusively masculine sites does not mean that they remained unproblematic preserves of patriarchal power. Far from it: as a single-sex milieu firmly located in the forefront of masculine public life, the coffeehouse was the seat of a whole host of anxieties about the proper regulation of masculine behavior.

No one knew this better than Joseph Addison and Richard Steele. Their periodical papers, the *Tatler,* the *Spectator,* and the *Guardian,* used the coffeehouse as a sort of virtual stage on which they might expose the foibles and follies of masculine comportment in the public sphere. The papers were at once entertaining and didactic, and they were an instant success in the highly competitive English literary marketplace. While in periodical publication, the *Spectator* was selling at the remarkable number of three to four thousand copies per day. Addison's "modest computation" was that each paper was read by about twenty people. The periodical essays of Addison and Steele are well known as the champions for a new social ethic of politeness and for locating this ethic in the coffeehouse milieu of the early eighteenth century. For this reason, the *Spectator* papers and their ilk figure prominently in accounts of the emergence of a "bourgeois public sphere" and a "culture of politeness" in post-Restoration Britain.[7] It is less often recognized in these accounts that the moral essays of the *Spectator* and the like were engaged in a wide-ranging challenge to the improper behavior that they found in the coffeehouses of early eighteenth-century London.

What sort of coffeehouse behavior caused the most concern? One of the major targets of the *Tatler* and the *Spectator* papers was the effeminate male (Figure 38). "Effeminacy" was a particularly fluid term of abuse in early modern England used to criticize a variety of perceived masculine vices and inadequacies. It was not exclusively associated with homosexuality, as is often assumed. The stock type characters of the fop, the beau, the town gallant, and the excessively Frenchified *petit maître* were seen as the bane of the polite coffeehouse society by Addison and Steele. These characters were understood to be men who devoted too much attention to the presentation of the self, and especially to putatively trivial (and feminine) matters like fashion, exhibitionism, overdecorous ceremony, and the protocols of politeness. Such precise attention to manners and propriety was considered women's work, and the man who demonstrated these qualities invited the censure of his peers. Abel Boyer defined a beau as a man who "has all the folly, vanity, and levity of a woman."[8] Such was the paradox of the gendered division of polite labor in genteel society: women bore the burden of maintaining the standards of etiquette, and yet femininity was also blamed for the excesses of that labor.

Foppery, then, was the result of men importing female politeness into the masculine public sphere. It is somewhat disinguous, therefore, to say that the female private sphere is "where the important action takes place" in Enlightenment sociability, for this ignores the restrictions placed on female participation in masculine single-sex milieus such as the coffeehouse and inflates the importance of domestic politeness outside of this carefully policed restriction. Especially in Britain, the "important action" of Enlightenment sociability did not take place in the salons. The action took place in the coffeehouses.

Figure 38. The Compleat Beau: Engraving; *Essay in Defense of the Female Sex* (1696), BL 1081.e.15. Courtesy of the British Library.

Philip Carter has noted that "men's participation within the public sphere provided opportunities not only for confirming one's masculinity but also for exposing oneself to ridicule."[9] In the vicious and verbose world of Augustan literary production, such an opportunity to scoff at the follies of others was not readily forsaken by either the polite essayists or Grub Street hacks of lesser repute. Both printed pamphlets and manuscript libels derided the effeminacy of London's fops. The *Tatler* ordered the servants at St. James's Coffeehouse and White's Chocolate House to ensure that effeminate pretty fellows be

Figure 39. William Hogarth, "Beau of Button's Coffeehouse" (c. 1720), (London: W. Dickenson, 1 March 1786), based on an original drawing by William Hogarth (c. 1720) in the collection of Samuel Ireland, aquatint engraving (1786); British Museum, Department of Prints and Drawings, BM Sat. no. 1702. Courtesy of the British Museum, London.

barred from entering these bastions of polite public sociability. Bickerstaff's disdain for these effeminate coffeehouse patrons bears a striking resemblance to the ridicule heaped upon the "mollies," another group of urban social deviants defined more by their sexuality than by the fops' obsession with self-display. In a like manner, the *Female Tatler* encouraged the purging from polite society of "all effeminate fops," or those "impudent beau-Jews . . . who so far from being admitted into civil society, ought to be expell'd [from] the nation."[10] The fop and the beau are often cast as French or Jewish in their manners — the implication being that native English manliness is free from the vices of wealthy foreigners.

Yet it would have been nearly impossible to ban the fop from coffeehouse society, for the coffeehouse was thought to be part and parcel of the fop's social round (Figure 39). Abel Boyer's stereotypical Sir John Foppington made

White's Chocolate House his "stage," "where after a quarter of an hour's compliment to himself in the great glass, he faces about and salutes the company," among whom this beau takes his snuff with due affectation and begins to discourse on matters of fashion, diet, or his affairs with various French ladies. Sir John is also said to frequent Tom's Coffeehouse "to learn some piece of news" or Will's Coffeehouse "to gather some fragments of wit," but his purpose in doing so is far from edification, but only to collect more material for his idle banter.[11] While the fop was a habitué of coffeehouse society, his fault lay in using the coffeehouse as a stage for self-serving or frivolous ends rather than as a place to share the news of the day in good company and engage in sober discourse about it.

Of course a beau was seen only in the eyes of his beholder: no one would admit to being a fop. The word "fop" was a term of abuse that one hurled at one's enemies rather than a means of self-identification. Although the term had been used to connote foolishness for centuries, it gained a particular association with urban fashionability by the later seventeenth century. To Daniel Defoe, the terms fool, fop, and beau were all synonymous. Similar terms became current in the later seventeenth and early eighteenth centuries, such as the "pretty fellow," the "beau," or the "*petit maître.*" Many of these terms were taken from the French, partly because their effeminacy and their stereotypically excessive devotion to the vicissitudes of fashion were commonly understood to be the peculiar vices of a court society, and no court was more degenerate in this respect than Versailles.[12] Despite the attempts by Augustan moralists to view the fop as an identifiable "other" who might be excluded from polite society, the stereotype emerged out of these moralists' concerns that the coffeehouse world was not what it should be. Instead of a civil space for learned discussion on serious matters, it was feared that the coffeehouse had become a venue for cheap gossip and egotistic self promotion. To purge the coffeehouses of foppery therefore required that the patrons learn to distinguish between politeness and priggishness, between tastefulness and ostentation, and between really valid news and worthless gossip.

This was no easy task, for such judgments were always conditional and subject to negotiation, if not outright contestation. Were the fops unwelcome intruders into this hallowed ground of good taste? Or, more troublingly, were the dictators of good taste themselves perhaps prone to the excesses of foppery? This was the conclusion reached by the poet who claimed that Will's Coffeehouse "is cramm'd eternally with beaus," including not only its literary wits but even the proprietor Will Urwin himself. While Will's Coffeehouse was the most prominent target, primarily because of its fame as the center of post-Restoration London's literary life, the problem of foppery in polite society was hardly limited to that locale alone: it was a vice endemic to all coffeehouses that catered to an elite clientele.[13]

The danger posed by this threat was substantial, for if carried to an extreme, coffeehouse foppery was thought to lead to the even more serious vices of atheism, debauchery, and a general disrespect for all authority. Such a "town-wit" was a man with no restraint whatsoever: "His mind [is] used to whistle up and down in the levities of fancy, and effeminated by the childish toyings of a rampant imagination finds it self indisposed for all solid imployment, especially the serious exercises of piety and virtue." One of the greatest fears about metropolitan coffeehouse society was that when its relative openness to all comers was combined with the freedom of discourse found there, it would become a vital breeding ground for atheism. When he deigns to consider matters more profound than the best way of adjusting his cravat, or powdering his wig, the "town-beau" reveals himself to be as impious as he is shameless: "His religion . . . is pretended Hobbism, and he swears the *Leviathan* may supply all the leaves of Solomon, yet he never saw it in his life . . . however, the rattle of it at coffee-houses, has taught him to laugh at spirits, and maintain there are no angels but those in petticoats, and therefore he defies heaven."[14] This then was the true danger of coffeehouse foppery: if no restraint in manners was upheld, then the floodgates would be thrown open and society would soon be awash with vice.

The critical discourse of the coffeehouses in particular was thought to promote the spread of atheist thinking. Coffeehouses were forums for talk and debate as much as they were simple drinking houses, and this emphasis on free speech was feared to be the first step on the road to free thought. Among the coffeehouse wits, "atheism . . . is not now owned with a blush, but on the contrary, esteemed a piece of gallantry, and an effect of that extraordinary wit in which we pretend to excell our ancestors," lamented one tract. Atheism was also understood more generally to be a product of urban society, and the London metropolis in particular. In the city, so the argument went, men were freed from the traditional ways of thinking and could therefore contemplate what had been heretofore unthinkable — a world without God. Visitors to London were often shocked at the toleration for freethinking that seemed to prevail in the city. Thomas Hunt reported to Matthew Henry that he found "much of Atheisme . . . and great coldness in religion, among such a concourse of people as frequent this citty" of London. To Robert Boyle, London was "this libertine city." This view has been endorsed by Michael Hunter, one of the most prominent historians of early modern atheism, who sees the metropolitan "culture of 'wit,' an educated but not scholarly environment in which intellectual agility was at a premium," as the most fertile breeding ground for unbelief in late seventeenth-century England. Of course the defenders of wit were at pains to emphasize that skillful intelligence and urbane matters hardly made one an atheist, for in and of itself "wit is no ways scurrilous and pro-fane."[15] Whether or not atheism actually flourished in the free and easy chatter of London's coffeehouses is beside the point, however, for the widespread belief that it did is indicative of the intense anxieties raised by the combination of an urban setting, the valorization of wit, and the predominantly masculine society found in the coffeehouses.[16]

A unifying concern in the many critiques of male coffeehouse manners was a desire to tame what the authors saw as an excessive taste for novelty, "gallan-try, and fashion" that prevailed in the coffeehouses of early eighteenth-century London.[17] Such a thirst for novelty was thought to be not only unbecoming of a man, but also a depraved misuse of the public sphere. It was a violation of the restraint, the good taste, and the decorum that were construed to be proper behavior in coffeehouse society. The pursuit of new things simply for the sake of their being new was considered to be an irrational vice that must be tamed. The worst offender in this regard was the newsmonger, and his natural home was the coffeehouse.

Attacks on the inordinate appetite of the English public for news were a commonplace staple of seventeenth-century satire and they were deployed most readily by servants of the crown who had an interest in controlling the flow of information to the public outside the confines of the court. Roger L'Estrange set forth his reasons for tightly controlling the news in 1663, not long after his appointment as chief licenser of the press for the restored mon-archy. Even "supposing the press in order [and] the people in their right wits," he declared, "a Publick Mercury should never have my vote; because I think it makes the multitude too familiar with the actions, and counsels of their superi-ours, too pragmaticall and censorious, and gives them, not only an itch, but a kind of colourable right, and licence, to be meddling with the government." This was printed, paradoxically, in the first issue of his own licensed news-paper, the *Intelligencer* (1663–66) whose only purpose he thought was "to redeem the vulgar from their former mistakes, and delusions, and to preserve them from the like for the time to come." Such were the fears of the Restora-tion court and its most vehement defenders, and these royalists were the prime motivators behind the various attempts to suppress the kingdom's coffee-houses in the later seventeenth century.[18]

Although the demand for news was great and the publishers of post-Restoration England worked hard to supply that demand with a growing number of titles, especially when they could get away with such activities during the lapses of the Licensing Act from 1679–1685 and after 1695, periodical news publication faced a serious legitimation crisis in early modern England. As we have seen, the lapsing of the licensing act in 1695 was not universally welcomed and did not herald a new age of an English "free press," although it has sometimes appeared so in retrospect. Early eighteenth-century serial publications were associated with the ephemeral, satirical, deeply partisan, and highly unreliable news and propaganda products of the seventeenth-century civil war and Restoration crises of authority.[19] The periodical was a genre akin to the scandalous and disreputable libel, and periodical prose writers were highly suspect and controversial figures.

Sir Roger L'Estrange gambled away much of his already tenuous social credibility by embarking on newswriting ventures such as the *Intelligencer* and even more so through his fiercely polemic journal the *Observator* (1681–87), but L'Estrange evidently thought that the risk was worth taking in order to counter the threat to the Stuart monarchy posed by whig politics in the 1680s. By dedicating the *Observator* "to the ignorant, the seditious, or the schismaticall Reader," L'Estrange eschewed the usual decorum of dedicating a publication upward to a worthy patron and instead chose to remonstrate downward to "the multitude," a populist strategy that was only marginally justified by its avowed purpose of reproving faction, by which he mainly meant chastising whigs. Although the *Observator* successfully managed to shift the terms of political debate in the early 1680s decisively in favor of the tories, L'Estrange never gained much respect for his propagandistic efforts and even he had to face the prospect of official prosecution on several occasions. Like so many other periodical prose writers, L'Estrange denied that he was in fact engaged in publishing a newspaper. "How long has it been news . . . to reply upon libells?" he asked: "How long has it been news; when the honour, and authority of the crown, and of the church are openly attacqued and defam'd in printed libells, to defend the government in printed replies?"[20] L'Estrange complained to the secretary of state Leoline Jenkins that his loyalist efforts in publishing the *Observator* had gone unrecognized and largely unrewarded. "I have Cassandra's fate upon me, not to be believed when I speak truth, nor am I supported against villains in the most necessary services I can render," he lamented. He would later cease publication of the *Observator* by royal command in early 1687.[21]

High-flying royalists such as L'Estrange were not the only ones concerned with restraining the English taste for news. Daniel Defoe had made the criticism of news writing and newsmongering a staple of his writing for the periodical the *Review* (1704–13). Defoe claimed that his was not any ordinary newspaper or propaganda piece, rather he took it as his task to offer "needful rectifications" to the "absurdities and contradictions" often found in the periodical press. The *Spectator* project borrowed heavily from Defoe's innovations in the *Review*; Addison and Steele adapted the club motif from Defoe's "Scandalous Club" in his journal, and they also reiterated his criticism of the periodical news industry in their papers.[22] Together, Addison and Steele expressed some of the most important criticism of the news culture of early eighteenth-century England through their *Spectator* project.

Like L'Estrange and Defoe before them, Addison and Steele used the newspaper form to convey their disapproval for the practice of newsmongering. Once we recognize this apparent contradiction, it becomes difficult if not impossible to make any simple association between the seventeenth-century news revolution and the emergence of a Habermasian public sphere. In its ideal form, the public sphere envisioned by the Spectatorial periodical essay was a carefully policed forum for urbane but not risqué conversation, for moral reflection rather than obsession with the news of the day or the latest fashions, and for temperate agreement on affairs of state rather than heated political debate. In other words, it was not envisioned as an open forum for competitive debate between ideologies and interests, but rather as a medium whereby a stable sociopolitical consensus could be enforced through making partisan political debate appear socially unacceptable in public spaces such as coffeehouses or in media like periodical newspapers.

For the new whigs such as Addison and Steele, just as much as for old tories like L'Estrange, coffeehouse discourse was best when it was politically tranquil. All parties, both Whig and Tory, shared an aversion to widening popular participation in the political public sphere. Tim Harris's arguments on the recourse by the Restoration court to appeals for popular support as a last-ditch resort apply with equal validity for the partisan political culture of the early eighteenth century. The popular politics with which recent historians have been so enamored were extremely unpopular to the politicians of late seventeenth- and early eighteenth-century England. Despite the practical necessity of such appeals to popular support in a cutthroat world in which even the dynastic succession remained in doubt, the politicization of the public sphere remained a move which was only made in extremis. Tarring his whig and dissenting opponents with the brush of vulgar popularity was a propagandistic stratgegy that L'Estrange could not resist using at every opportunity. For their part, Addison and Steele deplored the intrusion of "the rabble of mankind, that crowd our streets, coffee-houses, feasts, and publick tables" into the debates on the state of the political nation.[23] The major difference between the whig moralists and the chief Restoration tory propagandist was that the *Spectator* project shifted the burden of responsibility for controlling the public sphere from the repressive vigilance of the servants of the state to the self awareness of the individual. The "politeness" espoused by Mr. Spectator was a social ethic in which the regulation of proper behavior, both through external shaming as well as internalized guilt, was as important as social "polish" or an urban lifestyle. Whig politeness was a form of policing just as stringent, and just as socially exclusive, as tory persecution.[24]

The *Tatler* and the *Spectator* took on the appearance and the publishing schedule of a newspaper, and they were read alongside newspapers at coffee-house tables throughout Britain, but these periodicals were not themselves newspapers. Although the *Tatler* included some traditional "news" items in its pages when it began publication, such content gradually diminished over time, and it was entirely absent from the *Spectator* project. Addison proudly announced that "my paper has not a single word of news, a reflection in politicks, nor a stroke of party." Addison and Steele deemed traditional news to be either too controversial (i.e., factional) or too trivial, and they became increasingly critical of both its producers and its consumers in their writings. They understood that the periodicity of a newspaper created a constant expectation among the reading public that something "newsworthy" would occur on a regular basis.[25] Thus they claimed that the newswriter was bound to become the greatest advocate of continuing the war against France, because war stories filled copy and sold papers. Without a war, the newswriters would be forced to invent stories, as Steele claimed happened during the (relatively pacific) reign of Charles II, when one "could not furnish out a single paper of news, without lighting up a comet in Germany, or a fire in Moscow, [and] . . . prodigies were grown so familiar that they had lost their name." Even worse, Steele's Bickerstaff maintained, the style of the newswriters was so confusing and the reliability of their reports so tenuous that their writings "seize the noddles of such as were not born to have thoughts of their own." The consequences of reading such ill-mannered prose was severe: "The tautology, the contradictions, the doubts, and wants of confirmations, are what keep up imaginary entertainments in empty heads, and produce neglect of their own affairs, poverty, and bankruptcy, in many of the shop-statesmen; but turn the imaginations of those of a little higher orb into deliriums of dissatisfaction, which is seen in a continual fret upon all that touches their brains." In contrast, if newsreaders were fed with the right sort of edifying information — the kind that might "daily instil into them . . . sound and wholesome sentiments" — the vulgar public might be spared the confusion and the despair that ensued from reading the news offered by Grub Street hacks. News readers were therefore "the blanks of society," truly tabulae rasae, who could be altered for good or for ill by the kinds of works they read.[26]

Those who read the wrong papers were prone to become "newsmongers." Addison and Steele often caricatured the newsmonger as a man who had an inordinate interest in the affairs of other countries, and especially their matters of state. Richard Steele devoted several issues of his *Tatler* to the story of an upholsterer, known as "the greatest newsmonger in our quarter," who drove his business into bankruptcy and his family into poverty as a result of his chasing after news rather than attending to his affairs. Steele concludes by stating that he intended the story "for the particular benefit of those worthy citizens who spend more time in a coffeehouse than in their shops, and whose thoughts are so taken up with the affairs of the Allies [in the War of the Spanish Succession], that they forget their customers."27

The upholsterer's news obsession was presented as a particularly English, and even more so a tory, vice. Steele's Bickerstaff drew a parallel between the upholsterer's political fantasies and the chivalric delusions of Cervantes's Don Quixote. "The newspapers of this island are as pernicious to weak heads in England as ever books of chivalry to Spain," he declared. Although the upholsterer's chastisement is supposed to be aimed at the vices to which all Englishmen are prone, he is nevertheless clearly identified as a tory sympathizer: his favorite journals include tory publications such as the *Post Boy,* the *Moderator,* and the *Examiner;* among the whig papers, only Jacques de Fonvive's *Post-Man* caught his eye. In other papers, Bickerstaff and Mr. Spectator ridicule those readers who trust the veracity of John Dyer's high tory manuscript newsletters. Like Quixote, English Tories such as the upholsterer or Sir Roger de Coverley are consistently portrayed by Addison and Steele as hopelessly out-of-date, romantic daydreamers who may be enjoyed for the quaint humor, the warm companionship and entertainment their company provides, but they are also clearly marked out as unsuitable for serious political responsibility.28 It is another testament to the success of the *Spectator* project that the quixotic Tories such as de Coverley and the upholsterer became some of the most popular characters introduced in the papers.

Criticism of popular newsmongering had of course been the mainstay of Restoration-era complaints against the rise of the coffeehouses. Samuel Butler's Theophrastan characters included the "intelligencer" who "frequents clubs and coffee-houses [as] markets of news," along with a "newsmonger" who is "a retailer of rumour," and the "coffee-man" who attracts his customers primarily through allowing them to read and share the news. His caricatures were part of a commonplace satire of the late seventeenth-century coffeehouse news industry. These satires did not abate in the eighteenth century. Daniel Defoe cited approvingly Steele's story of the upholsterer and went on to advise the aspirant tradesman that "state news and politics . . . is none of

Figure 40. "The Blacksmith lets his iron grow cold attending to the taylor's news" (1772), line engraving, BM Sat. 5074; LWL, 772.6.0.2. Courtesy of the Lewis Walpole Library, Yale University.

his business." Letters to the "political upholsterer" became a regular feature in the whiggish newspaper the *Daily Courant* (1702–35) and graphic satires of tradesmen involved in news and public affairs to the detriment of their own business continued to be produced (Figure 40). Addison and Steele even invented a neologism for their newsmongering bête noire: a "quidnunc," from the Latin for "What now?" or "What's the news?" The name seems to have struck a chord with their readers, for the term remained in common currency well into the nineteenth century (Figure 41).[29]

Figure 41. "Quid nunc, or the upholsterer shaving" (1771), engraving, LWL 771.12.0.5. Courtesy of the Lewis Walpole Library, Yale University. The figure of Spectatorial satire, the political upholsterer is also derided as a "Quid nunc" in this print.

Aside from the waste of time involved in chasing after the inconsequential trivia of news, this sort of mania for information was also seen as suspect because it contributed to the degradation of the quality of coffeehouse discourse itself. This was the purpose behind the Spectatorial reform of coffeehouse society. To call a piece of news "coffeehouse discourse" in post-Restoration Britain was instantly to diminish its value and its trustworthiness, for it was equated with gossip, or mere rumor. Jonathan Swift protested that "it is a great deal below me to spread coffeehouse reports" and often declared that he did not bother to go to coffeehouses because they were unreliable gossip centers. Henry Compton, bishop of London, also claimed that he never went to coffeehouses nor "credited any news that came from them." Sir Leoline Jenkins, secretary of state for Charles II, thought it unwise to "measure the temper of the nation by the humour of our coffee houses," for he believed that "the bulke of the nation is not so injust, nor so ill natured," as the opinionated men who dominated coffeehouse conversations.[30] The purveyor of such rumors, the "coffeehouse statesman," or the "coffeehouse politician" was another stock figure of ridicule. And much like the newsmonger, he was seen as an inept commentator on affairs, more interested in self display than in making any substantial contribution to the formation of public opinion. He was an amateur, a veritable armchair critic who knew little of the real stakes involved in public affairs, and yet was always eager to offer his ill considered advice on those matters. A Restoration-era satire complained that "there's no man comes ... [to a coffeehouse], but he's a great master in state affairs, and can *ex tempore* dictate any thing (as he thinks) worthy to be acted by a council, or Parliament." The trope was taken up by Addison and Steele in their moral essays and the coffeehouse politician remained a stock figure of ridicule and remained so for more than a century afterward. In the Regency era, William Hazlitt could still find a receptive audience for a critical essay on coffeehouse politicians in his *Table Talk* (1821–22).[31]

In this respect, then, the irresponsible chatter of masculine coffeehouse politicians was hardly distinguishable from women's domestic gossiping. Such comparisons had been a standard trope in the satirical literature on coffeehouse conversation almost as soon as it became a phenomenon of note in Restoration London. A 1667 broadside proclaimed in doggerel verse that at the coffeehouse, "Here men do talk of everything, / With large and liberal lungs, / Like women at a gossiping." Another feared that "men by visiting these Stygian tap-houses [coffeehouses] will usurp upon [women's] prerogative of tatling, and soon learn to excel us in talkativeness: a quality wherein our sex has ever claimed preheminence."[32] These were precisely the sort of analogies that Addison and Steele sought to rob of their aptness through their efforts to purge coffeehouse conversation of its triviality, its unreliability, and thus, its effeminacy. Steele's *Tatler* claimed to have taken its title "in honour of" the fair sex, but its real intent was to reform the practice of discourse itself, to turn idle tattling into polite conversation. Daniel Defoe was less sanguine about the prospects for the perceived Spectatorial reform of coffeehouse discourse. "The tea-table among the ladies, and the coffeehouse among the men," he declared "seem to be places of new invention for a depravation of our manners and morals, places devoted to scandal, and where the characters of all kinds of persons and professions are handled in the most merciless manner, where reproach triumphs, and we seem to give ourselves a loose to fall upon one another in the most unchristian and unfriendly manner in the world."[33] In other words, there was still little difference between women's private gossip and men's public discourse.

It should not be thought that gossip and newsmongering were the only targets of the Spectatorial critique of coffeehouse talk. Addison and Steele also took aim at anyone whose conversation did not measure up to their standards of discursive decorum, the general rule of which was "That men should not talk to please themselves, but those that hear them." Thus their satires hit hard at all sorts of time-wasting coffeehouse orators, such as loquacious bores, boasters, projectors, pedants, sardonic laughers, over-zealous gesticulators, and even singers and whistlers. Steele's Isaac Bickerstaff called for "the utter extirpation of these [offending] orators and story-tellers, which I look upon as very great pests of society." Bickerstaff's pronouncement here was not intended to be universally applied; he offered a specific dispensation from the rule to the "fair sex," thereby further reinforcing the distinction between regulated, serious male discourse and feminine chatter, the regulation of which was a hopelessly lost cause to the censorious Isaac Bickerstaff. But it was crucial that masculine coffeehouse society be made safe for worthy conversation. The consequences of "the long and tedious harangues and dissertations which [the superficial coffeehouse statesmen] daily utter in private circles" were similar to those that Bickerstaff had claimed were also caused by newsmongering: "the breaking of many honest tradesmen, the seducing of several eminent citizens, the making of numberless malecontents, and . . . the great detriment and disquiet of Her Majesty's Subjects."[34]

The reformation of coffeehouse manners was a serious matter for Augustan moralists such as Addison and Steele because it cut to the heart of the social order that they envisioned for their new Britain. Coffeehouses were theoretically open to all subjects regardless of class or merit, and they were the prime sites for the activities upon which a prosperous urban and open society depended to flourish: political discourse, mercantile business, and cultural criticism. Women had little place in this scheme of things. Indeed several issues of the *Spectator* were devoted to the particular problems posed by the presence of women in the coffeehouses, mostly as servants or as proprietors. Such women were prone to become "idols," or the recipients of undue if not immodest attention from the men who patronized the coffeehouses in which these women worked. One letter to the paper complained that "these idols sit and received all day long the adoration of the youth . . . I know, in particular, goods are not entered as they ought to be at the Custom-House, nor law-reports perused at the Temple, by reason of one beauty who detains the young merchants too long near Change, and another fair one, who keeps students at her house when they should be at study."[35] Such was the danger of mixed company in the world of the coffeehouse. Even when their ostensible purpose there was only to serve the men, women were distractions from the serious business of masculine employments.

Even worse, thought the critics of coffeehouse society, the status of women workers in the coffeehouses as women located in (but not full participants of) the public sphere meant that they often had to endure the unwanted attention and suggestions of their patrons. One female coffeehouse-keeper complained to the *Spectator* in a letter that she "cannot help hearing the improper discourses [my customers] are pleased to entertain me with. They strive who shall say the most immodest things in my hearing: At the same time half a dozen of them loll at the bar staring just in my face, ready to interpret my looks and gestures, according to their own imaginations." It was difficult to conceive of a role for women in the ideal coffeehouse society that did not fit into the existing stereotypes of either the virtuous servant or the vicious prostitute. But what is even more interesting in the *Spectator*'s accounts of female coffeehouse workers is that the object of reform was not the women, but the men. It was the men who wasted their time doting on "idols" at the coffee-bar or who made lewd and improper suggestions to the coffee-woman who served them. Addison and Steele did not suggest that respectable women should not keep coffeehouses — indeed, they emphatically endorsed the suggestion that "it is possible a woman may be modest, and yet keep a publick house" — but they thought it necessary that male behavior in the coffeehouses be self-controlled.[36] The coffeehouse was a key site of masculine social discipline.

It is important to recognize that all of these anxieties about coffeehouse masculinity were voiced not only by the declared enemies of coffeehouse society but also by its own patrons. The wits of Will's Coffeehouse and their successors, Addison and Steele, who held court at Button's Coffeehouse, were all particularly concerned to police the boundaries of propriety in the coffeehouses because those locales were precisely the setting in which the leaders of the political, mercantile, and cultural orders of British society socialized (Figure 42). To a large extent, their criticisms of the fops, the beaus, the wits, the newsmongers, the politicians and even the simple bores of coffeehouse society were directed against themselves and their fellows. Foppery was a vice to which anyone was potentially prone, even a Joseph Addison or a Richard

Figure 42. Bernard Picart, "Les Free-Masons," engraving (1734), in *Religious Ceremonies and Customs of the Several Nations of the Known World*, 7 vols. (London: Nicholas Prevost, 1731–1739), Beinecke 1997 Folio 123, Plate 11, facing 6:203. Courtesy of the Beinecke Rare Book and Manuscript Library, Yale University. A portrait of Richard Steele is here placed at the center of a coffeehouse world in which the lodges of early British freemasonry flourished.

Steele, and thus they saw it as the particular duty of their new urban moralism to bring an awareness of these masculine failings to the attention of their readers.[37]

If the objects of the reform of male coffeehouse manners were clear, what then did the ideal coffeehouse society look like? Again, Addison and Steele provided the template in the *Spectator;* their essay in issue 49 represents the coffeehouse as "the place of rendezvous to all that live near it, who are thus turned to relish calm and ordinary life." The most judicious use of the coffeehouse, Steele claims, is by those "men who have business or good sense in their faces, and come to the coffeehouse either to transact affairs or enjoy conversation." These are men whose "entertainments are derived rather from Reason than Imagination," and their natural leader is a character Steele dubs "Eubulus," a wealthy but not ostentatious man who serves his fellows in "the office of a Council, a Judge, an Executor, and a Friend to all his Acquaintance, not only without the profits which attend such offices, but also without the deference and homage which are usually paid to them." Perhaps it is here in the idealized mental world of Richard Steele that we find Habermas's sober, rational, public sphere of private men coming together to exercise their reason in public. But it was difficult to find this ideal public sphere in the real coffeehouses of London.

Herein, then, lay much of the import and the urgency of Addison's claim that his Mr. Spectator desired to be known as the one who "brought philosophy out of closets and libraries, schools and colleges, to dwell in clubs and assemblies, at tea-tables, and in coffee-houses."[38] In other words, he wanted to make the coffeehouses and such places safe for philosophy, and to do so required that they be purged of the vice, disorder, and folly that Mr. Spectator so often observed within them. Much the same could be said of course of the tea table, that stereotypical breeding ground for "scandal" spread by female gossips (Figure 43).[39] These were not entirely the same sort of spaces, however: the coffeehouse was a male preserve and was clearly demarcated as a "public" house, while the tea table was seen as a space presided over by women, and was properly located within the "private" domestic household. Addison may have claimed that the *Spectator*'s appeal was universal, but this does not mean that he considered all of the spaces in which the journals should be received were equivalent. Addison and Steele understood far more than Habermas or his admirers that the practical public sphere of early eighteenth-century England was such a complex and variegated entity that it often defied the attempts of even its champions to describe it, let alone to discipline it.

No Place for a Lady: Women and the Coffeehouse Milieu

Despite the masculinist tenor with which coffeehouse society was infused, women were still important and vital participants in the functioning of the coffeehouses, even if their contributions were belittled by contemporaries. Could women participate in the newsmongering, the politicking, and the learned discussions that were taken to be the mainstay of masculine coffeehouse sociability? In theory, there is no reason why any woman who found her way into a coffeehouse could not have joined the conversations there, but in practice there is no evidence of any woman actually taking part in a coffeehouse debate. Understanding this absence requires that we take into consideration the distinctions of class and status as well as gender, for it was the women of England's social elite who were most significantly absent from coffeehouse society. The coffeehouses of London were simply no place for a lady who wished to preserve her respectability.

Figure 43. "The Tea Table" (c. 1710), engraving; LWL, Print 766.0.37. Courtesy of the Lewis Walpole Library, Yale University.

This is not to say that one cannot find any evidence of gentlewomen ever going to a coffeehouse, but the exceptions prove the rule. First and foremost, the cases are few and far between. Even the most indefatigable proponents of the openness of coffeehouses to genteel women have been able to uncover only a handful of references. Thomas Bellingham noted in his diary that one evening's socialization in Preston included meeting "with severall women att ye coffee house . . . and came home very late."[40] Was this a normal occasion? It seems unlikely: there is only one such reference in Bellingham's diary, and it is worth remembering that the locale was a Preston coffeehouse, a place far removed from the metropolitan ideal set by the numerous coffeehouses of London. It is also unclear who these women were: they may well have been the relatives or servants of the coffeehouse-keeper. In early eighteenth-century London, we learn from Jonathan Swift that "a gentlewoman from Lady Giffard's house," whom he supposed to be the mother of Esther Johnson, his beloved "Stella," "had been at the coffee house to inquire for" Mrs. Rebecca Dingley. Should we take this as evidence that gentlewomen regularly whiled away the hours in the coffeehouses and made them their haunts in the same way that Dryden turned Will's Coffeehouse into his second home? If so, it is surprising that there are no other references to Dingley's coffeehousing in Swift's voluminous correspondence with Stella or anyone else in his circle. Indeed there are few such references in any later Stuart sources.[41]

Some exceptional women may have moved with relative ease in the company of the coffeehouse, especially when they had specific business to attend to. Hester Pinney, as a successful single woman in the lace business, seems to have had no difficulties dealing with the stockjobbers at Garraway's and Jonathan's coffeehouses when she had to attend to business related to her investments in the South Sea Company and other joint-stock ventures, or to maintain her contacts with West India merchants. But there could have been few single women as successful as Pinney, for, as Richard Grassby notes, "spinsters exercising a trade or craft were the exception in propertied society."[42]

There are some special occasions when gentlewomen found acceptance as a part of coffeehouse society. The coffeehouses of Bath and Tunbridge, those famous watering holes for the social elite, served both men and women especially when they doubled as gambling houses. But Bath was not London. Furthermore, as favored locales for rest, recreation, and match-making, Bath and Tunbridge were particularly open to female sociability in ways that did not resemble the more businesslike social scene in the London coffeehouses. Another way in which the coffeehouses at Bath differed from those in London was that they strove to offer a haven from the partisan divisions and conflicts that were common in metropolitan coffeehouses. These coffeehouses were more like the "coffee-rooms" that might be found at an eighteenth-century opera house: both were mixed-sex variants on a single-sex template set by the male coffeehouse world of London. They adapted the cachet of sobriety and politeness attached to the male coffeehouses and translated it into a social milieu more characterized by leisure than by business. A similar sort of suspension of the usual gendered proprieties seems to have obtained in Paris during the fairs of St. Germain and St. Laurence, when French ladies would often frequent the cafés.[43]

Another important exception is the case of the auction, particularly sales of artworks. Coffeehouse auctions welcomed ladies as customers at their sales and auctioneers went out of their way to encourage women to feel comfortable during the course of a coffeehouse sale. Edward Millington offered separate accommodations for his prospective female purchasers when he conducted his sales at the Barbados Coffeehouse in Cornhill. But even here, where women were welcomed into a coffeehouse, a separate gallery for ladies was established, thus again reinforcing the sense that they were temporarily intruding upon a masculine preserve. The London auction "season" followed the movement of gentry families in and around the metropolis. Auctions were held "for the diversion and entertainment of the gentlemen, ladies, &c." in Epsom and Tunbridge Wells in the summer months, when much of the beau monde had migrated to drink the spa waters in these places. Presumably most women came to the auctions to purchase pictures fit for hanging in their houses, either in London or the country, although some were eager amateurs of the master painters as well. Lady Rutland, for example, was keen to acquire some of the best works from the 1682 auction of Sir Peter Lely's collection, although she commissioned a principal to do the actual bidding for her at auction. Many women may have attended the auctions not to make a purchase, but rather to acquaint themselves with the fundamentals of the art of painting and the social conventions of art appreciation by viewing the works for sale and by observing the tasteful purchases of other connoisseurs. This seems to be the case when Anna Larpent made her frequent "educational" visits to London art auctions in the later eighteenth century.[44]

Why were women not just permitted but actively invited into the coffeehouse world at auction time? An auction was a special event, a moment when the normal business of the coffeehouse was temporarily suspended or superseded by the more important business of conducting the sale. Women were especially welcome at auctions of fine art because they were acting in the service of their household. A lady who bid for a number of pictures at auction was presumably doing so in order to furnish her home with a judicious collection. Thus her intrusion into the normally masculine coffeehouse world could be justified as an exceptional occurrence that was necessary in order to further advance the prestige of her household.[45]

These important exceptions aside, we find abundant evidence that the rounds of urban genteel sociability were patterned differently for men as for women, although they were not mutually exclusive. An exemplary source of documentation for the different patterns of male and female urban elite sociability may be found in James Brydges's journal of his years in London from the beginning of 1697 to the end of the year 1702. Here Brydges meticulously recorded the patterns of his coffeehouse going, and although he often traveled around the town with his wife, it is remarkable that she never accompanied him to the coffeehouses he visited. On 1 October 1697, he noted that "my wife set me down at Tom's coffeehouse," while she went off on her own to make her own visits. When her visits were finished, Brydges's wife would return again to pick him up at the coffeehouse. Clearly, Mrs. Brydges saw the domestic visit as her particular social duty, while Mr. Brydges—a young gentleman on the make in London society—found his niche in the world of the coffeehouses.[46]

Entirely "separate spheres" for men and women did not exist in post-Restoration London, but neither was there one gender-neutral social world in which both men and women had an equal place. Perhaps it would be better to imagine two interlocking spheres of masculine and feminine activity, rather than two separate ones. Some putatively "public" activities, such as attending the theatre, shopping, going on walks, or visiting the pleasure gardens, were commonly engaged in by both men and women together, while others, such as club life and coffeehousing, remained a male preserve. Recognizing these differences might help to close the gap between the views of Kathleen Wilson, for whom "stridently gendered and exclusionary notions of political subjectivity . . . played central roles in consolidating oppositional categories of the domestic and public spheres," and those of Lawrence Klein, who emphasizes that "women were found in all sorts of places that . . . were public."[47] It is evident that Wilson and Klein are thinking of two sorts of public spheres, the former being the magisterial realm of state power and high politics and the latter being the world of commercialized leisure that developed independently of the state. In all of these cases in fact the degree of publicness (openness to all comers) and privateness (exclusivity) varied, and the principles of exclusion often varied along lines as diverse as class, status, political affiliation, regional identity, or ethnicity, as well as sex.

Just as it would be wrong to presume that gentlewomen had unfettered access to coffeehouse society, it would also be wrong to presume that all women were made to feel unwelcome in the coffeehouses. Women of a less exalted social status paradoxically found it much easier to enter a coffeehouse than their genteel sisters, not least because the majority of them were there to serve the male patrons.

Paula McDowell's study of female engagement with post-Restoration print culture has revealed much about the importance of women as hawkers of pamphlets and other forms of cheap print. It is unsurprising that these women often showed up in the London coffeehouses to sell their wares. McDowell takes pains to emphasize that these women were "anything but the passive distributors of *other* people's political ideas." Rather, they were powerful agents in shaping the modes and forms of political discourse of the time through their keen understanding of the tastes and desires for news and printed ephemera. The coffeehouse hawkers' local knowledge of their customers made its way back to the newswriters and Grub Street printers who produced the works sold.[48] This may have been the case, but these women hawkers can hardly be considered to have been full-fledged participants in the masculine public sphere to whose needs they catered. These poor and often illiterate women made their way into the coffeehouses, but were not considered to be a legitimate part of it. To be sure, McDowell is acutely aware of the limitations placed on these women by virtue of their class and their gender, and it was precisely these limitations that masked the work they performed in facilitating the flow of information in the coffeehouse milieu.

Most commonly, women were found in coffeehouses as the proprietors of these establishments: more than 20 percent of coffeehouse keepers who paid the poll taxes in 1692 and 1693 were women. These working women thus earned the title "coffee-woman." The term was not entirely an honorable one, however. Just as alewives were considered suspect figures because they opened up their homes in order to serve their customers, so were the coffee-women also open to charges that their business was not a licit one. The low social status of the coffeehouse-keeper only accentuated the coffee-woman's vulnerability to the solicitations of her customers, many of whom were of a higher social station than herself. The coffee-women Anne Rochford and Moll King were both subject to public satires in which their rise from a humble background to prosperous coffeehouse-keepers was tainted by the implication that they owed their success to prostitution rather than pure business acumen.[49] Despite their attempts to distinguish themselves from public houses that served alcohol, the coffeehouses fell prey to the same anxieties about urban immorality and disorder that plagued the taverns and alehouses.

During the 1690s, when such fears were seized upon and inflamed by the Societies for the Reformation of Manners, John Dunton published his discontent with the growing association between coffeehouses and the sins of bawdry. He thought

> That it is an horrid disgrace, considering the reproach that coffeehouses in by-places have now brought upon themselves, that any such should be suffered,

or at least that the numbers of them should not be regulated, it were becoming our magistrates to make an inquiry into these abuses, for what else can be thought to be the design of coffeehouses in such places, where most of the neighbourhood are men who work for their bread before they eat it, and where to be sure there is also an ale-house or two, of whose liquor labouring men have more need; such places serve only to ensnare apprentices and youngmen, who if they had not such temptations might perhaps never be debaucht. And it is also worthy the consideration of the magistrates, whether a young woman, or sometimes two together should be suffered to set up such houses, seeing 'tis highly reasonable to suspect they design rather to expose themselves to sale than their coffee. . . . This city is not without instances of coffee-womens having been debaucht, even in some of the best frequented and most populous places of the city, under their husbands noses, which demonstrates the inconveniency of exposing women at publick bars in this loose age, wherein few of 'em have so much virtue as to withstand the re-peated assaults which they must expect it so exposed, and therefore *its much more commendable to see none but men and boys in a coffeehouse*, except circumstances be such as can't admit of it.

Almost apologetically, Dunton added, "This is not designed as a satyr against all coffeehouses, nor yet against such as are kept by women of unspotted reputation, whereof there are diverse in and about the city; but certainly it must be allowed that being the weaker sex, they neither ought to expose themselves, nor to be exposed in such numbers by others to those abominable temptations."[50] Dunton's tirade reveals both the practical accessibility that working women had to coffeehouses as well as his intense anxieties about the propriety of such access.

Dunton's alarmist complaints may also be usefully read as a guide to the norms that were expected of coffeehouse society at the end of the seventeenth century. He notes that coffeehouses are not fit for areas of town inhabited by the laboring classes, who have more need of alehouses as a source of recreation and nourishment. Thus the only possible purpose a coffeehouse might have in such a neighborhood is as a front for a bawdy house. The coffeehouse was a fit place for gentlemen of leisure, Dunton suggests, but not for the lower classes, whose interests there must be licentious.

It is striking how often coffeehouse women are associated with prostitution by Dunton's contemporaries. Ned Ward's *London Spy* insinuated the women who frequent one widow's coffeehouse do so with the hope that "the lewdness of the Town" might bring "a cully [gullible person] in their way." The Swiss traveler to London, Cesar de Saussure, warned that many coffeehouses were but fronts for a brothel, in which, he advised, "you are waited on by beautiful, neat, well-dressed, and amiable, but very dangerous nymphs." Prostitution itself was understood at the time to be not just simply the exchange of sexual services for money, but rather part of a broader and more diffuse spectrum of sexual immorality. A "whore" was not necessarily a prostitute pure and simple, but a woman who was thought to have violated communal standards of sexual propriety. A sure-fire way of breaking these codes and thus gaining a reputation for immodesty was by frequenting public houses such as taverns, alehouses, or coffeehouses.[51]

Complaints that coffeehouse women were little more than whores were not entirely unfounded. Evidence from the London church courts and the quarter sessions records of the City of London document the accessibility of city coffeehouses to women, but most were either running the business or were servants.[52] Female patrons of coffeehouses were associated with either sexual immorality or some other form of criminal activity. For example, Elizabeth Way frequented coffeehouses and taverns with a group of men who were later accused of running a money laundering operation for clipped coins. Sometimes the sexual impropriety took place in the coffeehouse itself. The company at one coffeehouse in the parish of Clement Danes was startled by the sound of a woman's voice next door. Their curiosity thus piqued, one man from the crowd, Christopher Dent, peeped through a hole into the room, where he saw a woman named Hannah Barnes drinking sack with a man she called Parker. How long Dent continued to observe the two is unclear, but apparently it was long enough for him to see "Hannah lying on a bed in the room with her coats up above her belly, and Mr. Parker between her leggs, lying upon her and committing the foul crime of adultery with her."[53] It is not clear from this account whether the adjacent room was another part of the coffeehouse, or whether it was a separate tenement. But this raises another important matter to consider about the permeability of the coffeehouse space. The coffeehouse was also a domicile for the keeper and his family, and it was often located next to other private residences as well. Often the "coffeehouse" was little more than a special room in a private house that was reserved for serving coffee to guests.

This meant that the dividing line between the public space of the coffeehouse and the private space of the household was never clear-cut. If the public coffeehouse was just another room within a larger private domicile, then it was of course open to intrusion (and surveillance, as we have seen) from the other members of the household. While beginning to make her way as a lace retailer in London, Hester Pinney lodged above a coffeehouse, as well as over taverns and in the households of professionals. It was living above taverns, however, that especially raised the ire of her father. A Mrs. Lloyd also spent several nights at the Amsterdam Coffeehouse in 1715.[54] Women lodgers such as Pinney and Lloyd certainly must have overheard bits of coffeehouse gossip and perhaps even joined the company there on occasion while they lived in the building.

After this survey of the various ways in which women could find themselves a part of the coffeehouse scene, it can no longer be maintained that women were entirely excluded from the social world of the English coffeehouse. It seems just as clear, however, that it would be equally wrong to assume that women had the same unfettered access to the coffeehouses that men did. To do so would be to ignore the important ways in which daily life, and the spatial experience of it, was (and remains) fundamentally shaped by cultural notions of gendered propriety. In this way, the masculine ideal of the coffeehouse public sphere impinged upon the actual ways in which that space was put into practice. Even if women could and did enter into the metropolitan coffeehouses, they could never join the company there and feel entirely "at home" with the men.

Gender was not the only means by which access to the coffeehouse public sphere was restricted. The *Grub Street Journal* confidently asserted in 1732 that women and "people of mean fortune" do not frequent coffeehouses.[55] Social class, regional, professional or political affiliations, as well as idiosyncratic personal preferences all fractured the social world of the coffeehouse in smaller pieces — and they did not form a homogeneous whole. Coffeehouse society was more like a variegated set of separate publics rather than a unitary one. The resulting voice of the coffeehouses then sounded much more like the confused chatter of the tower of Babel than it did the product of a sober, rational, ideal speech situation. Controlling this chatter thus remained high on the agenda for everyone concerned with the state of public life in post-Restoration Britain, and one of the best means of control was to regulate access, either through formal legal means discussed in the previous chapter or through the self-scolding disciplinary chiding of the moralists discussed here.

A Civilized Society?

In 1723, the author of the periodical *Pasquin,* an imitator of the *Spectator* papers, offered a startling revision of the cultural history of English coffeehouses. Rather than describing the gradual acceptance of the coffeehouse as a legitimate part of the urban social scene, the journal told a story of the decline and fall of coffeehouse politeness. Introduced in the reign of Charles II, the coffeehouses of his reign partook in the general cultural renaissance provoked by the Restoration of the monarchy:

There were several coffeehouses then erected [after the Restoration], where assemblies of the literati professed to meet, and the town had due notice given them, at what hour the respective boards sat to speak sentences and say things worth the hearing. John Dryden took his place very solemnly every evening at Will's, which is remembered and duly honour'd for his sake, to this day. But these meetings expir'd with the reign of that prince or soon after; and all institutions which have succeeded since, have discover'd more affectation in the projectors of them, than any of that spirit which form'd the first assemblies of this kind. The coffeehouse where politeness is said to reside at present, may well enough be said to be but the leavings of *Pharsalia,* the epitome of what was once to be there seen.

Pasquin's author had evidently forgotten that Dryden had once been assaulted outside of Will's Coffeehouse by a gang of ruffians who had not taken kindly to his latest poetic satires. Nostalgia for the past is a sure sign that what was once a novel, and potentially threatening, institution has become thoroughly domesticated. By the 1720s, the coffeehouse had become an accepted fixture and a recognized center for what was increasingly being called "polite" society.[56]

The business of moral censure never went out of fashion, of course, and laments for the still hopelessly uncivil society found in the coffeehouses never ceased to issue from the pens of British moralists in the mid-eighteenth century. Nevertheless, the image of the coffeehouse had changed by the 1720s in the wake of the efforts of Addison and Steele and their ilk to refashion the coffeehouse as a center of respectable male manners for eighteenth-century Britain. Perhaps because of the remarkable success of the *Spectator* project, one finds a series of later eighteenth-century imitators who tried to continue the Spectatorial tradition, and in so doing they perpetuated the myth of the coffeehouse as a paragon of Augustan politeness. It was this myth that was later memorialized by later Victorian and twentieth-century antiquarian students of the coffeehouse and finally ensconced in the historical record by Jürgen Habermas, who relied primarily on these accounts for his influential discussion of the rise of the coffeehouse as an example of the emergence of what he called the "bourgeois public sphere."[57]

A powerful tension between accessibility and exclusivity runs throughout the history of the coffeehouse. This tension began with the very first coffeehouse societies, whose codes of conduct were adapted from the virtuoso sociability of great house visits but were then also merged with the more open atmosphere of the English public house. It is sometimes supposed that the relative freedom of the Augustan coffeehouse was replaced in the later eighteenth century by more restrictive gentleman's clubs. But club life went hand in hand with coffeehouse society, and it had been so from the very first coffeehouses at Tillyard's in Oxford, or Harrington's Rota Club in London.[58] Although they were public houses, and very few formal means of exclusion operated to keep undesirables out, we have seen that there were a whole host of informal means which operated to stratify coffeehouse society and to make it much less open to all comers as it might appear at first glance.

This should make us think twice before we draw any immediate and unqualified associations between the development of coffeehouse society and the rise of an unfettered and unproblematic public sphere. Public social life, and even more so, public politics were both always problematic in early modern Britain, and it is very difficult to find many normative champions of a Habermasian public sphere in the period. The public sphere in the political realm, as Habermas called it, was born out of the practical exigencies of partisan political conflict, but it found few outright defenders in the world of early modern political or social theory. Instead of a Habermasian public sphere, we find in early eighteenth-century political culture a number of advocates for a more "civilized" public life such as Addison, Steele, and their fellow travelers in the cooperative *Spectator* project. This was a public life which includes the coffeehouse at its center to be sure, but the purpose of this civilization of public life was not to carve out a space for the politics of democratic reason as the Habermasian paradigm would lead us to believe. They wanted a "civil" society, and this perhaps explains the growing popularity of the term among the literati of the British Enlightenment over the course of the eighteenth century, but they did not want a "bourgeois public sphere."[59] Their goal was not to prepare the ground for an age of democratic revolutions; it was to make the cultural politics of Augustan Britain safe for an elitist whig oligarchy.

Conclusion

Like the ever rising middle class or the ever separating masculine and feminine spheres, it seems that every era has had its consumer revolution and its own public sphere. These concepts are so capacious that they can be applied to almost any time and any place with a little imagination. All societies past and present have been "consumer societies" in the sense that they all require a variety of goods and services. What varies is the sorts of goods and services required, as well as the values placed on them at different times. Even Neolithic economies, we have been told, can be considered "the original affluent society." Likewise, all societies have in various ways made provision for a certain degree of public discourse. While Habermas thought his public sphere was surely a "category of bourgeois society" and thus historically traceable to the pre-(French) revolutionary rise of the bourgeoisie, most of the continued interest in his formulation has dropped his Marxisant teleology and recent scholarship has relentlessly sought to push back the point at which one can trace the emergence of a distinct sort of public sphere.[1] With the right ingenuity with regard to source material, one might well expect to soon read of claims for a "Paleolithic public sphere" from the ranks of archaeologists.

Surely the rise of coffee drinking and the development of the coffeehouse as a social institution did not simply usher in both a consumer revolution and a new public sphere to British society in the later seventeenth century. But they were remarkable innovations nevertheless, and the preceding chapters have sought to account for these novelties by understanding coffee and the coffee-houses through a detailed look at the historically specific ways in which seventeenth and early eighteenth-century consumers made sense of the new drink and the new institution. Careful attention to such apparently innocuous subjects as a hot drink and a public drinking establishment over the course of the seventeenth and eighteenth centuries has provided us with a useful optic through which we have seen the attitudes of early modern people in the British Isles toward matters as varied as economic culture, medical values, and ideas about foreign cultures, as well as the proper ordering of gender roles and urban social relations. Coffee had a very active social life in early modern Britain, and this study has endeavored to follow its datebook in every direction in which it ventured. In so doing, I have traveled well beyond the boundaries of the British Isles themselves: the history of British coffee took place in Mocha, Surat, and Cairo as much it did in London, Bath, and Edinburgh. British history can, and should, be enlivened by understanding it as an important part of a global history.[2] This book has also made many conceptual journeys: I have freely ranged far beyond the world of coffee and have drawn parallels between coffee and opium, coffeehouses and conventicles and barbershops, and so forth. It is only by understanding the relationships between coffee and coffeehouses and their near kin in the mental worlds of early modern people that we can begin to appreciate the significances that contemporaries brought to these novelties. Coffee culture became part and parcel of British daily life in the century after the Restoration through a gradual process of familiarization in which coffee and coffeehouses were compared and contrasted to other drinks — beers, ales, wines, herbal concoctions — and other public houses such as alehouses, taverns, or even barbershops. In this way, coffee gradually began to make sense to the early modern mind.

It has been much easier for present-day historians to make sense of the origins of coffee culture in early modern Britain than it had been for British people in the seventeenth century. With the growing popularity of the consumer revolution and the public sphere paradigms in the 1980s and 1990s, historians of early modern Britain have become ever more comfortable with the rise of coffee culture in the seventeenth and eighteenth centuries, perhaps all too comfortable. The rise of coffee has commonly received its due respect in these accounts over the course of a few cursory pages of discussion. In these brief reflections, readers have been invited to view the introduction of coffee and coffeehouses as a rather self-evident example of one of the many ways in which post-Restoration Britain was becoming a more democratic, a more socially fluid, a more commercial, a more "polite" and thus a rather more *modern* society than it had hitherto been.[3] The normative coffeehouse public sphere so carefully articulated by Addison and Steele as an ideal to strive for in their *Tatler* and *Spectator* essays has come alive as historical reality in the many studies of the consumer revolution, the public sphere and polite society over the past few decades. These new whig historians, most of whom are the products of a post-war generation and began to publish in the 1970s and 1980s have celebrated the rise of coffee culture along with describing it. In these triumphal accounts, the introduction of coffee and coffeehouses into British society was an undeniably good thing and a clear example of the way in which post-Restoration Britain was on its way to becoming a nation filled with William Blackstone's famously "polite and commercial people."[4]

In this way, post-Restoration coffee culture has played an important cameo role in some of the most important historical writing on the period in the last three decades. Coffee was one of those new commodities that formed part of the new "world of goods" celebrated by historians of the consumer revolution and it has been routinely mentioned along with chocolate, tea, clocks, china wares, calicoes, and all the other commodities that began to find their way into the shops and homes of early modern consumers. Even more so have coffee-houses found their way into histories of the new: they commonly form one part of the mise en scène for studies of the post-Restoration urban renaissance, a backdrop for the scientific debates which shaped the rise of experimental science, an important venue for the elaboration of the codes and conventions of polite culture, and of course as the prime site for the emergence of a "bour-geois public sphere" and the modern, democratic political culture and civil society that came with it. Although the efflorescence of coffee culture is ac-knowledged to be a crucial component of these grand narratives, the variety of contemporaries' responses to the new drink, and especially to the myriad of different coffeehouses, have rarely been explored in great detail.

It is often said that the devil is in the details, and this book has been an advocate for the devil insofar as this discussion complicates a story which has all too often been taken as read in the new whig histories of coffee. This account is "revisionist" insofar as it has insisted that there is no reason to believe that the rise of coffee culture should have been a success story; indeed the preceding chapters have gone to considerable effort to demonstrate that that there were many good reasons to think that coffee would fail to take hold and they have compelled us to recognize that the acceptance of coffee culture took much longer and faced much more resistance than more whiggishly inclined histories have tended to acknowledge.

This may provoke historians in a variety of different fields and specialties touched on here to reconsider their understandings of the role of coffee culture in their respective areas of interest. Historians of civility should recall the brutal caning of Titus Oates at the Amsterdam Coffeehouse and his use of a dish of coffee thrust in the eyes of his opponent in self defense — an incident which was not uncommon in early modern coffeehouses — as they consider their understandings of the role of the coffeehouse in the making of the eighteenth century's "culture of politeness." Normative codes of politeness, as Addison and Steele knew all too well, were necessary because they were so often breached in daily practice.

Historians of early modern science, many of whom have emphasized the importance of codes of civility and gentlemanly conduct on the emergence of scientific experiment and scientific argument, might want to ponder a bit further upon the reasons why the English virtuosi forged the social template for the coffeehouse little more than a decade before they established the more formal scientific institution of the Royal Society. The account of the invention of the coffeehouse offered here reverses what has become something of a received truth in the recent historiography of the scientific revolution: the coffeehouse was not simply one among many backdrops or stages upon which the development of experimental science was played out; it was *itself* the product of the cultural world forged by the virtuosi in Britain's age of scientific revolution. I have insisted that the British coffeehouse took the cultural shape that it did due to the intellectual proclivities and the social codes and conventions of the virtuosi. The scientific laboratory, the academic journal, the learned society and the coffeehouse were all products of the social and cultural legacy of virtuosity. Although this book is not itself a study in the history of science, it is very much a product of the exciting new ground broken by social historians of early modern science in the past few decades and it shares their deep concern with the social history of knowledge. The cultural world of early modern virtuosity uncovered by these historians affected more than the emergence of scientific thought and methods, important as these developments undoubtedly were, and this work has urged that the virtuosi be taken much more seriously as an important innovative force within early modern British culture.[5]

Economic historians interested in the cultural milieu which encouraged the financial and commercial revolutions of the late seventeenth and eighteenth centuries may want to reconsider their understandings of the ways in which new goods and services were received in this age of economic innovation. The commercial success of coffee and the social success of the coffeehouses did not just happen because overseas merchants were finally able to bring a naturally appealing liquor to English consumers. The success of coffee required, to invoke a well worn phrase in nearly every historical field save perhaps economic history, the *construction* of consumer demand for it. Economic historians have long recognized that post-Restoration Britain saw a "commercial revolution," quantifiably measurable in terms of the growth of overseas imports and exports, but the cultural history of that revolution has yet to be written.[6]

This book takes a step in that direction. I have placed great emphasis on the disproportionate influence of the virtuosi, a small subculture within England's social elite; and I have also attended to the quite proportional, but therefore massive, importance of the growth of metropolitan London in shaping the cultural contours of England's commercial revolution. The question of where the demand, and the productive capacity to feed that demand, for new things came from is one that has challenged students of economic history for centuries. It clearly vexed Max Weber: "A man does not 'by nature' wish to earn more and more money, but simply to live as he is accustomed to live and to earn as much as is necessary for that purpose. Wherever modern capitalism has begun its work of increasing the productivity of human labour by increasing its intensity, it has encountered the immensely stubborn resistance of this leading trait of pre-capitalistic labour." I have similarly contended here that consumers do not naturally desire new goods such as coffee; that desire had to be cultivated through the combination of various preexisting elements within a given culture. Understanding the origins of the new demand for coffee in early modern Britain may not offer the magic key that opens the door to understanding the rise of capitalism as a unique mode of economic and social organization, but they may help us appreciate some of the factors that led to the slow erosion of the bloody-minded consumer resistance to novel tastes, institutions, and fashions that characterized the old economic regime.[7] In this way, the rise of coffee and coffeehouses had an important role to play in Britain's prolonged bourgeois revolution.

Much the same could be said for the political consequences of coffee culture. Political historians of the post-Restoration era who wish to consider the ways in which the coffeehouse altered the conduct of political action and the means of political persuasion, as indeed they should, will want to take into account the extended struggle that the coffeehouses had to endure in order to achieve their legitimacy. While the mid-seventeenth-century emergence of the coffeehouse offers one of the most evident ways in which British politics after the Restoration was not a repeat performance of the early seventeenth century, neither should the history of the rise of the coffeehouse be understood in terms of the irrepressible emergence of a public sphere manqué. The rise of the coffeehouse expanded the limits of the politically possible in the decades after the Restoration, but the account offered here has argued that this only made coffeehouse politics all the more complex and all the more vexing for the managers of the British state at both the local and the national levels. There remains much room for further case studies of the political character and significance of individual coffeehouses such as the Amsterdam, Will's, Button's, Ozinda's or the Grecian, within the complex matrix of post-Restoration political culture. The role of the coffeehouse in the mid-eighteenth-century heyday of whig oligarchy and in later Hanoverian Britain also remains seriously understudied.[8] Detailed analyses of this sort will continue to illuminate more clearly the various ways in which coffeehouses made themselves an indispensable, and unavoidable, aspect of both popular and elite political repertoires in an age of recurrent party conflict and royal succession crises.

In its sympathy for the devil's details and in its forthright challenge to neo-whig platitudes, this book might easily be taken to be a thoroughly revisionist study of early modern coffee culture. There would be some truth to this reading, for later Stuart and early Hanoverian British history badly remains in need of the strong dose of revisionist debate that radically transformed studies of the early Stuart era some three decades earlier.[9] Although a bit of revisionist correction has been necessary along the way to correct the anachronistic and triumphalist whiggery of earlier accounts, a fresher "post-revisionist" perspective remains at the core of the story told here. While critical of simpler accounts of the rise of coffee culture, this book has worked hard to build a case for carefully considering the positive forces that shaped its ultimate success.

Caffeinated modernity was not waiting to happen in the seventeenth century, but certain elements within British society, such as the virtuosi who promoted coffee drinking and the overseas merchants who took to importing it in increasingly large quantities, were particularly receptive to encouraging the popularity of coffee drinking and promoting the coffeehouse as a central institution of urban life. The complex interactions between the various components of the early modern British social order in the making of British coffee culture have been at the heart of this account of the rise of coffee culture. This has not been a story of single causes or prime movers. Each step in the process of introducing coffee to British society set in motion a whole new set of actions, reactions and further transformations. The virtuosi may have introduced coffee into British society at the outset of the seventeenth century, but once they had done so, the meanings attributed to drinking coffee and even more so to frequenting coffeehouses became as variegated as early modern British society itself. British early modernity was remarkably flexible and, given the right circumstances, quite receptive to social and cultural innovation. The striking rise of coffee culture offers a remarkable example of just how much change the British old regime could accommodate.

Did coffee and coffeehouses matter in early modern Britain? The answer to this question depends of course on how one measures historical significance: if this is understood in terms of dramatic revolutions in state and society, then the answer must be "no." Coffee did not execute a reigning monarch, as the Rump Parliament did in 1649, nor did it force another king to flee his throne, as the Prince of Orange and his supporters did in late 1688. Yet neither was coffee a mere trifle, in the history of which "the anecdotal, the picturesque and the unreliable play an enormous part," as Fernand Braudel put it.[10] As colorful as its history may be, the story of the introduction of coffee into the British Isles reveals much about the ways in which early modern economic, social, and political relations were constituted. Coffee culture itself did not transform British society — this book has emphatically refused to argue for a "caffeine revolution" that inaugurated a modern work ethic or a more recognizably democratic civil society — but understanding the remarkable ways in which British coffee culture did emerge helps us understand how even a pre-modern society could adopt innovative consumption habits and could invent new social institutions such as the coffeehouse. Hard as it is for us today to imagine a world without coffee, it was even harder for early modern Britons to imagine what a world *with* coffee would be like. It is a testament to their flexible imaginations that they succeeded in creating a coffee world of their own.

Notes

Introduction

1. Hattox, *Coffee and Coffeehouses.*

2. Brewer, McKendrick, and Plumb, eds., *Birth of a Consumer Society;* Brewer and Porter, eds., *Consumption and the World of Goods;* Brewer, *Pleasures of the Imagination;* van Horn Melton, *Rise of the Public in Enlightenment Europe;* and Blanning, *Culture of Power and the Power of Culture.*

3. English virtuoso culture is further studied in Cowan, "An Open Elite."

4. Compare Porter, *Creation of the Modern World,* esp. 35–37.

5. For reviews of these historiographical problems see Cowan, "Refiguring Revisionisms," and Cowan, "Rise of the Coffeehouse."

6. Chaudhuri, *Trading World of Asia,* 388; see also Smith, "Accounting for Taste," the *problematique* for which is precisely the opposite of the one considered here. For Smith, the question is why coffee ultimately failed to gain the same mass market in England that tea did. This work is concerned with the problem of how *both* coffee and tea became acceptable consumer items in the first place.

7. Clark, "The 'Mother Gin' Controversy in the Early Eighteenth Century."

Part I. Coffee: From Curiosity to Commodity

1. Biddulph, "Part of a Letter of Master William Biddulph from Aleppo," 8:266. John Smith may well have observed coffee drinking in Constantinople before Biddulph: Smith, *True Travels, Adventures, and Observations of Captaine John Smith,* 25, as perhaps did

Sir Anthony Sherley in Aleppo: Denison Ross, *Sir Anthony Sherley and His Persian Adventure*, 14, 107, 186. The first printed mention of coffee in English occurred in the 1598 translation of van Linschoten, *Voyage of John Huyghen van Linschoten to the East Indies*, 1:157; Sandys, "Relation of a Journey Begun," in Purchas, *Hakluytus Posthumus*, 8:146; Thomas, *Religion and the Decline of Magic*, 17.

2. Mennell, *All Manners of Food*, 2.

3. Rumsey, *Organon Salutis*, sig. A6r; compare *Spectator*, no. 447 (2 Aug. 1712), 4:70–71; Becker, *Outsiders*, 41–58; Mennell, *All Manners of Food*, 1–19; Sherratt, "Alcohol and Its Alternatives," 16.

4. Bacon, *Letters and the Life of Francis Bacon*, 6:158; Woodhead, "'The Present Terrour of the World'?"; Pincus, "From Holy Cause to Economic Interest," 281–82; Rycaut, *Present State of the Ottoman Empire*, 3; Webster, *Great Instauration*, 248, 253, 274; Wear, "Early Modern Europe, 1500–1700," 309–10; Berry, *Idea of Luxury*, 102–11; Appleby, *Economic Thought and Ideology*, 41; De Vries, *Economy of Europe in an Age of Crisis*, 176–82.

5. Carter and Cullenberg, "Labor Economics and the Historian," 86 (quote), 116–17.

6. Davis, "English Foreign Trade, 1660–1700," 2:258; see also Davis, *Commercial Revolution*, 10–11; de Vries, *Economy of Europe in an Age of Crisis*, 187, although he also notes that price reduction itself cannot entirely account for these new demands; compare de Vries, "Between Purchasing Power and the World of Goods," 115.

7. Goodman, *Tobacco in History*, 38–39; Goodman, "Excitantia," 133; Goodman, *Tobacco in History*, 40–51.

8. Veblen, *Theory of the Leisure Class*; see also Campbell, *Romantic Ethic and the Spirit of Modern Consumerism*, 17–35, 49–57; McCracken, *Culture and Consumption*, 6–7, 93–103.

9. McKendrick, "Commercialization of Fashion," 52; Sherratt, "Introduction: Peculiar Substances," 5; Braudel, *Structures of Everyday Life*, 249–60, esp. 256–58 on coffee. Duncan, *Wholesome Advice Against the Abuse of Hot Liquors*, 12–13; Smith, "From Coffeehouse to Parlour," 152. For criticism of this line of argument, see Styles, "Product Innovation in Early Modern London."

10. Sombart, *Luxury and Capitalism*, 99–100; Mennell, *All Manners of Food*, 111; Elias, *Court Society*, esp. 66–77; Camporesi, *Exotic Brew*, 46.

11. Smith, "From Coffeehouse to Parlour," 151, 152; Smith, "Complications of the Commonplace"; and Smith, *Consumption and the Making of Respectability*.

12. Schivelbusch, *Tastes of Paradise*; Sherratt, "Introduction: Peculiar Substances," 3–4; Albrecht, "Coffee-Drinking as a Symbol of Social Change," 93.

13. Stallybrass and White, *Politics and Poetics of Transgression*, 97; Mintz, *Sweetness and Power*, 183–86.

14. Campbell, "Understanding Traditional and Modern Patterns of Consumption," 42.

15. Campbell, *Romantic Ethic and the Spirit of Modern Consumerism*, 89; compare Campbell, "Understanding Traditional and Modern Patterns of Consumption," 52–55. Similar arguments may be found in Mukerji, *From Graven Images*, and Schama, *Embarrassment of Riches*.

16. Cowan, "An Open Elite"; Peacham, *Compleat Gentleman*, 105.

17. Whitaker, "Culture of Curiosity," 75; Daston and Park, *Wonders and the Order of Nature,* quote at 218, see also 215–301. Virtuoso "curiosity" is also explored in: Benedict, *Curiosity;* Daston, "Neugierde als Empfindung und Epistemologie"; and Ginzburg, *Clues, Myths, and the Historical Method,* 60–76, 194–97.

18. Houghton, "English Virtuoso," 205; compare 191 n. 72; Caudill, "Some Literary Evidence"; Findlen, *Possessing Nature;* Eamon, *Science and the Secrets of Nature,* 314.

19. For the importance of court culture on the continental virtuosi, see Eamon, *Science and the Secrets of Nature,* esp. 222–29; and Findlen, *Possessing Nature.* On the exceptional nature of the Royal Society compared to other European scientific academies, see Biagioli, "Etiquette, Interdependence and Sociability in Seventeenth-Century Science."

20. Caudill, "Some Literary Evidence," ch. 8; Eamon, *Science and the Secrets of Nature,* 303; BL, Evelyn MS 39a, Out-Letters, no. 153 (4 Feb. 1659). See also: BL, Egerton MS 2231, fol. 172r. The virtuosic critique of the universities should not, however, obscure the important role played by the universities in supporting similar goals, such as scientific research and "oriental" studies: Frank, *Harvey and the Oxford Physiologists;* Toomer, *Eastern Wisedome and Learning.*

21. Levine, *Dr. Woodward's Shield,* 85–86, 114–29, 238–52; Lloyd, "Shadwell and the Virtuosi."

22. RSA, EL/S 1/90, fol. 179v. The most convincing explanation for Stubbe's grudge against the Royal Society is found in Cook, "Henry Stubbe and the Virtuosi-Physicians," 246–71.

23. The cultural stakes at issue in the battles between the ancients and moderns are skillfully illuminated in the works of Levine: *Dr. Woodward's Shield; Battle of the Books;* and *Between the Ancients and the Moderns.*

24. Hunter, *Science and Society,* 67–68, see also 172; Houghton, "English Virtuoso," 56; compare 211–13; Frank, *Harvey and the Oxford Physiologists,* 44; Shapin, *Social History of Truth.*

25. Westfall provides a more sympathetic understanding and definition of the virtuoso in *Science and Religion in Seventeenth-Century England,* 10–25, esp. 13–14. Daston, "Factual Sensibility," 464, 466, 467; elaborated in Daston and Park, *Wonders and the Order of Nature,* 215–53; compare Hunter, *Science and Society,* 17–18.

26. Some historians of early modern court and visual culture have also examined virtuosity: Smuts, *Court Culture and the Origins of a Royalist Tradition,* 152–54; Pace, "Virtuoso to Connoisseur"; Cowan, "Arenas of Connoisseurship"; and Cowan, "An Open Elite."

27. MacGregor, "Cabinet of Curiosities in Seventeenth-Century Britain," 152; Daston, "The Factual Sensibility," 452. BL, Evelyn MS 39a, Out-Letters, no. 382 (18 July 1676).

28. Webster, *Great Instauration,* 377; compare 218, 426–27; Cook, "Henry Stubbe and the Virtuosi-Physicians," 269. Webster's expansive notion of "puritanism" has been cogently criticized by Hunter, *Establishing the New Science,* 7–8; compare Hunter, *Science and Society,* 113. Webster, "Benjamin Worsley," 213–35; see also: Letwin, *Origins of Scientific Economics,* 131–38; and Pincus, "Neither Machiavellian Moment nor Possessive Individualism."

29. Webster, *Great Instauration,* 324–483; esp. 355–57, 422–27.

30. Webster, *Great Instauration,* 97, 99, 420–27, 502; Houghton, "History of Trades";

Hunter, *Science and Society,* ch. 4; Ochs, "Royal Society of London's History of Trades"; Eamon, *Science and the Secrets of Nature,* 342–45.

31. Muldrew, *Economy of Obligation;* Muldrew, "Hard Food for Midas."

Chapter 1. An Acquired Taste

1. Reinders and Wijsenbeek, *Koffie in Nederland,* 14–15; Rauwolf, *Collection of Curious Travels and Voyages,* 1:A7v, A8r, A8v. Compare Rauwolf, *Aigentliche Beschreibung,* sigs. iiir, iiiv, ivr–v. The author of the 1485 German *Herbarius zu Teutsch* claimed a similar motivation for his botanical travels: Arber, *Herbals,* 25.

2. Rauwolf, *Collection of Curious Travels and Voyages,* 1:a1r; compare Rauwolf, *Aigentliche Beschreibung,* sig. ivv; Dannenfeldt, *Leonhard Rauwolf,* 31–32.

3. Rauwolf, *Collection of Curious Travels and Voyages,* 1:a2r; compare Rauwolf, *Aigentliche Beschreibung,* sig. iv [*bis*]; Findlen, *Possessing Nature,* 159.

4. Rauwolf, *Collection of Curious Travels and Voyages,* 1:A4r; Parkinson, *Theatrum Botanicum,* 1623; Ray, *Philosophical Letters,* 270–71, 272–73; Birch, *History,* 4:400, 528. John Ray's translation of the work was celebrated in *Phil. Trans.,* 17, no. 200 (1693), 768–71.

5. Rauwolf, *Collection of Curious Travels and Voyages,* 1:92; compare Rauwolf, *Aigentliche Beschreibung,* 102. A substantial survey of the travel literature may be found in Schynder-von Waldkirch, *Wie Europa den Kaffee entdeckte.*

6. Olearius, *Voyages and Travels of the Ambassadors,* 322; Denison Ross, *Sir Anthony Sherley and His Persian Adventure,* 186; Herbert, *Relation of Some Yeares Travaile,* 150; Herbert, *Relation of Some Yeares Travaile,* 4th ed., 113; Howell, *New Volume of Letters,* 136; and Howell, *Epistolae Ho-Elianae,* 2:348.

7. Lithgow, *Most Delectable, and True Discourse,* sig. I3r; Finch in Purchas, *Hakluytus Posthumus,* 4:18; Herbert, *Relation of Some Yeares Travaile,* 150. See also Paldanus's editorial addition to Linschoten, *Voyage,* 1:157; Denison Ross, *Sir Anthony Sherley and His Persian Adventure,* 107.

8. Sandys in Purchas, *Hakluytus Posthumus,* 8:146; Biddulph in *Hakluytus Posthumus,* 8:266; Olearius, *Voyages and Travels,* 323, on the Persian "tea houses" or *Tzai Chattai Chane;* Hartlib, *Ephemerides* (4 Aug.–31 Dec. 1654), part 3 in *Hartlib Papers* [CD-ROM], 29/4/29A–B.

9. Herbert, *Relation of Some Yeares Travaile,* 150–51; see also Olearius, *The Voyages and Travels,* 298; Hattox, *Coffee and Coffeehouses,* 110–11, 113–14; Sandys in *Hakluytus Posthumus,* 8:146–47. Compare Biddulph in *Hakluytus Posthumus,* 8:266. Sandys in *Hakluytus Posthumus,* 8:146; Denison Ross, *Sir Anthony Sherley and His Persian Adventure,* 186–87.

10. Berry, *Idea of Luxury,* 68–69, 76 n. 11, 84 n. 13; Griffiths, *Youth and Authority,* 188–222; Clark, *English Alehouse,* esp. 145–68; Clark, "Alehouse and the Alternative Society"; Wrightson, "Puritan Reformation of Manners," 69–107; Burton, *Anatomy of Melancholy* (i:2:ii:2), 1:223; compare (ii:5:i:5), 2:250–51.

11. Daston and Park, *Wonders and the Order of Nature,* 21–67; Caudill, "Some Literary Evidence," esp. chs. 2–3; Findlen, *Possessing Nature,* 132–33; Browne, *Works of Sir Thomas Browne,* 1:166. The second edition of Howell, *Instructions for Forreine*

Travell, included a new appendix for traveling into Turkey and the Levant region, and Lupton, *Emblems of Rarities,* a sort of virtuoso's guide book to curiosities past and present, is full of information on the customs and cultures of Jews, Turks, and Indians.

12. Blount, *Voyage into the Levant,* sig. A2r–v; compare: Bacon, *Letters and the Life of Francis Bacon,* 2:10; Coryate, *Coryats Crudities,* sigs. C7r–C8r; Blount, *Voyage into the Levant,* 15, 42; Rumsey, *Organon Salutis,* sigs. A4v–A7v; Rumsey, *Organon Salutis,* 2nd ed. (1659); Aubrey, *"Brief Lives,"* 1:108–11; Pepys, *Diary,* 5:274; Bodl. MS Aubrey 6, fol. 102r.

13. Coryate, *Coryats Crudities,* sigs. B2v–B3r; compare Gerarde, *Herball or Generall Historie of Plantes,* 2d ed., sig. 2v; Gardiner, *Triall of Tobacco,* fol. 3r.

14. Olearius, *The Voyages and Travels,* sig. A2v.

15. Bacon's influence on the virtuosi of the seventeenth century was, to a certain extent, at odds with his own desire to purge scientific inquiry of the frivolity and "humanist embellishments" that he disdained in Renaissance natural history, which is well described in Findlen, "Francis Bacon and the Reform of Natural History," quote at 241.

16. Jones, *Ancients and Moderns,* 50–61; Daston, "Marvelous Facts and Miraculous Evidence," 111 (quoted); Bacon, *Francis Bacon,* 483, 798. Bacon may have been referring to the native Americans' use of coca mentioned in de Acosta, *Natural and Moral History of the Indies,* 245–46, or perhaps the East Indian betel he describes in his *History Natural and Experimental of Life and Death* (1638), in Bacon, *Works,* 14:361–62.

17. Bacon, *Sylva Sylvarum,* 738, in *Works,* 4:389–90; Bacon, *History Natural and Experimental of Life and Death,* in *Works,* 14:361–63.

18. Jorden, *Discourse of Naturall Bathes,* 128–29; Webster, *Great Instauration,* 468; Parkinson, *Theatrum Botanicum,* 1614, 1622–23.

19. Aubrey, *"Brief Lives,"* 2:206–7; Rumsey, *Organon Salutis,* 5, 19, sig. a4r. Rumsey was a great advocate of purgative remedies. The "instrument of health" after which his book was titled was a long whale-bone used to induce vomiting.

20. Bodl. MS Wood F.39, fol. 206r; *Mercurius Politicus,* no. 367 (11–18 June 1657), 7857; Rumsey, *Organon Salutis,* 2nd ed.; Rumsey, *Organon Salutis,* 3rd ed. (1664).

21. Rumsey, *Organon Salutis* (1657 ed.), sigs. b2r–v; compare Howell, *A New Volume of Letters,* 136; Sandys in Purchas, *Hakluytus Posthumus,* 8:146; Burton, *Anatomy of Melancholy* (ii.5.i.5), 2:250; Butler, *Satires and Miscellaneous Poetry and Prose,* 324; *Coffee-Houses Vindicated,* 3; John Evelyn, MS annotation to *Phil. Trans.,* vol. 21, no. 256 (Sept. 1699), 311 in BL shelfmark Eve.a.149; Plutarch, *Alcibiades,* § 23.3. These writers were most likely familiar with North's translation of Plutarch: *Lives of the Noble Grecians and Romanes,* 288.

22. Toomer, *Eastern Wisedome and Learning;* Champion, *Pillars of Priestcraft Shaken,* 106–16. Aubrey, *"Brief Lives,"* 1:299, 301–2. See also Houghton, "Discourse of Coffee," *Phil. Trans.,* vol. 21, no. 256 (1699), 312; compare Ellis, *Penny Universities,* 14–15; Webster, *Great Instauration,* 355.

23. [Antaki], *Nature of the Drink Kauhi.* The translation contains numerous errors, according to Hattox, *Coffee and Coffeehouses,* 154 n. 12, and compare 64–69. The humoral status of coffee was indeterminate before Pococke's translation, for it was claimed to be "cold and dry" in one of the earliest (1652) handbills promoting the drink: BL shelfmark C.20.f.2 (372).

24. Wood, *Life and Times*, 1:168–69 (quote), 416, 423, 468, 488–89; 2:300, 334, 396, 429. Evelyn, *Diary*, 1:14 [*bis*]; compare Evelyn, *Diary*, 2:18 and n. 4. Evelyn made a similar remark in his MS annotations to *Phil. Trans.*, vol. 21, no. 256 (1699), 313; see BL shelfmark Eve.a.149. I must thank Douglas Chambers for suggesting that I look at Evelyn's annotations to his library.

25. Frank, *Harvey and the Oxford Physiologists*, 28–30, 41; Willis, *Pharmaceuticae Rationalis*, 155; compare Rumsey, *Organon Salutis*, 1st ed., sigs. b2v–b3r; and Houghton, "A Discourse of Coffee," 316.

26. On Oxford science see Tyacke, "Science and Religion at Oxford Before the Civil War," esp. 86; as well as Frank, *Harvey and the Oxford Physiologists*; and Webster, *Great Instauration*. Hartlib, *Ephemerides* (4 Aug.–31 Dec. 1654), part 3, MS 29/4/29B in *Hartlib Papers* [CD-ROM].

27. Hartlib MSS 42/4/4A in *Hartlib Papers* [CD-ROM]; Crossley, ed., *Dr. John Worthington, Diary and Correspondence*, 1:127. Two copies of a similar extract from Tulpii, *Descriptio Herbæ Theê*, in the Hartlib MSS 65/11/1A–2B and 49/4/5 would indicate that Hartlib circulated information on tea as well. Oldenberg, *Oldenburg Correspondence*, 8:331, 333, 357, 358, 372, 387, 430, 513, 515; Anthony Wood obtained an original copy of Pococke's translation, now at Bodl. Wood 679 (2); see Wood, *Life and Times*, 1:201 n. 2. For full details of Pococke's translation and its reception, see Toomer, *Eastern Wisedome and Learning*, 166–67.

28. Stubbs, "John Beale . . . Part I"; Stubbs, "John Beale . . . Part II"; Mendyk, *"Speculum Britanniae,"* 138–41; and Leslie, "Spiritual Husbandry of John Beale." Hartlib MSS 52/161A-B, *Hartlib Papers* [CD-ROM]; compare Beale's recommendation of chocolate: Hartlib MSS 51/34A, *Hartlib Papers* [CD-ROM].

29. Hartlib MSS 51/63B–64A, *Hartlib Papers* [CD-ROM]; Boyle, *Works*, 6:449–52.

30. Hartlib MSS 51/43B (quoted); Hartlib MSS 15/2/61A–64B, esp. fols. 61A–B, *Hartlib Papers* [CD-ROM]; also printed in Webster, *Great Instauration*, 539–46, esp. 540–41. The attribution and dating of this tract are discussed in Webster, "Benjamin Worsley," 221–23. On Worsley's role in shaping the Navigation Act, see Webster, *Great Instauration*, 462–65; Brenner, *Merchants and Revolution*, 626–28; and Pincus, *Protestantism and Patriotism*, 47–49.

31. On West Indian plantations, see: RSA, JBO 2/79; compare Birch, *History*, 1:424; BL, Evelyn MS, In-Letters 2, no. 113 (24 Apr. 1671). On growing foreign plants in England: RSA, LBO 8/87; RSA, LBO Supp. 1/398–99. Beale's project was supported by no less than the king himself: BL, Sloane MS 856, fol. 37v. On similar lines: Hartlib MSS, 8/22/2A, *Hartlib Papers* [CD-ROM]. Boyle, *Works*, 6:438.

32. Skinner, "Thomas Hobbes and the Nature of the Early Royal Society," 238; Hunter, *Science and Society*, 34; Sprat, *History of the Royal Society*, 156.

33. Oldenberg, *Oldenburg Correspondence*, 3:384–85 (quote at 385). Shapin, *Social History of Truth*, 243–47; compare Caudill, "Some Literary Evidence," 62–79; McKeon, *Origins of the English Novel*, 100–102, 114–17; and Iliffe, "Foreign Bodies."

34. Birch, *History*, 2:9. Unfortunately, Goddard's paper on coffee seems not to have survived, and it does not receive mention in his obituary in Birch, *History*, 3:244–46. RSA, LBO 2/211; The Latin phrasing of the question for Harpur was "Num usus frequens liquoris *coffee*, unquam causetum apoplexiam, vel paralysin?" See also *Phil.*

Trans., vol. 1, no. 20 (17 Dec. 1666), 360. Oldenberg, *Oldenburg Correspondence*, 3:606 (quoted).

35. Ray, *Correspondence of John Ray*, 193; Birch, *History*, 4:540. Compare Reinders and Wijsenbeek, *Koffie in Nederland*, 108; RSA, JBO 9/151; RSA, JBO 9/157; Sloane, "Account of a Prodigiously Large Feather . . . and of the Coffee-Shrub," *Phil. Trans., vol. 18*, no. 208 (Feb. 1694), 61–64.

36. Houghton, "Discourse of Coffee," 317.

37. Evelyn, MS annotation to *Phil. Trans.*, vol. 21, no. 256 (1699), 317; see BL shelf-mark Eve.a.149. Compare John Beale's indignation at Houghton's defense of luxury trades in Boyle, *Works*, 6:449–50. Evelyn, *Diary*, 1:14–15 [*bis*]. The cause of this mess was, he thought, Charles II's squandering of his demesnes.

38. On coffee in Venice, see Horowitz, "The Nocturnal Rituals of Early Modern Jewry," 38–39; in France, Leclant, "Coffee and Cafés in Paris," and Franklin, *Le Café, le Thé, et le Chocolat;* in the Netherlands, Reinders and Wijsenbeek, *Koffie in Nederland;* on Europe in general, Albrecht, "Coffee-Drinking as a Symbol of Social Change," and Schneider, "Die neuen Getränke."

39. Findlen, *Possessing Nature*, ch. 3, esp. 132; see also: Daston, "Ideal and Reality of the Republic of Letters in the Enlightenment," 367–86; Goldgar, *Impolite Learning;* and Eamon, *Science and the Secrets of Nature.* Iliffe, "Foreign Bodies," explores some of the fissures in the cosmopolitan ideal. *Journal des Sçavans*, vol. 4, [no. 3] (28 Jan. 1675), 33–35; *Journal des Sçavans*, vol. 13, no. 4 (29 Jan. 1685), 46–49; *Journal des Sçavans*, vol. 24, no. 23 (11 June 1696), 420–22; Bayle, *Oeuvres Diverses*, 1:232–33, 284–86.

40. The Turkish reception of coffee occurred along different lines than the rest of Europe and is outlined in Hattox, *Coffee and Coffeehouses*, who estimates that there were approximately 600 coffeehouses in Istanbul by the later sixteenth century: 81, compare 160 n. 9. Reinders and Wijsenbeek, *Koffie in Nederland*, 41; *View of Paris, and Places Adjoining*, 24–25; and compare *Curious Amusements*, 55.

41. Wrigley, "Simple Model of London's Importance in Changing English Society and Economy."

Chapter 2. Coffee and Early Modern Drug Culture

Epigraph: Braudel, *Structures of Everyday Life*, 261.

1. Attempts to address this problem from a global perspective include Courtwright, *Forces of Habit*, and Jamieson, "Essence of Commodification."

2. Smith, "From Coffeehouse to Parlour," and Smith, *Consumption and the Making of Respectability.*

3. Montesquieu, *Persian Letters*, 86.

4. Camporesi, *Bread of Dreams*, 137 (quoted); for similar arguments, see Braudel, *Structures of Everyday Life*, 261; Ginzburg, *Ecstasies*, esp. 303–7; Goodman, *Tobacco in History*, 42–43; Goodman, "Excitantia," 133–35; compare Goodman, Lovejoy, and Sheratt, *Consuming Habits*, 230. Schmidt, "Tobacco," 613–14; Goodman, *Tobacco in History*, 43; Mathee, "Exotic Substances."

5. Compare Camporesi, *Bread of Dreams*, 138, 140. Opium and *nepenthe* could often be conflated in early modern herbals, as in Culpeper, *Culpeper's Complete Herbal*, 500.

6. See also the reservations in Pelling, *Common Lot,* 44, and a similar judgment for the French case in Mandrou, *Introduction to Modern France,* 219–20.

7. For example, BL, Harley MS 7316, fol. 3r; Schivelbusch, "Die trockene Trunkenheit des Tabaks." Gerarde, *Herball or Generall Historie of Plantes,* 1549; *Calendar of Court Minutes of the EIC, 1660–63* (Nov. 1662), 278; compare Parkinson, *Theatrum Botanicum,* 1582; *Poor Robin's Intelligence,* [26 October 1676]; Leadbetter, *The Royal Gauger,* 262. *Coculus India* was being imported to England as early as 1629, according to the Rate Book: Roberts, "Early History of the Import of Drugs into Britain," 175. Friedman, *Battle of the Frogs and Fairford's Flies,* 171–75; Hill, *The World Turned Upside Down,* 159–62, quote at 160.

8. Daston and Park, *Wonders and the Order of Nature,* 130.

9. Lears, *Fables of Abundance,* 26; Gerarde, *Herball or Generall Historie of Plantes,* sig. B4v; Webster, *Great Instauration,* 253; Parkinson, *Theatrum Botanicum,* 1614.

10. Boyle, *Works,* 6:728; Daston and Park, *Wonders and the Order of Nature,* 148; Monardes, *Ioyfvll Nevves ovt of the newe founde worlde.* Arnold, "Cabinets for the Curious," 188; the Apothecaries broke from the Grocers in 1614, and obtained royal privilege in 1617: Cook, *Decline of the Old Medical Regime,* 46–47.

11. Mun in McCulloch, ed., *Early English Tracts on Commerce,* 8. Mun's interest in the East India trade led him to disparage the development of the tobacco trade, see *Early English Tracts on Commerce,* 8–9, 19; Holmes, *Augustan England,* 185.

12. Roberts, "Early History of the Import of Drugs into Britain," 167, 168. Compare the similar sentiments cited in Findlen, *Possessing Nature,* 268; and Daston and Park, *Wonders and the Order of Nature,* 158; Webster, "Alchemical and Paracelsian Medicine," 330; Webster, *Great Instauration,* esp. 246–323; and Wear, "Early Modern Europe, 1500–1700," 309–10.

13. Culpeper, *English Physitian,* sig. A2v. See also Cook, *Decline of the Old Medical Regime,* 120–24; Webster, *Great Instauration,* 268; Culpeper, *English Physitian,* sig. A2v; compare Culpeper, *Physical Directory,* 2nd ed., sig. B2r; Matthews, "Herbals and Formularies," 196; [Fuller], *Anglorum Speculum,* esp. 2. Pinnell, *Philosophy Reformed and Improved,* 3rd ed., 78; Webster, *Great Instauration,* 284. Such views were not peculiar to England. Aignon went so far as to argue that even every province of France was supplied by God with sufficient resources to remedy all ailments: *Prestre Medecin,* 215, 208 [*bis*]. See also Guy Patin's criticisms of the French apothecaries summarized in Franklin, *Les Médicaments,* 28, 31.

14. Bright, *Treatise: Wherein is Declared the Sufficiencie of English Medicines,* 16, 12–13. The notion that the English climate necessitated a different diet from that of other countries was rather commonplace, as in Harrison, *Description of England,* 123–25. Compare Pelling, *Common Lot,* 34; Evelyn, *Mundus Muliebris,* 2nd ed., sig. A4r; *Eccentric Magazine,* 1:58–59.

15. See Paulli, *Treatise on Tobacco, Tea, Coffee, and Chocolate,* esp. 24–25, 132–33; compare Naironus, *Discourse on Coffee,* sig. A2r; and see Chaytor, *Papers of Sir William Chaytor,* 281; *Grand Concern of England Explained,* 21; Aignon, *Prestre Medecin,* 148, 210–13; *Collection for Improvement of Husbandry and Trade,* vol. 4, no. 88 (6 Apr. 1694); and compare BL, Add. MSS 51319, fol. 199r.

16. *Natural History of Coffee, Thee, Chocolate, Tobacco,* 26, 30; Birch, *History,* 2:465. Compare Paulli, *Treatise on Tobacco,* 88, 125.

17. Gardiner, *Triall of Tabacco,* fol. 3r; Dufour, *Manner of Making of Coffee, Tea, and Chocolate,* sigs. A2v–A3r; *Spectator,* no. 69 (19 May 1711), 1:294; compare also: *British Apollo,* supernumerary paper, [no. 3] (June [1708]); and Pollexfen, *Discourse of Trade, Coyn, and Paper Credit,* 59.

18. Linschoten, *Voyage,* 2:115–17. According to Linschoten, bangue was ingested, rather than smoked, in South Asia. Compare the account of Acosta's "Tractado" (1578) and Browne's African travels in Davenport, *Aphrodesiacs and Anti-Aphrodesiacs,* 104. Lémery, *Treatise of Foods,* 291–92, notes that the natives of Madagascar preferred to smoke their bangue. Fryer, *New Account of East India and Persia,* 1:230, 2:113, 1:92, 1:262–63, 3:100.

19. Howell, *New Volume of Letters,* 137; compare Burton, *Anatomy of Melancholy* (ii.5.i.5), 2:251. *Nepenthe* is the drug in Homer, *Odyssey,* book 4.221, and is described in the Loeb translation as "a drug to quiet all pain and strife, and bring forgetfulness of every ill."

20. RSA, JBO 8/284–85; JBO 8/285–86; JBO 8/286; JBO 8/288–89; compare JBO 8/290 and Ray, *Philosophical Letters,* 174. The Society's information on the plant was most likely derived from the works of Linschoten and Ray: Ray, *Philosophical Letters,* 234–35, quote at 235.

21. Boyle, *Works,* 2:103–8; RSA, RBO 1/212–16. See also RSA, RBO 2/138; and RBO 2/139. RSA, RBO 2/210.

22. RSA, RBO 3/48–49; RSA, RBO 3/48.

23. The story seems to have begun with Linschoten, *Voyage,* 1:209–11, compare 2:68–72, 2:212; and is repeated in BL, Sloane MS 1326, fol. 103r. See also Burton, *Anatomy of Melancholy* (ii.5.i.5), 2:250; RSA, RBO 1/216; Fryer, *New Account of East India and Persia,* 1:92.

24. Linschoten, *Voyage,* 2:113, 114; compare Fryer, *New Account of East India and Persia,* 3:99–100; Ray, *Philosophical Letters,* 58; Lémery, *Treatise of Foods,* 292–93; Rycaut in Oldenburg, *Oldenburg Correspondence,* 3:604; *Domestick Intelligence,* no. 11 (27–30 June 1681). [Hammond], *Work for Chimny-sweepers,* sig. E4v; this anonymous tract is attributed in Harley, "The Beginnings of the Tobacco Controversy," 38–39.

25. Two medical treatises on opium were published during the seventeenth century: Sala, *Opiologia;* and Jones, *Mysteries of Opium Reveal'd.* For examples of the medical use of opium, see Ward, *Diary of the Rev. John Ward,* 248, 266. Herbert, *Relation of Some Yeares Travaile,* 150–51. Bacon, *Works,* 14:361–63, quote at 361; see also Boyle, *Works,* 2:28, 6:726.

26. RSA, EL/S 1/90, fol. 181v. Although Stubbe himself saw the gentlemen virtuosi as dangerous interlopers into established medical privilege — on which see Cook, "Henry Stubbe and the Virtuosi-Physicians," 246–71 — he was as steeped in the culture of curiosity as any fellow of the Royal Society. Landsdowne, *Petty-Southwell Correspondence,* 117, 255. Culpeper, *Complete Herbal,* 203–5, quote at 205.

27. Lémery, *Treatise of Foods,* 292–93; compare Oldenburg, *Oldenburg Correspondence,* 3:604; Olearius, *Voyages and Travels of the Ambassadors,* 321; and *Athenian Mercury,* vol. 6, no. 4 (13 Feb. 1692).

28. Boyle, *Works*, 2:121–22. In the previous century, Paracelsus had queried whether there "is not a mystery of nature even in poison" (*Selected Writings*, 95), and toxic substances were part of the iatrochemical repertoire. See, for example, Pollock, *With Faith and Physic*, 105.

29. RSA, LBO 1/416. For a similar case, see RSA, RBO 3/90–92. The medical efficacy of viper poison was the object of much interest among Italian virtuosi, on which see Findlen, *Possessing Nature*, ch. 6, esp. 241–45. On the extreme early modern abhorrence of poisons, see Pelling, *Common Lot*, 36, 45–46; Bellany, "Mistress Turner's Deadly Sins," 188–89.

30. [Antaki], *Nature of the Drink Kauhi*, 4; *Natural History of Coffee*, 5–6; DuFour, *Manner of Making of Coffee*, 14; Duncan, *Wholesome Advice Against the Abuse of Hot Liquors*, esp. 55, 74–75, 215–16; *Ale-wives Complaint Against the Coffee-Houses*, 5; Duncan, *Wholesome Advice Against the Abuse of Hot Liquors*, 219; see also *Athenian Mercury*, vol. 1, no. 23 (1691), Q. 4.

31. Although excess heat was often blamed for infertility, "insufficient heat . . . loomed far larger in the [medical] literature [on impotency] than did its surplus." Laqueur, *Making Sex*, 102.

32. Olearius, *Voyages and Travels*, 322–23; Sandys in Purchas, *Hakluytus Posthumus*, 8:146; Denison Ross, *Sir Anthony Sherley and His Persian Adventure*, 186–87. Olearius' story is related in *Natural History of Coffee*, 5; Sandys' account is in *Vertues of Coffee*, 6.

33. On English conceptions of Turkish sexuality, see Bray, *Homosexuality in Renaissance England*, 75. MS annotation to *Phil. Trans.*, vol. 14, no. 155 (20 Jan. 1684/85), 441 in BL shelfmark Eve.a.149; compare the similar remarks in North, *Lives*, 2:176–77.

34. Naironus, *Discourse on Coffee*, 20; *Women's Petition Against Coffee*, quote at 6; see also: *Wandring-Whores Complaint*; *Maidens Complain[t] Against Coffee*; *Character of a Coffee-House with the Symptoms of a Town Wit*, 5; *Ale-Wives Complaint*, 5; a reprint of "The Women's Petition" (1674): *City-wifes Petition Against Coffee*; and Brown, *Essays Serious and Comical*, 34. *Womens Complaint Against Tobacco*; compare Duncan, *Wholesome Advice Against the Abuse of Hot Liquors*, 220.

35. T. J., *World Turned Upside Down*; *Parliament of Women*; *List of the Parliament of Women*, and *Account of the Proceedings of the New Parliament of Women*. See Underdown, *Revel, Riot, and Rebellion*, 211, and Davis, *Society and Culture in Early Modern France*, 124–51. Hughes, "Gender and Politics in Leveller Literature," 162–88.

36. Rochester, *Complete Poems*, 54–59; BL, Harley MS 7312, fol. 90r; BL, Harley MS 6914, fols. 11v–15v; BL, Harley MS 7315, fols. 284v–286r; Bodl. MS Don. b.8, 194–97; Day, ed., *Pepys Ballads*, 4:50; BL, Add. MSS 40060, fol. 78r; *Character of a Town-Miss*, 3. See also Weil, "Sometimes a Scepter Is Only a Scepter," 151.

37. *Wandring-Whores Complaint for Want of Trading*, 4. See also *Mens Answer to the Womens Petition Against Coffee*, 2. Compare Pincus, "Coffee Politicians Does Create," 823–24; Harris, *London Crowds in the Reign of Charles II*, 80–91.

38. Coe and Coe, *True History of Chocolate*, 90, 94–95, 154, 174–76; St. Serfe, *Tarugo's Wiles*, 18; *Natural History of Coffee, Thee, Chocolate, Tobacco*, 18 which paraphrases and plagiarizes Stubbe, *Indian Nectar*, 132–41; *Spectator*, nos. 365, 395 (29 Apr. 1712); (3 June 1712), 3:374; 3:480–81; Stubbe, *Indian Nectar*, 171, 129–30.

39. Stubbe, *Indian Nectar,* 142, 130. On Stubbe's Galenism see, cautiously, Jacob, *Henry Stubbe,* 46–49. Compare Foucault, *Care of the Self,* 105–44; Rouselle, *Porneia,* 19; Brown, *Body and Society,* 19–20; and Laqueur, *Making Sex,* 35–49, 103.

40. *Tatler,* no. 1 (12 Apr. 1709), 1:16; *Spectator,* no. 88 (11 June 1711), 1:375; *Oxford DNB,* s.v. "Francis White." See also *View of Paris and Places Adjoining,* 24–25; *Character of the Beaux,* 3.

41. Schivelbusch, *Tastes of Paradise,* 92. References to coffee drinking in Pepys and Wood are too numerous to mention. For their indulgences with chocolate and tea, see Pepys, *Diary,* chocolate: 1:178; 3:226–27; 4:5; 5:64; 5:139; drunk at a coffeehouse: 5:329; tea: 1:253; 6:327–28; 8:302. Wood, *Life and Times,* 1:189; 1:378; 1:466; 1:467–68; 2:15; 2:23–24; 2:27; 2:81; 2:89; 2:92.

42. Mintz, *Sweetness and Power,* 108–12; Smith, "Complications of the Commonplace," 263; and Goodman, "Excitantia," 132, 142 nn. 61–62. [Ward], *London Spy Compleat,* 11, 146, 203, 278–79, 290; *Spectator,* no. 269 (8 Jan. 1712), 2:551; *Spectator,* no. 568 (16 July 1714), 4:539; De Saussure, *Foreign View of England in 1725–1729,* 101; and Southerne, *Works,* 1:378.

43. Compare Ellis, *Penny Universities,* 49–57. Rumsey, *Organon Salutis,* 1st ed., sig. b3r; Chamberlayne, *Angliae notitia,* 1:45; compare Miège, *New State of England,* 2:37–38.

44. See, e.g., Wood, *Life and Times,* 1:502, 3:27; *Friendly Monitor,* 32; *Spectator,* no. 450 (6 Aug. 1712), 4:85; and compare Chartres, "Place of Inns in the Commercial Life of London and Western England," 327–29; Grassby, *Business Community of Seventeenth-Century England,* 177, 288.

45. *Coffee-Houses Vindicated,* 4; CUL, Add. MS. 91C, fol. 13r. Prynne, *Healthes Sicknesse;* Bury, *England's Bane;* Scrivener, *Treatise Against Drunkennesse;* and Darby, *Bacchanalia.*

46. Bodl. MS Rawlinson D.1136, p. 8.

47. Sherratt, "Alcohol and Its Alternatives," 13; *Mens Answer to the Womens Petition,* 2; *Ale-Wives Complaint Against the Coffee-Houses,* 4; *Women's Petition Against Coffee,* 5; *Character of a Coffee-House,* 3.

48. Scrivener, *Treatise Against Drunkenesse,* 114; [Defoe], *Poor Man's Plea,* 12. Stow, *Survey of the Cities of London and Westminster,* 1:257; Clark, *English Alehouse,* 108–11.

49. Brome, *Songs and Other Poems,* 43 (quoted), compare 58, 77–78, 80; *Pepys Ballads,* 4:243 (quoted), compare 5:98. 237. See also Oldham, *Poems,* 237; Jordan, *Lord Mayor's Show,* 5–6; *Night-Walkers. Poor Robin's Character of an Honest Drunken Curr,* 7 (quoted); *Wit at a Venture,* 77. Compare Pincus, "Coffee Politicians Does Create," 823, 825; and Klein, "Coffeehouse Civility," 41–42.

50. Phillips, *New News from Tory-Land and Tantivy-shire,* 4. Compare the Tory response: *Heraclitus Ridens,* no. 58 (7 Mar. 1682), 4. Smith, *Consumption and the Making of Respectability.*

51. Illich, *Medical Nemesis,* 63 n. 86. Depositions of Anne Covant (31 Dec. 1686) and Margaret Cooper (5 Jan. 1687), in CLRO, MC 6/462 B; and Campbell, *London Tradesman,* 188.

52. Franklin, *Le Café, le Thé, et le Chocolat,* 167; compare Porter and Porter, *Patient's Progress,* 132. Cook, *Decline of the Old Medical Regime in Stuart London,* esp. ch. 1 on

the "buyer's market": 28, as well as Porter and Porter, *Patient's Progress;* Porter, *Health for Sale;* and Cody, "No Cure, No Money."

53. *Essays Serious and Comical,* 101; BL shelfmark c.112.f.9 (21); compare Linschoten, *Voyage,* 2:65, 67; *English Lucian,* no. 12 (21–28 Mar. 1698).

54. BL shelfmark C.20.f.2 (372); repr. as figure 14 below; BL shelfmark C.20.f.2. (371); BL shelfmark c.112.f.9. (17); and *Of the Use of Tobacco, Tea, Coffee,* 13.

55. Willis, *Pharmaceuticae Rationalis,* 155; Pepys, *Diary,* 8:302; Nicolson, ed., *Conway Letters,* 231; Harvey, *Discourse of the Plague,* 12; BL, Add. MS 15226, fol. 59.

56. Old Bailey, Ref. T16860707-2 (William Booth; 7 July 1686); *Review,* vol. 1 [9], no. 43 (8 Jan. 1713), 86a. These apothecaries' probate records fail to reveal any exotic drinks among their stocks: CLRO, OCI 2151; CLRO, OCI 2333; CLRO, OCI 2358; PRO, PROB 4/17465; and PRO, PROB 4/8815.

57. Stubbe, *Indian Nectar,* 125; *Orbilius Vapulans,* 12; and *Character of a Coffee-House* (1665), 1; Goodman, *Tobacco in History,* 43–44; Duncan, *Wholesome Advice Against the Abuse of Hot Liquors,* 217; Findlen, *Possessing Nature,* 242–43; and Camporesi, *Bread of Dreams,* 73, 103.

58. Peacham, *Worth of a Penny,* 21; Porter, *Health for Sale,* 52; Cook, *Decline of the Old Medical Regime,* 83–86, 114; Porter, *Patient's Progress,* 130–32.

59. Porter, *Health for Sale,* 36, 41 (quoted); Porter and Porter, *Patient's Progress,* 33–52, 157–59; compare Jones, "Great Chain of Buying."

60. Naironus, *Discourse on Coffee,* sig. A2v; *Calendar of Treasury Books,* vol. 2, *1667–1668,* 95, 192, 196; Sainsbury, ed., *Calendar of the Court Minutes of the EIC, 1664–1667,* 373, 376, 393.

61. HMC, *Fifth Report,* 158; 12 Charles II, c. 13, and 12 Charles II, cc. 23, 24 (1660). On this legislation, see Chandaman, *English Public Revenue,* 41, now supplemented by Braddick, *Parliamentary Taxation in Seventeenth-Century England,* 201–3.

62. Tryon, *Wisdom's Dictates,* 128; see also Smith, "Enthusiasm and Enlightenment"; DuFour, *Manner of Making of Coffee,* 15; compare Lister, *Journey to Paris,* 35; [Chamberlayne], *Englands Wants,* 4; Jenner, "Bathing and Baptism," 213; BL, Add. MSS 32526, fol. 61r.

63. On the significant differences between the Atlantic "new merchants" and the entrenched monopoly traders, see Brenner, *Merchants and Revolution.*

Chapter 3. From Mocha to Java

1. Chaudhuri, *English East India Company,* 5.

2. Davis, *Commercial Revolution.* For recent studies of mercantilist practice, see Ormrod, *Rise of Commercial Empires,* and Zahediah, "Making Mercantilism Work."

3. Unfortunately, the records of the Levant Company do not survive with the same amount of detail provided by those of the East India Company and the account offered here is disproportionately devoted to the India Company's engagement with the coffee trade.

4. *CSP — Colonial East Indies, 1513–1616,* 393; İnalcik and Quataert, eds., *Economic and Social History of the Ottoman Empire,* 335–36.

5. Foster, ed., *Journal of John Jourdain, 1608–1617,* 82, 85, 86 (quoted).

6. Henry Middleton, "Sixth Voyage," in Purchas, *Hakluytus Posthumus,* 3:115–93;

Letters Received by the East India Company, vol. 1, passim; *CSP — Colonial East Indies, 1513–1616,* 744–45, 762, 769, 772.

7. *Letters Received by the East India Company,* 6:153–54, 166, *CSP — Colonial . . . East Indies, 1617–1621,* 270, 296, 298, 372, 593, 738 (quoted), 786, 790; *EFI, 1618–1621,* 243–45.

8. *EFI, 1618–1621,* 83, 143–44 (quoted), 295–96, 306, 311.

9. *EFI, 1624–1629,* 213 (quoted); *EFI, 1630–33,* 124 (quoted); *CSP — Colonial, East Indies, 1630–35,* 254; *EFI, 1634–36,* 215.

10. *EFI, 1634–1636,* 279, 300–302, 327; *EFI, 1637–1641,* 93; İnalcik and Quataert, eds., *Economic and Social History of the Ottoman Empire,* 331–35, 359.

11. *EFI, 1637–1641,* 103, 194, 242; *EFI, 1642–45,* 58–59, 93.

12. Terpstra, *De Opkomst der Westerkwartieren van de Oost-Indische Compagnie,* 80, 110–15, 127–36; Israel, *Dutch Primacy in World Trade,* 177–78; *EFI, 1646–1650,* 224; *EFI, 1651–1654,* 118; *CSP — Colonial, East Indies, 1622–1624,* 143; *EFI, 1646–1650,* 171.

13. *EFI, 1655–1660,* 145, 206; Coolhaas, ed., *Generale Missiven,* 310; Sainsbury, ed., *Calendar of the Court Minutes of the East India Company, 1655–1659,* xxxiv.

14. *EFI, 1655–1660,* 240–41; Sainsbury, ed., *Calendar of the Court Minutes of the East India Company, 1644–1649,* 261–62; Sainsbury, ed., *Calendar of the Court Minutes of the East India Company, 1650–1654,* 24; *EFI, 1661–1664,* 18, 30; BL, OIOL, B/26, 309; Chaudhuri, *Trading World of Asia,* 366–68.

15. *EFI, 1655–1660,* 322; *EFI, 1661–1664,* 22, 187–88, 208, 319; *EFI, 1665–1667,* 17; BL, OIOL, E/3/88, fols. 34r, 136r–v, 210v; *EFI, 1665–1667,* 21 (quoted), 170, 174; BL, OIOL B/26, 592; *EFI, 1668–1669,* 180; Chaudhuri, *Trading World of Asia,* 360–61.

16. BL, OIOL, E/3/89, fol. 219r; E/3/91, fol. 99v; B/26/635, 807, 824, B/30/533; E/3/87, fol. 108r; E/3/90, 23r (quoted), 24r (quoted).

17. Davis, *Aleppo and Devonshire Square,* 38; PRO, SP 105/155, 31r; SP 105/154, fol. 136v; SP 105/145, 111–12; İnalcik and Quataert, eds., *Economic and Social History of the Ottoman Empire, 1300–1914,* 507–8; Loughead, "East India Company in English Domestic Politics," 132–59; Wood, *History of the Levant Company,* 103–5.

18. BL, OIOL, B/36, fol. 122b; PRO, SP 105/154, fol. 127r; Folger MS L.c. 1117 (25 Aug. 1681); PRO, SP 105/145, 109, 113; SP 105/154, fol. 129r; BL, OIOL B/36, fols. 123r–v, 164; compare the report in HRHC, Bulstrode MS (14 Oct. 1681), which improbably reports a gift of 10,000 guineas.

19. PRO, PC 2/69, 300, 302, 313, 329, 342–43, 346, 413–14. *Impartial Protestant Mercury,* no. 69 (16–20 Dec. 1681); Folger MS L.c. 1205 (13 Apr. 1682); BL, OIOL B/37, fol. 12a.

20. Folger MS L.c. 1577 (19 Aug. 1684); Chaudhuri and Israel, "English and Dutch East India Companies and the Glorious Revolution of 1688–89," 430–32, 436; Das Gupta, *Indian Merchants and the Decline of Surat,* ch. 2; Folger MS L.c. 1582 (30 Aug. 1684); BL, OIOL E/3/92, fol. 104v; Luttrell, *Brief Historical Relation,* 2:634, 3:146–47, 3:190, 4:176–77.

21. Folger MS L.c. 2543 (5 Nov. 1695); GL, MS 9563, fols. 53r, 83r–84v, 87r, 91r, 93r; BL, OIOL, E/92, 105r, 186v, 173v; Ovington, *Voyage to Surat in the Year 1689,* 270–71; BL, OIOL, E/94, fols. 119v, 170r.

22. Folger MS L.c. 3024 (25 July 1706), L.c. 3075 (23 Nov. 1706), L.c. 3157 (1 Jan. 1708), L.c. 3287 (4 Dec. 1708); BL, OIOL, E/3/95, fol. 179r (quoted); B/48/18, 25, 29, 267, 300; E/3/96, fols. 85v–87r, 197, 275v–278r; E/3/97, fols. 1r–4v, 155v–158v, 315r–320r.

23. BL, OIOL E/3/97, fol. 156r; *Review,* 8:4 (3 Apr. 1711), 14b. The price data in Smith, "Accounting for Taste," 191, do not support the observations of contemporaries.

24. BL, OIOL B/51/759; B/53/117; E/3/99, fols. 129v, 278r; G/17/1, part 1, fols. 12–13, 14–15; Chaudhuri, *Trading World of Asia,* 368–83; BL, Add. MS 19291.

25. Bowen, *Elites, Enterprise and the Making of the British Overseas Empire,* ch. 3; Styles, "Product Innovation in Early Modern London."

26. BL, OIOL, B/26/279, 356, 402.

27. GL, MS 9563, fol. 53r; *Domestick Intelligence,* no. 24 (26 Sept. 1679); BL, OIOL, B/30/105–6; B/41/80, 261–62. Francia was a substantial wine importer and is identified in Jones, "London Overseas-Merchant Groups," 442, and Jones, *War and Economy,* 270.

28. BL, OIOL, B/36, fol. 146b; B/37, fol. 169b; B/38, fol. 174a; B/41, fol. 80a; B/40 fol. 225a. On Gambier, see PRO, C/108/132; and Ormrod, *Rise of Commercial Empires,* 200, 330.

29. For a similar process in the Dutch coffee market, see Glamann, *Dutch-Asiatic Trade,* 39–40; BL, OIOL, B/30/531; B/36, fol. 43a; B/39, fols. 273b–274a; B/40, fol. 225a; B/39, fols. 8a–b, 215b–216a.

30. *Impartial Protestant Mercury,* no. 44 (20–23 Sept. 1681); Folger MS L.c. 1282 (3 Oct. 1682); MS L.c. 2225 (21 Sept. 1693); L.c. 3182 (27 May 1708); *The Cargo's of Seven East-India Ships* (1664), BL shelfmark C.112.f.9 (118); BL, OIOL B/37, fols. 98a, 214b; B/48/133, 149; B/51/115, 510, 716.

31. BL, OIOL, B/37, fols. 101a, 146a; B/44, fols. 185a–b, 186a; Folger MS L.c. 3024 (25 July 1706).

32. Chaudhuri, *English East India Company,* 169–71; BL, OIOL B/36, fols. 123a, 128b, 163a.

33. BL, OIOL B/37, fol. 37a, 165b; B/38, fols. 22b, 85b, 221b, 273b, 275a; B/39, fols. 178a, 181b–182a; B/41, fol. 79a.

34. Folger MS L.c. 1925 (9 Mar. 1688); BL, OIOL B/39, fols. 59a, 61b, 138b, 141a; B/40, fols. 47a, 48a.

35. BL, OIOL B/46, fol. 92b; B/48/405; B/48/493; B/51/201; B/52/152; B/51/536; B/52/643; B/54/111.

36. Glamann, *Dutch-Asiatic Trade,* 29; Ormrod, *Rise of Commercial Empires,* chs. 2–3; Folger MS L.c. 1455 (20 Oct. 1683).

37. İnalcik and Quataert, eds., *Economic and Social History of the Ottoman Empire,* 508; Glamann, *Dutch-Asiatic Trade,* 186.

38. BL, Add. MS 36785, fol. 47r, but compare PRO, CO 388/2/6; PRO, Cust 3/3; Broadbent, *Domestick Coffee-Man,* 6–8; Douglas, *Supplement to the Description of the Coffee-Tree,* 41–42.

39. Davis, Ralph, "English Foreign Trade, 1700–1770," 302–3; Smith, "Accounting for Taste," 185.

40. Schumpeter, *Overseas English Trade Statistics,* 60; PRO, CO 390/5; BL, Add. MS

38330; Ormrod, *Rise of Commercial Empires,* 182; Ashton, *Economic History of England,* 151, 161.

41. 1 W&M sess. 2, c. 6; 4&5 W&M c. 5, §13; 6&7 W. III c. 7; 9&10 W.III c. 14; 12&13 W.III c. 11; 3&4 Anne c. 4; 6 Anne c. 22; 7 Anne c. 7; 10 Anne c. 26; Ormrod, *Rise of Commercial Empires,* 184–85.

42. *Calendar of Treasury Books,* Shaw, ed., vol. 9, *1689–1692,* 1062–63; BL, OIOL B/54/293, 406; Clark, *Guide to English Commercial Statistics,* 67, 106; Brewer, *Sinews of Power,* 51–52; Winslow, "Sussex Smugglers."

43. Smith, "Accounting for Taste." Ormrod, *Rise of Commercial Empires,* 182, 184.

44. Smith, "Accounting for Taste."

45. Chaudhuri, *Trading World of Asia,* 388.

46. Douglas, *Arbor Yemensis,* 16–20; Reinders and Wijsenbeek, *Koffie in Nederland,* 23, 25; Jamieson, "Essence of Commodification," 281–82; İnalcik and Quataert, eds., *Economic and Social History of the Ottoman Empire,* 725.

47. Smith, "Sugar's Poor Relation," 72; Smith, "Accounting for Taste," 209.

48. Jones and Spang, "Sans-culottes, *sans café, sans tabac*"; Smith, "Accounting for Taste," 212; Mintz, *Sweetness and Power;* George, *London Life in the Eighteenth Century,* 14 (quoted); Chapman, ed., *Johnson's Journey to the Western Islands,* 50; Boswell, *Life of Johnson,* 222, 734.

Part II. Inventing the Coffeehouse

1. OED, s.v. "public house."

2. CLRO, CS Bk., vol. 2, fol. 299b; CS Bk., vol. 4, fol. 317; *Spectator,* no. 24 (28 Mar. 1711), 1:104; (6 June 1712), 3:490–93.

3. The earliest known silver coffee pot (1681–82) is held at VAM M.398–1921; Snodin and Styles, *Design and the Decorative Arts,* 135.

4. Broadbent, *Domestick Coffee-Man,* 12.

5. *Propositions for changing the excise, now laid upon coffee, chacholet, and tea;* Lightbody, *Every Man His own Gauger,* 62–63; Smith, "Complications of the Commonplace," 263; Broadbent, *The Domestick Coffee-Man,* 3–4.

6. *Answer to a Paper set forth by the Coffee-Men;* Lightbody, *Every Man His own Gauger,* 62–63, quoted.

7. PRO, SP 29/378/48; CLRO, CS Bk., vol. 4, fol. 317; *Spectator,* no. 49, 26 Apr. 1711), 1:209–210, quoted.

8. CLRO, Common Hall Minute Books, vol. 5, fols. 460v–461r; CLRO, Journals of the Court of Common Council, vol. 4, fols. 30v ff.; *Life and Character of Moll King,* 7–8; *Spectator,* no. 31 (5 Apr. 1711), 1:132; no. 403 (12 June 1712), 3:509; no. 24 (28 Mar. 1711), 1:104.

9. Gibson Wood, "Picture Consumption in London at the End of the Seventeenth Century"; Ogden and Ogden, *English Taste in Landscape;* Watt, *Cheap Print and Popular Piety;* Cowan, "Arenas of Connoisseurship"; Cowan, "An Open Elite."

Chapter 4. Penny Universities?

1. Barry, "Bourgeois Collectivism?" 84.

2. Wood, *Life and Times,* 1:168; 1:188–89; compare 2:212–13.

3. Wood, *Life and Times,* 1:201. On Tillyard, in addition to the following, see also 1:203, 244, 350, 477; 2:229, 3:134.

4. Clark, *British Clubs and Societies;* Allen, "Political Clubs in Restoration London"; Wood, *Life and Times,* 1:466.

5. Wood, *Life and Times,* 1:472–73. See also Turnbull, "Peter Stahl, the First Public Teacher of Chemistry at Oxford."

6. Wood, *Life and Times,* 2:147.

7. Wallis, "Dr. Wallis' Letter Against Mr. Maidwell," 314. For a detailed discussion of the debate, see Caudill, "Some Literary Evidence," 339–48.

8. Wallis, "Dr. Wallis' Letter Against Mr. Maidwell," 315–16, 328; compare Caudill, "Some Literary Evidence," 344–45, 373.

9. Wood, *Life and Times,* 2:300 and 2:429; 2:332; 2:56; 2:334. Wood's general view of the state of scholarship and public mores after the Restoration was a generally pessimistic one: 1:296–97, 301, 509–10.

10. See, respectively, Wood, *Life and Times,* 2:279; 3:235; 3:263; 2:93; 2:60; and 2:332–33. See also 2:531. North, *Lives,* 2:291–92; and of Thomas Tenison as recorded in Evelyn, *Diary,* 4:367–68. Goldgar, *Impolite Learning,* 228–31.

11. CUL, T.II.29, Item 1, fol. 2r; Wood, *Life and Times,* 2:396; Bodl. MS Tanner 102, fol. 115; and Cooper, *Annals of Cambridge,* 3:515. Compare Caudill, "Some Literary Evidence," 368; Aubertin-Potter and Bennett, *Oxford Coffee Houses,* 14.

12. Bodl. MS Wood F.39, fol. 347r; fol. 351v; Bodl. MS Wood F.44, fol. 111; compare fol. 131.

13. The best source of information on the early history of London coffeehouses is Houghton, *Collection for the Improvement of Husbandry and Trade,* no. 458 (2 May 1701). John Aubrey thought that the first London coffeehouse had been set up by one Bowman, a "Coachman to Mr. Hodges a Turkey Merchant," but Houghton's story tells us that Bowman learned the trade from Rosée, and he began his own trade only after Rosée had left the country. See Aubrey, *Brief Lives,* 1:108–111. Compare: *Athenian Mercury,* vol. 9, no. 5 (1692), q. 2; Bradley, *Virtue and Use of Coffee,* 21–22; Ellis, *Penny Universities,* 30–33.

14. Compare Shapin and Schaffer, *Leviathan and the Air-Pump,* 292; and see Johns, *Nature of the Book,* 231; Worden, *Rump Parliament,* 403 (quoted). Houghton, *Husbandry and Trade Improv'd,* 2:126; GL, MS 3018/1, fol. 140r; BL, Add. MS 10116, fol. 33r. Rugge's journals attest to his own interest in some of the characteristic objects of virtuosic curiosity, particularly strange news from foreign lands, natural marvels, exotic animals, and monstrous births. See, e.g., BL, Add. MS 10117, fols. 84v–85r, 112v, 113r–v, 114v, 118r.

15. *Kingdoms Intelligencer,* 2:50 (8–15 Dec. 1662), 89; *Intelligencer,* 2nd series, no. 7 (23 Jan. 1664/65).

16. Aubrey, *Brief Lives,* 1:289. See also Russell Smith, *Harrington and His Utopia,*

101. On Harrington and Neville, see Pincus, "Neither Machiavellian Moment nor Possessive Individualism," 719. *Humble Petition of Divers Well-Affected Persons;* and *Proposition in Order to the Proposing of a Commonwealth or Democracie.* On the Bow Street club, see Ashley, *John Wildman,* 142. The facetious *Decrees and Orders of the Committee of Safety of the Commonwealth of Oceana* refers to the "politick casuists of the coffee club in Bow Street."

17. Harrington, *Political Works of James Harrington,* 110–11, here 111; Routledge, ed., *Calendar of the Clarendon State Papers,* 4:264; *Political Works of James Harrington,* 856–57. For further details on the Restoration regime's inquiry into the seditious designs of the Bow Street club, see PRO, SP 29/41/32; SP 29/46/30; *CSPD 1661–62,* 347. Fears that the Commonwealth club-men might continue to plot against the monarchy persisted: *CSPD 1663–64,* 161, 392; PRO, SP 29/81/109. Pepys, *Diary,* 1:61 concurs with Aubrey, *Lives,* 1:289; compare Russell Smith, *Harrington and His Utopia,* 108.

18. Aubrey, *Lives,* 1:289; Harrington, *Political Works of James Harrington,* 814, 117; compare Russell Smith, *Harrington and His Utopia,* 101; Pepys, *Diary,* 1:13; Hunter, *Science and Society in Restoration England,* 77.

19. Aubrey, *Lives,* 1:289; Pepys, *Diary,* 1:20–21; Harrington, *Political Works of James Harrington,* 117; Woolrych, "Introduction," 129; Worden, "Harrington's 'Oceana,'" 136–37; and Strumia, "Vita Istituzionale Della Royal Society," 522. Compare Hill, *Experience of Defeat,* 191, 200–201.

20. Harrington, *Political Works of James Harrington,* 859; Hirst, "Locating the 1650s in England's Seventeenth Century," 367.

21. Pepys, *Diary,* 1:14; 1:17; 1:61; also 1:20–21; Aubrey, *Brief Lives,* 2:148. On Petty and the Hartlib circle, see Webster, *Great Instauration,* 70–76, 81–84; Harrington, *Political Works of James Harrington,* 814. The key text in this tradition was Stefano Guazzo's *La Civil Conversazione* (1574), which was translated into English by George Petty and Bartholomew Young in 1581–1584. See Findlen, *Possessing Nature,* 104–5.

22. The major sources of information on Rota members are Aubrey, *Brief Lives,* 1:289; and Wood, *Athenae Oxonienses,* 3:1119. See also Russell Smith, *Harrington and His Utopia,* 102–3. Strumia, "Vita Istituzionale Della Royal Society," 520–23; compare Hunter, *Establishing the New Science,* 8–9, and Johns, *Nature of the Book,* 471 n. 50.

23. On the Venetian precedent for balloting procedures at the Rota and the Royal Society, see Wootton, "Ulysses Bound?" 349–50. On Robert Boyle's rules for conducting scientific debate civilly, see Shapin and Schaffer, *Leviathan and the Air-Pump,* 72–76. See also Biagioli, "Etiquette, Interdependence and Sociability in Seventeenth-Century Science," which places the codes of civility that governed the Royal Society in their European context.

24. Ward, *Diary of the Rev. John Ward,* 116. The dangerous precedent set by the Rota may also have prompted the author (possibly Robert Hooke) of the 1660 sequel to Bacon's *New Atlantis* to emphasize that the men of Solomon's House "dare not divulge" *arcana imperii.* See R.H., *New Atlantis begun by the Lord Verulam,* 39. Although the Library of Congress catalog attributes the work to Richard Haines (1633–1685), Hooke's authorship is suggested in Johns, *Nature of the Book,* 478–79, and Freeman, "Proposal for an English Academy in 1660," 297–300. For the persistence of the notion

that the Royal Society had been established to "draw mens minds off from the bitterness of party," see *Spectator*, no. 262 (31 Dec. 1711), 2:519.

25. *Censure of the Rota upon Mr. Milton's Book;* Underdown, *Freeborn People*, 72; Allen, *Clubs of Augustan London*, 15–19; Russell Smith, *Harrington and His Utopia*, 99; I have been unable to locate the tract *Rump's Seminary . . . by the Coffee Club at Westminster* (1659? Thomason Tract E.1956) cited by Russell Smith. *Late Letter from the Citty of Florence, written by . . . a counsellor of the Rota;* Tatham, *Dramatic Works of John Tatham*, 289.

26. Butler, *Hudibras*, 184, 175; [Butler?], *Censure of the Rota;* Butler, *Satires and Miscellaneous Poetry and Prose*, 324–27. See also Butler's general satires on virtuosos in *Satires and Miscellaneous Poetry and Prose*, 167–68, and *Characters*, 121–24, 247–48, and the commentary in Nicolson, *Pepys' Diary and the New Science*, 122–57. *Rota or, News from the Common-wealths-mens Club*, in BL shelfmark C.20.f.2.

27. BL, Evelyn MS 39a (out-letters), no. 329 (unfoliated); St. Serfe, *Tarugo's Wiles*, 20. See Woolrych's assessment of the Rota in *Complete Prose Works of John Milton*, 7:130. Levine, *Dr. Woodward's Shield;* see also Johns, *Nature of the Book*, 456–57.

28. *Character of a Coffee-House with the Symptomes of a Town-Wit*, 1. On the Calves-Head Club myths, see Allen, *Clubs of Augustan London*, 58–67; and Lund, "Guilt By Association." Leigh, *Censure of the Rota upon Mr. Driden's Conquest of Granada*, sig. A2r. Compare Hirst, "Locating the 1650s in England's Seventeenth Century," 367 n. 36.

29. Caudill, "Some Literary Evidence," 380. For the success of public lectures on science held in early eighteenth-century London coffeehouses, see Stewart, *Rise of Public Science*, xxxii, 29, 117–19, 143–44, 174–81, 210, 251; Stewart, "Philosophers in the Counting Houses"; and Stewart, "Other Centres of Calculation."

30. *Collection for the Improvement of Husbandry and Trade*, no. 461 (23 May 1701). This text elaborates on comments first published in Houghton, "A Discourse of Coffee," *Philosophical Transactions*, no. 256 (Sept. 1699), 317.

31. M.P., *Character of Coffee and Coffee-Houses*, 9; *Poor Robin's Intelligence* (25 Sept.–2 Oct. 1677); [Richard Leigh], *The Transproser Rehears'd*, 48. *Coffee Scuffle*, quatrains 3, 5. The BL copy of this work includes a barely legible MS annotation stating: "This is thought to be made by one Woolmoth on Evans [?] . . . and Sir James Langham." Compare Ward, *London Spy Compleat*, 137. Coffeehouses specializing in Latin conversation continued to flourish into the eighteenth century: William Hogarth's father, Richard, kept one. See Paulson, *Hogarth*, 14–15.

32. *Coffee Scuffle*, quatrains 9, 13; *News from the Coffee-House*, BL Luttrell Collection II; the verse was repeated in a Lord Mayor's pageant performed on 29 Oct. 1675 in [Thomas Jordan], *Triumphs of London*, 23. St. Serfe, *Tarugo's Wiles*, 19–21; on the Royal Society's forays into blood transfusion, see Nicolson, *Pepys' Diary and the New Science*, 55–99, and for their connections with the London coffeehouses: Johns, "Coffee, Print, and Argument," and idem, *Nature of the Book*, 553.

33. *Coffee Scuffle* was countered by a tract entitled *Juniper Lecturer Corrected*, the author of which attempted to demonstrate his erudition by composing his response in Latin. For related critiques of coffeehouse learning, see Klein, "Coffeehouse Civility, 1660–1714," 35–36.

34. Klein, *Shaftesbury and the Culture of Politeness*, 12; Pincus, "Coffee Politicians

Does Create," 822–30; Klein, "Coffeehouse Civility," 39; Elias, *Court Society;* for the contested nature of gentility, see Corfield, "Rivals: Landed and Other Gentlemen."

35. Bryson, *From Courtesy to Civility;* Shapin, *Social History of Truth,* as well as in Findlen, *Possessing Nature,* and Johns, *Nature of the Book.* Klein, *Shaftesbury and the Culture of Politeness,* 11–13.

36. Shapin, "The House of Experiment in Seventeenth-Century England," 381; Howarth, *Lord Arundel and His Circle,* and compare Girouard, *Life in the English Country House,* 170–79. The centrality of London to late seventeenth-century virtuoso culture is emphasized in Hunter, *Science and Society.*

37. Fisher, "The Development of London as a Centre of Conspicuous Consumption in the Sixteenth and Seventeenth Centuries"; Stone, *Crisis of the Aristocracy,* 357–63, 385–98, 623–25; Stone, "Residential Development of the West End of London in the Seventeenth Century"; Heal, *Hospitality in Early Modern England.* These themes are central to Whyman, *Sociability and Power,* and Rosenheim, *Emergence of a Ruling Order,* 215–52.

38. *Brief Description of the Excellent Vertues of that Sober and Wholesome Drink,* BL shelfmark C.20.f.2. (377). See also *Character of a Coffee-House* (1665), 2; M.P., *Character of Coffee and Coffee-Houses* (1661), 5–6; and *Character of a Coffee-House with the Symptomes of a Town-Wit* (1673), 3; compare Ellis, *Penny Universities,* xv; and see Sennett, *Fall of Public Man,* 81–82.

39. Goldgar, *Impolite Learning,* 236; Roche, *France in the Enlightenment,* 540; Goldsmith, *Exclusive Conversations,* 69 (quote); compare Gordon, *Citizens Without Sovereignty,* 93–112, 127–28, and Goodman, *Republic of Letters,* 122; *Spectator,* no. 119 (17 July 1711), 1:487; compare *Lucubrations of Isaac Bickerstaff,* 1:v.

40. The best discussion of the etiquette of the virtuoso visit is found in Findlen, *Possessing Nature,* 97–150; but the English case is also well documented in Caudill, "Some Literary Evidence," 1–266; Biagioli, "Etiquette, Interdependence and Sociability in Seventeenth-Century Science"; Johns, "Coffee, Print, and Argument," and especially his *Nature of the Book,* 444–542; [Boyer], *Letters of Wit, Politicks and Morality,* 216.

41. For examples, see Bodl. MS Tanner 22, fol. 41r; and LMA, Acc. 1128/177, fol. 9r.

42. Although taverns were thought to cater to a more genteel clientele, they were still associated with immoral behavior: Clark, *English Alehouse,* 11–14; Westhauser, "Friendship and Family in Early Modern England." Clark, *English Provincial Society,* 156; Clark, "Alehouse and the Alternative Society"; and contrast with Collinson, *Religion of Protestants,* 103–5, 109, 132, 148, 203–7, 216–17, as well as Collinson, *Godly People* 407–8.

43. *Coffee-Houses Vindicated,* quotes at 1, 5. The reference is to Cicero's letter to Lucius Lucceius, *Epistolae Ad familiares,* 5.12. For an incident of coffeehouse drunkenness, see Hearne, *Remarks and Collections of Thomas Hearne,* 390.

44. Hooke, *Diary,* 463–70. Mulligan, "Self-Scrutiny and the Study of Nature," 325, 327. Hooke's coffeehousing had not abated by the later 1680s and 1690s, as evidenced by the frequent notices in Hooke, "Diary"; Iliffe, "Material Doubts"; Johns, *Nature of the Book,* 554–60; Johns, "Flamsteed's Optics"; compare Shapin, "Who Was Robert Hooke?" 261.

45. Hooke, *Diary,* 429; Mulligan, "Self-Scrutiny and the Study of Nature," quote at 327, compare 311–12; *Excerpt Out of a Book, Shewing, That Fluids Rise Not in the Pump,* BL shelfmark 536.d.19 (6); Johns, "Flamsteed's Optics," 81–84.

46. Hooke, *Diary*, 13; 64; 210; 232; quote at 358; 88; 82; 225; quote at 313.

47. Pepys, *Diary*, 10:71, 11:62–63; 5:27–28; 5:12 (quote); 5:108.

48. Pepys, *Diary*, 5:123; 4:263; 5:290 (quote); see also his coffeehouse meetings with Daniel Whistler, FRS: 5:14; and 5:274; Pepys, *Diary*, 4:361–62 (quote).

49. Pepys, *Diary*, insects: 1:317–18. That discussions of spontaneous generation were current in virtuoso circles is clear from the copious references provided by R. C. Latham in his note 1 for this entry; *Diary*, inventions: 4:256–57; 4:263; natural phenomena: 3:35–36; 4:365; 5:346; medicine and chemistry: 4:378.

50. For painters, see Pepys, *Diary*, 3:2 — although on this occasion Pepys was stood up by Samuel Cooper the portrait painter; 9:139; 9:140; composers: 1:63; political economy: 4:22–23; 5:45; Roman history: 4:434.

51. Pepys, *Diary*, 5:37 (quote). Will's Coffeehouse would soon become the favorite haunt of London's literati, see Lillywhite, *London Coffee Houses*, 655–59 and Matthew, ed., *Oxford DNB*, s.v. "William Urwin." Pepys, *Diary*, 4:212; 5:63; 5:83. On the Royal Society's "history of trades," see Houghton, "History of Trades"; Ochs, "Royal Society of London's History of Trades"; Eamon, *Science and the Secrets of Nature*, 342–45; Pepys, *Diary*, 5:34 (quote); 5:274 (quote); also present that evening was the physician Daniel Whistler, FRS.

52. Pepys, *Diary*, common discourse: 4:353; 5:44; office business: 4:380; 4:287; 5:119; 5:293; 6:28; 7:89; rumors: 4:438; social gossip: 5:1; 4:281; 5:18; 5:23–24; political gossip: 4:322; 5:35; 5:142; 5:186; 5:355; 4:80; 4:163; 5:356–57; 6:108. Shame: 9:248; compare 9:103–4, where he notes that the speech lasted well over three hours.

53. Pepys, *Diary*, 4:162. The book was Balthazar Gerbier's *Counsell to Builders* (1663). On his news reading and purchasing practices, see Pepys, *Diary*, 4:297; 6:128; 6:162; 6:305; 9:38; 9:161; and esp. 6:305 n. 3 on the newsbooks bound in the Pepys Library. Pepys might go to a coffeehouse "to hear news," as in 5:321.

54. For a brief survey of Brydges's early years in London, see Collins Baker and Baker, *Life and Circumstances of James Brydges*, 11–12, 17–23. Brydges's later role as a prominent patron of scientific and technological learning in the early eighteenth century is well documented in Stewart, *Rise of Public Science*.

55. Huntington, MS ST 26/1–2 (unfoliated) (9 June 1697); (15 July 1697); (12 Sept. 1697); (18 Oct. 1697); (18 Nov. 1698); (23 Dec. 1700); Collins Baker and Baker, *Life and Circumstances of James Brydges*, 41.

56. Huntington, MS ST 26/1–2 (3 Feb. 1701), at the Goat Tavern.

57. Matthew, ed., *Oxford DNB*, s.v. "Francis White"; compare Swift, *Prose*, 4:28, 12:50; Congreve, *William Congreve*, 20. Huntington, MS ST 26/1–2 (12 July 1697) and (7 Aug. 1697); compare *Tatler*, no. 1 (12 Apr. 1709), 1:16. For more political discourse at White's, see Huntington, MS ST 26/1–2 (6 Feb. 1698). For Derwentwater: MS ST 26/1–2 (6 Aug. 1697). See also the queries on natural history at White's on 8 Sept. 1697. For Tom's: MS ST 26/1–2 (21 Aug. 1697).

58. Huntington, MS ST 26/1–2 (7 Oct. 1697), see also (26 Apr. 1698), (12 May 1698), (2 June 1698), (9 Dec. 1700); for his medical consultations: (6 Aug. 1700), (9 Aug. 1700). Collins Baker and Baker, *Life and Circumstances of James Brydges*, 11–12, calculates forty-three Royal Society dinners; Huntington, MS ST 26/1–2 (3 Apr. 1700), see also (1 Dec. 1700).

59. This conclusion is based on the absence of nearly any significant discussion of coffeehouse activities in Brydges's voluminous personal correspondence. I have examined Huntington, MS ST 57/1–8, out-letters (1693–1713).

60. Huntington, MS ST 57/4, 153. Brydges's views were much influenced by the experience of the trial of Henry Sacheverell and its aftermath; see Huntington, MS ST 57/4, 52–58, esp. 55.

61. Brydges purchased art and books primarily through dealers such as Reinier Leers, in Rotterdam, John Senserf, who also resided in Rotterdam, and Louis du Livier, a wine merchant in Bayonne, although he also relied upon friends such as the Inspector General Charles Davenant and the Amsterdam banker John Drummond. On Brydges's collecting, see Collins Baker and Baker, *Life and Circumstances of James Brydges,* 63–92; Stewart, *Rise of Public Science,* 155; and Ormrod, "Origins of the London Art Market, 1660–1730," 177–78, 181, 182.

62. This is not to say that Augustan peers had no need for coffeehouse socializing. The diary of the Second Baron Ossulston for much of Queen Anne's reign demonstrates the centrality of the coffeehouse to urban aristocratic sociability, especially during the London parliamentary "season." See Jones, "London Life of a Peer in the Reign of Anne," 145–48, 150–51.

63. Westerhauser, "Friendship and Family in Early Modern England," 524–25; Evelyn, *Diary and Correspondence,* 3:381; Evelyn, *Diary,* 4:367–68; MS annotation to *Phil. Trans.,* no. 155 (20 Jan. 1685), 441; BL shelfmark Eve.a.149.

64. Sharpe and Zwicker, *Refiguring Revolutions,* 7; *Diary and Correspondence of John Evelyn,* 590 (quote); for Hooke, see Iliffe, "Material Doubts," and compare: Boyle, *Works,* 2:163; Eamon, *Science and the Secrets of Nature,* 331; Jenner, "The Politics of London Air." Evelyn, *Character of England,* 27; BL, Evelyn MS 39(a), no. 72 (unfoliated).

65. Shapin, "Who Was Robert Hooke?" 261; compare: Boyle, *Works,* 2:182–83; 6:95; Nicolson, *London Diaries,* 189–90, 307–8; 188; 204, 267; Locke, *Correspondence of John Locke,* 6:132. See Bodl. MS Ballard 5, fol. 27; and compare Toland, *Collection of Several Pieces of Mr. John Toland,* 2:296.

66. Bodl. MS Lister 3, fol. 157; Heinemann, "John Toland and the Age of Reason," 49–50. On Toland's coffeehousing, see Champion, *Republican Learning,* 61, 93, 168, 243; Daniel, *John Toland,* 144–47, and compare Jacob, *Newtonians and the English Revolution,* 226; Jacob, *Radical Enlightenment,* 151; Shaftesbury, *Life, Unpublished Letters, and Philosophical Regimen,* 68; Shaftesbury, *Characteristics,* 2:165, 327–30; 1:53 (quote); see also Cowan, "Reasonable Ecstasies," 137–38.

67. Byrd, *London Diary,* 111.

Chapter 5. Exotic Fantasies and Commercial Anxieties

1. Evelyn, *Diary,* 4:389–90 [emphasis in original]. On the same day, Evelyn also saw a live crocodile from the West Indies.

2. Folger MS L.c. 1579 (23 Aug. 1684); L.c. 1580 (26 Aug. 1684); L.c. 1582 (30 Aug. 1684); *London Gazette* no. 2072 (24–28 Sept. 1685); no. 1174 (15–19 Feb. 1677); Stow, *Survey of the Cities of London and Westminster,* vol. 1, bk. 3, facing 230–31; and

Chartres, "Place of Inns in the Commercial Life of London and Western England, 1660–1760," 101. The notoriety of the Belle Savage as an exhibition site was such that it became a source of strained simile for doggerel poetasters, as in NAL/V&A, MS D25.F38, 755.

3. *London Gazette*, no. 1973 (13–16 Oct. 1684); no. 1974 (16–20 Oct. 1684); no. 1977 (27–30 Oct. 1684). The rhinoceros probably remained at the Belle Savage until 14 April 1686: *London Gazette*, no. 2122 (18–22 Mar. 1686); no. 2002 (22–26 Jan. 1685). The print was by Francis Barlow (1626–1704) and is reproduced in Clarke, *Rhinoceros from Dürer to Stubbs*, 40.

4. Daston and Park, *Wonders and the Order of Nature*, esp. 291–92; Houghton, "English Virtuoso in the Seventeenth Century"; and Cowan, "Open Elite."

5. *Mens Answer to the Womens Petition*, 2; *Coffee-Houses Vindicated*, quotes at 3, 2, 3, respectively; Lillywhite, *London Coffee Houses*, 602–10. On trade tokens, see Akerman, *Examples of Coffee House . . . Tokens*, 3; Burn, *Descriptive Catalogue of the London . . . Coffee-House Tokens*, 16, 21, 89–90. For Oxford: Aubertin-Potter and Bennett, *Oxford Coffee Houses*, 17. For an exegesis of the significance of the "Turk's Head" signs compatible with the one offered here, see Matar, *Islam in Britain*, 115–16.

6. For sherbets: *Mercurius Publicus* (16–23 Apr. 1663), 4:16, 249; *Intelligencer*, 2nd ser., no. 7 (23 Jan. 1665). There were nine bagnios in London by the end of Queen Anne's reign: Lillywhite, *London Coffee Houses*, 95–96. On the café Procope: Leclant, "Coffee and Cafés in Paris," 90–91; *Curious Amusements*, 55.

7. Said, *Orientalism*. On the reception of Said's work, see Prakash, "Orientalism Now." Although Said's account claimed to encompass primarily the period following the late eighteenth century, at times he reached back to include the early modern "orientalism" of Antoine Galland, Barthélemy d'Herbelot, Edward Pococke, as well as earlier writers: *Orientalism*, 3; and compare 63–73.

8. On seventeenth-century scholarly orientalism, see Champion, *Pillars of Priestcraft Shaken*, 102–5; and Toomer, *Eastern Wisedome and Learning*. On the fragility of early modern British imperialism, see Colley, *Captives*, and Wilson, *Island Race*.

9. Morley, *Memoirs of Bartholomew Fair*; Porter, *Health for Sale*, 94–111, esp. 109–10. This fascination was, of course, a Europe-wide phenomenon; French parallels to the English case are explored in Isherwood, *Farce and Fantasy*, esp. 16, 24.

10. Park and Daston, "Unnatural Conceptions." On the role of the fair as a hybrid between patrician and popular cultures, see Stallybrass and White, *Politics and Poetics of Transgression*, 27–43; and compare Agnew, *Worlds Apart*, 27, 31, 46–50; Chartres, "Place of Inns in the Commercial Life of London and Western England," 38–39. Harris, "Problematising Popular Culture"; and Reay, *Popular Cultures in England*, 198–218. On the wide appeal of cheap print in the pre-coffeehouse age, see Watt, *Cheap Print and Popular Piety*.

11. Thomas, "Cleanliness and Godliness in Early Modern England," 58; compare: Jenner, "Bathing and Baptism," 197; Jorden, *Discourse of Naturall Bathes*. Sandys, *Travels*, 12; R.H., *New Atlantis begun by the Lord Verulam*, 73. John Evelyn visited a bagnio while in Venice: Evelyn, *Diary*, 2:430–31.

12. Chamberlen, *Vindication of Publick Artificiall Baths*; compare *Publique Bathes*

Purged; and see Webster, *Great Instauration*, 261, 298. For the first London bagnio, see Haworth, *Description of the Duke's Bagnio*, 35.

13. *True Account of the Royal Bagnio*, 4, 6; Uffenbach, *London in 1710*, 164. Uffenbach provides the most detailed firsthand account of a bagnio, but compare Hooke, "Diary," 80, and see Ned Ward's facetious account of a visit to a bagnio in *London Spy Compleat*, 216–24; Thompson, *Quacks of Old London*, 268.

14. On the disparagement of luxury in this period see: Berry, *Idea of Luxury*; Hundert, *Enlightenment's "Fable,"* ch. 4; Goldsmith, "Liberty, Luxury, and the Pursuit of Happiness," 225–51; Gunn, *Beyond Liberty and Property*, 96–119; and Sekora, *Luxury*; contrast these works with the important corrective offered by de Vries, "Luxury in the Dutch Golden Age in Theory and Practice." BL shelfmark 551.a.32.(60); and *Loyal Protestant, and True Domestick Intelligence*, no. 39 (19 July 1681).

15. *True Account of the Royal Bagnio*, 4, 6; *London Gazette*, no. 1556 (14–18 Oct. 1680); Ward, *London Spy Compleat*, 216–18. Wits: *Loyal Intelligence*, no. 3 (31 Mar. 1680); Sermons: *Some Reflections on Mr. P—n*, 40–41, which intimates that the preacher was a nonconformist, or at least sympathetic to dissent; Monmouth: *Protestant (Domestick) Intelligence*, no. 74 (19 Mar. 1680). Art auction: *London Gazette*, no. 2240 (5–9 May 1687).

16. *London Gazette*, no. 1560 (28 Oct.–1 Nov. 1680); no. 1599 (14–17 Mar. 1681); no. 2042 (15–18 June 1685); no. 2334 (29 Mar.–2 Apr. 1688); Haworth, *Description of the Duke's Bagnio*, 15; *London Gazette*, no. 1723 (22–25 May 1682); no. 2452 (9–13 May 1689).

17. Chartres, "Place of Inns in the Commercial Life of London and Western England," 342; Trumbach, *Sex and the Gender Revolution*, 139, 142, 147, 164–65, 182–83, 334, 369–70, 376; *OED*, 2nd ed., s.v. "bagnio." Stow, *Survey of the Cities of London and Westminster* (1720), 317; Byrd, *London Diary*, 136, 143, 146. Such references are numerous in Byrd's diary. Boswell, *Boswell in Holland*, 45–46.

18. Much the same could be said for the eighteenth-century fashion for portraiture *à la turque*, on which see Pointon, *Hanging the Head*, ch. 5. For even more wide-ranging studies of the early modern English appropriation of oriental material culture, see Allen, *Tides in English Taste*, 1:192–217, and Berg, "Manufacturing the Orient," 385–419.

19. The classic account is Turner, *Ritual Process*, esp. ch. 5. The subversive potentials of this sort of inversion are emphasized in Davis, *Society and Culture in Early Modern France*, 124–51.

20. Recent anthropologies of consumption have tended to reject any distinction between traditional and modern modes of social consumption. See Appadurai, *Modernity at Large*, and Miller, *Theory of Shopping*. For the persistence of an orientalist coffeehouse mystique well into the nineteenth century, see Fisher, *Travels of Dean Mahomet*, 149–52; Castle, *Masquerade and Civilization*, 60–62, and compare: Defoe, *Roxana*, 140, 214–17; Walkowitz, "Going Public," 3–4; Williams, *Dream Worlds*, 66–73; Finkelstein, *Dining Out*, 97–98. Compare Appadurai, *Modernity at Large*, 83–84.

21. A similar process of "cleansing public amusements of their immoral image" was also necessary for the success of the late Victorian department store, as in Rappaport, "Halls of Temptation," quote at 83. Barbon, *Discourse of Trade*, 14; on the novelty of

Barbon's legitimation of consumer demand, see Berry, *Idea of Luxury*, 108–18, and Appleby, *Economic Thought and Ideology*, 168–83.

22. Pelling, "Barber-Surgeons, the Body and Disease," 95; and for more detail Pelling, *Common Lot*, 222–24; on an early Jacobean barbershop, see *Pepys Ballads*, 2:43; Smuts, *Court Culture and the Origins of a Royalist Tradition*, 57–58.

23. Useful information on James Salter and his coffeehouse may be found in: Caudill, "Some Literary Evidence," 381–85; Lillywhite, *London Coffee-Houses*, 194–95; GL, Print Room, Norman collection, *London Inns and Taverns*, 5:41; Faulkner, *Historical and Topographical Description of Chelsea*, 373–78; Ashton, *Social Life in the Reign of Queen Anne*, 1:129–32; and Timbs, *Curiosities of London*, 75–76, 542.

24. BL, Sloane MS 4046, fol. 342; *Catalogue of the Rarities . . . at Don Saltero's Coffee-House* (1729). For the similarity between items in Saltero's coffeehouse and those collected by Sir Hans Sloane, see King, "Ethnographic Collections," 230, 240 n. 33.

25. *British Apollo*, vol. 1, no. 102 (28 Jan.–2 Feb. 1708/9); vol. 1, no. 117 (23–25 Mar. 1709); vol. 2, no. 40 (10–12 Aug. 1709); vol. 2, no. 43 (19–24 Aug. 1709); vol. 2 (5 Oct. [*sic*]–7 Sept. 1709); *Tatler*, no. 34 (28 June 1709), 1:252, 254, 253–54; compare *Tatler*, no. 195 (8 July 1710), 3:51–52; and no. 226 (19 Sept. 1710), 3:179–80. *Tatler*, no. 216 (26 Aug. 1710), 3:133; compare no. 221 (7 Sept. 1710), 3:153–57; no. 236 (12 Oct. 1710), 3:219; and *Spectator*, no. 21 (24 Mar. 1711), 1:91.

26. Uffenbach, *London in 1710*, 161; contrast with his judgment on the Royal Society's museum on 98, and compare Findlen, *Possessing Nature*, 147–49; Thoresby, *Diary of Ralph Thoresby*, 2:376; *Catalogue of the Rarities . . . at Don Saltero's Coffee-House* (1729), 4–7.

27. Bodl. MS Smith 45, 19. On the catalogue as a genre, see Findlen, *Possessing Nature*, 36–44, and Chartier, *Order of Books*, 69–71; *Catalogue of the Rarities . . . at Don Saltero's Coffee-House*, 26th ed. (1770s?). See also the numerous Don Saltero catalogues in BL shelfmarks 1401.c.37, and 1474.b.40.

28. Bowack, *Antiquities of Middlesex*, 1:13; Burney, *Evelina*, 187; Franklin, *Autobiography of Benjamin Franklin*, 103; Lillywhite, *London Coffee-Houses*, 194–95.

29. Hooke, *Diary*, 358, and 232, where Hooke saw the prints of Benjamin Woodroffe, FRS; Caudill, "Some Literary Evidence," 381; Bagford, "Letter Relating to the Antiquities of London," lxiii. On Conyers's archaeological work, see Hunter, *Science and the Shape of Orthodoxy*, 184–85; *Athenian Mercury*, 4:16 (21 Nov. 1691); compare *English Lucian*, no. 7 (14–21 Feb. 1698), and no. 11 (14–21 Mar. 1698) (quoted).

30. On the spectacles at the fairs, see Altick, *Shows of London*, and Irving, *John Gay's London*, ch. 5. Bodl. MS D.D. Weld. c.13/3/1, cited in Rosenheim, *Emergence of a Ruling Order*, 237. See also Nicholas Blundell's visit to see the antelope at Holborn in *Great Diurnal of Nicholas Blundell*, 2:155. These displays pre-dated the Restoration, as documented amply in Stone, *Crisis of the Aristocracy*, 389–90.

31. Hooke, *Diary*, 174, 178, 184. Compare: HMC, vol. 6, *Seventh Report*, pts. 1–2, 465a; *City Mercury*, no. 1 (4 Nov. 1675). The admission incident provoked an apprentices' riot: HMC, vol. 6, *Seventh Report*, pts. 1–2, 471a; *True and Perfect Description of the Strange and Wonderful Elephant*; *Full and True Relation of the Elephant*; *Elephant's Speech to the Citizens and Countrymen of England*; Etherege, *Man of Mode*, 1:487–88 (28–29).

32. Evelyn, *Diary,* 2:39–40. Compare: Hooke, *Diary,* 423; Lister, *Journey to Paris,* 182; Landsdowne, *Petty-Southwell Correspondence,* 95; IHR (microfilm), Thynne MSS, vol. 77, fol. 129r; Bodl. MS Tanner 21, fol. 111v; Pepys, *Diary,* 2:166 and 4:298. Compare Evelyn, *Diary,* 3:256, and Pepys, *Private Correspondence and Miscellaneous Papers,* 1:62; Ward, *London Spy,* 173; CLRO, Ward Presentments, 242B, Farringdon extra (1685).

33. Compare Isherwood, *Farce and Fantasy,* 3–5, 33, and see Chartier, *Forms and Meanings,* 89; *Essay in Defence of the Female Sex,* 94; see also Levine, *Dr. Woodward's Shield,* 324 n. 34.

34. On the rarity of women as visitors to curiosity cabinets, see Findlen, *Possessing Nature,* 141–44; and for the Royal Society, compare the case of Margaret Cavendish, Duchess of Newcastle, in Nicolson, *Pepys' Diary and the New Science,* 104–14, and Whitaker, *Mad Madge,* 298–300. On elite women at Bartholomew Fair see HMC, *Twelfth Report,* appendix, pt. 5: *Manuscripts of . . . Duke of Rutland,* 27; BL, Add. MSS 32095, fol. 36r.

35. HMC, vol. 6, *Seventh Report,* pts. 1–2, 473a; Lister, *Journey to Paris in the Year 1698,* 182.

36. Many of these examples may be found in the seventeenth-century handbills collected in BL shelfmarks N.Tab.2026/25 and C.121.b.2. See also Pepys, *Diary,* 9:398, 9/406–7; Evelyn, *Diary,* 3:198, 3:255–56; and Nicolson, *London Diaries,* 204, 267; Bacon, *Novum Organon* (1620), 2:29, in Bacon, *Works,* 14:138; compare Bacon, *Advancement of Learning* (1605), bk. 2, in *Francis Bacon,* 176–77. For the Royal Society's adoption of this program, see Sprat, *History of the Royal Society,* 83.

37. Park and Daston, "Unnatural Conceptions," 47–51, 53; BL shelfmark N.Tab.2026/25 (33).

38. For early eighteenth-century examples, compare BL, Sloane MS 5246, fols. 11r, 53v; and for the late sixteenth century: Mullaney, "Strange Things, Gross Terms, Curious Customs," 69; BL shelfmark N.Tab.2026/25 (24) (quoted).

39. Todd, *Imagining Monsters,* 156, 157; Fabaron, "Le commerce des monstres," 95–112; *Spectator,* no. 412 (23 June 1712), 3:541. Compare: *Tatler,* no. 108 (17 Dec. 1709), 2:155.

40. Park and Daston, "Unnatural Conceptions," 34; Compare Watt, *Cheap Print and Popular Piety,* 165; Wilson, *Island Race;* Outram, *Enlightenment,* 63–79; Looney, "Cultural Life in the Provinces," 41; Semonin, "Monsters in the Marketplace," 69–81; *Tatler,* no. 20 (26 May 1709), 1:159–60; compare no. 4 (19 Apr. 1709), 1:40. For an earlier auction sale of an elephant, see *London Gazette* (23–26 Feb. 1685), and compare Verney, *Memoirs of the Verney Family,* 4:269.

41. Wilson, "Three Ladies of London" (1584), in *Select Collection of Old English Plays,* quotes at 6:306 and 6:276; Livy, *History of Rome,* bk. 39, chaps. 6–7; (Evelyn to the countess of Sunderland, 13 Apr. 1679, London), in BL Evelyn MS 39b (out-letters, vol. 2). On the ubiquity of the Asian luxury trope in Roman thought, see Berry, *Idea of Luxury,* 68–69.

42. On the association of luxury with effeminacy in English culture, see Pocock, *Machiavellian Moment,* 430–31; Pocock, *Virtue, Commerce, and History,* 114; Barker-Benfield, *Culture of Sensibility,* 104–53; and Cowan, "Reasonable Ecstasies," 126–27.

Compare Evelyn, *Diary,* 5:156. For a satire on women's fashion, see D'Urfey, *Collin's Walk Through London,* 102–4.

43. Tatham, *Knavery in All Trades; Cup of Coffee; Satyr Against Coffee; Character of a Coffee-House* (1665), 1.

44. M.P., *Character of Coffee and Coffee-Houses* (1661), 1; *Character of a Coffee-House with the Symptomes of a Town-Wit* (1673), 2; the print is also reprinted as [Hancock], *Touchstone or, Trial of Tobacco.*

45. Ward, *London Spy,* 15, 197, 205. Compare Ward's *Vulgus Britannicus,* part 4, canto 12, 139, in which coffee is called a "Jewish liquor"; Ward, *School of Politicks;* Ward, *Rambling Rakes;* and *Urania's Temple,* 8.

46. On Lloyd's, see Gibb, *Lloyd's of London,* esp. 1–57, and Dawson, "London Coffee-Houses and the Beginnings of Lloyd's"; for the rest, see Dickson, *Financial Revolution in England,* 490, 503–6; Neal, *Rise of Financial Capitalism,* 22–25, 33, 46. For whale oil, *London Gazette,* no. 1843 (16–19 July 1683).

47. Chaudhuri, *English East India Company,* 170, 202. For an early book auction in Naples, see Hobson, "Sale by Candle in 1608"; for Dutch book auctions: van Eeghen, *Amsterdamse Boekhandel 1680–1725;* HMC, *Twelfth Report, Appendix, Part 9,* 65; *London Gazette,* no. 1140 (19–23 Oct. 1676); Meyers, Harris, and Mandlebrote, eds., *Under the Hammer;* Cowan, "Arenas of Connoisseurship."

48. Cowan, "Art in the Auction Market of Later Seventeenth-Century London"; *London Gazette,* no. 2630 (22–26 Jan. 1691).

49. Borsay, *English Urban Renaissance,* 140–43; *London Gazette,* no. 3201 (13–16 July 1696); no. 1363 (9–12 Dec. 1678), quoted; CUL, Add. MS 1, fol. 39; BL, Evelyn MS, 39b, vol. 2, no. 470; Bodl. MS Rawlinson Letters 114, fols. 250–54; Bodl. MS Rawlinson Letters 91, fols. 468r–469r; BL, Harley MS 3777, fol. 150r. See also the catalogues for early eighteenth-century auctions of curiosities held in Amsterdam in BL shelfmark S.C. 467 (1–5).

50. See also Cowan, "Arenas of Connoisseurship," and Cowan, "Art in the Auction Market of Later Seventeenth-Century London"; *London Gazette,* no. 2343 (30 Apr.–3 May 1688); no. 2227 (21–24 Mar. 1687); on the popularity of the unicorn's horn among the curious, see Schnapper, *Collections et Collectionneurs,* 1:88–94, and Caudill, "Some Literary Evidence," 150, 153–55. Compare the similar sales of exotica in *London Gazette,* no. 2608 (6–10 Nov. 1690); no. 2824 (1–5 Dec. 1692).

51. BL shelfmark 1402.g.1 (1); see also: *London Gazette* no. 2334 (29 Mar.–2 Apr. 1688); *Catalogue,* GL Broadside 11–49; *London Gazette,* no. 2773 (6–9 June 1692).

52. Hooke, *Diary* (16 Nov. 1678), 384; Hooke, "Diary" (18, 20 Mar. 1689), 107; (5 Apr. 1689), 111; Hooke, *Diary* (22 May 1678), 359 (quote); (30 Oct. 1676), 255; (28 May 1678), 360; (15 May 1678), 358; Hooke, "Diary" (11 Mar. 1689), 105; (12 Mar. 1689), 105; ([21] Mar. 1689), 108; (18 May 1689), 122; (25, 27 May 1689), 124; Hooke, *Diary* (27 May 1678), 360; Hooke, "Diary" (14 May 1689), 121; (28 May 1689), 124.

53. Cowan, "An Open Elite"; Wanley, *Diary* (19 Apr 1722), 1:139; compare (4 Dec. 1721), 1:125, and BL, Harley MS 7055, fol. 242.

54. North, *Lives of the Norths,* 3:199–200; Huygens, *Oeuvres Complètes,* 9:380, my translation.

55. Huygens, *Journaal* (31 Jan. 1692), 2:13; (5 Apr. 1694), 2:331; (15 Feb. 1696), 2:572.

56. *London Gazette*, no. 1407 (12–15 May 1679); Hooke, *Diary* (13 May 1679), 358; *Bibliotheca Digbeiana*, in Bodl. MS Wood E.14, no. 3; *Smith's Currant Intelligence*, no. 19 (13–17 Apr. 1680), noted by Hooke, *Diary* (17 Apr. 1680), 443.

57. *London Gazette*, no. 2155 (12–15 July 1686); *Catalogue des livres Francois, Italiens & Espagnols*.

58. BL shelfmark 1402.g.1 (53), [Wing C7672]; compare *London Gazette*, no. 2607 (3–7 Nov. 1690); Hooke, *Diary* (14 Dec. 1680), 460; Huygens, *Journaal* (20 Mar. 1695), 2:464; compare Ogden and Ogden, *English Taste in Landscape*, 89, 93 n. 37; Evelyn, *Diary* (21 June 1693), 5:144–45; Huygens, *Journaal* (24 Mar. 1695), 2:464; Hooke, *Diary* (27 May 1689), 124.

59. *London Gazette*, no. 2526 (23–27 Jan. 1689).

60. BL, Sloane MS 647, fols. 122r–v; compare the variants in: Huntington, MS EL 8771; BL, Add. MS 21094, fols. 67v–68r; BL, Harley MS 7315, fols. 89v–91v; Bodl. MS Firth c.15, pp. 28–30; NAL, Forster & Dyce MS D.25.F.37, p. 53. Internal evidence strongly suggests that this satire was composed around 1672 and the abortive outbreak of the last Anglo-Dutch War.

61. *At Amsterdamnable-Coffee-House;* the reference is to the notorious Amsterdam Coffeehouse. *Catalogue of Books of the Newest Fashion* ([1693], n.p.), BL shelfmark 8122.e.10.; BL, Add. MS 34729, fol. 267r–v; BL, Add. MS 40060, fols. 45r–46v; *Auction of State Pictures*.

62. *Poor Robin's Intelligence* (3–10 Apr. 1676); *Copy of Verses*, BL shelfmark C.39.k.6. (39); *Catalogue of Batchelors; Charecters of Some Young Women; Catalogue of the Bowes of the Town; Continuation of a Catalogue of Ladies* (1691); *Mercurius Matrimonialis; Continuation of a Catalogue of Ladies . . . the 6th of this Instant July* [1702?]; *Pepys Ballads*, W.G. 4:234; compare 5:418, 5:420; 5:433.

63. E. P. Thompson argues that wife-selling "in its ritual form" did not take place until the very late seventeenth and eighteenth century, in *Customs in Common*, 442, and his conclusions are supported by Ingram, *Church Courts, Sex and Marriage*, 207 n. 47; Trumbach, *Sex and the Gender Revolution*, 267, 384–87; and Weeks, *Sex, Politics and Society*, 78–79 n. 32; compare Menefee, *Wives for Sale*, 2, 31, 211–12, and Stone, *Road to Divorce*. See, however, Thomas D'Urfey's humorous ballad "The Hopeful Bargain" in *Wit and Mirth*, 258–60; and Menefee, *Wives for Sale*, 195.

64. *Athenian Mercury*, vol. 2, no. 13 (7 July 1691); *Catalogue of Jilts;* the practice began with the publication of *Wandring Whore*.

65. On Dunton's association with the Societies for the Reformation of Manners, see Dabhoiwala, "Prostitution and Police in London," 246–59; but also compare the account of Dunton's (early modern) pornographic style in Turner, "Pictorial Prostitution."

66. See the complaints of Jonathan Swift in his letter to the *Tatler*, no. 230 (28 Sept. 1710), 3:191–96; as well as in his *Journal to Stella* (18 Sept. 1710), 1:22.

67. [Buckeridge], "Dedication," sig. A2v; Bodl. MS Smith 48, pp. 209–10; Shaftesbury, *Characteristics*, 2:258–59.

68. BL, Evelyn MS, In-Letters 14 [unfoliated], no. 1581 (21 Nov. 1962); Evelyn MS 39b, Out-Letters 2 [unfoliated], no. 615 (1 Aug. 1689); no. 617 (19 Aug. 1689). The

Tunbridge Wells sale in question was advertised in *London Gazette*, no. 2477 (22–25 July 1689), and an eight-page catalogue was published: Millington, *Collection of Curious Prints*.

69. Evelyn, *Diary and Correspondence*, Bray, ed., 682, and BL Evelyn MS 39b, Out-Letters 2, no. 616 (12 Aug. 1689) and compare no. 658 (16 July 1692) for Evelyn's regrets at the auctioning of Robert Boyle's library.

70. Bray, ed., *Diary and Correspondence*, 679. Evelyn's views were shared by John Aubrey, his virtuoso contemporary, see: Hunter, *John Aubrey*, 65–66; BL Evelyn MS 39b, Out-Letters 2, no. 617 (19 Aug. 1689); Evelyn, *Diary* (21 June 1693), 5:144–45; BL Evelyn MS 39b, Out-Letters 2, no. 721 (5 Feb. 1695); and Evelyn, *Numismata*, 199. See also Evelyn, *Memoires for My Grand-son*, 51.

Part III. Civilizing the Coffeehouses

1. North, *Examen*, 141. This passage had been composed well before its publication, however: North died in 1734.

2. [Kennett], *Complete History of England* 3:336; Hume, *History of England*, 4:281; [Ralph], *History of England*, 1:297; Hallam, *Constitutional History of England*, 2:170–71 (quote at 170); Macaulay, *History of England*, 1:360–62, quotes at 360, 361; on Macaulay's concept of a "fourth estate," see Clive, *Macaulay*, 124–25.

3. Ellis, *Penny Universities*, 94. For similar views see Siebert, *Freedom of the Press in England*, 296. Cranfield, *Press and Society*, 20–21.

4. There have of course been many varieties of whig histories. I use the uncapitalized term here to refer to the sense of inevitable and triumphal modernization warned against in Butterfield, *Whig Interpretation of History;* some of the complexities relating to this terminology are discussed in Patterson, *Nobody's Perfect*, 1–35.

5. On Habermas's reception history, see Cowan, "What Was Masculine About the Public Sphere?"; Goodman, "Public Sphere and Private Life"; and Ellis, "Coffee-Women, *The Spectator* and the Public Sphere." Recent accounts of the coffeehouse in a Habermasian vein include van Horn Melton, *Rise of the Public in Enlightenment Europe*, 240–50, and Blanning, *Culture of Power and the Power of Culture*, 159–61.

6. Pincus, "Coffee Politicians Does Create"; Houston and Pincus, "Introduction," in *Nation Transformed*, 14, 18; Sommerville, *News Revolution in England*, esp. 75–84; Bucholz, *Augustan Court*, 149, 200, 248; Brewer, *Pleasures of the Imagination*, quote at 37 and see ch. 1. Compare also Zook, *Radical Whigs and Conspiratorial Politics*, 6–7; Klein, "Coffeehouse Civility, 1660–1714"; and contrast the rather different perspective in Berry, "Rethinking Politeness in Eighteenth-Century England." Jacob, "Mental Landscape of the Public Sphere," 96.

7. Clark, *English Society;* Scott, *England's Troubles;* on the mutual incompatibility of these two revisionist accounts of post-Restoration England, see Cowan, "Refiguring Revisionisms." Compare also Claydon, "Sermon, the 'Public Sphere' and the Political Culture of Late Seventeenth-Century England." Miller, *After the Civil Wars*, 60–64, and Raymond, "Newspaper, Public Opinion and the Public Sphere," both offer unusually non-whiggish accounts of Restoration coffeehouse politics.

8. This expansive view of the early modern English state is articulated in works such

as Goldie, "Unacknowledged Republic"; Hindle, *State and Social Change;* and Sacks, "Corporate Town and the English State." For a later period, see Eastwood, *Government and Community in the English Provinces.*

9. Braddick and Walter, eds., *Negotiating Power in Early Modern Society,* and Griffiths, Fox, and Hindle, eds., *Experience of Authority;* Braddick, *State Formation in Early Modern England,* 432.

Chapter 6. Before Bureaucracy

1. Lillywhite, *London Coffee Houses,* 655–59; Ellis, *Penny Universities,* 58–69; Matthew, ed., *Oxford DNB,* s.v. "William Urwin"; Blundell, *Great Diurnal,* 1:35.

2. Blundell, *Great Diurnal,* 2:103, 2:156, 2:157, 2:158, 2:207, 2:207, 2:208; Boswell, *Boswell's London Journal,* 286; Boswell, *Life of Johnson,* 770.

3. On the stark urban-rural divide with regard to possession of hot drink accoutrements, see Estabrook, *Urbane and Rustic England,* 148–49.

4. The rapid profusion of coffeehouses throughout the British Isles is documented in Pincus, "Coffee Politicians Does Create," 812–14; Aubertin-Potter and Bennett, *Oxford Coffee Houses,* 42–43; Biggins, "Coffeehouses of York," 50–60; Borsay, *English Urban Renaissance,* 145; Wilson, *Sense of the People,* 30, 32, 290, 305; Money, "Taverns, Coffee Houses and Clubs," 24; CLRO, Alchin Box H/103, no. 12.

5. Hatton, *New View of London,* 1:30; compare Miège, *Present State of Great Britain,* 1:137; Ellis, *Penny Universities,* xiv; Ashton, *Social Life in the Reign of Queen Anne,* 1:214; Burnett, "Coffee in the British Diet, 1650–1900," 38; *Calendar of Treasury Books, 1689–1692* (24 Dec. 1689), vol. 9, 344.

6. Weatherill, *Consumer Behaviour and Material Culture in Britain,* 26–27; and compare the data to similar effect in Shammas, *Pre-Industrial Consumer in England and America,* 182. On the late appearance of coffee and tea accoutrements in Essex, see Steer, ed., *Farm and Cottage Inventories of Mid-Essex,* 24, 258.

7. The definition of "dealer" for excise purposes was not defined. It is tempting to assume that the reference is to coffeehouses, but it is more likely that the excise collectors sought out those coffee merchants who sold in sufficient quantities to be worth collecting the tax. Many of these dealers may indeed have also been substantial coffeehouse-keepers, but a direct correlation cannot be assumed.

8. Blundell, *Great Diurnal,* 3:77, 3:109, and Bodl. MS Ballard 17, fol. 126; Chartres, "Food Consumption and Internal Trade," 176.

9. Blundell, *Great Diurnal,* 1:178–79, 1:239, 1:284, 1:309, 1:310, 2:33, 3:170; compare Barry, "Press and the Politics of Culture," 62–63.

10. CLRO, Alchin Box H/103, no. 12. Population figures are usually given by parish and not ward, but I have used the ward returns in Brett-James, *Growth of Stuart London,* 500, as a rough guide for comparison.

11. Compare the results based on hearth tax returns in Power, "Social Topography of Restoration London," 202–6; *London and Westminster Directory for the Year 1796.*

12. 3 William & Mary, c. 6, the London assessment records for which have served as an important source for the demographic and socioeconomic history of the City; Glass, "Notes on the Demography of London at the End of the Seventeenth Century"; Glass,

"Socio-Economic Status and Occupations in the City of London"; and Glass, ed., *London Inhabitants Within the Walls 1695.*

13. Alexander, "Economic and Social Structure of the City of London," 15–16; and Glass, "Socio-Economic Status and Occupations in the City of London," 378–79.

14. Alexander, "Economic and Social Structure of the City of London," 81, 135–36; *Ale-Wives Complaint Against the Coffee-Houses;* Chamberlayne, *Angliae notitia,* 1:45; and Miège, *New State of England,* 2:37–38.

15. *Review,* 5:129 (22 Jan. 1709), 515; Campbell, *London Tradesman,* 281; Earle, *City Full of People,* 92; Earle, "Middling Sort in London," 143–44; Earle, *Making of the English Middle Class,* 353 n. 126; *Case Between the Proprietors of News-Papers, and the Subscribing Coffee-Men,* 8–9.

16. Alexander, "Economic and Social Structure of the City of London," 137.

17. Earle, "Middling Sort in London," 144; compare Earle, *Making of the English Middle Class,* 109, Table 4.3.

18. The data gathered in Table 8 is the product of invaluable archival indexes at the PRO and the CLRO and the kindness of Dr. David M. Mitchell and Dr. Simon Smith, both of whom supplied me with several important references. On the overrepresentation of the wealthy in probate sources see Shammas, *Pre-Industrial Consumer in England and America,* 19. CLRO, MC 1/177•122 (1671); CLRO, MC 1/128•56 (1671); CLRO, MC1/174•120 (3 Nov. 1670); MC 1/199B•153 (1682).

19. Muldrew, *Economy of Obligation;* BL, Add. MS 61615, fols. 35r–v (quoted); BL, Sloane MS 4047, fol. 155; BL, Sloane MS 4046, fols. 343, 345, 347; BL, Sloane MS 3516, fol. 100; BL, Sloane MS 4046, fol. 343 (quoted); *Case of the Coffee-Men of London and Westminster,* 23 (quoted).

20. Pepys, *Diary* (3 Feb. 1664), 5:37; Westminster, St. Paul's Covent Garden, Churchwarden's Accounts, H 453 (1671), fol. 15r; *Calendar of Treasury Books,* vol. 7 (9 Aug. 1683), 889.

21. Westminster, St. Paul's Covent Garden, Churchwarden's Accounts, H 473, unfoliated; H 476 [1696 book], 38, and [1697 book], [30]; Boswell, *Life of Johnson,* 770; see also Matthew, *Oxford DNB,* s.v. "William Urwin."

22. *Case Between the Proprietors of News-Papers, and the Coffee-Men of London and Westminster,* 13; Borsay, *English Urban Renaissance,* 145.

23. Alexander, "Economic and Social Structure of the City of London," 137. Miles is closely associated with the stock-jobbing trade in Bodl. MS Ballard 47, fol. 8r; Matthew, ed., *Oxford DNB,* s.v. "Edward Lloyd"; Gibb, *Lloyd's of London;* Archenholz, *A Picture of England,* 200; Matthew, ed., *Oxford DNB,* s.v. "Francis White"; *Life and Character of Moll King,* 13; *Tom K—g's: or the Paphian Grove;* Berry, "Rethinking Politeness."

24. Saussure, *Foreign View of England,* 102; compare Macky, *Journey Through England,* 1:168–69, and Hilliar, *Brief and Merry History of Great Britain,* 21–23; Chaney, *Lifestyles.*

25. *London Gazette,* no. 1355 (11–14 Nov. 1678); no. 1978 (30 Oct.–3 Nov. 1684); Key, "Political Culture and Political Rhetoric of County Feasts and Feast Sermons, 1654–1714"; Key, "Localism of the County Feast in Late Stuart Political Culture." Macky, *Journey Through England,* 1:168; Lillywhite, *London Coffee Houses,* 132–35, 144–45, 200, 202–3, 237–38, 310, 319–20, 414–15, 431, 510–12, 560–61; Uffenbach, *London in 1710,* 27–28, 97, 142, 149, 151, 182, 188.

26. Lillywhite, *London Coffee Houses*, 387–90, 622–29, 147–49, 282–86, 198–99; Olson, *Anglo-American Politics*, 95–97, 125–28; Hancock, *Citizens of the World*, 88–89; Byrom, *Private Journal and Literary Remains*, 1:42; Lillywhite, *London Coffee Houses*, 156–58; *Spectator*, no. 609 (20 Oct. 1714), 5:81; Pittis, *Dr. Radcliffe's Life and Letters*, 46.

27. *CSPD Jan. 1–Apr. 30, 1683*, 184–86; Dr. Williams, Roger Morrice's Entering Books, Q. 413 (4 Jan. 1689); Folger MS L.c. 1346 (6 Mar. 1683); Monod, *Jacobitism and the English People*, 105–6; Horowitz, *Parliament, Policy, and Politics*, 220 n. 67; Lillywhite, *London Coffee Houses*, 288; Bodl. MS Carte, fol. 100v; *Englishman*, no. 36 (26 Dec. [1713]), 144–48.

28. Lillywhite, *London Coffee Houses*, 163–66, 432–33; Colley, "Loyal Brotherhood and the Cocoa Tree"; Macky, *Journey Through England*, 1:168, 1:124.

29. *Observator*, 1:61 (12 Oct. 1681); 1:123 (15 Apr. 1682); 1:217 (4 Oct. 1682); 1:227 (21 Oct. 1682); 1:274 (18 Jan. 1683); 1:343 (23 May 1683); 1:355 (12 June 1683); 1:403 (14 Sept. 1683); 1:450 (5 Dec. 1683); *Loyal Protestant*, no. 74 (8 Nov. 1681); no. 85 (3 Dec. 1681); no. 93 (22 Dec. 1681); *Spectator*, no. 521 (28 Oct. 1712), 4:355–56; Lund, "Guilt by Association."

30. Robert Darnton's model of a "communication circuit" for news in old regime France also fits well with the image of post-Restoration London offered here; see his *Forbidden Best-Sellers of Pre-Revolutionary France*, 188–91, and Darnton, "An Early Information Society."

31. The interrelated nature of oral, print, and manuscript communication in early modern England has now been well mapped out in works such as Fox, *Oral and Literate Culture in England*; Love, *Culture and Commerce of Texts*, ch. 5; Johns, *Nature of the Book*, and Bellany, *Politics of Court Scandal*, ch. 1; compare Durkheim, *Division of Labor in Society*. On the role of urbanization in Durkheimian theory, see Saunders, *Social Theory and the Urban Question*, 38–51.

32. Folger MS L.c. 3043 (7 Sept. 1706); *London Gazette*, no. 2430 (21–25 Feb. 1689); *Impartial Protestant Mercury*, no. 62 (22–25 Nov. 1681); *Extracts from the Records of the Burgh of Edinburgh*, 1701–1718, 15.

33. *Cup of Coffee* (quoted); PRO, SP 29/99/7; Magalotti, *Lorenzo Magalotti at the Court of Charles II*, 124 (quoted); LC, MS 18124, vol. 1, fol. 10r; Folger MS L.c. 657 (n.d.), MS L.c. 755 (6 Mar. 1678); MS L.c. 1415 (9 Aug. 1683).

34. PRO, SP 29/211/28; *Observator*, no. 15 (21 May 1681); *Loyal Protestant*, no. 25 (31 May 1681); PRO, SP 29/333/155; SP 29/416/part 2/120; SP 29/437/24; *Extracts from the Records of the Burgh of Edinburgh*, 1681–1689, 148; PRO, SP 29/417/part 1/82.

35. PRO, SP 29/437/24; HMC, *Eleventh Report*, appendix, part 7, 20; PRO, SP 29/433/part 2/142; HMC, vol. 7, n.s., *Manuscripts of the House of Lords*, 1706–1708, 52; PRO, SP 29/433/part 2/142; PRO, SP 29/433/part 2/139.

36. *Loyal Protestant*, no. 239 (1 Mar. 1683); CLRO, CS Bk, vol.6, fol. 127b; *Case of the Coffee-Men of London and Westminster*, 13–15; PRO, SP 9/217; Harris, "Newspaper Distribution During Queen Anne's Reign"; *Collection for the Improvement of Husbandry and Trade*, 5:108 (24 Aug. 1694); *Commons Journals*, 9:690.

37. Folger MS L.c. 1452 (16 Oct. 1683); PRO, SP 29/433/part 2/139–141; BL, Add. MS 4194, fol. 343r.

38. *Pasquin,* no. 28 (22 Apr. 1723); *Case of the Coffee-Men of London and Westminster; Case Between the Proprietors of News-Papers, and the Subscribing Coffee-Men; Case Between the Proprietors of News-Papers, and the Coffee-Men of London and Westminster.*

39. PRO, SP 29/51/10.I; GL, MS 3018/1, fol. 140r; Lillywhite, *London Coffee Houses,* 382, 254–55; compare Johns, *Nature of the Book,* 111; Folger MS L.c. 1202 (4 Apr. 1682); compare PRO, 29/419/9; *Publick Occurances,* no. 1 (25 Sept. 1690); Dunton, *Life and Errors,* 1:217; *Collection for Improvement of Husbandry and Trade,* 12:583 (24 Sept. 1703); Dunton, *Life and Errors,* 235.

40. PRO, SP 29/373/125; *For Information to All People; London Gazette,* no. 1993 (22–24 Dec. 1684); Mark Knights, *Politics and Opinion in Crisis 1678–81,* 173; Baldwin, *Mercurius Anglicus,* no. 2 (10–13 Oct. 1681); *Impartial Protestant Mercury,* no. 50 (11–14 Oct. 1681). Compare *Kingdoms Intelligencer,* 3:25 (15–22 June 1663); *Smith's Currant Intelligence,* no. 17 (6–10 Apr. 1680).

41. Swift, *Journal to Stella,* 1:3, 1:25, 1:56–58, 1:72, 1:135, 1:167 (quoted), 1:225; Swift, *Journal to Stella,* 1:183; *London Gazette,* no. 1440 (4–8 Sept. 1679); Wildman, *Advertisement from Their Majesties Post-Office;* Ashley, *John Wildman,* 282–89; Toland, *Collection of Several Pieces of Mr. John Toland,* 2:296–314. For similar cases of indiscretion with coffeehouse letters: BL, Add. MS 38847, fols. 113r, 114r; HMC, *Calendar of the Stuart Papers,* vol. 3, 79–80; and Bodl. MS Carte 125, fol. 100v.

42. Swift, *Journal to Stella,* 1:246; Lillywhite, *London Coffee Houses,* 237–38.

43. Boulton, *Neighborhood and Society,* 293; on neighborhood and urban identity, see Archer, *Pursuit of Stability,* 74–83. Compare Wrightson, *Earthly Necessities,* 75–79.

44. Davis, *History of Shopping,* 101; Uglow, *Hogarth,* 39–40; Lillywhite, *London Signs.* Martin Lister admired the royal discipline imposed on Parisian shops in *Journey to Paris in the Year 1698,* 17. Saussure, *Foreign View of England,* 102; CLRO, Court of Aldermen Repertories, 58, fol. 84r; *Tatler,* no. 18 (21 May 1709), 1:145 (quoted); compare *Spectator,* no. 28 (2 Apr. 1711), 1:115–18.

45. Ellis, *Penny Universities,* 36–37; Akerman, *Examples of Coffee House, Tavern, and Tradesmen's Tokens;* and Burn, *Descriptive Catalogue of . . . Coffee-House Tokens.* Coffeehouses were not the only shops to issue such tokens, nor were they limited to London. A coffeehouse in Aylesbury, Buckinghamshire, seems to have issued two halfpenny tokens in 1670: Buckinghamshire County Record Office, "Turk's Head," 17–19. Muldrew, "Hard Food for Midas"; van der Wee, "Money, Credit, and Banking Systems," 300.

46. Burn, *Descriptive Catalogue,* lxxvi–lxxvii; LC MS 18124, vol. 3, fol. 230r. The two most prominent proclamations were issued on 16 Aug. 1672 and 19 Feb. 1675. PRO, PC 2/63, 25; PC 2/63, 57; PC 2/63, 273 (quoted); Mathias, *Transformation of England,* 190–208.

47. Goldie, "Unacknowledged Republic"; Hindle, *State and Social Change in Early Modern England;* GL, MS 594/2, St. Stephen Walbrook, Vestry Minutes (19 Dec. 1674, 13 May 1675, 29 Apr. 1680). The various coffeehouses included Holcher's, Maddison's, the Berge Yard, Cragg's, and Powell's.

48. GL, MS 4069/1–2, Cornhill Ward, Wardmote Inquest Book, vol. 1, fols. 316v, 322r, 353r, 437r, 469r, 473r, 483r; Armet, ed., *Extracts from the Records of the Burgh of*

Edinburgh, 1701–1718, 139, 146, 160; LMA, MJ/SBB/601a, 25. I am grateful to A. J. Cassidy, archivist for the Hertfordshire County Record Office, for information on Hertfordshire.

49. GL, MS 68, Vintry Wardmote Inquest Minutes, see esp. fol. 84r; CLRO, MS 020D, 2 vols., 1:364; Bodl. MS D. 129, fol. 29.

50. Heal, *Hospitality in Early Modern England,* 55–56, 317–18; *CSPD July 1–Sept. 30, 1683,* 286–87, 342; Swift, *Journal to Stella,* 1:130; Ehrman et al., *London Eats Out,* 31–47.

51. *OED,* s.v. "restaurant"; Spang, *Invention of the Restaurant;* Matthew, ed., *Oxford DNB,* s.v. "Pontack"; Byng, *Torrington Diaries,* 182–83.

52. *(True) Domestick Intelligence,* no. 90 (11–14 May 1680). On English inns, see Chartres, "The Place of Inns in the Commercial Life of London and Western England," and Everitt, "English Urban Inn, 1560–1760"; PRO, SP 29/47/118; PRO, SP 35/13/7; Folger MS L.c. 2176 (9 May 1693); Hunter, "English Inns, Taverns, Alehouses and Brandyshops," 80–81.

53. PRO, C 6/244/2; Scott, *Algernon Sidney and the Restoration Crisis,* 175–78; Everitt, "English Urban Inn, 1560–1760," 174–75; and Kishlansky, *Parliamentary Selection,* 196–97; Holmes, *British Politics in the Age of Anne,* 461 n. 51; Harris, *London Crowds in the Reign of Charles II,* 28.

54. Hunter, "Legislation, Proclamations and Other National Directives Affecting Inns"; 15 Car. II, c. 10, § xiv; *Extracts from the Records of the Burgh of Glasgow, 1663–1690,* 172; *Extracts from the Records of the Burgh of Edinburgh, 1665–1680,* 287.

55. CLRO, Misc. MSS 95.10; CLRO, SM 47, unfoliated (Apr. 1676); LMA, MJ/SBB/289, 17–19; LMA, MJ/SBB/294, 24; LMA, MJ/SBB/315, 53–54; LMA, MJ/SBB/316, 23; LMA, MJ/SBB/302, 51; LMA, MJ/SBB/303, 57–58; LMA, MJ/SBB/316, 23; Jeaffreson, ed., *Middlesex County Records,* 4:36; LMA, MJ/SBB/282, 34; LMA, MJ/SP/1676/Jan. 2; *CSPD 1689–90,* 374–75; CLRO, SM 62, unfoliated (Apr. 1692); CLRO, Aldermen Repertories 96:227; CLRO, SM 62, unfoliated (May 1692); CLRO, Aldermen Repertories 96:432, 440; GL, MS 60, fol. 22r; GL, MS 4069/2, fol. 491v; CLRO, LV (B), 1701; MJ/SBB/755, 55. Many records of licensed victualers may have been destroyed at some point, for the City of London's victualing license series are limited for the seventeenth century.

56. Cunnington, *Records of the County of Wiltshire,* 266; Lancashire County Record Office, QSP 643/14–15 (10 Jan. 1688); CUL, T.II.29, quote at item 1, fol. 2r; Bodl. MS Rawlinson D.1136, 75, 78.

57. CLRO, Common Council Journals, 47, fol. 179r; CLRO, Common Hall Minute Books, 5, fol. 416r; LMA, MJ/SBB/436, 38; LMA, MJ/SBB/437, 45; LMA, MJ/SBB/467, 47; GL, MS 68, fol. 16r; GL, MS 4069/2, fol. 497v, fol. 501v; for an incident of magisterial vendetta, see LMA, MJ/SBB/420, 44; PRO, SP 29/51/10.I.

58. LMA, MJ/SBB/391, 45; LMA, MJ/SBB/401, 44; LMA, MJ/SBB/394, 48; CLRO, SM 53, unfoliated (Oct. 1682); CLRO, Common Council Journals, 49, fol. 404v; Mayor's precept (26 Feb. 1686) in CLRO, Alchin Box H/103 (15, no. 2); PRO, SP 29/417/part 1/77; *CSPD 1682,* 485; PRO, SP 29/422/part 2/110; PRO, SP 29/422/part 2/151.

59. Folger MS L.c. 1367 (24 Apr. 1683); MS L.c. 1530 (1 May 1684); MS L.c. 1532 (6

May 1684); MS L.c. 1608 (30 Oct. 1684); *CSPD 1684–85,* 305. CLRO, Sessions Papers, Box 2, depositions concerning remarks made against Sir John Moore [c. Oct. 1681], Information of T. Novell; Lillywhite, *London Coffee Houses,* 80–83. Folger MS L.c. 1510 (15 Mar. 1684). *Excommunicato capiendo* writs were a powerful and controversial means of punishing dissenters: Horle, *Quakers and the English Legal System,* 44–46, 53, 231–32, 250–53 nn. 112, 117, 132.

60. PRO, SP 29/421/102; CLRO, Sessions Minute Book 53; Journals of the Court of Common Council, 49, fol. 404v. For the broader campaign, see Harris, "Was the Tory Reaction Popular?"; *Observator,* vol. 1, no. 285 (7 Feb. 1683).

61. LMA, MJ/OC/1, fol. 14r; *Observator,* vol. 9, no. 29 (22–26 Apr. 1710).

62. Franklin, *Café, le Thé, et le Chocolat,* 202–6; and Franklin, *Dictionnaire Historique,* 434–35; *Extracts from the Records of the Burgh of Glasgow, 1663–1690,* 72.

63. PRO, CUST 48/1, 51–52. On the cause for grievance behind this petition, see *Calendar of Treasury Books 1672–1675,* vol. 4, 59, 132; PRO, CUST 48/4, 30–31; and compare PRO, CUST 48/3, 134–36.

64. *Extracts from the Records of the Burgh of Edinburgh, 1665–1680,* 211; GL, MS 4069/2, fol. 281v; CLRO, Ward Presentments, 242B, St. Dunston & St. Bride in Farringdon without (1690), 36; Cordwainer (1698), 47; 242C, Aldgate (1703); 242D, Farringdon extra (1706) and Broadstreet Ward (1712); 242E, Cordwainer Street (1714), Part of Farringdon extra (1718), and Tower (1720); 243A, Aldersgate in and out (1728); 243C, Bridge Within (1750). For a general complaint by citizens about the encroachments made by interlopers not in possession of the freedom, see CLRO, Sessions Papers, Box 3 (3 Apr. 1688).

65. Westminster, St. Paul's Covent Garden, Churchwarden's Accounts, H 449 (1667), unfoliated; H 450 (1668), fols. 5r, 21r; H 452 (1670), fol. 22r; H 453 (1671), fol. 21r; H 454 (1672), fol. 22r; H 455 (1673), [p. 23]; H 456 (1675), fol. 22r; H 461 (1680), unfoliated; H 462 (1681), unfoliated; H 466 (1686), unfoliated; GL, MS 9583/2, part I, fols. 23v, 53r.

66. *Mercurius Anglicus,* no. 8 (13–17 Dec. 1679); *Athenian Mercury* (9 Sept. 1693), 11:18, q. 2; *Athenian Mercury* (24 Feb. 1694), 13:6; and *Observator,* 1:94 (13–17 Mar. 1703). On the Reformation of Manners campaigns against public houses, see Shoemaker, "Reforming the City"; and Craig, "Movement for the Reformation of Manners," 103–50.

67. CLRO, Sessions Papers, Box 3 (7 Dec. 1692); CLRO, Alderman repertories 95, fol. 63b; Luttrell, *Brief Historical Relation,* 3:118, 4:352, 5:161; LMA, MJ/SBB/551, 37; Clark, Longleat House newsletter copies, vol. 304–4, fols. 50r, 55r–v; Shoemaker, *Prosecution and Punishment,* 157–58, 263; *Extracts from the Records of the Burgh of Edinburgh, 1689–1701,* 20–21; Edinburgh, MS Laing III.394, 38–39, 307–13; *Extracts from the Records of the Burgh of Edinburgh, 1701–1718,* 71.

68. LMA, WJ/SP/1718/October (petition); LMA, WJ/OC I, fol. 4; LMA, MJ/OC/1, fols. 8v–9r; Matthew, ed., *Oxford DNB,* s.v. "Francis White."

69. Hunt, "Conquering Desires"; Huntington MS HM 1264, 149–51, quote at 150; PRO, CUST 48/3, 24–25, 71–72; [Bevan?], "Proposal for Raising 125,000 l." (c. 1710) in GL, Broadside 13–19; PRO, T 1/100/90, fol. 331; *Calendar of Treasury Papers 1708–1714,* 162; Bodl. MS Rawlinson D.360, fol. 84r; compare Brooks, "Taxation, Finance, and Public Opinion, 1688–1714," 248–49, 284, 293, 307.

70. BL, Add. MS 51319, fol. 117v (quoted), and see fol. 119r; on the maladministration of the coffee excises see: PRO, PC 2/65, 199; PRO, T 48/88, 29–30; and PRO, CUST 48/2, 217, 219–20, 232–33; PRO, CUST 48/3, 129, 130, 131–33; 1 W & M, sess. 2, c. 3. See *Calendar of Treasury Books,* vol. 10, 4 pts., January 1693 to March 1696, 285. Coffee remained subject to both customs and excise duties, however: Hoon, *Organization of the English Customs System,* 86; Clark, *Guide to English Commercial Statistics,* 110.

71. For the larger informational economy, see Smith, "Function of Commercial Centers in the Modernization of European Capitalism."

72. Hence perhaps the symbiotic relationship between the coffeehouse and the more formalized gentleman's club: Clark, *British Clubs and Societies;* Langford, *Englishness Identified,* 253–54.

73. Cain and Hopkins, *British Imperialism;* Pallares-Burke, "*Spectator* Abroad"; Bodl. MS Ballard 47, fol. 8r; Hoppit, "Myths of the South Sea Bubble"; BL, Harley MS 7317, fol. 126v; Harley MS 7319, fols. 182r, 196r, 366r, 367r.

Chapter 7. Policing the Coffeehouse

1. Harrington, *Political Works,* 856–57; BL, Stowe MS 185, fol. 175r; Slaughter, ed., *Ideology and Politics on the Eve of Restoration,* 56.

2. PRO, SP 29/47/118; PRO, SP 29/51/10.I; Love, *Culture and Commerce,* 74; Miller, *After the Civil Wars,* 60.

3. Compare Seaward, *Cavalier Parliament,* 73, 257; Hyde, *Life of Edward Earl of Clarendon,* 2:298–99.

4. SCA, Court Books, Lib. D, fol. 143b; HMC, 12th rpt., App., Part VII, *Manuscripts of Sir Henry Le Fleming,* 52; PRO, PC 2/63, 173; PRO, SP 29/294/64; LC, MS 18124, vol. 3, fol. 154r.

5. PRO, SP 29/311/112; PRO, PC 2/63, 252; CLRO, Journals of the Court of Common Council, 47, fol. 179v (quoted); PRO, PC 2/63, 259; Steele, *Bibliography of Royal Proclamations,* 3, no. 2359; 2, no. 824.

6. Steele, *Bibliography,* 1, no. 3595; BL, Add. MS 25124, fol. 53r; HL, HA 4685, Hastings MSS, Box 40 (Christina Hastings to Earl of Huntingdon, Nov. 1675); see also: (Ralph Verney to Edmund Verney, 6 Dec. 1675); (Edmund Verney to Ralph Verney, 9 Dec. 1675); and (Edmund Verney to John Verney, 27 Dec. 1675) in Princeton Verney MSS, microfilm reel 29; [Nedham?], *Paquet of Advices and Animadversions,* 4; HMC, vol. 8, *Ninth Report,* 66; (William Fall to Sir Ralph Verney, 11 Nov. 1675) in Princeton, Verney MSS, microfilm reel 29.

7. Pincus, "Coffee Politicians Does Create," 828–29. PRO, PC 2/65, 79; compare: PRO, SP 29/376/80; CLRO, Journals of the Court of Common Council, 48 (pt. 1), fols. 189r–91r; *Proclamation for the Suppression of the Coffeehouses;* Steele, *Bibliography,* 1, no. 3622; *London Gazette* (27–30 Dec. 1675); Folger MS L.c. 269 (30 Dec. 1675); PRO, PC 2/65, 81; Folger MS L.c. 270 (1 Jan. 1676); SCA, Court Books, Lib. D, fol. 296a.

8. BL, Add. MSS 29555, fol. 288r; (Edmund Verney to Ralph Verney, 3 Jan. 1676); (Ralph Verney to Edmund Verney, 3 Jan. 1676) both in Princeton, Verney MSS, microfilm reel 29.

9. BL, Add. MSS 29555, fol. 292r; PRO, PC 2/65, 86; compare: (Ralph Verney to

Edmund Verney, 3 Jan. 1676) in Princeton, Verney MSS, microfilm reel 29; Folger MS L.c. 273 (8 Jan. 1676).

10. PRO, SP 29/378/40; BL, Add. MS 32518, fol. 228r.

11. PRO, SP 29/378/48; BL, Add. MS 32518, fol. 228r; compare North, *Lives,* 1:197–98; PRO, PC 2/65, 88; PRO, PC 2/65, 92–93; *CSPD 1675–76,* 503; Steele, *Bibliography,* 1, no. 3625; *Additional Proclamation Concerning Coffee-Houses; London Gazette,* no. 1059 (10–13 Jan. 1676); LC, MS 18124, vol. 5, fol. 3v.

12. (Edmund Verney to Ralph Verney, 10 Jan. 1676) in Princeton, Verney MSS, microfilm reel 29; Ellis, *Penny Universities,* 93–94; Pincus, "Coffee Politicians Does Create," 831; (Edmund Verney to Ralph Verney, 6 Jan. 1676) in Princeton, Verney MSS, microfilm reel 29 (quoted); Bodl. MS Don. b.8, 557; De F. Lord, ed., *Poems on Affairs of State,* 1:283. Compare [Defoe], *Review,* vol. [9], no. 76 (28 Mar. 1713), 151; PRO, SP 29/378/76–77, 79; Folger MS L.c. 275 (13 Jan. 1676), quoted.

13. PRO, PC 2/65, p. 293; PRO, SP 29/383/132; HRHC Bulstrode MS (30 June 1676); Folger MS L.c. 354 (28 July 1676).

14. PRO, SP 29/385/245–246 [renumbered 325–26], quote at fol. 336r; compare: PRO, SP 29/391/45; HRHC, Bulstrode newsletter (15 Sept. 1676); Beinecke, Osborn MS N 10810; BL, Add. MS 36988, fol. 199r; PRO, SP 29/379/43; Haley, *First Earl of Shaftesbury,* 403–5.

15. Beinecke, Osborn MS N 10810; HRHC, Bulstrode newsletters (20 Oct. 1676). Compare PRO, SP 29/385/250; Folger MS Xd.529, no. 2 (4 Nov. 1676); Muddiman, *King's Journalist,* 205–7.

16. PRO, PC 2/65, 439–40; PRO, PC 2/65, 442; CLRO, Misc. MSS 19.4; CUL, T.II.29, item no. 24 (24 Jan. 1677).

17. PRO, SP 29/391/45; PRO, 29/394/111; PRO, 29/394/174; Dr. Williams, Roger Morrice's Entring Book, vol. 1, P.58. The manuscript was likely printed later as *The Last Memorial of the Spanish Ambassador* (London: Francis Smith, 1681).

18. PRO, PC 2/66, 108; BL, Add. MS 32095, fol. 38r; Bodl. MS Carte 79, fols. 126r–v; (Francis Benson to Sir Leoline Jenkins, 11 Sept. 1677) in HL, HM 30314; PRO, PC 2/66, 108; PRO, 29/396/115, 116; *CSPD 1677–78,* 339; *CSPD 1677–78, 338.*

19. *Extracts from the Records of the Burgh of Edinburgh, 1665–1680,* 322–23; Hume Brown, ed., *Register of the Privy Council of Scotland* (1676–1678), 278, 283.

20. Lillywhite, *London Coffee Houses,* 80–83, 216–24; PRO, SP 29/401/60; PRO, SP 29/405/98; PRO, SP 29/401/96. On Sing's role as a Catholic newswriter, see PRO, SP 29/396/115, 116; he was later thought to receive a 20s. per week pension "to go about to coffee-houses and publick meetings to disparage the discoverers of the [popish] plot": Old Bailey, Ref. 016810228–2 (28 Feb. 1681).

21. Folger MS L.c. 876 (20 Dec. 1679); *(True) Domestick Intelligence,* no. 48 (19 Dec. 1679); *Haarlem Courant,* no. 4 (6 Jan. 1680); Knights, *Politics and Opinion in Crisis,* 172–73.

22. *Coppy of the Journal Book of the House of Commons,* 33; NLS, MS 14407, fols. 72–73; Grey, *Debates of the House of Commons,* 7:380–85; HRHC, Bulstrode newsletters (27 Oct. 1680); compare Knights, *Politics and Opinion in Crisis,* 276, n. 125; Bodl. MS F. 39, fol. 27v.

23. Hence the popularity of anti-newswriter satires such as *Iter Oxoniense*; Harris, "Venerating the Honesty of a Tinker."

24. PRO, PC 2/68, 323, 334; *London Gazette*, no. 1469 (15–18 Dec. 1679); *True Domestick Intelligence*, no. 48 (19 Dec. 1679); PRO, PC 2/68, 359; *Domestick Intelligence*, no. 54 (9 Jan. 1680); Crist, "Francis Smith and the Opposition Press," 131–32; 118; LC, MS 18124, vol. 7, fol. 19; PRO, PC 2/68, 477, 495, 512; Folger MS L.c. 934 (15 May 1680); *London Gazette*, no. 1509 (3–6 May 1680); no. 1513 (12 May 1680).

25. Hume Brown, ed., *Register of the Privy Council of Scotland* (1681–82), 1, 21; *Book of the Old Edinburgh Club*, vol. 16, 104; *Smith's Protestant Intelligence*, no. 2 (1–4 Feb. 1681); Hume Brown, ed., *Register of the Privy Council of Scotland* (1681–82), 52.

26. CLRO, rep. 86, fol. 178r; PRO, SP 29/417/37.

27. LC, MS 18124, vol. 6, fol. 267; HRHC, Bulstrode newsletters (6 Sept. 1679); [Harris], *Domestick Intelligence*, no. 53 (6 Jan. 1680); IHR (microfilm), Coventry MSS 6, fols. 210 (quoted), 215, 217, 218, 242; *Loyal Protestant*, no. 18 (7 May 1681).

28. *Currant Intelligence*, no. 26 (19–23 July 1681); Knights, *Politics and Opinion in Crisis*, 173; *CSPD 1680–81*, 371; *Grand Juries Address*, 2; Atherton, "This Itch Grown a Disease," 44, 58; Folger MS L.c. 1055 (19 Mar. 1681).

29. PRO, SP 29/413, part 2/169; compare: PRO, SP 29/413, part 2/170; PRO, SP 29/414/55; PRO, SP 29/414, part 1/55:i.

30. PRO, SP 29/423, part 2/98; PRO, SP 29/431/69; PRO, SP 29/433, part 2/140; Folger MS L.c. 1398 (5 July 1683); compare PRO, SP 29/433/142; Lillywhite, *London Coffee Houses*, 170; Greaves, *Secrets of the Kingdom*, 254–55.

31. PRO, SP 29/417, part 1/51. Elford's coffeehouse had previously come under suspicion for allowing Henry Muddiman's newsletter to be read publicly: PRO, SP 29/ 385/250; Muddiman, *King's Journalist*, 205–6. PRO, SP 29/425, part 3, unfoliated/ 138, 33.

32. Folger MS L.c. 1210 (25 Apr. 1682); Lillywhite, *London Coffee Houses*, 191; Folger MS L.c. 882 (3 Jan. 1680).

33. Folger MS L.c. 908 (4 Mar. 1680); LC, MS 18124, vol. 7, fol. 26; PRO, SP 29/415, part 2/178; PRO, SP 29/416, part 2/120; Folger MS L.c. 1294 (31 Oct. 1682); PRO, SP 29/427, part 1, unfoliated/23; PRO, SP 29/428, part 1/26 i.

34. PRO, SP 29/422/26; *Observator*, no. 140 (20 May 1682); compare *Diaries of the Popish Plot*, 116. PRO, SP 29/437/15.

35. Folger MS L.c. 1005 (8 Nov. 1680); *English Gazette*, no. 3 (25–29 Dec. 1680); Folger MS L.c. 1024 (24 Dec. 1680); Crist, "Francis Smith and the Opposition Press," 222–23; CLRO, Aldermen Rep. 87, fol. 126r.

36. PRO, SP 29/422, part 2/158; PRO, SP 29/422, part 2/164; Folger MS L.c. 1250 (29 July 1682); compare LC, MS 18124, vol. 8, unnumbered fol. between fol. 33 and fol. 34 (25 Mar. 1682); vol. 8, fol. 108; *London Mercury*, no. 34 (28 July–1 Aug. 1682); *Observator*, no. 104 (27 Feb. 1682); no. 123 (15 Apr. 1682); no. 184 (5 Aug. 1682).

37. Folger MS L.c. 1296 (4 Nov. 1682); MS L.c. 1306 (28 Nov. 1682). The trained bands were directly responsible to the crown: Allen, "The Role of the London Trained Bands in the Exclusion Crisis." Wrightson, "Politics of the Parish in Early Modern England"; Goldie, "Unacknowledged Republic."

38. PRO, SP 29/417/36; PRO, SP 29/417, part 1/79; *English Intelligencer*, no. 3 (28 July 1679).

39. PRO, SP 29/417, part 1/82.

40. Folger MS L.c. 1298 (9 Nov. 1682); PRO, SP 29/422, part 2/110; PRO, SP 29/422, part 2/151; Folger MS L.c. 1390 (19 June 1683).

41. HMC, *Seventh Report*, pts. 1–2, 480b; Folger MS L.c. 1240 (11 July 1682); SCA, Court Books, Lib. D, fol. 350a; Lib. D, fol. 350b; Lib. F, fol. 16b; PRO, SP 29/436, part 1/44; compare McDowell, *Women of Grub Street*, 60.

42. LC, MS 18124, vol. 9, fol. 10; Folger MS L.c. 1390 (19 June 1683).

43. Bury, *Advice to the Commons*, 49; SCA, Court Books, Lib. F, fols. 36a–37b, 68b, 81b; Steele, *Bibliography*, 1, no. 3859; Luttrell, *Brief Historical Relation*, 1:431; SCA, Supplementary Documents, Series I, Box A, Envelope 2,ii (10 Feb. 1688); HMC, *Report on the Manuscripts of the Marquis of Ormonde*, vol. 2, 364; Steele, *Bibliography*, 2, no. 952; *CSPD 1686–87*, no. 281, 73.

44. PRO, SP 31/1/141; Dr. Williams, Morrice Entring Book, vol. 1, P.599; Folger MS L.c. 1765 (25 Jan. 1687); Clark, Longleat House newsletter copies, vol. 2, fol. 102r; Dr. Williams, Morrice Entring Book, vol. 1, P.563.

45. BL, Add. MS 4194, fol. 337r, 341v; Clark, Longleat House newsletter copies, vol. 304–3, fol. 109r; BL, Add. MS 4194, fol. 416r; Bodl. MS Don c.38, fol. 299r; Luttrell, *Brief Historical Relation*, 1:467.

46. CLRO, Journals of the Court of Common Council, 50 (pt. 1), fols. 355r–v; Luttrell, *Brief Historical Relation*, 1:471; Steele, *Bibliography*, 1, no. 3888; Steele, *Bibliography*, 1, no. 3889; CLRO, Journals of the Court of Common Council, 50 (pt. 1), fols. 355v–356r. On the nature of Williamite propaganda in late 1688, see Claydon, *William III and the Godly Revolution*, 24–63.

47. Steele, *Bibliography*, 3, no. 2746; Steele, *Bibliography*, 3, no. 2747; Luttrell, *Brief Historical Relation*, 1:478, 1:489; Steele, *Bibliography*, 2, nos. 1000, 1004, 1005, 1006; *London Gazette*, no. 2400 (15–17 Nov. 1688).

48. *Commons Journals*, 10:43, 45, 10:273; Cobbett, *Parliamentary History of England*, 5: cols. 164–68, quote at 5:165; Grey, *Debates of the House of Commons*, 9:142–47; Hanson, *Government and the Press*, 76–83; Rea, *English Press in Politics*; *Commons Journals*, 11:438, 11:439.

49. Luttrell, *Parliamentary Diary*, 395; Folger MS L.c. 2685 (22 Oct. 1696); L.c. 2686 (24 Oct. 1696); Luttrell, *Brief Historical Relation*, 4:204; Cocks, *Parliamentary Diary*, 180; Gibbs, "Press and Public Opinion: Prospective," 241; see also Gibbs, "Government and the English Press."

50. Folger MS L.c. 2685 (22 Oct. 1696), L.c. 2686 (24 Oct. 1696); *Commons Journals*, 11:567; Hoppit, ed., *Failed Legislation*, 212; *Commons Journals*, 11:765, 11:767; 11:774, 11:777; Hoppit, ed., *Failed Legislation*, 216; Cobbett, *Parliamentary History*, 5: col. 1164; compare Matthew, ed., *Oxford DNB*, s.v. "Edward Lloyd."

51. Folger MS L.c. 2676 (1 Oct. 1696); SCA, court books, Lib. F, fols. 119a, 121b,. 143b–144a, 146b; SCA, Supplementary Documents, series I, box F, envelope 25, petition vs. hawkers (n.d.); Hoppit, ed., *Failed Legislation*, 184, 190, 202, 206; Johns, *Nature of the Book*, 154–57; Folger MS L.c. 2768 (18 Feb. 1701).

52. Gibbs, "Government and the English Press," 89; Hanson, *Government and the Press*, 8–10; Gunn, *Beyond Liberty and Property*, 90–92.

53. Luttrell, *Brief Historical Relation*, 1:516; Monod, *Jacobitism and the English*

People, 105–6; Lillywhite, *London Coffee Houses,* 135–36, 432–33; Bodl. MS Aubrey 13, fol. 85r.

54. For precedents to this political tactic, see Bellany, *Politics of Court Scandal in Early Modern England;* Fox, *Oral and Literate Culture in England 1500–1700,* chs. 6–7; Folger MS L.c. 2072 (10 Nov, 1691); L.c. 2115 (3 Nov. 1692); L.c. 2217 (2 Sept. 1693); L.c. 2293 (27 Feb. 1694); Luttrell, *Brief Historical Relation,* 2:304, 2:606, 2:608, 2:613.

55. *CSPD 1689–90,* 53 (quoted); *London Gazette,* no. 2429 (18–21 Feb. 1689); Luttrell, *Brief Historical Relation,* 2:202; PRO, SP 44/351, 3; HMC, *Report on the Manuscripts of the Duke of Buccleuch & Queensbury,* vol. 2, 144, 322; Folger MS L.c. 2020 (25 May 1689).

56. Folger MS L.c. 2073 (12 Nov. 1691); L.c. 2074 (14 Nov. 1691); L.c. 2214 (16 Aug. 1693); *Commons Journals,* 10:62–64; Grey, *Debates of the House of Commons,* 9:183, 188–90, quote at 189; CLRO, Sessions Papers, Box 3, 8 July 1689; Luttrell, *Brief Historical Relation,* 2:253.

57. HMC, *Twelfth Report . . . Manuscripts of the House of Lords, 1689–1690,* 40; Folger MS L.c. 2389 (23 Oct. 1694); Snyder, "Newsletters in England," 8–9; Love, *Culture and Commerce of Texts,* 12; Richards, *Party Propaganda Under Queen Anne,* 58; Defoe, "Correspondence Between De Foe and John Fransham," 261.

58. Old Bailey, Ref. T16931206–60 (6 Dec. 1693); Luttrell, *Brief Historical Relation,* 3:521, 3:542, 3:547, 4:206; 5:287, 5:602; Folger MS L.c. 2537 (22 Oct. 1695); *Commons Journals,* 11:710, 14:256, 14:268; *Flying Post,* no. 692 (12–14 September 1699); HMC, *Fourteenth Report,* Portland MSS, vol. 4, 248; Addison, *Freeholder,* no. 22 (5 Mar. 1716), 132.

59. *CSPD May 1690–Oct. 1691,* 263. See also Dawson, "London Coffee-Houses and the Beginnings of Lloyd's," 82; PRO, PC 2/73, 253; PRO, SP 32/6/34 (quoted); PRO, SP 32/12/246; *POAS,* 5:40; HMC, *Report on the Manuscripts of the Marquess of Downshire,* vol. 1, 483, compare 482, 489; Luttrell, *Brief Historical Relation,* 4:448, 3:17, 3:513, 3:533; Folger MS L.c. 2508 (17 Aug. 1695); Matthew, ed., *Oxford DNB,* s.v. "Pontack"; Folger MS L.c. 2529 (3 Oct. 1695); *CSPD July 1–31 Dec. 1695 and addenda 1689–95,* 72–73.

60. Folger MS L.c. 2378 (2 Oct. 1694); L.c. 2560 (17 Dec. 1695); HL, MS HM 30659, no. 60 (19 Mar. 1696); no. 61 (26 Mar. 1696); Folger MS L.c. 2593 (7 Mar. 1696).

61. Folger MS L.c. 2626 (21 May 1696); L.c. 2650 (16 July 1696); L.c. 2492 (6 July 1695).

62. Steele, *Bibliography,* 1, no. 4315; Luttrell, *Brief Historical Relation,* 5:157, 5:132, 5:143; *Observator,* no. 2 (8 Apr. 1702).

63. PRO, SP 34/2/64, fol. 97; HMC, *Fourteenth Report,* Portland MSS, vol. 4, 258; *CSPD 1703–4,* pp. 471, 477; Luttrell, *Brief Historical Relation,* 5:287; PRO, SP 34/3/115, fol. 176; compare PRO, SP 34/8/62, fol. 98; *Commons Journals,* 14:269–70, 4:336–37; *Observator,* vol. 6, no. 60 (24–27 Sept. 1707); compare Matthew, ed., *Oxford DNB,* s.v. "John Tutchin," and Black, *English Press in the Eighteenth Century,* 156.

64. HMC, *Manuscripts of the House of Lords, 1706–1708,* vol. 7, n.s., 50–52; *Lords Journals,* 18:307.

65. Downie, *Robert Harley and the Press;* [Defoe], *Review,* 5:108 (4 Dec. 1708), 430b; compare 8:2 (29 Mar. 1711), 7a.

66. Harris, "Newspaper Distribution During Queen Anne's Reign"; Defoe, *Letters of Daniel Defoe*, 108–18, 388 (quoted); Downie, *Robert Harley and the Press*, 69–70.

67. Monod, *Jacobitism and the English People*, ch. 6 and passim; compare Rogers, "Popular Protest in Early Hanoverian London"; and Wilson, *Sense of the People*, 101–17.

68. Folger MS L.c. 3944 (10 Sept. 1715); *Weekly Journal or Saturday's Post*, no. 15 (23 Mar. 1716); no. 76 (24 May 1718); *Post-Boy*, no. 4411 (2–5 Nov. 1717); Hyland, "Liberty and Libel," 875; PRO, SP 35/3/78/1–6.

69. PRO, SP 35/13/6; SP 35/13/7; SP 35/13/17; *Weekly Journal or Saturday's Post*, no. 98 (25 Oct. 1718); PRO, SP 35/13/28.

70. PRO, SP 35/13/32; SP 35/13/33; SP 35/13/36; *Weekly Journal, or, British Gazetteer* (1 Nov. 1718), 1192; PRO, SP 35/13/59; *Weekly Journal or Saturday's Post*, no. 100 (8 Nov. 1718); Old Bailey, Ref. T17181205-53 (5 Dec. 1718).

71. PRO, SP 35/13/31, quoted; SP 35/14/36.

72. Compare Lund, "Guilt by Association," and Cowan, "Mr. Spectator and the Coffeehouse Public Sphere"; Cobbett, *Parliamentary History of England*, 20:328–29.

73. The distinction between a normative and a practical public sphere is introduced in Cowan, "What Was Masculine About the Public Sphere?" 133–34.

74. Muddiman, *King's Journalist*, 200–201.

75. IHR (microfilm), Thynne MSS 25, fol. 424r; and see *Dialogue Between an Exchange and Exchange Alley*, 1–2; LMA, MJ/SBB/401, 41; *Heraclitus Ridens*, no. 12 (19 Apr. 1681); *Heraclitus Ridens* (1713).

76. *Review*, vol. [9], no. 76 (28 Mar. 1713), S 152a.

Chapter 8. Civilizing Society

1. The reading of these images here revises that offered in Cowan, "What Was Masculine About the Public Sphere?" 134.

2. *CSPD 1683*, 351–52.

3. Shepard, *Meanings of Manhood in Early Modern England*; Gowing, *Domestic Dangers*; *Spectator*, no. 49 (26 Apr. 1711), 1:208; compare *Tatler*, no. 10 (3 May 1709), 1:89.

4. Habermas, *Structural Transformation*; Sennett, *Fall of Public Man*.

5. The particularly whig politics of this enterprise is described in Cowan, "Mr. Spectator and the Coffeehouse Public Sphere."

6. Wortley Montagu, *Complete Letters*, 1:314; *Gray's Inn Journal*, 2:50–54; for a ladies' coffeehouse in Bath, see Smollett, *Expedition of Humphrey Clinker*, 40 (quoted); compare Vickery, *Gentleman's Daughter*, 258, 342 n. 82.

7. *Spectator*, no. 10 (12 Mar. 1711), 1:44; Habermas, *Structural Transformation*; Klein, *Shaftesbury and the Culture of Politeness*; Brewer, *Pleasures of the Imagination*.

8. Carter, *Men and the Emergence of Polite Society*, 144–46; [Boyer], *English Theophrastus*, 3rd ed., 53.

9. Gordon, "Philosophy, Sociology, and Gender," 903; Carter, "Men About Town," 57.

10. Bodl. MS Firth c.15/181–82; NAL/V&A, MS D25.F38/618–19; *Twelve Inge-*

nious *Characters,* 30–36; and *Character of the Beaux; Tatler,* no. 26 (9 June 1709), 1:200, 198–200; compare Ward, *History of the London Clubs,* 28–29, and BL, Harley MS 7315, fols. 224v, 285r; *Female Tatler,* 5–6.

11. [Boyer], *English Theophrastus,* 55–56; compare *Essay in Defence of the Female Sex,* 72; and Anon., *Country Gentleman's Vade Mecum,* 31; [Ward], *London Spy Compleat,* 144–45, 201–5; *Female Tatler,* 49, 78.

12. Carter, "Men About Town," 40–41; Defoe, *Compleat English Tradesman* (1726), 2:231. See Shaftesbury's critique of court culture discussed at length in Klein, *Shaftesbury and the Culture of Politeness,* 175–94; and compare *View of Paris,* 18.

13. BL, Harley MS 7317, fol. 126v, and in BL, Harley MS 7319, fol. 366r. Compare *Essay in Defence of the Female Sex,* 79; for criticisms of the beaus at Tom's Coffeehouse, see: *Humours and Conversations of the Town,* 59; [D'Aulnoy], *Memoirs of the Court of England,* pt. 2, 42 [repeated in new pagination]; and *Female Tatler,* 64.

14. *Character of a Coffee-House with the Symptomes of a Town-Wit,* 5; T.O., *True Character of a Town Beau,* 2; which is repeated verbatim in the following: [Symson], *Farther Essay Relating to the Female Sex,* 113–14; *Character of a Town-Gallant,* 7; and ibid., 2nd ed., 4. Compare *News from Covent-Garden.* On Hobbism as a "coffeehouse philosophy," see Mintz, *Hunting of Leviathan,* 137, and Shapin and Schaffer, *Leviathan and the Air Pump,* 292–93.

15. Bodl. MS Smith 45/147; compare Jacob, *Radical Enlightenment,* 89; Jacob, *Henry Stubbe,* 84; Hunter, *Science and Society in Restoration England,* 164; and Redwood, *Reason, Ridicule and Religion,* 30, 41, 66, 175; *Remarques on the Humours and Conversations of the Town,* 69; Bodl. MS Eng Letters e.29, fol. 209r; Boyle, *Works,* 5:515; Hunter, *Science and the Shape of Orthodoxy,* 233, and see Hunter, "Witchcraft and the Decline of Belief"; [Flecknoe], *Treatise of the Sports of Wit* [sig. A3v].

16. Champion, *Pillars of Priestcraft Shaken,* 7, esp. n. 24, 187; compare Jacob, *Newtonians and the English Revolution,* 226; and Jacob, *Radical Enlightenment,* 151.

17. *Spectator,* no. 49 (26 Apr. 1711), 1:209.

18. For the early Stuarts, see Sharpe, *Personal Rule of Charles I,* 646–47, 684–90; on the later Stuarts, Fraser, *Intelligence of the Secretaries of State;* L'Estrange, *Intelligencer,* no. 1 (31 Aug. 1663); and compare no. 32 (21 Apr. 1664), 257; Pincus, "Coffee Does Politicians Create"; compare Cowan, "Rise of the Coffeehouse in Restoration England Reconsidered."

19. Johns, "Miscellaneous Methods"; Johns, *Nature of the Book,* 174–75; 539–40; and compare the rather more whiggish accounts in Sutherland, *Restoration Literature,* 233–44; Ford, "Growth of the Freedom of the Press"; and Siebert, *Freedom of the Press in England,* with Treadwell, "Stationers and the Printing Acts," 755–76; Bellany, *Politics of Court Scandal in Early Modern England,* ch. 2; Raymond, *Invention of the Newspaper.*

20. Schwoerer, *Ingenious Mr. Henry Care,* 138–40; Turner, "Sir Roger L'Estrange's Deferential Politics in the Public Sphere"; *Observator in Dialogue,* 1: unpaginated introduction. On L'Estrange's vernacular prose style, see Birrell, "Sir Roger L'Estrange: The Journalism of Orality"; for the wider context of this brand of loyalist populism, see Harris, "Venerating the Honesty of a Tinker," *Observator,* no. 325 (23 Apr 1683), quoted, and compare no. 326 (25 Apr. 1683) with Defoe's similar denial in *Review of the Affairs of France* 5:1 (27 Mar. 1708).

21. PRO, SP 29/425, part 2/75; see also SP 29/431/47; Folger MS L.c. 1761 (15 Jan. 1687); Luttrell, *Brief Historical Relation*, 1:392, 396.

22. [Defoe], *Review*, 1:1 (19 Feb. 1704) p. 4; compare Downie, "Stating Facts Right About Defoe's *Review*"; Downie, "Reflections on the Origins of the Periodical Essay."

23. Harris, "Venerating the Honesty of a Tinker." Compare the political sociology of L'Estrange, *Memento treating of the rise, progress, and remedies of seditions*, with *Tatler*, no. 153 (1 Apr. 1710), 2:361, quoted.

24. Gordon, "Voyeuristic Dreams"; France, *Politeness and Its Discontents*, 53–73.

25. Greenough, "Development of the *Tatler*," 633–63, and see Sherman, *Telling Time*, 128–29; *Spectator*, no. 262 (31 Dec. 1711), 2:517 (quoted). Compare *Spectator*, no. 124 (23 July 1711), 1:507. For a contemporary critique of the seventeenth-century press on the same grounds, see Sommerville, *News Revolution in England*.

26. *Tatler*, no. 18 (21 May 1709), 1:148–50, quote at 149–50; compare no. 11 (5 May 1709), 1:102; no. 42 (16 July 1709), 1:305–6; no. 74 (29 Sept. 1709), 1:512; *Spectator*, no. 452 (8 Aug. 1712), 4:90–94; *Tatler*, no. 178 (30 May 1710), 1:471 (quoted). Steele invokes an understanding of the physiological consequences of reading that was commonplace in early modern England: Johns, *Nature of the Book*, ch. 6; *Spectator*, no. 10 (12 Mar. 1711), 1:46 (quoted); and compare no. 4 (5 Mar. 1711), 1:18.

27. *Tatler*, no. 155 (6 Apr. 1710), 2:369–73, quote at 373. The character is further developed in nos. 160 (18 Apr. 1710), 2:393–97; 178 (30 May 1710), 2:467–73; 180 (3 June 1710), 2:478–82; and 232 (3 Oct. 1710), 3:199–203.

28. *Tatler*, no. 178 (30 May 1710), 2:471 (quoted); no. 232 (3 Oct. 1710), 3:201; compare no. 155 (6 Apr. 1710), 2:371; no. 178 (30 May 1710), 2:469; no. 18 (21 May 1709), 1:150; no. 214 (22 Aug. 1710), 3:125; *Spectator*, no. 43 (19 Apr. 1711), 1:182–83; *Freeholder*, no. 22 (5 Mar. 1716), 132; Paulson, *Don Quixote in England*, esp. 20–31.

29. Butler, *Characters*, 129, 177, 256–58; compare M.P., *Character of Coffee and Coffee-Houses*; *Character of a Coffee-House with the Symptoms of a Town-Wit*; Defoe, *Compleat English Tradesman* (1726), 31, 32 (quoted), and compare 38; *Tatler*, no. 10 (3 May 1709), 1:89; compare: *Spectator*, no. 625 (26 Nov. 1714), 5:136–37; *OED*, s.v. "quidnunc," and for its particular association with coffeehouses: *Letter from the Quidnunc's at St. James's Coffee-House*.

30. Bodl. MS Wood, F. 40, fol. 72; *Letters Addressed from London to Sir Joseph Williamson*, 1:73; Swift, *Correspondence*, 1:462 (quoted), 1:601, 1:344; Clark, Longleat House newsletter copies, vol. 1, fol. 431r; PRO, SP 104/3, fols. 16r–v (quoted).

31. *City and Country Mercury*, no. 10 (8–11 July [1667]) (quoted); *Tatler*, no. 84 (22 Oct. 1709), 2:36; *Tatler*, no. 125 (26 Jan. 1710), 2:237; and [Defoe], *Vindication of the Press*; BM Sat. nos. 2010 (c. 1733), 5073 (1772), 5074 (1772), 5923 (1781); Woodward and Cruikshank, "Public House Politicians!! N. 11" (1807), LWL, print 807.1.2.1.1; Hazlitt, *Complete Works*, 8:185–204; compare Brewer, *Party Ideology and Popular Politics*, 140–41.

32. *News from the Coffeehouse; Women's Petition Against Coffee*, 3–4 (quoted); compare: M.P., *Character of Coffee and Coffee-Houses*, 4; *Mens Answer to the Womens Petition Against Coffee*, 4–5; and *City-Wifes Petition, against Coffee*, [2].

33. *Tatler*, no. 1 (12 Apr. 1709), 1:15; compare especially *Spectator*, no. 247 (13 Dec.

1711), 2:458–62, on the femininity of idle talk. Compare here also Shevelow, *Women and Print Culture,* 94–98; and Rawson, *Satire and Sentiment,* 209–11; Defoe, *Compleat English Tradesman* (1987 ed.), 133–34; compare here *Spectator,* no. 457 (14 Aug. 1712), 4:111–13.

34. For projectors: *Spectator,* no. 31 (5 Apr. 1711), 1:127–32; on pedants: no. 105 (30 June 1711), 1:436–38; laughers: *Guardian,* no. 29 (14 Apr. 1713), 125–26; gesticulators: no. 84 (17 June 1713), 305–7; singing and whistling: *Spectator,* no. 145 (16 Aug. 1711), 2:73; *Tatler,* no. 264 (16 Dec. 1710), 3:337, 338 (quoted). On this important essay, compare Sherman, *Telling Time,* 131–33; *Tatler,* no. 268 (26 Dec. 1710), 3:351–52 (quoted).

35. Copley, "Commerce, Conversation, and Politeness," 68; *Spectator,* no. 87 (9 June 1711), 1:371; compare *Case Between the Proprietors of News-Papers,* 12–13.

36. The reformation of male manners proposed by Addison and Steele is the subject of Maurer, *Proposing Men; Spectator,* no. 155 (28 Aug. 1711), 2:107; compare also James Miller, *Coffee-House,* 27–28.

37. Smithers, *Life of Joseph Addison,* 92, 242–44, 281, 315–17; *Englishman,* ser. 1, no. 36 (26 Dec. [1713]), 144–48; see Pope's enigmatic comments on Addison and Steele in Spence, *Observations, Anecdotes, and Characters,* 1:80, and compare Ketcham, *Transparent Designs,* 202 n. 24.

38. *Spectator,* no. 49 (26 Apr. 1711), 1:210, 209–10; no. 10 (12 Mar. 1711), 1:44 (quoted). This statement is a variation on Cicero, *Tusculan Disputations,* 5.4.10, and the reading here should be compared with Klein, *Shaftesbury and the Culture of Politeness,* 36–37, 42; Klein, "Gender, Conversation, and the Public Sphere," 100, 109–10; and Brewer, *Pleasures of the Imagination,* 103.

39. *Spectator,* no. 606 (13 Oct. 1714), 5:72; compare no. 300 (13 Feb. 1712), 3:73; no. 376 (12 May 1712), 3:415; and for the tea-table ideal, see *Guardian,* no. 2 (13 Mar. 1713), 46; no. 16 (30 Mar. 1713), 86.

40. Hewitson, ed., *Diary of Thomas Bellingham,* 44. The social status of the women mentioned here is unclear. Compare the readings in Pincus, "Coffee Politicians Does Create," 816; and Klein, "Gender, Conversation, and the Public Sphere," 115 n. 29.

41. Longe, ed., *Martha Lady Giffard,* 250–51; Hooke, *Diary* (2 Oct. 1675), 184, contains an entry which reads: "At Mans. Dind with Mr. Boyle and Lady Ranelaugh." It is unclear whether Hooke visited Man's *before* dining with Boyle and his sister, or whether they joined him for dinner at the coffeehouse. Given the abundant evidence for Hooke's peripatetic nature throughout the rest of his diaries, I am inclined to accept this reading in favor of that offered in Pincus, "Coffee Politicians Does Create," 816.

42. Sharpe, "Dealing with Love"; Grassby, *Business Community of Seventeenth-Century England,* 153.

43. Borsay, *English Urban Renaissance,* 249, although even here compare 272, where Borsay states that "the ladies and gentlemen went their separate ways . . . the latter to the coffeehouses," as a part of the daily routine at Bath; Toland, *Collection of Several Pieces of Mr. John Toland,* 2:105; Burney, *Evelina,* 39; Rocque, *Voyage to Arabia the Happy,* 294–95.

44. BL 1402.g.1 (12); *London Gazette,* no. 2477 (22–25 July 1689); no. 2578 (24–28

July 1690); no. 2584 (14–18 Aug. 1690); no. 2585 (18–21 Aug. 1690); no. 2781 (4–7 July 1692). On the resort season, see Borsay, *English Urban Renaissance,* 141–42; HMC, *Twelfth Report, Rutland,* 2:67–68; Brewer, "Cultural Consumption in Eighteenth-Century England," 380.

45. See the Countess of Rutland's household management in HMC, *Twelfth Report,* 2:15–18.

46. HL, Stowe MS 26/1–2 (1 Oct. 1697), quoted; (22 Apr. 1701). On the social significance of the domestic visit—and thus the prominent potentials for social power it afforded to gentlewomen skilled in the practice of polite sociability—see Whyman, *Sociability and Power in Late Stuart England.*

47. Wilson, *Island Race,* 40; Klein, "Gender and the Public/Private Distinction," 103.

48. McDowell, *Women of Grub Street,* 60, 84–85, 102–3, and 17 (quoted), 60–61.

49. Alexander, "Economic and Social Structure of the City of London," 136; *OED,* s.v. "coffee-woman." Dabhoiwala, "Prostitution and Police in London," 42; compare Clark, *English Alehouse,* 79; Hanawalt, *"Of Good and Ill Repute,"* 108; *Life and Character of Moll King;* and *Velvet Coffee-Woman.*

50. [John Dunton], *Night-Walker,* 2:8–9 (my emphasis); compare 1:17. For a comprehensive review of the circumstances surrounding the publication of this periodical, see Dabhoiwala, "Prostitution and Police in London," 246–59.

51. [Ward], *London Spy,* 27; Saussure, *Foreign View of England,* 102; Gowing, *Domestic Dangers;* Dabhoiwala, "Prostitution and Police in London," esp. 1–92, 93; and Hitchcock, *English Sexualities,* 94–101.

52. LMA, DL/C/237 (17 May 1678) Cutt vs. Jacombe; LMA, DL/C/244, fols. 95v–96v (4 May 1694) Wollasten vs. Jennings; LMA, DL/C/245, fols. 4–7 (20 Jan. 1696) Branch vs. Palmer. I would like to thank Dr. Jennifer Melville for kindly drawing my attention to these references.

53. CLRO, Sessions Papers Box 2 (1679–86), Sept. 1682 Sessions, 29 Aug. 1682. For other examples drawn from the London church court records, see Earle, *City Full of People,* 242, 252, 300 n. 223. For an example of a coffeehouse that also served as a bawdy house, see the indictment of Mary Hambleton's coffeehouse in Dabhoiwala, "Prostitution and Police in London," 53; LMA, DL/C/245, fols. 194–210, quote at fol. 207r.

54. The ways in which putatively public concerns were embedded in the structure of the private lives of the middle class is explored at length and with great insight in Hunt, *Middling Sort;* Sharpe, "Dealing with Love." Ryder, *Diary of Dudley Ryder,* 124.

55. *Grub Street Journal,* no. 145 (12 Oct. 1732).

56. *Pasquin,* no. 87 (29 Nov. 1723); *Domestick Intelligence,* no. 49 (23 Dec. 1679); Bodl. MS Don. c.38, fol. 276v; Klein, "Coffeehouse Civility"; Klein, "Politeness and the Interpretation of the British Eighteenth Century."

57. *Censor,* 2:61 (12 Mar. 1717); *Weekly Journal or Saturdays Post,* no. 288 (2 May 1724); *Grub Street Journal,* no. 142 (21 Sept. 1732), no. 145 (12 Oct. 1732); *Common Sense,* no. 67 (13 May 1738); Timbs, *Clubs and Club Life in London;* Lillywhite, *London Coffee Houses;* Ellis, "Coffee-Women, *The Spectator* and the Public Sphere."

58. Beljame, *Public et les Hommes de Lettres,* 264–65; Sennett, *Fall of Public Man,* 81, 84; compare Langford, "British Politeness and the Progress of Western Manners," 62–

63, and his *Englishness Identified,* esp. 179–80, 253–54, 284. Witness also the extensive documentation of the interlocking associations between coffeehouses and clubbing in Clark, *British Clubs and Societies;* Allen, *Clubs of Augustan London;* Timbs, *Clubs and Club Life in London.*

59. Compare Jacob, "Mental Landscape of the Public Sphere," and Cowan, "What Was Masculine About the Public Sphere?" 149–50.

Conclusion

1. Sahlins, *Stone Age Economics,* ch. 1. With regard to English history, Steven Pincus points to the post-Restoration era, in Pincus and Houston, eds., *A Nation Transformed;* but the concept is used for much earlier periods in Norbrook, *Writing the English Republic,* and Lake and Questier, "Puritans, Papists, and the 'Public Sphere' in Early Modern England." Similar trepidations about the malleability of the term "consumer society" have been recently voiced in Brewer, "Error of Our Ways."

2. Berg, "In Pursuit of Luxury," offers another provocative example.

3. Prominent examples of this include Brewer, *Pleasures of the Imagaination,* 34–40, and Porter, *Creation of the Modern World,* 35–37.

4. Rather different appraisals of this postwar new whig historiography can be found in Cowan, "Review of Laura Brown"; Laqueur, "Roy Porter"; Hitchcock, "New History from Below"; and Clark, *Revolution and Rebellion.*

5. See also Cowan, "An Open Elite."

6. The history of credit relations pioneered in Muldrew, *Economy of Obligation,* and Muldrew, "Hard Food for Midas," offers an important basis for a cultural history of the commercial revolution. For an attempt to reconcile the quantitative and the qualitative elements of early modern consumer culture, see de Vries, "Luxury in the Dutch Golden Age in Theory and Practice."

7. Weber, *Protestant Ethic and the Spirit of Capitalism,* 60. The other side of this equation is, of course, the origin of the desire to increase productivity. This issue has recently been taken up by de Vries, "Industrial Revolution and the Industrious Revolution," and Hatcher, "Labour, Leisure and Economic Thought Before the Nineteenth Century."

8. Compare Scott, *England's Troubles;* for examples of localized studies, see Harris, "Grecian Coffeehouse and Political Debate in London," and Berry, "Rethinking Politeness." On early nineteenth-century coffeehouse politics, see McCalman, "Ultra-radicalism and Convivial Debating Clubs in London"; Aspinall, *Politics and the Press;* Herzog, *Poisoning the Minds of the Lower Orders;* and Barrell, "Coffeehouse Politicians."

9. For further discussions, see Cowan, "Refiguring Revisionisms," and Lake, "Retrospective."

10. Braudel, *Structures of Everyday Life,* 256.

Bibliography

All locations are London unless otherwise noted.

Abbreviations

BAC	British Art Center, New Haven, Connecticut
Beinecke	Beinecke Rare Book and Manuscript Library, Yale University, New Haven, Connecticut
BL	British Library
BM Sat.	British Museum, Department of Prints and Drawings, English cartoons and satirical prints, 1320–1832
Bodl.	Bodleian Library, Oxford
Clark	William Andrews Clark Library, UCLA, Los Angeles, California
CLRO	Corporation of London Record Office, London
Commons Journals	*Journals of the House of Commons*
CSP	*Calendar of State Papers*
CUL	Cambridge University Library, Cambridge
Dr. Williams	Dr. Williams Library, London
ECS	*Eighteenth-Century Studies*
Edinburgh	Edinburgh University Library, Edinburgh
EFI	*English Factories in India*
EHR	*English Historical Review*
Folger	Folger Shakespeare Library, Washington D.C.
GL	Guildhall Library, London

HJ   *Historical Journal*
HMC   Historical Manuscripts Commission
Huntington   Huntington Library, San Marino, California
HRHC   Harry Ransom Humanities Center, University of Texas at Austin
IHR   Institute of Historical Research, Senate House, London
LC   Library of Congress, Washington, D.C.
LMA   London Metropolitan Archives (formerly the Greater London Record Office), London
Lords Journals   *Journals of the House of Lords*
LWL   Lewis Walpole Library, Yale University, Farmington, Connecticut
NAL/V&A   National Art Library at the Victoria and Albert Museum, London
NLS   National Library of Scotland, Edinburgh
OIOL   Oriental and India Office Library; division of the British Library, London
Old Bailey   Proceedings of the Old Bailey London, 1674–1834; (www.oldbaileyonline.org)
P&P   *Past & Present*
Princeton   Princeton University, Firestone Library, Princeton, New Jersey
PRO   Public Record Office, National Archives, London
RSA   Royal Society Archives, London
SCA   Stationer's Company Archives, London
Westminster   Westminster Archives Centre, London
VAM   Victoria and Albert Museum, London

Printed Primary Sources

PERIODICALS

Athenian Mercury, 19 vols. (John Dunton, 1691–97).

British Apollo, 117 issues, 12 monthly papers and two quarterly books (J. Mayo, 1708–9).

City and Countrey Mercury, 33 issues (1667).

City Mercury (1692).

City Mercury (Andrew Clark, 1675).

Collection for Improvement of Husbandry and Trade, 12 vols. (Randal Tayler, 1692–1703).

Commonsense, or, The Englishman's journal, 354 issues (J. Purser, 1737–43).

Currant Intelligence, 24 issues (John Smith, 1680). Becomes: *Smith's Currant Intelligence* beginning with no. 10 (13–16 March 1679).

Current Intelligence, 24 issues (John Macock, 1666).

Domestick Intelligence, nos. 1–55 (Benj. Harris (1679–81). Becomes *Protestant (Domestick) Intelligence; Or news from both City and Country,* nos. 56–114 (Benj. Harris, 1680–81).

Domestick Intelligence, nos. 1–155 (Thomas Benskins, 1681–82).

Domestick Intelligence, 17 issues (Benjamin Harris, 1683).

English Gazette (W.E., 1680).

English Intelligencer (Thomas Burrell, 1679).

English Lucian, nos. 1–15 (John Harris, 1698).

Englishman, Rae Blanchard, ed. (Clarendon Press, 1955).

Female Tatler, Fidelis Morgan, ed. (Dent, 1992).

Gray's Inn Journal, 2 vols. (W. Faden, 1756).

Grub Street Journal (J. Roberts, 1730–37).

Guardian (1713), John Calhoun Stephens, ed. (Lexington: University Press of Kentucky, 1982).

Haarlem Courant (1680).

Heraclitus Ridens, 82 issues (B[enjamin] T[ooke], 1681–82).

Impartial Protestant Mercury, 100 issues [out of 115] (R. Janeway, 1681–82).

Intelligencer (1728–29), James Woolley, ed. (Oxford: Clarendon, 1992).

Intelligencer, 4 vols. (Richard Hodgkinson, 1663–66).

Journal des Sçavans (Amsterdam: Chez Pierre le Grand, 1669–1796).

Kingdoms Intelligencer, 3 vols. (R. Hodgkinson and Tho. Newcomb, 1660–63).

London Gazette (Oxford and London, 1660–1700).

Loyal Protestant, and True Domestick Intelligence, 247 issues (Nat. Thompson, 1681–83).

Medleys for the Year 1711 (John Darby, 1712).

Mercurius Anglicus, 51 issues (Robert Harford, 1679–80). Becomes *True News: or, Mercurius Anglicus,* with no. 11 (24–27 December 1679).

Mercurius Anglicus, 3 issues (Richard Baldwin, 10–17 October 1681).

Mercurius Honestus, or Tom Tell-Truth, 1 issue (1660).

Mercurius Politicus, 514 vols. (Thomas Newcomb, 1650–60).

Mercurius Publicus, 4 vols. (Richard Hodgkinson, 1660–63).

Observator (J. How, 1702–12).

Observator in Dialogue, 3 vols. (J. Bennet, 1684–87).

Pasquin, nos. 1–120 (J. Peele, 1722–24).

Philosophical Transactions, vols. 1–12 ((1665–78); vols. 13–65 (1683–1775).

Poor Robin's Intelligence (A. Purflow, 1676–77).

Post-Boy (R. Baldwin, 1695–1728).

Publick Occurrences, 1 issue (Boston: Benjamin Harris, 25 September 1690).

Review of the Affairs of France (1704–13) in *Defoe's Review,* Arthur Wellesley Secord, ed., 22 vols. (New York: Columbia University Press, 1938). References are to the volume and issue numbers of the originals, and not the reprint, volumes.

Smith's Protestant Intelligence, 22 issues (F. Smith, 1681).

Spectator (1711–14), Donald F. Bond, ed., 5 vols. (Oxford: Clarendon, 1965).

Tatler (1709–11), Donald F. Bond, ed., 3 vols. (Oxford: Clarendon, 1987).

True Domestick Intelligence (N. Thompson, 1679–80).

Weekly Advertisements of things lost and stollen, 3 issues (Peter Lillicray, 1669).

Weekly Journal, or, British Gazetteer (James Read, 1715–30).

Weekly Journal or Saturday's Post (Nathaniel Mist, 1716–28)

Weekly Pacquet of Advice from Rome, 5 vols. (Langley Curtis, 1678–83).

BOOKS

Account of the Proceedings of the New Parliament of Women (J. Coniers, 1683).

Ackermann, Rudolph, *Microcosm of London* (1808–1810).

Additional proclamation concerning coffee-houses (Bill & Barker, 1676).

Ale-wives Complaint against the Coffee-Houses (John Tomson, 1695).

Answer to a Paper set forth by the Coffee-Men (1680s?–90s?), Wing A3334.

Antaki, Dawud ibn Umar, *Nature of the Drink Kauhi, or Coffe* [Edward Pococke, trans.], (Oxford: Henry Hall, 1659).

Archenholz, Johann Wilhelm von, *Picture of England* (Dublin: P. Byrne, 1791).

At Amsterdamnable-Coffee-House on the 5th Of November next ([1684]).

Aubrey, John, *Brief Lives,* Andrew Clark, ed., 2 vols. (Oxford: Clarendon, 1898).

Auction of State Pictures (1710).

Bacon, Francis, *Francis Bacon,* Brian Vickers, ed. (Oxford: Oxford University Press, 1996).

——, *Letters and the Life of Francis Bacon,* James Spedding, ed., 7 vols. (Longmans, 1861–1874).

——, *Works of Francis Bacon,* Basil Montagu, ed., 17 vols. (Pickering, 1825–34).

Bagford, John, "Letter Relating to the Antiquities of London," in John Leland, *Joannis Lelandi Antiquarii de Rebus Britannicis Collectanea,* Thomas Hearne, ed., 6 vols. (Oxford, [1715]), 1: lviii–lxxxvi.

Barbon, Nicholas, *Discourse of Trade* (1690), J. Hollander, ed. (Baltimore: Johns Hopkins Press, 1905).

Bayle, Pierre, *Oeuvres Diverses,* 5 vols. (1727; reprint, New York: Georg Olms, 1964–82).

Bibliotheca Digbeiana, in Bodl. MS Wood E.14, no. 3.

Biddulph, William, "Part of a Letter of Master William Biddulph from Aleppo" (1600), in Samuel Purchas, *Hakluytus Posthumus or Purchas His Pilgrimes,* 20 vols. (1625; reprint, Glasgow: James MacLehose and Sons, 1900), vol. 8.

Birch, Thomas, *History of the Royal Society of London,* 4 vols. (1756–57; reprint, New York: Johnson Reprint, 1968).

Blackmore, Richard, *Discommendatory Verses* ([1700]).

Blount, Henry, *Voyage into the Levant* (Andrew Crooke, 1636).

Blundell, Nicholas, *Great Diurnal of Nicholas Blundell of Little Crosby, Lancashire,* J. J. Bagley, ed., 3 vols., Record Society of Lancashire and Cheshire, vol. 110 (1968–72).

Bond, Richmond P., ed., *New Letters to the Tatler and Spectator* (Austin: University of Texas Press, 1959).

Book of the Old Edinburgh Club, vol. 16 (Edinburgh: Constable, 1928).

Boswell, James, *Boswell in Holland, 1763–1764,* Frederick A. Pottle, ed. (New York: McGraw-Hill, 1952).

——, *Boswell's London Journal, 1762–1763,* Frederick A. Pottle, ed. (New York: McGraw-Hill, 1950).

——, *Life of Johnson,* R. W. Chapman, ed. (1791; reprint, Oxford: Oxford University Press, 1980).

Bowack, John, *Antiquities of Middlesex,* 2 vols. (W. Redmayne, 1705–6).

Bowler, Dom Hugh, ed., *London Sessions Records, 1605–85* (Catholic Record Society, 1934).

Boyer, Abel, *English Theophrastus,* 3rd ed. (1702; reprint, Bernard Lintott, 1708).

——, *Letters of Wit, Politicks and Morality* (J. Hartley, 1701).

Boyle, Robert, *Works,* Thomas Birch, ed., 6 vols. (1772; reprint, Hildesheim: Georg Olms, 1966).

Bradley, Richard, *Virtue and use of Coffee, with Regard to the Plague* (Eman. Matthews, [1721]).

Brief Description of the Excellent Vertues of that Sober and Wholesome Drink, Called Coffee (Paul Greenwood, 1674).

Bright, Timothy, *Treatise: wherein is declared the sufficiencie of English medicines, for cure of all diseases* (Henrie Middleton, 1580).

Broadbent, Humphrey, *Domestick Coffee-Man* (E. Curll, 1722).

Brome, Alexander, *Songs and Other Poems,* 3rd ed. (Henry Brome, 1668).

Brown, Thomas, *Essays Serious and Comical* (B. Bragg, 1707).

Browne, *Works of Sir Thomas Browne,* S. Wilkin, ed., 4 vols. (Pickering, 1836).

Buckeridge, Banbrigg, "Dedication to Sir Robert Child," in Roger de Piles, *Art of Painting and the Lives of the Painters* (J. Nutt, 1706).

Burney, Fanny, *Evelina,* Edward A. Bloom, ed. (1778; reprint, Oxford: Oxford University Press, 1968).

Burton, Robert, *Anatomy of Melancholy,* Nicolas K. Kiessling, Thomas C. Faulkner, and Rhonda L. Blair, eds., 3 vols. (Oxford: Clarendon, 1989–94).

Bury, Edward, *England's Bane* (Tho. Parkhurst, 1677).

Bury, Jacob, *Advice to the Commons within all his Majesties Realms and Dominions* (Henry Hills, 1685).

Butler, Samuel, *Characters,* Charles W. Daves, ed. (Cleveland: Case Western Reserve University, 1970).

——, *Satires and Miscellaneous Poetry and Prose,* René Lamar, ed. (Cambridge: Cambridge University Press, 1928).

Butler, Samuel[?], *Censure of the Rota* (1660).

Byng, John, *Torrington Diaries: A selection from the tours of the Hon. John Byng,* C. Bruyn Andrews, ed. (Eyre and Spottiswoode, 1954).

Byrd, William, *London Diary (1717–1721) and Other Writings,* Louis B. Wright and Marion Tinling, eds. (Oxford: Oxford University Press, 1958).

Byrom, John, *Private Journal and Literary Remains of John Byrom,* Richard Parkinson, ed., 2 vols. in 4 (Manchester: Chetham Society, 1854–55).

Calendar of State Papers, Colonial Series (1860–).

Calendar of State Papers, Domestic (1856–).

Calendar of State Papers, Venetian (1856–).

Calendar of Treasury Books (1904–).

Calendar of Treasury Books and Papers, 1556–57–1745, 11 vols. (1868–1903).

Campbell, R., *London Tradesman* (T. Gardner, 1747).

Cartwright, J. J., ed., *Wentworth Papers, 1705–1739* (Wyman, 1883).

Case Between the Proprietors of News-Papers, and the Coffee-Men of London and Westminster (R. Walker, [1728]).

Case Between the Proprietors of News-Papers, and the Subscribing Coffee-Men (E. Smith, [1729]).

Case of the Coffee-Men of London and Westminster (G. Smith, [1728]).

Catalogue des livres Francois, Italiens & Espagnols ([1699]), BL, S.C. 73 (4).

Catalogue of batchelors, attenders on the womens auction [1691].

Catalogue of Books of the Newest Fashion [1693], BL, 8122.e.10.

Catalogue of Jilts, Cracks, Prostitutes, Night-Walkers (R.W., 1691).

Catalogue of the Bowes of the Town [10 July 1691].

Catalogue of the Rarities to be seen at Don Saltero's Coffee-House in Chelsea (Tho. Edlin, 1729).

Catalogue of the Rarities to be seen at Don Saltero's Coffee-House in Chelsea, 26th ed. (Tho. Edlin, [177?]), BL 1651/1662.

Catalogue, being an extraordinary and great collection of Antiques, Original drawings, and other curiosities (1714), GL Broadside 11–49.

Censure of the Rota upon Mr. Milton's Book (1659).

Chamberlayne, Edward, *Angliae Notitia*, 2 vols., 2nd ed. (1671; reprint, R. Chiswel, 1672).

——, *Englands Wants* (J. Martyn, 1667).

Chamberlen, Peter, *Vindication of Publick Artificiall Baths and Bath-Stoves* (1648).

Chapman, R. W., ed., *Johnson's Journey to the Western Islands of Scotland* (Oxford University Press, 1924).

Character of a Coffee-House (1665).

Character of a Coffee-House with the Symptomes of a Town-Wit (Johnathan Edwin, 1673).

Character of a Town-Gallant (W.L., 1675).

Character of a Town-Gallant, 2nd ed. [Rowland Reynolds, 1680]).

Character of a Town-Miss (Rowland Reynolds, 1680).

Character of the beaux (1696).

Charecters of some young women [1691].

Chaytor, William, *Papers of Sir William Chaytor of Croft (1639–1721)*, M. Y. Ashcroft, ed. (Northallerton: North Yorkshire County Record Office Publications, no.33; January 1984).

Christie, W. D., ed., *Letters Addressed from London to Sir Joseph Williamson while Plenipotentiary at the Congress of Cologne in the years 1673 and 1674*, 2 vols., Camden Society, new series, nos. 8–9 (Camden Society, 1874).

City-wifes Petition Against Coffee (A.W., 1700).

Cobbett, William, *Parliamentary History of England*, 36 vols. (1806–20; reprint, New York: AMS, 1966).

Cocks, Richard, *Parliamentary Diary of Sir Richard Cocks, 1695–1702*, D. W. Hayton, ed. (Oxford: Clarendon, 1996).

Coffee-Houses Vindicated (J. Lock, 1673).

Coffee-Houses Vindicated (J. Lock, 1675)

Coffee Scuffle (London, 1662), [BL 11622.bb.11].

Coleman, George, *Circle of Anecdote and Wit: To which is added, a choice selection of toasts and sentiments* (J. Bumpus, 1821).

Congreve, William, *William Congreve: Letters and Documents*, John C. Hodges, ed. (New York: Harcourt Brace & World, 1964).

Continuation of a catalogue of ladies [1691].

Continuation of a catalogue of ladies [1702?].

Coolhaas, W. Ph., ed., *Generale Missiven van Gouverneurs-Generaal en Raden aan Heren XVII der Verenigde Oostindische Compagnie* (The Hague: Nijhoff, 1960).

Coppy of the Journal Book of the House of Commons for the Sessions of Parliament (1680).

Copy of Verses, containing, a catalogue of young wenches (London: P. Brooksby, n.d.), BL C.39.k.6. (39).

Coryate, Thomas, *Coryats Crudities* (W.S., 1611).

Country Gentleman's Vade Mecum (John Harris, 1699).

Crossley, James, ed., *Diary and Correspondence of Dr. John Worthington,* Remains Historical and Literary . . . Lancaster and Chester, 3 vols. (Manchester: Chetham Society, 1847–86).

Culpeper, Nicholas, *Culpeper's Complete Herbal* (1653; reprint, Ware: Wordsworth, 1995).

———. *English Physitian* (Peter Cole, 1652).

———. *Physical Directory,* 2nd. ed. (Peter Cole, 1650).

Cunnington, Howard, *Records of the County of Wiltshire being extracts from the Quarter Sessions Great Rolls of the Seventeenth Century* (Devizes, 1932).

Cup of Coffee: Or, Coffee in Its Colours (1663).

Curious Amusements (D. Browne, 1714).

Darby, Charles, *Bacchanalia* (E. Whitlock, 1698).

D'Aulnoy, Marie Catherine, Countess of Dunois, *Memoirs of the Court of England,* 2 parts (J. Woodward, 1708).

Day, W. G., ed., *Pepys Ballads,* 5 vols. (Cambridge: D. S. Brewer, 1987).

De Acosta, Joseph, *Natural and Moral History of the Indies,* Clements R. Markham, ed., First Series, no. 60 (Hakluyt Society, 1880).

De F. Lord, G., and others, eds., *Poems on Affairs of State,* 7 vols. (New Haven: Yale University Press, 1963–75).

De Gray Birch, Walter, *Historical Charters and Constitutional Documents of the City of London* (Whiting, 1887).

De la Rocque, Jean, *Voyage to Arabia Felix* (E. Symon, 1732).

De Piles, Roger, *Art of Painting and the Lives of the Painters* (J. Nutt, 1706).

De Saussure, Cesar, *Foreign View of England in 1725–1729,* Mme van Muyden, trans. and ed. (Caliban, 1995).

Decrees and Orders of the Committee of Safety of the Commonwealth of Oceana (1659).

Defence of Tabacco (Richard Field, 1602).

Defoe, Daniel, *Compleat English Tradesman* (1726; reprint, Gloucester: Alan Sutton, 1987).

———. *Compleat English Tradesman* (1726), 2 vols. (1745; reprint, New York: Burt Franklin, 1970).

———. "Correspondence Between De Foe and John Fransham of Norwich, 1704–1707," *Notes and Queries,* 5th ser., 3 (3 April 1875).

———. *Letters of Daniel Defoe,* George Harris Healey, ed. (Oxford: Oxford University Press, 1955).

———. *Poor Man's Plea* (A. Baldwin, 1698).

——. *Roxana*, David Blewett, ed. (1724; reprint, Penguin, 1982).

——. *Vindication of the Press* (T. Walker, 1718).

Dennis, John, *Poems in Burlesque* (1692).

Dialogue between an Exchange and Exchange Alley (1681).

Diderot, Denis, *Rameau's Nephew and Other Works,* Jacques Barzun and Ralph H. Bowen, trans. (Indianapolis: Bobbs-Merrill, 1964).

Douglas, James, *Arbor Yemensis fructum Cofè ferens* (Thomas Woodward, 1727).

——. *Supplement to the Description of the Coffee-Tree* (Thomas Woodward, 1727).

Dufour, Philippe Sylvestre, *Manner of Making of Coffee, Tea, and Chocolate,* John Chamberlain, trans. (1671; reprint, William Crook, 1685).

Duncan, Daniel, *Wholesome Advice Against the Abuse of Hot Liquors* (H. Rhodes, 1706).

Dunton, John, *Life and Errors of John Dunton,* 2 vols. (1818; reprint, New York: Burt Franklin, 1969).

——, *Night-Walker,* 2 vols. (James Orme, 1696–97).

D'Urfey, Thomas, *Collin's Walk Through London and Westminster* (John Bullord, 1690).

——, *Wit and Mirth: or Pills to Purge Melancholy* (W. Pearson, 1719)

Earle, John, *Microcosmography,* Alfred S. West, ed. (1633, reprint, of 5th ed.; Cambridge: Cambridge University Press, 1951).

Eccentric Magazine, 2 vols. (G. Smeeton, 1812–13).

Elephant's Speech to the Citizens and Countrymen of England at his First being Shewn at Bartholomew-Fair (1675).

Elliott, T. H., ed., *State Papers Domestic Concerning the Post Office in the Reign of Charles II* (Bath: Postal History Society, 1964).

Ellis, Frank H., ed., *Swift vs. Mainwaring: The Examiner and the Medley* (Oxford: Clarendon Press, 1985).

Endlesse Queries (1659).

Essay in Defence of the Female Sex (1696; reprint, New York: Source Book, 1970).

Essays Serious and Comical (B. Bragg, 1707).

Etherege, George, *Man of Mode,* W. B. Carnochan, ed. (1676; reprint, Lincoln: University of Nebraska Press, 1966).

Evelyn, John, *Character of England,* 3rd ed. (John Crooke, 1659).

——, *Diary and Correspondence of John Evelyn, FRS,* William Bray, ed., 4 vols. (Henry G. Bohn, 1863).

——, *Diary of John Evelyn,* E. S. de Beer, ed., 6 vols. (Oxford: Clarendon, 1955).

——, *Memoires for My Grand-son,* ed. Geoffrey Keynes (1704; reprint, Oxford: Nonesuch, 1926).

——, *Numismata* (Benjamin Tooke, 1697).

Evelyn, Mary, *Mundus Muliebris,* 2nd ed. (R. Bentley, 1690).

Excerpt out of a book, shewing, that fluids rise not in the pump, in the syphon, and in the barometer, by the pressure of air, but propter Fugaam vacui (undated) in BL 536.d.19 (6).

Extracts from the Records of the Burgh of Edinburgh, 1665–80, Marguerite Wood, ed. (Edinburgh: Oliver and Boyd, 1950).

Extracts from the Records of the Burgh of Edinburgh, 1681–89, Helen Armet and Marguerite Wood, eds. (Edinburgh: Oliver and Boyd, 1954).

Extracts from the Records of the Burgh of Edinburgh, 1689–1701, Helen Armet, ed. (Edinburgh: Oliver and Boyd, 1962).

Extracts from the Records of the Burgh of Edinburgh, 1701–18, Helen Armet, ed. (Edinburgh: Oliver and Boyd, 1967).

Extracts from the Records of the Burgh of Glasgow, 1663–90 (Glasgow: Scottish Burgh Records Society, 1905).

Extracts from the Records of the Burgh of Glasgow, 1691–1717 (Glasgow: Scottish Burgh Records Society, 1908).

Extracts from the Records of the Burgh of Glasgow, 1718–38 (Glasgow: Scottish Burgh Records Society, 1909).

Faulkner, Thomas, *Historical and Topographical Description of Chelsea and Its Environs* (J. Tilling, 1810).

Flecknoe, Richard, *Treatise of the Sports of Wit* (Simon Neals, 1675).

For Information to All People Where to Deliver their Letters by the Penny Post [1680].

Foster, William, ed., *English Factories in India [EFI]*, old series, 13 vols. (Oxford: Clarendon, 1906–23).

——, *Journal of John Jourdain, 1608–17* (Hakluyt Society, 1905).

Franklin, Benjamin, *Autobiography of Benjamin Franklin,* Charles W. Eliot, ed. (1771–88; reprint, New York: P. F. Collier, 1909).

Friendly Monitor, laying open the crying sins (Sam. Crouch, 1692).

Fryer, John, *New Account of East India and Persia, being nine years travels 1672–1681,* 3 vols., Hakluyt Society, second series, nos. 19, 21, 39 (Hakluyt Society, 1909–15).

Full and True Relation of the Elephant that is Brought over into England from the Indies, and Landed at London, August 3d. 1675 (William Sutten, 1675).

Fuller, Thomas, *Anglorum Speculum, or the Worthies of England* (John Wright, 1684).

Gardiner, Edmund, *Triall of Tabacco* (Mathew Lownes, 1610).

Gerarde, John, *Herball or Generall Historie of Plantes* (John Norton, 1597).

——, *Herball or Generall Historie of Plantes,* 2nd ed., Thomas Johnson, ed. (Adam Norton, 1633).

Glanville, Joseph, *Blow at Modern Sadducism in Some Philosophical Considerations About Witchcraft,* 4th ed. (E. Cotes, 1668).

Grand Concern of England Explained (1673).

Grand Juries Address and Presentments to the Mayor and Aldermen of the City of Bristol (Edinburgh: Andrew Anderson, 1681).

Greene, Douglas C., ed., *Diaries of the Popish Plot* (Delmar, N.Y.: Scholars' Facsimiles and Reprints, 1977).

Grey, Anchitell, *Debates of the House of Commons, from the year 1667 to the year 1694,* 10 vols. (D. Henry and R. Cave, 1763).

Gronow, Rees Howell, *Reminiscences and Recollections of Captain Gronow: Being Anecdotes of the Camp, Court, Clubs and Society, 1810–60,* John Raymond, ed. (New York: Viking, 1964).

Hammond, John, *Work for Chimny-sweepers: or a warning for tabacconists* (T. Este, 1602).

Hancock, John, *Touchstone or, Trial of Tobacco* (1676).

Harrington, James, *Political Works of James Harrington,* J. G. A. Pocock, ed. (Cambridge: Cambridge University Press, 1977).

Harrison, William, *Description of England,* Georges Edelen, ed. (1587; reprint, New York: Dover, 1994).

Hartlib Papers, CD-ROM (Ann Arbor, Mich.: UMI, 1995).

Harvey, Gideon, *Discourse of the Plague* (Nat. Brooke, 1665).

Hatton, Edward, *New View of London,* 2 vols. (1708).

Haworth, Samuel, *Description of the Duke's Bagnio* (Samuel Smith, 1683).

Hazlitt, W. C., ed., *Select Collection of Old English Plays,* 4th ed. (Reeves and Turner, 1874).

Hazlitt, William, *Complete Works of William Hazlitt,* P. P. Howe, ed., 21 vols. (New York: AMS, 1967).

Hearne, Thomas, *Remarks and Collections of Thomas Hearne,* H. E. Salter, ed., vol. 9 (August 10, 1725–March 26, 1728), Oxford Historical Society, o.s., vol. 65 (Oxford: Clarendon, 1914).

Heraclitus Ridens, 2 vols. (Benjamin Tooke, 1713).

Herbert, Thomas, *Relation of Some Yeares Travaile, begvnne anno 1626,* 4th ed. (R. Everingham, 1677).

——, *Relation of Some Yeares Travaile, begvnne anno 1626,* 1st ed. (William Stansby et al., 1634).

Hewitson, Anthony, ed., *Diary of Thomas Bellingham: An Officer under William III* (Preston: George Toulmin & Sons, 1908).

Hickelty Pickelty (1708).

Hilliar, Anthony, *Brief and Merry History of Great Britain* (J. Roberts, [c. 1710]).

Historical Manuscripts Commission, [HMC], *Reports* (HMSO, 1871–).

Hooke, Robert, "Diary" (November 1688–10 March 1690; 5 December 1692–8 August 1693), in *Early Science in Oxford,* R. T. Gunther, ed., vol. 10 (Oxford, 1935), pp. 69–265.

——, *Diary of Robert Hooke, 1672–1680,* Henry W. Robinson and Walter Adams, eds. (Taylor & Francis, 1935).

Hoppit, Julian, ed., *Failed Legislation, 1660–1800* (Hambledon, 1997).

Howell, James, *Epistolae Ho-Elianae,* 6th ed., 4 vols. (Thomas Guy, 1688).

——, *Instructions for Forreine Travell,* 2nd ed. (W.W., 1650).

——, *New Volume of Letters partly philosophicall, politicall, historicall* (T.W., 1647).

Humble Petition of Divers Well-Affected Persons, delivered the 6th day of July, 1659 (Thomas Brewster, 1659).

Hume, David, *History of England,* 4 vols. (Albany: B. D. Packard, 1816).

Hume Brown, P. ed., *Register of the Privy Council of Scotland,* 3rd ser., vol. 5 (1676–78) (Edinburgh: H. M. General Register House, 1912),

Humours and Conversations of the Town (R. Bentley, 1693).

Huygens, Christiaan, *Oeuvres Complètes,* 22 vols. (The Hague: Martinus Nijhoff, 1898–1950).

Huygens, Constantijn, *Journaal van Constantijn Huygens, den Zoon,* 2 vols. (Utrecht,

1876–77), Werken Uitgegeven door het Historisch Genootschap, new series, nos. 23, 25.

Hyde, Henry, *Life of Edward Earl of Clarendon, Lord High Chancellor of England*, 2 vols. (Oxford: Oxford University Press, 1857).

Iter Oxoniense, or, The going down of the asses to Oxenford (1681).

Jeaffreson, J. C., ed., *Middlesex County Records*, 4 vols. (Middlesex County Records Society, 1886–92).

Jones, John, *Mysteries of Opium Reveald* (Richard Smith, 1700).

Jordan, Thomas, *Lord Mayor's Show . . . performed on Monday, September xxx, 1682* (T. Burnel, 1682).

——, *Triumphs of London* (J. Macock, 1675).

Jorden, Edward, *Discourse of Naturall Bathes, and Minerall Waters*, 3rd ed. (Thomas Harper, 1633).

Juniper Lecturer Corrected and his Latin, Pagan, Putid Nonsense Paraphrazed (1662).

Kennett, White, *Complete History of England*, 3 vols. (B. Aylmer, 1706).

Larkin, James F., ed., *Stuart Royal Proclamations, Volume II: Royal Proclamations of King Charles I, 1625–1646* (Oxford: Clarendon, 1983).

Larkin, James F., and Paul L. Hughes, eds., *Stuart Royal Proclamations, Volume I: Royal Proclamations of King James I, 1603–1625* (Oxford: Clarendon, 1973).

Landsdowne, Marquis of, ed., *Petty-Southwell Correspondence, 1676–1687* (Constable and Company, 1928).

Lankaster, Edwin, ed., *Correspondence of John Ray* (Ray Society, 1848).

Leadbetter, Charles, *Royal Gauger; or gauging made perfectly easy*, 7th ed. (J. and F. Rivington et al., 1776).

Leigh, Richard, *Censure of the Rota upon Mr. Driden's Conquest of Granada* (Oxford, 1673).

——, *Transproser Rehears'd: or the fifth act of Mr. Bayes's Play* (Oxford, 1673).

Lémery, Louis, *Treatise of Foods* (John Taylor, 1704).

L'Estrange, Roger, *L'Estrange No Papist* (H. Brome, 1681).

——, *L'Estrange's Case in a Civil Dialogue between Ezekiel and Ephraim* (H. Brome, 1680).

——, *Memento Treating of the Rise, Progress, and Remedies of Seditions*, 2nd ed. (1662; reprint, Joanna Brome, 1682).

Letter from the Quidnunc's at St. James's Coffee-House and the Mall, London [Dublin: 1724].

Letters Received by the East India Company, 6 vols. (Sampson Low, 1896–1902).

Life and Character of Moll King (W. Price, [1747]).

Lightbody, James, *Every Man His Own Gauger* (G. C., [1695?]).

Linschoten, Jan Huyghen van, *Voyage of John Huyghen van Linschoten to the East Indies*, Arthur Coke Burnell and P. A. Tiele, eds., 2 vols., Hakluyt Society First Series, nos. 70–71 (Hakluyt Society, 1885).

List of the Parliament of Women (T.N., 1679).

Lister, Martin, *Journey to Paris in the year 1698*, R. P. Stearns, ed. (1699; reprint, Urbana: University of Illinois Press, 1967).

Lithgow, William, *Most Delectable, and True Discourse, of an admired and painefull peregrination from Scotland, to the most famous Kingdomes in Europe, Asia, and Affricke* (Nicholas Okes, 1614).

Locke, John, *Correspondence of John Locke,* E. S. de Beer, ed., vol. 6 (Oxford: Clarendon, 1981).

——, *Political Essays,* Mark Goldie, ed. (Cambridge: Cambridge University Press, 1997).

London and Westminster Directory for the Year 1796 (T. Fenwick, [1796]).

Longe, Julia G., ed., *Martha Lady Giffard: Her Life and Correspondence (1664–1722) A Sequel to the Letters of Dorothy Osborne* (George Allen, 1911).

Lugt, Frits, *Répertoire des Catalogues de Ventes Publiques,* vol. 1: "Première Periode vers 1600–1825" (The Hague: M. Nijhoff, 1938).

Lupton, Donald, *Emblems of Rarities* (London: Nicholas Okes, 1636).

Luttrell, Narcissus, *Brief Historical Relation of State Affairs from September 1678 to April 1714,* 6 vols. (Oxford: Oxford University Press, 1857).

——, *Parliamentary Diary of Narcissus Luttrell, 1691–1693,* Henry Horwitz, ed. (Oxford: Clarendon, 1972).

M.P., *Character of Coffee and Coffee-Houses* (John Starkey, 1661).

Macaulay, Thomas Babington, *History of England from the Accession of James II,* C. H. Firth, ed., 6 vols. (1848; reprint, Macmillan, 1913).

Macky, John, *Journey Through England in familiar letters from a gentleman here to his friend abroad,* 2 vols. (J. Hooke, 1722–24).

Magalotti, Lorenzo, *Lorenzo Magalotti at the Court of Charles II,* W. E. Knowles Middleton, ed., (Waterloo: Wilfrid Laurier University Press, 1980).

Maidens complain[t] against coffee (J. Jones, 1663).

Mandeville, Bernard, *Fable of the Bees, or Private Vices, Publick Benefits* (1732), F. B. Kaye, ed., 2 vols. (1924; reprint, Indianapolis: Liberty Fund, 1988).

Mens Answer to the Womens Petition against Coffee (1674).

Mercurius Matrimonialis, [1702?].

Miège, Guy, *New State of England under Their Majesties K. William and Q. Mary* (H.C., 1691).

Miller, James, *Coffee-House* (J. Watts, 1737).

Millington, Edward, *Collection of Curious Prints, Paintings, and Limnings, by the Best Masters* [1689], BL, 1402.g.1[12].

Monardes, Nicolas, *Ioyfvll Nevves ovt of the newe founde worlde,* John Frampton, trans. (Willyam Norton, 1577).

Montagu, Mary Wortley, *Complete Letters of Lady Mary Wortley Montagu,* Robert Halsband, ed., 3 vols. (Oxford: Clarendon, 1965).

Montesquieu, *Persian Letters,* C. J. Betts, trans. (Penguin, 1993).

Mun, Thomas, *Discovrse of Trade,* 2nd ed. (1621) in J. R. McCulloch, ed., *Early English Tracts on Commerce* (1856; reprint, Cambridge: Cambridge University Press, 1954).

Naironus, Antonius Faustus, *Discourse on Coffee* (Geo. James, 1710).

Natural History of Coffee, Thee, Chocolate, Tobacco (Christopher Wilkinson, 1683).

Nedham, Marchamont?, *Paquet of Advices and Animadversions* (1676).

News from Covent-Garden or the Town Gallants Vindication (J.T., 1675).

News from the Coffee-House (E. Crowch, 1667).

Nicolson, Majorie Hope, ed., *Conway Letters: The Correspondence of Anne, Viscountess Conway, Henry More, and Their Friends, 1642–1684* (New Haven: Yale University Press, 1930).

Nicolson, William, *London Diaries of William Nicolson, Bishop of Carlisle 1702–1718,* Clyve Jones and Geoffrey Holmes, eds. (Oxford: Clarendon, 1985).

Night-Walkers; or, the Loyal HUZZA (P. Brocksby, 1682).

North, Roger, *Examen* (Fletcher Gyles, 1740).

——, *Lives of the Right Hon. Francis North, Baron Guilford; the Hon. Sir Dudley North; and the Hon. and Rev. Dr. John North,* Augustus Jessop, ed., 3 vols. (George Bell, 1890).

North, Thomas, *Liues of the noble Grecians and Romanes, compared together by . . . Plutarke of Chaeronea* (Thomas Vautroullier, 1579).

Of the Use of Tobacco, Tea, Coffee, Chocolate, and Drams (H. Parker, 1722).

Oldenburg, Henry, *Correspondence of Henry Oldenburg,* A. R. Hall and M. B. Hall, eds., 13 vols. (Madison: University of Wisconsin Press, 1965–86).

Oldham, John, *Poems of John Oldham,* Harold F. Brooks, ed. (Oxford: Clarendon, 1987).

Olearius, Adam, *Voyages and Travels of the Ambassadors sent by Frederick Duke of Holstein, to the Great Duke of Muscovy, and the King of Persia,* John Davies, trans. (Thomas Dring, 1662).

Orbilius Vapulans (1662).

Ovington, John, *Voyage to Surat in the Year 1689,* H. G. Rawlinson, ed. (1696; reprint, Oxford University Press, 1929).

Paracelsus, *Selected Writings,* Jolande Jacobi, ed. (Princeton: Princeton University Press, 1951).

Parkinson, John, *Theatrum Botanicum* (Tho. Cotes, 1640).

Parliament of Women (W. Wilson, 1646).

Paulli, Simon, *Treatise on Tobacco, Tea, Coffee, and Chocolate,* Dr. James, trans. (1665; reprint, T. Osborn, 1746).

Peacham, Henry, *Compleat Gentleman* (Francis Constable, 1634).

——, *Worth of a Penny, or, a Caution to Keep Money* (William Lee, 1667).

Pepys, Samuel, *Diary of Samuel Pepys,* R. C. Latham and W. Matthews, eds., 11 vols. (1971).

——, *Private Correspondence and Miscellaneous Papers of Samuel Pepys 1679–1703,* J. R. Tanner, ed., 2 vols. (G. Bell, 1926).

Phillips, John, *New News from Tory-Land and Tantivy-shire* (1682).

Pinnell, H., *Philosophy Reformed and Improved in four profound tractates,* 3rd ed. (M.S., 1657).

Pittis, William, *Dr. Radcliffe's Life* (Dublin: Pat Dugan, 1724).

Plutarch, *Alcibiades,* in *Plutarch's Lives with an English Translation,* Bernadotte Perrin, trans., 11 vols. (Cambridge, Mass.: Harvard University Press, 1914–16).

Poetical Contest between Toby and a Minor-Poet of B-tt-n's Coffee-House (Ferdinando Burleigh, [1714?]).

Pollexfen, *Discourse of Trade, Coyn, and Paper Credit* (B. Aylmer, 1697).

Poor Robin's Character of an Honest Drunken Curr (E.C., 1675).

Pope, Alexander, *Poems of Alexander Pope,* John Butt, ed. (New Haven: Yale University Press, 1963).

Proclamation for the Suppression of the Coffeehouses (Bill & Barker, 1675).

Proposition in Order to the Proposing of a Commonwealth or Democracie [1659].

Propositions for Changing the Excise, now laid upon coffee, chacholet, and tea [1680s? 1690s?]. Wing T1451A.

Prynne, William, *Healthes Sicknesse* (1628).

Publiqe Bathes Purged (1648).

Purchas, Samuel, *Hakluytus Posthumus or Purchas His Pilgrimes,* 20 vols. (1625; reprint, Glasgow: James MacLehose, 1900).

R.H. [Robert Hooke?], *New Atlantis begun by the Lord Verulam, Viscount St. Alban's,* Manly P. Hall, ed. (1660; reprint, Los Angeles: Philosophical Research Society, 1985).

Ralph, James, *History of England: During the Reigns of K. William, Q. Anne, and K. George I,* 2 vols. (Daniel Browne, 1744).

Rauwolf, Leonhard, *Aigentliche Beschreibung der Raiss inn die Morgenlaender* (1583; reprint, Graz: Akademische Druck- u. Verlagsanstalt, 1971).

——, *Collection of Curious Travels and Voyages,* John Ray, ed., 2 vols. (S. Smith & B. Walford, 1693).

Ray, John, *Correspondence of John Ray* (Ray Society, 1848).

——, *Philosophical Letters,* W. Derham, ed. (W. and J. Innys, 1718).

Rebellions Antidote (George Croom, 1685).

Remarks upon Remarques (A.C., 1673).

Remarques on the Humours and Conversations of the Town (Allen Banks, 1673).

Rochester, earl of, John Wilmot, *Complete Poems of John Wilmot, Earl of Rochester,* David M. Vieth, ed. (New Haven: Yale University Press, 1968).

Rocque, John de la, *Voyage to Arabia the Happy* (G. Strahan, 1726).

Rollins, Hyder Edward, ed., *Pepys Ballads,* 8 vols. (Cambridge, Mass.: Harvard University Press, 1931).

Rota or, News from the Common-weaths-mens Club (n.d.).

Routledge, F. J., ed., *Calendar of the Clarendon State Papers,* 5 vols. (Oxford: Clarendon, 1932).

Rumsey, William, *Organon Salutis* (R. Hodgkinsonne, 1657).

——, *Organon Salutis,* 2nd ed. (D. Pakeman, 1659).

——, *Organon Salutis,* 3rd ed. (S. Speed, 1667).

Rycaut, Paul, *Present State of the Ottoman Empire* (John Starket and Henry Brome, 1668).

Ryder, Dudley, *Diary of Dudley Ryder, 1715–1716,* William Matthews, ed. (Methuen, 1939).

Sachse, W. L., ed., *Diurnal of Thomas Rugg, 1659–61,* Camden 3rd series, 91 (Camden Society, 1961).

Sainsbury, Ethel Bruce, ed., *Calendar of the Court Minutes of the East India Company,* 11 vols. (Oxford: Clarendon, 1907–38).

St. Serfe, Thomas, *Tarugo's Wiles, or the Coffee-House: A Comedy* (Henry Herringman, 1668).

Sala, Angelo, *Opiologia* (Nicholas Okes, 1618).

Sandys, George, *Relation of Iourney begun An. Dom. 1610* (W. Barrett, 1615).

Satyr Against Coffee [1674?].

Satyr Against Wit (Samuel Crouch, 1700).

Saussure, Cesar de, *Foreign View of England in 1725–1729,* M. van Muyden, ed. (Hampstead: Caliban, 1995).

Scrivener, Matthew, *Treatise against Drunkennesse* (Charles Brown, [1680]).

Shaftesbury, third earl of, Anthony Ashley Cooper, *Characteristics of Men, Manners, Opinions, Times,* John M. Robertson, ed., 2 vols. (1711; reprint, Indianapolis: Bobbs-Merrill, 1964).

——, *Life, Unpublished Letters, and Philosophical Regimen of Anthony, Earl of Shaftesbury,* Benjamin Rand, ed. (New York: Macmillan, 1900).

Sheridan, Frances, *Memoirs of Miss Sidney Bidulph* (J. Dodsley, 1767).

Slaughter, Thomas P., ed., *Ideology and Politics on the Eve of Restoration: Newcastle's Advice to Charles II* (Philadelphia: American Philosophical Society, 1984).

Sloane, Hans, "An Account of a Prodigiously Large Feather . . . and of the Coffee-Shrub," *Philosophical Transactions* 208 (February 1694).

Smith, John, *True Travels, Adventures, and Observations of Captaine Iohn Smith, in Europe, Asia, Affrica, and America, from anno Domini 1593. to 1629* (I.H., 1630).

Smollett, Tobias, *Expedition of Humphrey Clinker,* Lewis M. Knapp, ed., with revisions by Paul-Gabriel Boucé (1771; reprint, Oxford: Oxford University Press, 1984).

Some Reflections on Mr. P — n, Lecturer at the Bagnio in N — te-Street (A. Baldwin, 1700).

Southerne, Thomas, *Works of Thomas Southerne,* Robert Jordan and Harold Love, eds., 2 vols. (Oxford: Clarendon, 1988).

Spence, Joseph, *Observations, Anecdotes, and Characters of Books and Men,* James M. Osborn, ed., 2 vols. (Oxford: Clarendon, 1966).

Sprat, Thomas, *History of the Royal Society,* Jackson I. Cope and Harold Whitmore Jones, eds. (1667; reprint, St. Louis: Washington University Press, 1958).

Steele, Richard, *Lucubrations of Isaac Bickerstaff Esq.,* 4 vols. (Charles Lillie, 1710).

Steele, Robert, ed., *Bibliography of Royal Proclamations of the Tudor and Stuart Sovereigns . . . 1485–1714,* 3 vols. (Oxford: Oxford University Press, 1910).

Steer, Francis W., ed., *Farm and Cottage Inventories of Mid-Essex, 1635–1749,* Essex Record Office Publications, no. 8 (Colchester: Wiles & Son, 1950).

Stow, John, *Survey of the Cities of London and Westminster,* John Strype, ed., 2 vols. (A. Churchill et al., 1720).

Stubbe, Henry, *Indian Nectar, or a discourse concerning chocolata* (J.C., 1662).

Swift, Johnathan, *Correspondence,* David Wooley, ed., 4 vols. (Frankfurt: Peter Lang, 1999–).

——, *Journal to Stella,* Harold Williams, ed., 2 vols. (Oxford: Clarendon, 1948).

——, *Prose Writings of Jonathan Swift,* 14 vols. (Oxford: Blackwell, 1939–68).

Symson, Ez., *Farther Essay Relating to the Female Sex* (A. Roper, 1696).

T.J., *World Turned Upside Down* (John Smith, 1647).

T.O., *True Character of a Town Beau* (Randal Taylor, 1692).

Tatham, John, *Dramatic Works of John Tatham,* James Maidment and W. H. Logan, eds. (H. Sotheran, 1879).

——, *Knavery in All Trades: Or, the Coffee-House* (J.B., 1664).

Thirsk, Joan, and J. P. Cooper, eds., *Seventeenth-Century Economic Documents* (Oxford: Clarendon, 1972).

Thoresby, Ralph, *Diary of Ralph Thoresby,* Joseph Hunter, ed., 2 vols. (H. Colburn, 1830).

Toland, John, *Collection of Several Pieces of Mr. John Toland,* 2 vols. (J. Peele, 1726).

Tom K — g's: or the Paphian Grove (J. Robinson, 1738).

True Account of the Royal Bagnio (Joseph Hindmarsh, 1680).

True and Perfect Description of the Strange and Wonderful Elephant (J. Conniers, [1675]).

Tryon, Thomas, *Wisdom's Dictates* (Thos. Salisbury, 1691).

Twelve Ingenious Characters (S. Norris, 1680).

Uffenbach, Zacharias Conrad von, *London in 1710,* W. H. Quarrell and Margaret Mare, eds. and trans. (Faber & Faber, 1934).

Urania's temple (Rich. Baldwin, 1695).

Velvet Coffee-Woman (Simon Green, 1728).

Verney, Margaret M., ed., *Memoirs of the Verney Family from the Restoration to the Revolution, 1660 to 1696,* vol. 4 (Longman, 1899).

Vertues of Coffee set forth in the works of the Lord Bacon his Natural Hist. (W.G., 1663).

View of Paris, and places adjoining (John Nutt, 1701).

Voltaire, *Portable Voltaire,* Ben Ray Redman, ed. (New York: Penguin, 1968).

Wallis, John, "Dr. Wallis' Letter Against Mr. Maidwell [c. 1700]," Thomas W. Jackson, ed., in *Collectanea,* 1st series, C. R. L. Fletcher, ed., Publications of the Oxford Historical Society, vol. 5 (Oxford: Clarendon, 1885).

Wandring Whore, parts 1–5 (1660–61).

Wandring-Whores Complaint for want of Trading (Merc. Dean, 1663).

Wanley, Humfrey, *Diary of Humfrey Wanley, 1715–1726,* C. E. Wright and Ruth C. Wright, eds., 2 vols. (Bibliographical Society, 1966).

Ward, Edward, *History of the London Clubs* (J. Dutten, 1709).

——, *London Spy Compleat,* 4th ed. (J. How, 1709).

——, *Rambling Rakes* (J. How, 1700).

——, *School of Politicks* (Richard Baldwin, 1690).

——, *Vulgus Britannicus* (James Woodward, 1710).

Ward, John, *Diary of the Rev. John Ward, Vicar of Stratford-upon-Avon, 1648–79,* Charles Severn, ed. (Henry Colburn, 1839).

Wildman, John, *Advertisement from their Majesties Post-Office* (1690).

Willis, Thomas, *Pharmaceuticae Rationalis,* 2 parts (Thomas Dring, 1679).

Wit at a Venture (Johnathan Edwin, 1674).

Women's Petition Against Coffee (1674).

Womens Complaint Against tobacco (1675).

Wood, Anthony, *Life and Times of Anthony Wood,* Andrew Clark, ed., 5 vols., Oxford Historical Society nos. 19, 21, 26, 30, 40 (Oxford: Clarendon, 1891–1900).

Secondary Sources

Agnew, Jean-Christophe, *Worlds Apart: The Market and the Theater in Anglo-American Thought, 1550–1750* (Cambridge: Cambridge University Press, 1986).

Aignon, M., *Le Prestre Medecin, ou discours physique sur l'établissement de la medecine* (Paris: Laurent D'Houry, 1696).

Akerman, John Yonge, *Examples of Coffee House, Tavern, and Tradesmen's Tokens: Current in London in the Seventeenth Century* (1847).

Albrecht, Peter, "Coffee-Drinking as a Symbol of Social Change in Continental Europe in the Seventeenth and Eighteenth Centuries," *Studies in Eighteenth-Century Culture* 18 (1988).

Alexander, James M. B., "Economic and Social Structure of the City of London," Ph.D. Thesis, London School of Economics, 1989.

Allen, B. Sprague, *Tides in English Taste (1619–1800): A Background for the Study of Literature,* 2 vols. (1937; reprint, New York: Pageant Books, 1958).

Allen, David, "Political Clubs in Restoration London," *HJ* 19:3 (1976).

——, "Role of the London Trained Bands in the Exclusion Crisis, 1678–81," *EHR* 87 (1972).

Altick, Richard, *Shows of London* (Cambridge, Mass.: Harvard University Press, 1978).

Anderson, Sonia, *English Consul in Turkey: Paul Rycaut at Smyrna, 1667–1678* (Oxford: Clarendon, 1989).

Andrew, Donna, "Popular Culture and Public Debate: London 1780," *HJ* 39:2 (1996).

Appadurai, Arjun, "How to Make a National Cuisine: Cookbooks in Contemporary India," *Comparative Studies in Society and History* 30 (1988).

——, *Modernity at Large: Cultural Dimensions of Globalization* (Minneapolis: University of Minnesota Press, 1996).

Appadurai, Arjun, ed., *Social Life of Things: Commodities in Cultural Perspective* (Cambridge: Cambridge University Press, 1986).

Appleby, Joyce, *Economic Thought and Ideology in Seventeenth-Century England* (Princeton: Princeton University Press, 1978).

Aravamudan, Srinivas, "Lady Wortley Montagu in the *Hammam:* Masquerade, Womanliness, and Levantization," *ELH,* 62:1 (1995).

Arber, Agnes, *Herbals: Their Origin and Evolution,* 3rd ed. (Cambridge: Cambridge University Press, 1986).

Archer, Ian, *Pursuit of Stability: Social Relations in Elizabethan London* (Cambridge: Cambridge University Press, 1991).

Ariès, Philippe, "Introduction," to *History of Private Life: Passions of the Renaissance,* Roger Chartier, ed., Arthur Goldhammer, trans. (Cambridge, Mass.: Harvard University Press, 1989).

Arnold, Ken, "Cabinets for the Curious: Practicing Science in Early Modern English Museums" (Ph.D. diss., Princeton University, 1991).

Ashley, Maurice, *John Wildman: Plotter and Postmaster* (New Haven: Yale University Press, 1947).

Ashton, John, *Social Life in the Reign of Queen Anne: Taken from Original Sources,* 2 vols. (Chatto & Windus, 1882).

Ashton, T. S., *Economic History of England: The Eighteenth Century* (New York: Barnes and Noble, 1955).

Aspinall, Arthur, *Politics and the Press, c. 1780–1850* (Home & Van Thal, 1949).

Atherton, Ian, "This Itch Grown a Disease: Manuscript Transmission of News in the Seventeenth Century," *Prose Studies,* 21:2 (1998).

Aubertin-Potter, Norma and Alyx Bennett, *Oxford Coffee Houses, 1651–1800* (Kidlington, Oxford: Hampden, 1987).

Backsheider, Paula, *Daniel Defoe: His Life* (Baltimore: Johns Hopkins University Press, 1989).

Bailyn, Bernard, *Ideological Origins of the American Revolution,* enlarged ed. (Cambridge, Mass.: Harvard University Press, 1992).

Baker, Keith Michael, "Defining the Public Sphere in Eighteenth-Century France: Variations on a Theme by Habermas," in *Habermas and the Public Sphere,* Craig Calhoun, ed. (Cambridge: MIT Press, 1991).

——, *Inventing the French Revolution* (Cambridge: Cambridge University Press, 1990).

Barker, Hannah, *Newspapers, Politics and Public Opinion in Late Eighteenth-Century England* (Oxford: Clarendon, 1998).

Barker, Hannah, and Elaine Chalus, eds., *Gender in Eighteenth-Century England* (Longman, 1997).

Barker-Benfield, G. J., *Culture of Sensibility: Sex and Society in Eighteenth-Century Britain* (Chicago: University of Chicago Press, 1992).

Barrell, John, "Coffeehouse Politicians," *Journal of British Studies,* 43:2 (April 2004).

Barry, Jonathan, "Bourgeois Collectivism? Urban Association and the Middling Sort," in *Middling Sort of People: Culture, Society and Politics in England, 1550–1800,* Jonathan Barry and Christopher Brooks, eds. (Basingstoke: Macmillan, 1994).

——, "Identité Urbaine et Classes Moyennes dans l'Angleterre Moderne," *Annales ESC* (July-Aug. 1993), no. 4.

——, "Press and the Politics of Culture," in *Culture, Politics and Society in Britain 1660–1800,* Jeremy Black and Jeremy Gregory, eds. (Manchester: Manchester University Press, 1991).

Becker, Howard, *Outsiders* (1953; reprint, New York: Free Press, 1963).

Beljame, Alexandre, *Le Public et les Hommes de Lettres en Angleterre au Dix-Huitième Siècle 1660–1744 (Dryden–Addison–Pope),* 2nd ed. (Paris: Hachette, 1897).

Bellany, Alastair, "Mistress Turner's Deadly Sins: Sartorial Transgression, Court Scandal and Politics in Early Stuart England," *Huntington Library Quarterly* 58:2 (1996).

——, *Politics of Court Scandal in Early Modern England: News Culture and the Overbury Affair, 1603–1660* (Cambridge: Cambridge University Press, 2002).

Benedict, Barbara M., *Curiosity: A Cultural History of Early Modern Inquiry* (Chicago: University of Chicago Press, 2001).

Berg, Maxine, "In Pursuit of Luxury: Global History and British Consumer Goods in the Eighteenth Century," *P&P* 182 (2004).

——, "Manufacturing the Orient: Asian Commodities and European Industry (1500–1800)," in *Prodotti e Techniche d'Oltremare Nelle Economie Europee Secc. XIII–XVIII,* Simonetta Cavaciocchi, ed. (Florence: Le Monnier, 1998).

Berry, Christopher, *Idea of Luxury: A Conceptual and Historical Investigation* (Cambridge: Cambridge University Press, 1994).

Berry, Helen, "Early Coffee House Periodical and Its Readers: The Athenian Mercury, 1691-1697," *London Journal* 25:1 (2000).

——, " 'Nice and Curious Questions': Coffee Houses and the Representation of Women in John Dunton's *Athenian Mercury,*" *Seventeenth Century* 12:2 (Autumn 1997).

———, "Rethinking Politeness in Eighteenth-Century England: Moll King's Coffee House and the Significance of 'Flash Talk,' " *Transactions of the Royal Historical Society* 5th ser. (2001).

Biagioli, Mario, "Etiquette, Interdependence and Sociability in Seventeenth-Century Science," *Critical Inquiry* 22 (Winter 1996).

Bianchi, Marina, "In the Name of the Tulip: Why Speculation?" in *Consumers and Luxury: Consumer Culture in Europe, 1650–1850* (Manchester: Manchester University Press, 1999).

Biggins, James M., "Coffeehouses of York," *York Georgian Society: Annual Report* (1953–54).

Birrell, T. A., "Sir Roger L'Estrange: The Journalism of Orality," in *Cambridge History of the Book in Britain,* vol. 4, *1557–1695,* John Barnard and D. F. McKenzie, eds. (Cambridge: Cambridge University Press, 2001).

Black, Jeremy, *English Press in the Eighteenth Century* (Croom Helm, 1987).

———, "Underrated Journalist: Nathaniel Mist and the Opposition Press During the Whig Ascendancy," *British Journal for ECS,* 10 (1987).

Blanchard, Rae, "Was Sir Richard Steele a Freemason?" *PMLA,* 63:3 (1948).

Blanning, T. C. W., *Culture of Power and the Power of Culture: Old Regime Europe 1660–1789* (Oxford: Oxford University Press, 2002).

Borsay, Peter, *English Urban Renaissance: Culture and Society in the Provincial Town, 1660–1770* (Oxford: Clarendon, 1989).

Boulton, Jeremy, *Neighborhood and Society: A London Suburb in the Seventeenth Century* (Cambridge: Cambridge University Press, 1987).

Bourke, Algernon, *History of White's,* 2 vols. (Waterlow, 1892).

Bowen, H. V., *Elites, Enterprise and the Making of the British Overseas Empire, 1688–1775* (Macmillan, 1996).

Braddick, Michael, *Nerves of State: Taxation and the Financing of the English State, 1558–1714* (Manchester: Manchester University Press, 1996).

———, *Parliamentary Taxation in Seventeenth-Century England* (Bury St Edmonds, Suffolk: Royal Historical Society, 1994).

———, *State Formation in Early Modern England c. 1500–1700* (Cambridge: Cambridge University Press, 2000).

Braddick, Michael, and John Walter, *Negotiating Power in Early Modern Society: Order, Hierarchy and Subordination in Britain and Ireland* (Cambridge: Cambridge University Press, 2001).

Braudel, Fernand, *Structures of Everyday Life: The Limits of the Possible,* Siân Reynolds, trans. (1979; reprint, New York: Harper & Row, 1981).

———, *Wheels of Commerce,* Siân Reynolds, trans. (1979; reprint, New York: Harper & Row, 1982).

Bray, Alan, *Homosexuality in Renaissance England* (Boston: Gay Men's Press, 1982).

Brenner, Robert, *Merchants and Revolution* (Princeton: Princeton University Press, 1993).

Brett-James, Norman G., *Growth of Stuart London* (Allen & Unwin, 1935).

Brewer, John, "Cultural Consumption in Eighteenth-Century England: The View of the Reader," in *Frühe Neuzeit — Frühe Moderne? Forschungen zur Vielschichtigkeit von*

Übergangsprozessen, Rudolf Vierhaus, ed. (Göttingen: Vandenhoeck & Ruprecht, 1992).

——, "Error of Our Ways: Historians and the Birth of Consumer Society," public lecture at the Royal Society, Carlton House Terrace, London, 23 September 2003.

——, *Party Ideology and Popular Politics at the Accession of George III* (Cambridge: Cambridge University Press, 1976).

——, *Pleasures of the Imagination: English Culture in the Eighteenth Century* (New York: Farrar, Straus & Giroux, 1997).

——, *Sinews of Power: War, Money, and the English State, 1688–1783* (New York: Knopf, 1989).

——, "This, That, and the Other: Public, Social, and Private in the Seventeenth and Eighteenth Centuries," in *Shifting the Boundaries,* Dario Castiglione and Lesley Sharpe, eds. (Exeter: University of Exeter Press, 1995).

Brewer, John, Neil McKendrick, and J. H. Plumb, eds., *Birth of a Consumer Society: The Commercialization of Eighteenth-Century England* (Hutchinson, 1982).

Brewer, John, and Roy Porter, eds., *Consumption and the World of Goods* (Routledge, 1992).

Brooks, Colin, "Taxation, Finance, and Public Opinion, 1688–1714" (Ph.D. thesis, Cambridge University, 1970).

Brown, Peter, *Body and Society: Men, Women, and Sexual Renunciation in Early Christianity* (New York: Columbia University Press, 1988).

Bryson, Anna Clare, *From Courtesy to Civility* (Oxford: Oxford University Press, 1998).

Bucholz, Robert, *Augustan Court: Queen Anne and the Decline of Court Culture* (Stanford: Stanford University Press, 1993).

Buckinghamshire County Record Office, "Turk's Head: An Aylesbury Coffee-house?" *Annual Report and List of Accessions* (Aylesbury, 1990).

Burke, Peter, *Art of Conversation* (Ithaca: Cornell University Press, 1993).

Burn, Jacob Henry, *Descriptive Catalogue of the London Traders, Tavern, and Coffee-House Tokens* (Privately Printed, 1855).

Burnett, John, "Coffee in the British Diet, 1650–1900," in *Kaffee im Spiegel europäischer Trinksitten,* Daniela U. Ball, ed. (Zurich: Johann Jacobs Museum, 1991).

Butterfield, Herbert, *Whig Interpretation of History* (G. Bell, 1931).

Cain, P. J., and A. G. Hopkins, *British Imperialism: Innovation and Expansion, 1688–1914* (Longman, 1993).

Campbell, Colin, *Romantic Ethic and the Spirit of Modern Consumerism* (Oxford: Blackwell, 1987).

——, "Understanding Traditional and Modern Patterns of Consumption in Eighteenth-Century England: A Character-Action Approach," in *Consumption and the World of Goods,* Brewer and Porter, eds. (Routledge, 1992).

Camporesi, Piero, *Bread of Dreams: Food and Fantasy in Early Modern Europe,* David Gentilcore, trans. (1980; reprint, Chicago: University of Chicago Press, 1989).

——, *Exotic Brew: The Art of Living in the Age of Enlightenment,* Christopher Woodall, trans. (1990; reprint, Cambridge: Polity, 1994).

Carter, Philip, *Men and the Emergence of Polite Society, Britain, 1660–1800* (Longman, 2001).

———, "Men About Town," in Barker and Chalus, eds., *Gender in Eighteenth-Century England* (Longman, 1997).

Carter, Susan B., and Stephen Cullenberg, "Labor Economics and the Historian," in *Economics and the Historian,* Thomas G. Rawski et al., eds. (Berkeley: University of California Press, 1996).

Castle, Terry, *Masquerade and Civilization* (Stanford: Stanford University Press, 1986).

Caudill, Randall L.-W., "Some Literary Evidence of the Development of English Virtuoso Interests in the Seventeenth Century, With Particular Reference to the Literature of Travel" (D. Phil. thesis, Oxford University, 1975).

Champion, Justin, *Pillars of Priestcraft Shaken: The Church of England and Its Enemies, 1660–1730* (Cambridge: Cambridge University Press, 1992).

———, *Republican Learning: John Toland and the Crisis of Christian Culture, 1696–1722* (Manchester: Manchester University Press, 2003).

Chandaman, C. D., *English Public Revenue, 1660–1688* (Oxford: Clarendon, 1975).

Chaney, David, *Lifestyles* (Routledge, 1996).

Chartier, Roger, *Cultural Origins of the French Revolution,* Lydia G. Cochrane, trans. (Durham: Duke University Press, 1991).

———, *Forms and Meanings: Texts, Performances, and Audiences from Codex to Computer* (Philadelphia: University of Pennsylvnia Press, 1995).

———, ed., *History of Private Life: Passions of the Renaissance,* Arthur Goldhammer, trans. (Cambridge, Mass.: Harvard University Press, 1989).

———, *On the Edge of the Cliff: History, Language, and Practices,* Lydia Cochrane, ed. (Baltimore: Johns Hopkins University Press, 1997).

———, *Order of Books: Readers, Authors, and Libraries in Europe between the Fourteenth and Eighteenth Centuries,* Lydia G. Cochrane, trans. (1992; reprint, Stanford: Stanford University Press, 1994).

Chartres, John, "Food Consumption and Internal Trade," in *London, 1500–1700: The Making of the Metropolis* (Longman, 1986).

———, "Place of Inns in the Commercial Life of London and Western England, 1660–1760" (Ph.D. diss., Cambridge University, 1973).

Chaudhuri, K. N., *English East India Company: The Study of an Early Joint-Stock Company, 1600–1640* (Frank Cass, 1965).

———, *Trading World of Asia and the English East India Company, 1660–1760* (Cambridge: Cambridge University Press, 1978).

Chaudhuri, K. N.. and Jonathan Israel, "English and Dutch East India Companies and the Glorious Revolution of 1688–89," in *Anglo-Dutch Moment: Essays on the Glorious Revolution and Its World Impact* (Cambridge: Cambridge University Press, 1991).

Clark, J. C. D., *English Society, 1660–1832* (Cambridge: Cambridge University Press, 2000).

———, *Revolution and Rebellion: State and Society in England in the Seventeenth and Eighteenth Centuries* (Cambridge: Cambridge University Press, 1986).

Clark, G. N., *Guide to English Commercial Statistics, 1696–1782* (Royal Historical Society, 1938).

Clark, Peter, "Alehouse and the Alternative Society," in *Puritans and Revolutionaries:*

Essays in Seventeenth-Century History Presented to Christopher Hill, Donald Pennington and Keith Thomas, eds. (Oxford: Clarendon, 1978).

——, *British Clubs and Societies, 1580–1800: The Origins of an Associational World* (Oxford: Clarendon, 2000).

——, *English Alehouse: A Social History, 1200–1830* (Longman, 1983).

——, *English Provincial Society from the Reformation to the Revolution: Religion, Politics and Society in Kent, 1500–1640* (Hassocks: Harvester, 1977).

——, " 'Mother Gin' Controversy in the Early Eighteenth Century," *Transactions of the Royal Historical Society,* 5th ser., 38 (1988).

——, *Sociability and Urbanity: Clubs and Societies in the Eighteenth-Century City* (Leicester: Victorian Studies Centre, University of Leicester, 1986).

Clarke, T. H., *Rhinoceros From Dürer to Stubbs, 1515–1799* (Sotheby's, 1986).

Claydon, Tony, *William III and the Godly Revolution* (Cambridge: Cambridge University Press, 1996).

——, "Sermon, the 'Public Sphere' and the Political Culture of Late Seventeenth-Century England," in Lori Anne Ferrell and Peter McCullough, eds., *English Sermon Revised: Religion, Literature and History, 1600–1750* (Manchester: Manchester University Press, 2001).

Clery, E. J., "Women, Publicity, and the Coffee-House Myth," *Women: A Cultural Review,* 2:2 (1991).

Clive, John, *Macaulay: The Shaping of the Historian* (New York: Knopf, 1974).

Cody, Lisa, " 'No Cure, No Money,' or the Invisible Hand of Quackery: The Language of Commerce, Credit, and Cash in Eighteenth-Century British Medical Advertisements," in *Studies in Eighteenth-Century Culture,* Julie Candler Hayes and Timothy Erwin, eds., vol. 28 (Baltimore: Johns Hopkins University Press, 1999).

Coe, Sophie D., and Michael D. Coe, *True History of Chocolate* (Thames & Hudson, 1996).

Colley, Linda, *Captives: Britain, Empire and the World, 1600–1850* (Cape, 2002).

——, *In Defiance of Oligarchy: The Tory Party, 1714–60* (Cambridge: Cambridge University Press, 1982).

——, "Loyal Brotherhood and the Cocoa Tree: The London Organization of the Tory Party, 1727–1760," *HJ,* 20 (1977).

Collins Baker, C. H., and M. I. Baker, *Life and Circumstances of James Brydges, First Duke of Chandos, Patron of the Liberal Arts* (Oxford: Clarendon, 1949).

Collinson, Patrick, *Godly People: Essays on English Protestantism and Puritanism* (Hambledon, 1983).

——, *Religion of Protestants: The Church in English Society, 1559–1625* (Oxford: Clarendon, 1979).

Cook, Harold J., *Decline of the Old Medical Regime in Stuart London* (Ithaca: Cornell University Press, 1986).

——, "Henry Stubbe and the Virtuosi-Physicians," in *The Medical Revolution of the Seventeenth Century,* Roger French and Andrew Wear, eds. (Cambridge: Cambridge University Press, 1989).

Cooper, Charles Henry, *Annals of Cambridge,* 5 vols. (Cambridge: Warwick, 1842–52, 1908).

Copley, Stephen, "Commerce, Conversation, and Politeness," *British Journal for Eighteenth-Century Studies* 18 (1995).

Corfield, Penelope J., "Walking the City Streets: The Urban Odyssey in Eighteenth-Century England," *Journal of Urban History* 16:2 (Feb. 1990).

——, "Rivals: Landed and Other Gentlemen," in N. B. Harte and Roland Quinalt, eds., *Land and Society in Britain 1700–1914* (Manchester: Manchester University Press, 1996).

Courtwright, David T., *Forces of Habit: Drugs and the Making of the Modern World* (Cambridge, Mass.: Harvard University Press, 2001).

Cowan, Brian, "Arenas of Connoisseurship: Auctioning Art in Later Stuart London," in *Art Markets in Europe, 1400–1800*, Michael North and David Ormrod, eds. (Aldershot: Ashgate, 1998).

——, "Art in the Auction Market of Later Seventeenth-Century London," in *Mapping Markets for Paintings in Europe, 1450–1800*, Neil De Marchi and Hans van Miegroet, eds. (Turnhout, Belgium: Brepols, 2005).

——, "Mr. Spectator and the Coffeehouse Public Sphere," *ECS* 37:3 (2004).

——, "Open Elite: Virtuosity and the Peculiarities of English Connoisseurship," *Modern Intellectual History* 1:2 (2004).

——, "Reasonable Ecstasies: Shaftesbury and the Languages of Libertinism," *Journal of British Studies* 37:2 (April 1998).

——, "Refiguring Revisionisms," *History of European Ideas* 29:4 (2003).

——, "Review of Laura Brown, *Fables of Modernity*," H-Albion, H-Net Reviews, January, 2003. URL: *http://www.h-net.msu.edu/reviews/showrev.cgi?path=178661046324333*

——, "Rise of the Coffeehouse Reconsidered," *HJ* 47:1 (2004).

——, "What Was Masculine About the Public Sphere? Gender and the Coffeehouse Milieu in Post-Restoration England," *History Workshop Journal* 51 (2001).

Craig, A. G., "Movement for the Reformation of Manners, 1688–1715" (Ph.D. diss., University of Edinburgh, 1980).

Cranfield, G. A., *Press and Society: From Caxton to Northcliffe* (Longman, 1978).

Crist, Timothy, "Francis Smith and the Opposition Press in England, 1660–1688" (Ph.D. diss., Cambridge University, 1977).

Cust, Richard, and Peter G. Lake, "Sir Richard Grosvener and the Rhetoric of Magistracy," *Bulletin of the Institute of Historical Research* 54:129 (1981).

Daniel, Stephen H., *John Toland: His Methods, Manners, and Mind* (Kingston: McGill-Queen's University Press, 1984).

Dannenfeldt, Karl H., *Leonhard Rauwolf: Sixteenth-Century Physician, Botanist and Traveler* (Cambridge, Mass.: Harvard University Press, 1968).

Darnton, Robert, "Early Information Society: News and the Media in Eighteenth-Century Paris," *American Historical Review* 105:1 (Feb. 2000).

——, "Enlightened Revolution?" *New York Review of Books* (24 Oct. 1991).

——, *Forbidden Best-Sellers of Pre-Revolutionary France* (New York: Norton, 1995).

Das Gupta, Ashin, *Indian Merchants and the Decline of Surat, c. 1700–1750* (1979; reprint, New Delhi: Manohar, 1994).

Daston, Lorraine, "Factual Sensibility," *Isis* 79 (1988).

——, "Ideal and Reality of the Republic of Letters in the Enlightenment," *Science in Context* 4 (1991).

——, "Marvelous Facts and Miraculous Evidence," *Critical Inquiry* 18 (1991).

——, "Neugierde als Empfindung und Epistemologie in der frümodernen Wissenschaft," in Andreas Grote, ed., *Macrocosmos in Microcosmo: Die Welt in der Stube; Zur Geschichte des Sammelns 1450 bis 1800* (Opladen: Lesket Budrich, 1994).

Daston, Lorraine, and Katherine Park, *Wonders and the Order of Nature, 1150–1750* (New York: Zone, 1998).

Davenport, John, *Aphrodisiacs and Anti-Aphrodisiacs: Three Essays on the Power of Reproduction* (1869).

Davis, Dorothy, *A History of Shopping* (Routledge, 1965).

Davis, Natalie Zemon, *Society and Culture in Early Modern France* (Stanford: Stanford University Press, 1975).

Davis, Ralph, *Aleppo and Devonshire Square: English Traders and the Levant in the Eighteenth Century* (Macmillan, 1967).

——, *Commercial Revolution: English Overseas Trade in the Seventeenth and Eighteenth Centuries* (Historical Association, 1967).

——, "English Foreign Trade, 1660–1700," *Economic History Review*, n.s., 7:2 (1954).

——, "English Foreign Trade, 1700–1770," *Economic History Review*, n.s., 15:2 (1962).

——, *Rise of the English Shipping Industry in the Seventeenth and Eighteenth Centuries* (Macmillan, 1962).

Davison, Lee Krim, "Public Policy in an Age of Economic Expansion: The Search for Commercial Accountability in England, 1690–1750" (Ph.D. diss., Harvard University, 1990).

Dawson, Warren R., "London Coffee-Houses and the Beginnings of Lloyd's," in *Essays by Divers Hands, being the Transactions of the Royal Society of Literature of the UK*, Sir Henry Imbert-Terry, ed., n.s., vol. 11 (Oxford University Press, 1932).

de Vries, Jan, "Between Purchasing Power and the World of Goods: Understanding the Household Economy in Early Modern Europe," in *Consumption and the World of Goods*, John Brewer and Roy Porter, eds. (Routledge, 1993).

——, *Economy of Europe in an Age of Crisis, 1600–1750* (Cambridge: Cambridge University Press, 1976).

——, "Industrial Revolution and the Industrious Revolution," *Journal of Economic History* 54:2 (June 1994).

——, "Luxury in the Dutch Golden Age in Theory and Practice," in *Luxury in the Eighteenth Century: Debates, Desires and Delectable Goods*, Maxine Berg and Elizabeth Eger, eds. (New York: Palgrave, 2003).

Denison Ross, E., *Sir Anthony Sherley and His Persian Adventure* (Routledge, 1933).

Dickson, P. G. M., *Financial Revolution in England* (Macmillan, 1967).

Dobrée, Bonamy, *English Literature in the Early Eighteenth Century, 1700–1740* (Oxford: Clarendon, 1959).

Douglas, Mary, and Baron Isherwood, *World of Goods: Towards an Anthropology of Consumption* (Harmondsworth: Penguin, 1978).

Downie, J. A., "Reflections on the Origins of the Periodical Essay: A Review Article," *Prose Studies* 12:3 (Dec. 1989).

——, *Robert Harley and the Press: Propaganda and Public Opinion in the Age of Swift and Defoe* (Cambridge: Cambridge University Press, 1979).

——, "Stating Facts Right About Defoe's *Review*," *Prose Studies* 16:1 (April 1993).

Durkheim, Emile, *Division of Labor in Society*, W. D. Halls, trans. (1893; reprint, New York: Free Press, 1984).

Eamon, William, *Science and the Secrets of Nature* (Princeton: Princeton University Press, 1994).

Earle, Peter, *City Full of People: Men and Women of London, 1650–1750* (Methuen, 1994).

——, *Making of the English Middle Class: Business, Society and Family Life in London 1660–1730* (Berkeley: University of California Press, 1989).

——, "Middling Sort in London," in *Middling Sort of People: Culture, Society and Politics in England, 1550–1800,* Jonathan Barry and Christopher Brooks, eds. (Basingstoke: Macmillan, 1994).

Eastwood, David, *Government and Community in the English Provinces, 1700–1870* (Houndmills: Macmillan, 1997).

Ehrman, Edwina and others, *London Eats Out: Five Hundred Years of Capital Dining* (Museum of London, 1999).

Elias, Norbert, *Court Society,* Edmund Jephcott, trans. (1969; reprint, New York: Pantheon, 1983).

Ellis, Aytoun, *Penny Universities: A History of the Coffee-Houses* (Secker & Warburg, 1956).

Ellis, Markman, "Coffee-Women, *The Spectator* and the Public Sphere in the Early Eighteenth Century," in *Women and the Public Sphere: Writing and Representation, 1700–1830,* Elizabeth Eger, Charlotte Grant, Clíona O'Gallchoir and Penny Warburton, eds. (Cambridge: Cambridge University Press, 2001).

Estabrook, Carl B., *Urbane and Rustic England: Cultural Ties and Social Spheres in the Provinces, 1660–1780* (Manchester: Manchester University Press, 1998).

Everitt, Alan, "English Urban Inn, 1560–1760," in his *Landscape and Community* (Hambledon, 1985).

Fabaron, Élisabeth, "Le commerce des monstres dans les foires et les tavernes de Londres au XVIIIe siècle," in *Commerce(s) en Grande-Bretagne au XVIIIe Siècle,* Suzy Halimi, ed. (Paris: Publications de la Sorbonne, 1990).

Farge, Arlette, *Subversive Words: Public Opinion in Eighteenth-Century France,* Rosemary Morris, trans. (1992; reprint, University Park: Penn State Press, 1994).

Farrington, Benjamin, *Francis Bacon: Philosopher of Industrial Science* (Macmillan, 1973).

Fincham, Kenneth and Peter Lake, "Popularity, Prelacy and Puritanism in the 1630s: Joseph Hall Explains Himself," *EHR* 111:443 (1996).

Findlen, Paula, "Francis Bacon and the Reform of Natural History in the Seventeenth Century," in *History and the Disciplines: The Reclassification of Knowledge in Early Modern Europe* (Rochester, N.Y.: University of Rochester Press, 1997).

——, *Possessing Nature: Museums, Collecting, and Scientific Culture in Early Modern Italy* (Berkeley: University of California Press, 1994).

Finkelstein, Joanne, *Dining Out: A Sociology of Modern Manners* (Cambridge: Polity, 1989).

Fisher, F. J., "Development of London as a Centre of Conspicuous Consumption in the Sixteenth and Seventeenth Centuries," in *Essays in Economic History,* E. M. Carus-Wilson, ed. (1948; reprint, Edward Arnold, 1962).

Fisher, Michael H., *Travels of Dean Mahomet: An Eighteenth-Century Journey Through India* (Berkeley: University of California Press, 1997).

Fissell, Mary E., *Patients, Power, and the Poor in Eighteenth-Century Bristol* (Cambridge: Cambridge University Press, 1991).

Ford, Douglas, "Growth of the Freedom of the Press," *EHR* 4:13 (Jan. 1889).

Foucault, Michel, *Care of the Self,* Robert Hurley, trans. (1984; reprint, New York: Vintage, 1986).

——, *Discipline and Punish: The Birth of the Prison,* Alan Sheridan, trans. (New York: Vintage, 1977).

Fox, Adam, *Oral and Literate Culture in England, 1500–1700* (Oxford: Clarendon, 2001).

France, Peter *Politeness and Its Discontents: Problems in French Classical Culture* (Cambridge: Cambridge University Press, 1992).

Frank, Robert G., Jr., *Harvey and the Oxford Physiologists: Scientific Ideas and Social Interaction* (Berkeley: University of California Press, 1980).

Franklin, Alfred, *Café, le Thé, et le Chocolat,* La Vie Privée d'Autrefois, vol. 13 (Paris: Plon, 1893).

——, *Dictionnaire Historique des Arts* (Paris: H. Welter, 1906).

——, *Médicaments,* La Vie Privée d'Autrefois, vol. 9 (Paris: Plon, 1891).

——, *La Vie de Paris sous la Régence,* Vie Privée d'Autrefois, vol. 21 (1727; reprint, Paris: Plon, 1897).

Fraser, Peter, *Intelligence of the Secretaries of State and their Monopoly of Licensed News, 1660–1688* (Cambridge: Cambridge University Press, 1956).

Freeman, E., "Proposal for an English Academy in 1660," *Modern Language Review* 19 (1924).

Friedman, Jerome, *Battle of the Frogs and Fairford's Flies* (New York: St. Martin's, 1993).

Furbank, P. N., and W. R. Owens, "Defoe and Sir Andrew Politick," *British Journal for Eighteenth-Century Studies,* 17 (1994).

——, "Defoe, the De la Faye Letters and *Mercurius Politicus,*" *British Journal for Eighteenth-Century Studies,* 23 (2000).

Gallagher, Catherine, *Nobody's Story: The Vanishing Acts of Women Writers in the Marketplace, 1670–1820* (Berkeley: University of California Press, 1994).

George, M. Dorothy, *London Life in the Eighteenth Century* (New York: Capricorn, 1965).

Geuss, Raymond, *Idea of a Critical Theory: Habermas and the Frankfurt* School (Cambridge: Cambridge University Press, 1981).

Gibb, D. E. W., *Lloyd's of London: A Study in Individualism* (Macmillan, 1957).

Gibbs, G. C., "Government and the English Press, 1695 to the Middle of the Eighteenth Century," in *Too Mighty to be Free: Censorship and the Press in Britain the Netherlands,* A. C. Duke and C. A. Tamse (Zutphen: De Walburg Pers, 1987).

——, "Press and Public Opinion: Prospective," in *Liberty Secured? Britain Before and After 1688,* J. R. Jones, ed. (Stanford: Stanford University Press, 1992).

Gibson-Wood, Carol, "Picture Consumption in London at the End of the Seventeenth Century," *Art Bulletin,* 84:3 (Sept. 2002): 491–500.

Ginzburg, Carlo, *Clues, Myths, and the Historical Method* (Baltimore: Johns Hopkins University Press, 1989).

——, *Ecstasies: Deciphering the Witches' Sabbath* (New York: Viking, 1990).

Girouard, Mark, *Life in the English Country House* (New Haven: Yale University Press, 1978).

Glamann, Kristof, *Dutch-Asiatic Trade, 1620–1740* (The Hague: Nijhoff, 1958).

Glass, D. V., "Notes on the Demography of London at the End of the Seventeenth Century," *Daedalus* 97 (1968).

——, "Socio-Economic Status and Occupations in the City of London at the End of the Seventeenth Century," in *Studies in London History: Presented to Philip Edmund Jones,* A. E. J. Hollaender and William Kellaway, eds. (1969).

——, ed., *London Inhabitants within the Walls 1695,* Publications of the London Record Society, vol. 2 (London Record Society, 1966).

Goldgar, Anne, *Impolite Learning: Conduct and Community in the Republic of Letters, 1680–1750* (New Haven: Yale University Press, 1995).

Goldie, Mark, "Unacknowledged Republic: Officeholding in Early Modern England," in Tim Harris, ed., *The Politics of the Excluded, c. 1500–1850* (Houndmills: Palgrave, 2001).

Goldsmith, Elizabeth C., *Exclusive Conversations: The Art of Interaction in Seventeenth-Century France* (Philadelphia: University of Pennsylvania Press, 1988).

Goldsmith, M. M., "Liberty, Luxury, and the Pursuit of Happiness," in *Languages of Political Theory in Early-Modern Europe,* Anthony Pagden, ed. (Cambridge: Cambridge University Press, 1987).

Goodchild, Peter, " 'No Phantastical Utopia but a Reall Place': John Evelyn, John Beale, and Backbury Hill, Herefordshire," *Garden History* 19 (1991).

Goodman, Dena, "Public Sphere and Private Life: Toward a Synthesis of Current Historiographical Approaches to the Old Regime," *History and Theory* 31 (1992).

——, *Republic of Letters: A Cultural History of the French Enlightenment* (Ithaca: Cornell University Press, 1994).

Goodman, Jordan, "Excitantia: Or, how Enlightenment Europe took to soft drugs," in *Consuming Habits,* Jordan Goodman, Paul E. Lovejoy, and Andrew Sherratt, eds. (Routledge, 1995).

——, *Tobacco in History: The Cultures of Dependence* (Routledge, 1993).

Goodman, Jordan, Paul E. Lovejoy, and Andrew Sherratt, eds., *Consuming Habits* (Routledge, 1995).

Gordon, Daniel, *Citizens Without Sovereignty: Equality and Sociability in French Thought, 1670–1789* (Princeton: Princeton University Press, 1994).

——, "Philosophy, Sociology, and Gender in the Enlightenment Conception of Public Opinion," *French Historical Studies* 17:4 (Fall 1992).

Gordon, Scott Paul, "Voyeuristic Dreams: Mr. Spectator and the Power of Spectacle," *Eighteenth Century: Theory and Interpretation* 1995 36(1).

Gowing, Laura, *Domestic Dangers: Women, Words, and Sex in Early Modern London* (Oxford: Clarendon, 1996).

Grassby, Richard, *The Business Community of Seventeenth-Century England* (Cambridge: Cambridge University Press, 1995).

Greaves, Richard, *Secrets of the Kingdom: British Radicals from the Popish Plot to the Revolution of 1688–89* (Stanford: Stanford University Press, 1992).

Greenough, C. N., "The Development of the *Tatler,* Particularly in Regard to News," *PMLA* 31:4, new series 24:4 (1916).

Griffiths, Paul, *Youth and Authority: Formative Experiences in England, 1560–1640* (Oxford: Clarendon, 1996).

Gunn, J. A. W., *Beyond Liberty and Property: The Process of Self-Recognition in Eighteenth-Century Political Thought* (Kingston: McGill-Queen's University Press, 1983).

Habermas, Jürgen, "Further Reflections on the Public Sphere," in *Habermas and the Public Sphere,* Craig Calhoun, ed. (Cambridge, Mass.: MIT Press, 1992).

——, *Structural Transformation of the Public Sphere: An Inquiry into a Category of Bourgeois Society* (1962; reprint, Cambridge, Mass.: MIT Press, 1989).

Haggerty, George E., *Men in Love: Masculinity and Sexuality in the Eighteenth Century* (New York: Columbia University Press, 1999).

Hagstrum, Jean H., *Sex and Sensibility: Ideal and Erotic Love from Milton to Mozart* (Chicago: University of Chicago Press, 1980).

Haley, K. H. D., *First Earl of Shaftesbury* (Oxford: Clarendon, 1968).

Hallam, Henry, *Constitutional history of England, from the accession of Henry VII to the death of George II,* 2 vols. (John Murray, 1850).

Hanawalt, Barbara, *"Of Good and Ill Repute": Gender and Social Control in Medieval England* (New York: Oxford University Press, 1998).

Hancock, David, *Citizens of the World: London Merchants and the Integration of the British Atlantic Community, 1735–1785* (Cambridge: Cambridge University Press, 1995).

Hanson, Lawrence, *Government and the Press, 1695–1763* (Oxford: Oxford University Press, 1936).

Harley, David, "Beginnings of the Tobacco Controversy," *Bulletin of the History of Medicine* 67 (1993).

Harris, Jonathan, "Grecian Coffeehouse and Political Debate in London, 1688–1714," *London Journal* 25:1 (2000).

Harris, Michael, "Newspaper Distribution During Queen Anne's Reign," *Studies in the Book Trade* (Oxford, 1975).

Harris, Tim, *London Crowds in the Reign of Charles II: Propaganda and Politics from the Restoration until the Exclusion Crisis* (Cambridge: Cambridge University Press, 1987).

——, "Problematising Popular Culture," in *Popular Culture in England c. 1500–1850* (Basingstoke: Macmillan, 1995).

——, " 'Venerating the Honesty of a Tinker': The King's Friends and the Battle for the Allegiance of the Common People in Restoration England," in *Politics of the Excluded, c. 1500–1850,* Tim Harris, ed. (Houndmills: Palgrave, 2001).

——, "Was the Tory Reaction Popular? Attitudes of Londoners Towards the Persecution of Dissent," *London Journal* 1987–88 13(2).

Hatcher, John, "Labour, Leisure and Economic Thought before the Nineteenth Century," *P&P* no. 160 (Aug. 1998).

Hattox, Ralph S., *Coffee and Coffeehouses: The Origins of a Social Beverage in the Medieval Near East* (Seattle: University of Washington Press, 1985).

Heal, Felicity, *Hospitality in Early Modern England* (Oxford: Clarendon, 1990).

Heinemann, F. H., "John Toland and the Age of Reason," *Archiv für Philosophie* 4:1 (September 1950).

Held, David, *Introduction to Critical Theory: Horkheimer to Habermas* (Berkeley: University of California Press, 1980).

Herzog, Don, *Poisoning the Minds of the Lower Orders* (Princeton: Princeton University Press, 1998).

Hill, Christopher, *Experience of Defeat: Milton and Some Contemporaries* (New York: Penguin, 1984).

———, *World Turned Upside Down* (New York: Viking, 1972).

Hindle, Steve, *State and Social Change in Early Modern England, c. 1550–1640* (Houndmills: Macmillan, 2000).

Hirst, Derek, "Locating the 1650s in England's Seventeenth Century," *History* 81 (1996).

Hitchcock, Tim, *English Sexualities, 1700–1800* (Macmillan, 1997).

———, "New History from Below," *History Workshop Journal* 57:1 (Spring 2004).

Hobson, Anthony, "Sale by Candle in 1608," *Library* 26:3 (1971).

Holmes, Geoffrey, *Augustan England: Professions, State and Society, 1680–1730* (Allen & Unwin, 1982).

———, *British Politics in the Age of Anne,* 2nd ed. (Hambledon, 1987).

Holmes, Geoffrey and W. A. Speck, *Divided Society: Party Conflict in England, 1694–1716* (Edward Arnold, 1967).

Hoon, Elizabeth Evelynola, *Organization of the English Customs System, 1696–1786* (New York: D. Appleton-Century, 1938).

Hoppit, Julian, "Myths of the South Sea Bubble," *Transactions of the Royal Historical Society* 6th ser. (2002).

Horle, Craig W., *Quakers and the English Legal System, 1660–1688* (Philadelphia: University of Pennsylvania Press, 1988).

Horowitz, Eliot, "Nocturnal Rituals of Early Modern Jewry," *Association for Jewish Studies Review* 14 (1989).

Horowitz, Henry, *Parliament, Policy, and Politics in the Reign of William III* (Manchester: Manchester University Press, 1977).

Houghton, Walter, "English Virtuoso in the Seventeenth Century," *Journal of the History of Ideas* 3 (1942).

———, "History of Trades," *Journal of the History of Ideas* 2 (1941): 33–60.

Houston, Alan and Steve Pincus, eds., *Nation Transformed: England After the Restoration,* (Cambridge: Cambridge University Press, 2001).

Howarth, David, *Lord Arundel and His Circle* (New Haven: Yale University Press, 1985).

Hughes, Ann, "Gender and Politics in Leveller Literature," in Susan D. Amussen and Mark A. Kishlansky, eds., *Political Culture and Cultural Politics in Early Modern England: Essays Presented to David Underdown* (Manchester: Manchester University Press, 1995).

Hundert, E. J., *Enlightenment's "Fable": Bernard Mandeville and the Discovery of Society* (Cambridge: Cambridge University Press, 1994).

Hunt, Margaret, "Conquering Desires: Women, War and Identities in Eighteenth-Century Britain," paper presented at the 11th Berkshire Women's History Conference (6 June 1999).

——, *Middling Sort: Commerce, Gender, and the Family in England, 1680–1780* (Berkeley: University of California Press, 1996).

Hunter, J. Paul, *Before Novels: The Cultural Contexts of Eighteenth Century English Fiction* (New York: Norton, 1990).

Hunter, Judith, "English Inns, Taverns, Alehouses and Brandyshops: The Legislative Framework, 1495–1797," in *World of the Tavern: Public Houses in Early Modern Europe* (Aldershot: Ashgate, 2002).

——, "Legislation, Proclamations and Other National Directives Affecting Inns, Taverns, Alehouses, Brandy Shops and Punch Houses, 1552 to 1757" (Ph.D. diss., University of Reading, 1994).

Hunter, Michael, *Establishing the New Science: The Experience of the Early Royal Society* (Woodbridge: Boydell, 1989).

——, *John Aubrey and the Realm of Learning* (New York: Science History Publications, 1975).

——, *Science and Society in Restoration England* (Cambridge: Cambridge University Press, 1981).

——, *Science and the Shape of Orthodoxy: Intellectual Change in the late Seventeenth Century Britain* (Woodbridge: Boydell, 1995).

——, "Witchcraft and the Decline of Belief," *Eighteenth-Century Life* 22:2 (1998).

Hyland, P. B. J., "Liberty and Libel: Government and the Press during the Succession Crisis in Britain, 1712–1716," *EHR* 101:401 (Oct. 1986).

Iliffe, Robert, "Foreign Bodies: Travel, Empire and the Early Royal Society of London, Part 1: Englishmen on Tour," *Canadian Journal of History* 33:3 (1998).

——, "Material Doubts: Hooke, Artisan Culture, and the Exchange of Information in 1670s London," *British Journal for the History of Science,* 28 (1995).

Illich, Ivan, *Medical Nemesis: The Expropriation of Health* (New York: Pantheon, 1976).

İnalcik, Halil and Donald Quataert, eds., *Economic and Social History of the Ottoman Empire, 1300–1914* (Cambridge: Cambridge University Press, 1994).

Ingram, Martin, *Church Courts, Sex and Marriage in England, 1570–1640* (Cambridge: Cambridge University Press, 1987).

Irving, William Henry, *John Gay's London* (Cambridge, Mass.: Harvard University Press, 1928).

Isherwood, Robert M., *Farce and Fantasy: Popular Entertainment in Eighteenth-Century Paris* (Oxford: Oxford University Press, 1986).

Israel, Jonathan, *Dutch Primacy in World Trade, 1585–1740* (Oxford: Clarendon, 1989).

Jacob, James R., *Henry Stubbe: Radical Protestantism and the Early Enlightenment* (Cambridge: Cambridge University Press, 1983).

Jacob, Margaret C., "Mental Landscape of the Public Sphere: A European Perspective," *ECS* 28:1 (Fall 1994).

———, *Newtonians and the English Revolution, 1689–1720* (Hassocks, Sussex: Harvester, 1976).

———, *Radical Enlightenment: Pantheists, Freemasons, and Republicans* (Allen & Unwin, 1981).

Jamieson, Ross W., "Essence of Commodification: Caffeine Dependencies in the Early Modern World," *Journal of Social History* 35:2 (2001).

Jenner, Mark, "Bathing and Baptism: Sir John Floyer and the Politics of Cold Bathing," in *Refiguring Revolutions: Aesthetics and Politics from the English Revolution to the Romantic Revolution* (Berkeley: University of California Press, 1998).

———, "Politics of London Air: John Evelyn's *Fumifugium* and the Restoration," *HJ* 38:3 (1995).

Johns, Adrian, "Flamsteed's Optics and the Identity of the Astronomical Observer," in *Flamsteed's Stars: New Perspectives on the Life and Work of the First Astronomer Royal (1646–1719)*, Frances Willmoth, ed. (Bury St. Edmunds: Boydell, 1997).

———, "Coffee, Print, Authorship and Argument," in *Cambridge History of Seventeenth-Century Science*, Lorraine Daston and Katherine Park, eds. (Cambridge: Cambridge University Press, forthcoming).

———, "Miscellaneous Methods: Authors, Societies and Journals in Early Modern England," *British Journal for the History of Science* 33 (2000).

———, *Nature of the Book: Print and Knowledge in the Making* (Chicago: University of Chicago Press, 1998).

Jones, Clyve, "The London Life of a Peer in the Reign of Anne: A Case Study from Lord Ossulston's Diary," *London Journal* 16:2 (1991).

Jones, Clyve, and Geoffrey Holmes, eds., *London Diaries of William Nicolson, Bishop of Carlisle, 1702–1718* (Oxford: Clarendon, 1985).

Jones, Colin, "Bourgeois Revolution Revivified: 1789 and Social Change," in *Rewriting the French Revolution* (Oxford: Oxford University Press, 1991).

———, "Great Chain of Buying: Medical Advertisement, the Bourgeois Public Sphere, and the Origins of the French Revolution," *American Historical Review* 101:1 (Feb. 1996).

Jones, Colin, and Rebecca Spang, "Sans-culottes, *sans café, sans tabac*: Shifting Realms of Necessity and Luxury in Eighteenth-Century France," in *Consumers and Luxury: Consumer Culture in Europe, 1650–1850*, Maxine Berg, ed. (Manchester: Manchester University Press, 1999).

Jones, D. W., "London Overseas-Merchant Groups at the End of the Seventeenth Century and the Moves Against the East India Company" (D.Phil., Oxon., 1970).

———, *War and Economy in the Age of William III and Marlborough* (Oxford: Blackwell, 1988).

Jones, Richard Foster, *Ancients and Moderns: A Study of the Rise of the Scientific Movement in Seventeenth-Century England*, 2nd ed. (New York: Dover, 1961).

Ketcham, Michael G., *Transparent Designs: Reading, Performance, and Form in the Spectator Papers* (Athens: University of Georgia Press, 1985).

Key, Newton E., "Localism of the County Feast in Late Stuart Political Culture," *Huntington Library Quarterly* 58:2 (1996).

———, "Political Culture and Political Rhetoric of County Feasts and Feast Sermons, 1654–1714," *Journal of British Studies* 33 (July 1994).

King, J. C. H., "Ethnographic Collections: Collecting in the Context of Sloane's Catalogue of 'Miscellanies,'" in *Sir Hans Sloane: Collector, Scientist, Antiquary, Founding Father of the British Museum,* Arthur MacGregor, ed. (British Museum, 1994).

Kishlansky, Mark, *Parliamentary Selection: Social and Political Choice in Early Modern England* (Cambridge: Cambridge University Press, 1986).

Klein, Lawrence, "Coffeehouse Civility, 1660–1714: An Aspect of Post-Courtly Culture in England," *Huntington Library Quarterly* 59:1 (1997).

——, "Figure of France: The Politics of Sociability in England, 1660–1715," *Yale French Studies* 92 (1997).

——, "Gender and the Public/Private Distinction in the Eighteenth Century: Some Questions about Evidence and Analytic Procedure," *ECS* 29:1 (1995).

——, "Gender, Conversation, and the Public Sphere," in *Textuality and Sexuality: Reading Theories and Practices,* Judith Still and Michael Worton, eds. (Manchester: Manchester University Press, 1993).

——, "Politeness and the Interpretation of the British Eighteenth Century," *Historical Journal* 45:4 (2002).

——, "Rise of Politeness in England, 1660–1714" (Ph.D. Diss., Johns Hopkins University, 1983).

——, *Shaftesbury and the Culture of Politeness: Moral Discourse and Cultural Politics in Early Eighteenth-Century England* (Cambridge: Cambridge University Press, 1994).

Knapp, Jeffrey, "Elizabethan Tobacco," in *New World Encounters,* Stephen Greenblatt, ed. (Berkeley: University of California Press, 1993).

Knights, Mark, *Politics and Opinion in Crisis, 1678–81* (Cambridge: Cambridge University Press, 1994).

Lake, Peter, "Retrospective: Wentworth's Political World in Revisionist and Post-Revisionist Perspective," in *Political World of Thomas Wentworth, Earl of Strafford,* Julia Merritt, ed. (Cambridge: Cambridge University Press, 1996), 252–283.

——, "Review Article," *Huntington Library Quarterly* 57:2 (1994).

Lake, Peter, and Michael Questier, "Puritans, Papists, and the 'Public Sphere' in Early Modern England: the Edmund Campion Affair in Context," *Journal of Modern History,* 72:3 (2000).

Landes, Joan, *Women and the Public Sphere in the Age of the French Revolution* (Ithaca: Cornell University Press, 1988).

Landry, Donna, "Alexander Pope, Lady Mary Wortley Montagu and the Literature of Social Comment," in *Cambridge Companion to English Literature, 1650–1740,* Steven Zwicker, ed. (Cambridge: Cambridge University Press, 1998).

Langford, Paul, "British Politeness and the Progress of Western Manners: An Eighteenth-Century Enigma," *Transactions of the Royal Historical Society,* 6th ser., vol. 7 (1997).

——, *Englishness Identified: Manners and Character, 1650–1850* (Oxford: Oxford University Press, 2000).

——, *Polite and Commercial People: England, 1727–1783* (Oxford: Oxford University Press, 1992).

Laqueur, Thomas, *Making Sex: Body and Gender from the Greeks to Freud* (Cambridge, Mass.: Harvard University Press, 1990).

——, "Roy Porter, 1946–2002: A Critical Appreciation," *Social History* 29:1 (2004).

Lears, Jackson, *Fables of Abundance: A Cultural History of Advertising in America* (New York: Basic Books, 1994).

Leclant, Jean, "Coffee and Cafés in Paris, 1644–1693," in *Food and Drink in History,* Robert Forster and Orest Ranum, eds., Patricia Ranum, trans. (1951; reprint, Baltimore: Johns Hopkins University Press, 1979).

Leslie, Michael, "Spiritual Husbandry of John Beale," in *Culture and Cultivation in Early Modern England: Writing and the Land* (Leicester: Leicester University Press, 1992).

Letwin, William, *Origins of Scientific Economics* (Garden City, N.Y.: Doubleday, 1964).

Levin, Jennifer, *Charter Controversy in the City of London, 1660–1688, and its Consequences* (Athlone, 1969).

Levine, Joseph, *Battle of the Books: History and Literature in the Augustan Age* (Ithaca: Cornell University Press, 1991).

——, *Between the Ancients and the Moderns: Baroque Culture in Restoration England* (New Haven: Yale University Press, 1999).

——, *Dr. Woodward's Shield: History, Science, and Satire in Augustan England* (1977; reprint, Ithaca: Cornell University Press, 1991).

Lillywhite, Bryant, *London Coffee Houses* (Allen & Unwin, 1963).

——, *London Signs: A Reference Book of London Signs from the Earliest Times to About the Mid-Nineteenth Century* (Allen & Unwin, 1972).

Limouze, Arthur S., "Study of Nathaniel Mist's Weekly Journals" (Ph.D. diss., Duke University, 1947).

Lloyd, Claude, "Shadwell and the Virtuosi," *PMLA* 44 (1929).

Looney, J. Jefferson, "Cultural Life in the Provinces: Leeds and York, 1720–1820," in *First Modern Society: Essays in English History in Honour of Lawrence Stone,* A. L. Beier, David Cannadine, and James M. Rosenheim, eds. (Cambridge: Cambridge University Press, 1989).

Loughead, Philip, "East India Company in English Domestic Politics, 1657–1688" (D.Phil., Oxon., 1980).

Love, Harold, *Culture and Commerce of Texts: Scribal Publication in Seventeenth-Century England* (Amherst: University of Massachusetts Press, 1998).

Lund, Roger D., "Guilt By Association: The Atheist Cabal and the Rise of the Public Sphere in Augustan England," *Albion* 34:3 (Fall 2002).

MacGregor, Arthur, "Cabinet of Curiosities in Seventeenth-Century Britain," in *Origins of Museums: The Cabinet of Curiosities in Sixteenth- and Seventeenth-Century Europe,* Oliver Impey and Arthur MacGregor, eds. (Oxford: Oxford University Press, 1985).

Mackie, Erin, ed., *Commerce of Everyday Life: Selections from the Tatler and the Spectator* (Basingstoke: Macmillan, 1998).

——, *Market à la Mode: Fashion, Commodity, and Gender in the Tatler and Spectator Papers* (Baltimore: Johns Hopkins University Press, 1997).

MacLeod, Christine, "1690s Patent Boom: Invention or Stock-Jobbing," *Economic History Review* 2nd ser., 39:4 (1986).

Mandrou, Robert, *Introduction to Modern France, 1500–1640: An Essay in Historical Psychology,* R. E. Hallmark, trans. of 2nd ed. (1974; reprint, New York: Holmes & Meier, 1975).

Manley, Lawrence, *Literature and Culture in Early Modern London* (Cambridge: Cambridge University Press, 1995).

Matar, Nabil, *Islam in Britain, 1558–1685* (Cambridge: Cambridge University Press, 1998).

Mathee, Rudi, "Exotic Substances: the introduction and global spread of tobacco, coffee, cocoa, tea, and distilled liquor, sixteenth to eighteenth centuries," in *Drugs and Narcotics in History*, Roy Porter and Miklulas Teich, eds. (Cambridge: Cambridge University Press, 1995).

Mathias, Peter, *Transformation of England: Essays in the Economic and Social History of England in the Eighteenth Century* (London: Methuen, 1979).

Matthew, Colin and others, eds., *Oxford DNB* (Oxford: Oxford University Press, 2004).

Matthews, L. G., "Herbals and Formularies," in *The Evolution of Pharmacy in Britain*, F. N. L. Poynter, ed. (1965).

Maurer, Shawn Lisa, *Proposing Men: Dialectics of Gender and Class in the Eighteenth-Century English Periodical* (Stanford: Stanford University Press, 1998).

Maza, Sarah, *Private Lives and Public Affairs: The Causes Célèbres of Pre-Revolutionary France* (Berkeley: University of California Press, 1993).

——, "Women, the Bourgeoisie, and the Public Sphere: Response to Daniel Gordon and David Bell," *French Historical Studies* 17:4 (Fall 1992).

McCalman, Iain, "Ultra-radicalism and Convivial Debating Clubs in London, 1795–1838," *EHR* 102 (1987).

McCloskey, D. N., "Economics of Choice: Neoclassical Supply and Demand," in *Economics and the Historian*, Thomas G. Rawski et al., eds. (Berkeley: University of California Press, 1996).

McCracken, Grant, *Culture and Consumption* (Bloomington and Indianapolis: University of Indiana Press, 1988).

McDowell, Paula, *Women of Grub Street: Press, Politics, and Gender in the London Literary Marketplace, 1678–1730* (Oxford: Clarendon, 1998).

McFadden, George, *Dryden: The Public Writer, 1660–1685* (Princeton: Princeton University Press, 1978).

McKendrick, Neil, "Commercialization of Fashion," in *Birth of a Consumer Society: The Commercialization of Eighteenth-Century England,* John Brewer, Neil McKendrick, and J. H. Plumb, eds. (London: Hutchinson, 1982).

McKeon, Michael, *Origins of the English Novel, 1600–1740* (Baltimore: Johns Hopkins University Press, 1987).

Mendyk, Stan A. E., *"Speculum Britanniae": Regional Study, Antiquarianism, and Science in Britain to 1700* (Toronto: University of Toronto Press, 1989).

Menefee, Samuel P., *Wives for Sale: An Ethnographic Study of British Popular Divorce* (Oxford: Basil Blackwell, 1981).

Mennell, Stephen, *All Manners of Food: Eating and Taste in England and France from the Middle Ages to the Present,* 2nd ed. (1985; reprint, Urbana: University of Illinois Press, 1996).

Meyers, Robin, Michael Harris, and Giles Mandlebrote, eds., *Under the Hammer: Book Auctions Since the Seventeenth Century* (British Library, 2001).

Miller, Daniel, *Theory of Shopping* (Cambridge: Polity, 1998).

Miller, John, *After the Civil Wars: English Politics and Government in the Reign of Charles II* (Longman, 2000).

———, "Public Opinion in Charles II's England," *History* 80 (1995).

Mintz, Samuel I., *Hunting of Leviathan: Seventeenth Century Reactions to the Materialism and Moral Philosophy of Thomas Hobbes* (Cambridge: Cambridge University Press, 1962).

Mintz, Sidney, *Sweetness and Power: The Place of Sugar in Modern History* (New York: Viking, 1985).

Money, John, "Taverns, Coffee Houses and Clubs: Local Politics and Popular Articulacy in the Birmingham area in the Age of the American Revolution," *Historical Journal* 14 (1971).

Monod, Paul, *Jacobitism and the English People, 1688–1788* (Cambridge: Cambridge University Press, 1989).

Morley, Henry, *Memoirs of Bartholomew Fair* (Chapman and Hall, 1859).

Muddiman, J. G., *King's Journalist, 1659–1689* (Bodley Head, 1923).

Mukerji, Chandra, *From Graven Images: Patterns of Modern Materialism* (New York: Columbia University Press, 1983).

Muldrew, Craig, *Economy of Obligation: The Culture of Credit and Social Relations in Early Modern England* (Macmillan, 1998).

———, "'Hard Food for Midas': Cash and Its Social Value in Early Modern England," *P&P* 170 (Feb. 2001).

Mullaney, Steven, "Strange Things, Gross Terms, Curious Customs: The Rehearsal of Cultures in the Late Renaissance," in *Representing the English Renaissance,* Stephen Greenblatt, ed. (Berkeley: University of California Press, 1988).

Mulligan, Lotte, "Self-Scrutiny and the Study of Nature: Robert Hooke's Diary as Natural History," *Journal of British Studies* 35:3 (July 1996).

Neal, Larry, *Rise of Financial Capitalism: International Capital Markets in the Age of Reason* (Cambridge: Cambridge University Press, 1990).

Newdigate-Newdegate, Lady Anne Emily, *Cavalier and Puritan in the Days of the Stuarts* (Smith, Elder & Co., 1901).

Nicolson, Marjorie Hope, *Pepys' Diary and the New Science* (Charlottesville: University Press of Virginia, 1965).

Norbrook, David, *Writing the English Republic: Poetry, Rhetoric and Politics, 1627–1660* (Cambridge: Cambridge University Press, 1999).

Novak, Maximillian, *Daniel Defoe: Master of Fictions* (Oxford: Oxford University Press, 2000).

———, *William Congreve* (New York: Twayne, 1971).

Ochs, Kathleen, "Royal Society of London's History of Trades," *Notes and Records of the Royal Society* 39 (1985).

Ogden, Henry and Margaret Ogden, *English Taste in Landscape in the Seventeenth Century* (Ann Arbor: University of Michigan Press, 1955).

Olson, Alison Gilbert, *Anglo-American Politics, 1660–1775: The Relationship Between Parties in England and Colonial America* (New York: Oxford University Press, 1973).

Ormrod, David, "Art and Its Markets," *Economic History Review,* 52:3 (1999).

——, "Origins of the London Art Market, 1660–1730," in *Art Markets in Europe, 1400–1800,* Michael North and David Ormrod, eds. (Aldershot, UK: Ashgate, 1998).

——, *Rise of Commercial Empires: England and the Netherlands in the Age of Mercantilism, 1650–1770* (Cambridge: Cambridge University Press, 2003).

Outram, Dorinda, *The Enlightenment* (Cambridge: Cambridge University Press, 1995).

Ozouf, Mona, "Public Opinion at the End of the Old Regime," *Journal of Modern History* 60 (suppl.) (1988).

Pace, Claire, "Virtuoso to Connoisseur: Some Seventeenth-Century English Responses to the Visual Arts," *Seventeenth Century* 2:2 (1987).

Pallares-Burke, "*Spectator* Abroad: The Fascination of the Mask," *History of European Ideas* 22:1 (1996).

Park, Katherine and Lorraine J. Daston, "Unnatural Conceptions: The Study of Monsters in Sixteenth- and Seventeenth-Century France and England," *P&P* 92 (1981).

Patterson, Annabel, *Nobody's Perfect: A New Whig Interpretation of History* (New Haven: Yale University Press, 2002).

Paulson, Ronald, *Don Quixote in England: The Aesthetics of Laughter* (Baltimore: Johns Hopkins University Press, 1998).

——, *Hogarth: The "Modern Moral Subject," 1697–1732* (New Brunswick, N.J.: Rutgers University Press, 1991).

Pears, Iain, *Discovery of Painting: The Growth of Interest in the Arts in England, 1680–1760* (New Haven: Yale University Press, 1988).

Pelling, Margaret, "Barber-Surgeons, the Body and Disease," in A. L. Beier and Roger Finlay, eds., *London, 1500–1700: The Making of the Metropolis* (Longman, 1986).

——, *Common Lot: Sickness, Medical Occupations and the Urban Poor in Early Modern England* (Longman, 1998).

Peltonen, Markku, *Classical Humanism and Republicanism in English Political Thought, 1570–1640* (Cambridge: Cambridge University Press, 1995).

Phillipson, Nicholas, "Politics and Politeness in the Reigns of Anne and the Early Hanoverians," in *Varieties of British Political Thought, 1500–1800,* J. G. A. Pocock, ed. (Cambridge: Cambridge University Press, 1993).

Pincus, Steve, " 'Coffee Politicians Does Create': Coffeehouses and Restoration Political Culture," *Journal of Modern History* 67 (Dec. 1995).

——, "From Butterboxes to Wooden Shoes: The Shift in English Popular Sentiment from Anti-Dutch to Anti-French in the 1670s," *HJ* 38:2 (1995).

——, "From Holy Cause to Economic Interest," in *Nation Transformed?* Steven Pincus and Alan Houston, eds. (Cambridge: Cambridge University Press, 2001).

——, "Neither Machiavellian Moment nor Possessive Individualism: Commercial Society and the Defenders of the English Commonwealth," *American Historical Review* 103:3 (June 1998).

——, "Popery, Trade, and Universal Monarchy: The Ideological Context of the Outbreak of the Second Anglo-Dutch War," *EHR* no. 422 (Jan. 1992).

——, *Protestantism and Patriotism: Ideologies and the Making of English Foreign Policy, 1650–1668* (Cambridge: Cambridge University Press, 1996).

——, "Reconceiving Seventeenth-Century Political Culture," *Journal of British Studies* 38:1 (Jan. 1999).

Pocock, J. G. A., *Machiavellian Moment* (Princeton: Princeton University Press, 1975).

——, *Virtue, Commerce, and History* (Cambridge, UK: Cambridge University Press, 1985).

Pointon, Marcia, *Hanging the Head: Portraiture and Social Formation in Eighteenth-Century England* (New Haven: Yale University Press, 1993).

Pollock, Linda, *With Faith and Physic: The Life of a Tudor Gentlewoman Lady Grace Mildmay, 1552–1620* (Collins and Brown, 1993).

Porter, Dorothy and Roy Porter, *Patient's Progress: Doctors and Doctoring in Eighteenth-Century England* (Stanford: Stanford University Press, 1989).

Porter, Roy, *Creation of the Modern World: The Untold Story of the British Enlightenment* (New York: Norton, 2000).

——, *Health for Sale: Quackery in England, 1660–1850* (Manchester: Manchester University Press, 1989).

Power, M. J., "Social Topography of Restoration London," in *London, 1500–1700*, A. L. Beier and Roger Finlay, eds. (Longman, 1986).

Prakash, Gyan, "Orientalism Now," *History and Theory* 34:3 (1995).

Rappaport, Erika, "'Halls of Temptation': Gender, Politics, and the Construction of the Department Store in Late Victorian London," *Journal of British Studies* 35:1 (1996).

Rawson, Claude, *Satire and Sentiment, 1660–1830* (Cambridge: Cambridge University Press, 1994).

Raymond, Joad, *Invention of the Newspaper : English Newsbooks, 1641–1649* (Oxford: Oxford University Press, 1996).

——, "Newspaper, Public Opinion and the Public Sphere in the Seventeenth Century," *Prose Studies* 21:2 (Aug. 1998).

Robert Rea, *The English Press in Politics, 1760–1774* (Lincoln: University of Nebraska Press, 1963).

Reay, Barry, *Popular Cultures in England, 1550–1750* (Longman, 1998).

Redwood, John, *Reason, Ridicule and Religion* (Cambridge, Mass.: Harvard University Press, 1976).

Reinders, Pim and Thera Wijsenbeek, eds., *Koffie in Nederland: vier eeuwen cultuurgeschiedenis* (Delft: Walburg, 1994).

Richards, James O., *Party Propaganda Under Queen Anne: The General Elections of 1702–1703* (Athens: University of Georgia Press, 1972).

Roberts, Marie Mulvey, "Pleasures Engendered by Gender: Homosociality and the Club," in *Pleasure in the Eighteenth Century,* Roy Porter and Marie Mulvey Roberts, eds. (Basingstoke: Macmillan, 1996).

Roberts, R. S., "The Early History of the Import of Drugs into Britain," in *Evolution of Pharmacy in Britain* (Springfield, Ill., Charles C. Thomas, 1965).

Roche, Daniel, *France in the Enlightenment,* Arthur Goldhammer, trans. (1993; reprint, Cambridge, Mass.: Harvard University Press, 1998).

Rogers, Nicholas, "Popular Protest in Early Hanoverian London." *P&P,* 79 (1978).

Rogers, Pat, *Grub Street: Studies in a Subculture* (Metheun, 1972).

Rosenheim, James M., *Emergence of a Ruling Order: English Landed Society, 1650–1750* (Longman, 1998).

Rouselle, Aline, *Porneia: On Desire and the Body in Antiquity,* trans. Felicia Pheasant (1983; reprint, Oxford: Basil Blackwell, 1988).

Rousseau, G. S. and Roy Porter, "Introduction," in *Exoticism in the Enlightenment,* G. S. Rousseau and Roy Porter, eds. (Manchester: Manchester University Press, 1990).

Russell, Conrad, *Parliaments and English Politics, 1621–1629* (Oxford: Clarendon, 1979).

Russell Smith, H. F., *Harrington and his Utopia: A Study of a Seventeenth-Century Utopia and its Influence in America* (Cambridge: Cambridge University Press, 1914).

Sacks, David Harris, "Corporate Town and the English State: Bristol's 'Little Businesses' 1625–1641," *P&P* 110 (1986).

Sahlins, Marshall, *Culture and Practical Reason* (Chicago: University of Chicago Press, 1976).

———, *Stone Age Economics* (New York: Aldine De Gruyter, 1972).

Said, Edward, *Orientalism* (New York: Vintage, 1978).

Saunders, Peter, *Social Theory and the Urban Question,* 2nd ed. (New York: Holmes & Meier, 1986).

Schama, Simon, *Embarrassment of Riches: An Interpretation of Dutch Culture in the Golden Age* (Berkeley: University of California Press, 1988).

Schivelbusch, Wolfgang, "Die trockene Trunkenheit des Tabaks," in *Rausch und Realität: Drogen im Kulturvergleich,* Gisela Völger, ed., 2 vols. (Cologne: Das Museum, 1981).

———, *Tastes of Paradise: A Social History of Spices, Stimulants, and Intoxicants,* David Jacobson, trans. (1980; reprint, New York: Vintage, 1992).

Schmidt, Peer, "Tobacco—Its Use and Consumption in Early Modern Europe," in *Prodotti e Techniche D'Oltremare nelle Economie Europee Secc. XIII-XVIII,* Simonetta Cavaciocchi, ed. (Florence: Le Monnier, 1998).

Schnapper, Antoine, *Collections et Collectionneurs dans la France du XVIIe Siècle,* 2 vols. (Paris: Flammarion, 1988–94).

Schneider, Jürgen, "Die neuen Getränke: Schokolade, Kaffee und Tee (16.–18. Jahrhundert)," in *Prodotti e Techniche D'Oltremare nelle Economie Europee Secc. XIII–XVIII,* Simonetta Cavaciocchi, ed. (Paris: Le Monnier, 1998).

Schumpeter, E. B., *Overseas English Trade Statistics, 1697–1808* (Oxford: Oxford University Press, 1960).

Schwoerer, Lois, *Ingenious Mr. Henry Care: Restoration Publicist* (Baltimore: Johns Hopkins University Press, 2001).

———, "Women's Public Political Voice in England: 1640–1740," in *Women Writers and the Early Modern English Political Tradition,* Hilda Smith, ed. (Cambridge: Cambridge University Press, 1998).

Schynder-von Waldkirch, Antoinette, *Wie Europa den Kaffee entdeckte: Reiseberichte der Barockzeit als Quellen zur Geschichte des Kaffees* (Zurich: Jacobs Suchard Museum, 1988).

Scott, Jonathan, *Algernon Sidney and the Restoration Crisis, 1677–1683* (Cambridge: Cambridge University Press, 1991).

———, *England's Troubles: Seventeenth-Century Political Instability in European Context* (Cambridge: Cambridge University Press, 2000).

Seaward, Paul, *Cavalier Parliament and the Reconstruction of the Old Regime, 1661–1667* (Cambridge: Cambridge University Press, 1988).

Sekora, John, *Luxury: The Concept in Western Thought, Eden to Smollett* (Baltimore: Johns Hopkins University Press, 1977).

Semonin, Paul, "Monsters in the Marketplace: The Exhibition of Human Oddities in Early Modern England," in *Freakery: Cultural Spectacles of the Extraordinary Body,* Rosemarie Garland Thomson, ed. (New York: New York University Press, 1996).

Sennett, Richard, *Fall of Public Man* (New York: Norton, 1972).

Shammas, Carol, *Pre-Industrial Consumer in England and America* (Oxford: Clarendon, 1990).

Shapin, Steven and Simon Schaffer, *Leviathan and the Air-Pump: Hobbes, Boyle and the Experimental Life* (Princeton: Princeton University Press, 1985).

Shapin, Steven, "House of Experiment in Seventeenth-Century England," *Isis* 79 (1988).

——, *Social History of Truth: Civility and Science in Seventeenth-Century England* (Chicago: University of Chicago Press, 1994).

——, "Who Was Robert Hooke?" in *Robert Hooke: New Studies,* Michael Hunter and Simon Schaeffer, eds. (Bury St. Edmunds: The Boydell Press, 1989).

Sharpe, Kevin, "Personal Rule of Charles I," in *Before the English Civil War,* Howard Tomlinson, ed. (Macmillan, 1983).

——, *The Personal Rule of Charles I* (New Haven: Yale University Press, 1992).

Sharpe, Kevin and Steven Zwicker, "Introduction," in *Refiguring Revolutions: Aesthetics and Politics from the English Revolution to the Romantic Revolution,* Sharpe and Zwicker, eds. (Berkeley: University of California Press, 1998).

Sharpe, Pamela, "Dealing with Love: The Ambiguous Independence of the Single Woman in Early Modern England," *Gender and History* 11:2 (1999).

Shepard, Alexandra, *Meanings of Manhood in Early Modern England* (Oxford: Oxford University Press, 2003).

Sherman, Stuart, *Telling Time: Clocks, Diaries, and English Diurnal Form, 1660–1785* (Chicago: University of Chicago Press, 1996).

Sherratt, Andrew, "Alcohol and its Alternatives: Symbol and Substance in Pre-Industrial Cultures," in *Consuming Habits,* Jordan Goodman, Paul E. Lovejoy, and Andrew Sherratt, eds. (Routledge, 1995).

——, "Introduction: Peculiar Substances," in *Consuming Habits,* Jordan Goodman, Paul E. Lovejoy, and Andrew Sherratt, eds. (Routledge, 1995).

Shevelow, Kathryn, *Women and Print Culture: The Construction of Femininity in the Early Periodical* (Routledge, 1989).

Shoemaker, Robert B., *Gender in English Society, 1650–1850* (Longman, 1998).

——, *Prosecution and Punishment: Petty Crime and the Law in London and Middlesex, c. 1660–1725* (Cambridge: Cambridge University Press, 1991).

——, "Reforming the City: The Reformation of Manners Campaign in London, 1690–1738," in *Stilling the Grumbling Hive: The Response to Social and Economic Problems in England, 1689–1750* (New York: St. Martin's, 1992).

Siebert, F. S., *Freedom of the Press in England, 1476–1776: The Rise and Decline of Government Control* (Urbana: University of Illinois Press, 1965).

Simmel, Georg, *On Individuality and Social Forms: Selected Writings,* D. N. Levine, ed. and trans. (Chicago: University of Chicago Press, 1971).

Skinner, Quentin, "Thomas Hobbes and the Nature of the Early Royal Society," *HJ* 12 (1969).

Smith, Nigel, "Enthusiasm and Enlightenment: Of Food, Filth, and Slavery," in *Country and the City Revisited: England and the Politics of Culture, 1550–1850,* Gerald Maclean, Donna Landry, and Joseph P. Ward, eds. (Cambridge: Cambridge University Press, 1999).

Smith, S. D., "Accounting for Taste: British Coffee Consumption in Historical Perspective," *Journal of Interdisciplinary History* 27:2 (1996).

——, "Sugar's Poor Relation: Coffee Planting in the British West Indies, 1720–1833," *Slavery and Abolition* 19:3 (1998).

Smith, Woodfruff D., "Complications of the Commonplace: Tea, Sugar, and Imperialism," *Journal of Interdisciplinary History* 23:2 (1992).

——, *Consumption and the Making of Respectability, 1600–1800* (Routledge, 2002).

——, "From Coffeehouse to Parlour: The consumption of coffee, tea and sugar in northwestern Europe in the seventeenth and eighteenth centuries," in *Consuming Habits,* Goodman, Lovejoy, and Sherratt, eds. (Routledge, 1992).

——, "Function of Commercial Centers in the Modernization of European Capitalism," *Journal of Economic History* 44:4 (1984).

Smithers, Peter, *Life of Joseph Addison,* 2nd ed. (Oxford: Clarendon, 1968).

Smuts, Malcolm R., *Court Culture and the Origins of a Royalist Tradition in Early Stuart England* (Philadelphia: University of Pennsylvania Press, 1987).

Snodin, Michael, and John Styles, *Design and the Decorative Arts: Britain, 1500–1900* (Harry Abrams, 2001).

Snyder, Henry, "Newsletters in England, 1689–1715, with special reference to John Dyer — a byway in the history of England," in *Newsletters to Newspapers: Eighteenth-Century Journalism,* Donovan H. Bond and William R. McCleod, eds. (Morgantown, W. Va.: School of Journalism, West Virginia University, 1977).

Sombart, Werner, *Luxury and Capitalism,* W. R. Dittmar, trans. (1913; reprint, Ann Arbor: University of Michigan Press, 1967).

Sommerville, C. John, *News Revolution in England: Cultural Dynamics of Daily Information* (New York: Oxford University Press, 1996).

Spang, Rebecca, *Invention of the Restaurant: Paris and Modern Gastronomic Culture* (Cambridge, Mass.: Harvard University Press, 2000).

Stallybrass, Peter, and Allon White, *Politics and Poetics of Transgression* (Ithaca: Cornell University Press, 1986).

Stephen, Leslie, *English Literature and Society in the Eighteenth Century* (1903).

Stewart, Larry, *Rise of Public Science: Rhetoric, Technology, and Natural Philosophy in Newtonian Britain, 1660–1750* (Cambridge: Cambridge University Press, 1992).

——, "Other Centres of Calculation, or, Where the Royal Society Didn't Count," *British Journal for the History of Science* 32 (1999).

——, "Philosophers in the Counting House," in P. O'Brien, ed., *Urban Achievement in Early Modern Europe* (Cambridge: Cambridge University Press, 2001).

Stone, Lawrence, *Crisis of the Aristocracy, 1558–1641* (1965 reprint, with corrections; Oxford: Clarendon, 1979).

——, "Residential Development of the West End of London in the Seventeenth Century," in *After the Reformation: Essays in Honor of J. H. Hexter*, Barbara C. Malament, ed. (Philadelphia: University of Pennsylvania Press, 1980).

——, *Road to Divorce: England, 1530–1987* (Oxford: Oxford University Press, 1990).

Strumia, Anna M., "Vita Istituzionale Della Royal Society Seicentesca in Alcuni Studi Recenti," *Rivista Storica Italiana* 98:2 (1986).

Stubbs, Mayling, "John Beale, Philosophical Gardener of Herefordshire," 2 parts, *Annals of Science* 39 (1982) and 46 (1989).

Styles, John, "Product Innovation in Early Modern London," *P&P* 168 (2000).

Supple, B. E., *Commercial Crisis and Change in England, 1600–1642* (Cambridge: Cambridge University Press, 1964).

Sutherland, James, *Restoration Literature, 1660–1700: Dryden, Bunyan and Pepys*, Oxford History of English Literature, vol. 6 (Oxford: Oxford University Press, 1969).

Sutherland, James, *Restoration Newspaper and Its Development* (Cambridge: Cambridge University Press, 1986).

Terpstra, Heert, *Opkomst der Westerkwartieren van de Oost-Indische Compagnie* (The Hague: Nijhoff, 1918).

Thale, Mary, "Women in London Debating Societies in 1780," *Gender and History* 7:1 (1995).

Thirsk, Joan, *Economic Policy and Projects: The Development of a Consumer Society in England* (Oxford: Oxford University Press, 1976).

——, "New Crops and their Diffusion: Tobacco-Growing in Seventeenth-Century England," in *Rural Change and Urban Growth, 1500–1800*, C. W. Chalkin and M. A. Havinden, eds. (1974).

Thomas, Keith, "Cleanliness and Godliness in Early Modern England," in *Religion, Culture and Society in Early Modern Britain: Essays in Honour of Patrick Collinson*, Anthony Fletcher and Peter Roberts, eds. (Cambridge: Cambridge University Press, 1994).

——, *Man and the Natural World: Changing Attitudes in England, 1500–1800* (1983; reprint, Oxford: Oxford University Press, 1996).

——, *Religion and the Decline of Magic* (New York: Scribner's, 1971).

Thompson, C. J. S., *Quacks of Old London* (1928; reprint, New York: Barnes & Noble, 1993).

Thompson, E. P., *Customs in Common: Studies in Traditional Popular Culture* (New York: New Press, 1991).

Timbs, John, *Clubs and Club Life in London with anecdotes of its famous coffee houses, hostelries, and taverns from the seventeenth century to the present time* (Chatto & Windus, 1899).

——, *Curiosities of London: Exhibiting the Most Rare and Remarkable Objects of Interest in the Metropolis* (1855).

Todd, Dennis, *Imagining Monsters: Miscreations of the Self in Eighteenth-Century England* (Chicago: University of Chicago Press, 1995).

Toomer, G. J., *Eastern Wisedome and Learning: The Study of Arabic in Seventeenth-Century England* (Oxford: Clarendon, 1996).

Treadwell, Michael, "Stationers and the Printing Acts at the End of the Seventeenth Century," in *The Cambridge History of the Book in Britain,* vol. 4, *1557–1695,* John Barnard and D. F. McKenzie, eds. (Cambridge: Cambridge University Press, 2002).

Trevelyan, George, *England Under Queen Anne: Blenheim* (Longman, 1930).

Trumbach, Randolph, *Sex and the Gender Revolution Volume One: Heterosexuality and the Third Gender in Enlightenment London* (Chicago: University of Chicago Press, 1998).

Tully, James, ed., *Meaning and Context: Quentin Skinner and his Critics* (Princeton: Princeton University Press, 1988).

Turnbull, George Henry, "Peter Stahl, the First Public Teacher of Chemistry at Oxford," *Annals of Science, 9* (1953).

Turner, Dorothy, "Sir Roger L'Estrange's Deferential Politics in the Public Sphere," *Seventeenth Century* 13:1 (1998).

Turner, James Grantham "Pictorial Prostitution: Visual Culture, Vigilantism, and 'Pornography' in Dunton's *Night-Walker,*" in *Studies in Eighteenth-Century Culture,* vol. 28 (Baltimore: Johns Hopkins University Press, 1999).

Turner, Victor, *Ritual Process: Structure and Anti-Structure* (Ithaca: Cornell University Press, 1969).

Tyacke, Nicholas, "Science and Religion at Oxford before the Civil War," in *Puritans and Revolutionaries,* Donald Pennington and Keith Thomas, eds. (Oxford: Clarendon, 1976).

Uglow, Jenny, *Hogarth: A Life and a World* (Faber and Faber, 1998).

Underdown, David, *Freeborn People: Politics and the Nation in Seventeenth-Century England* (Oxford: Clarendon, 1996).

——, *Revel, Riot, and Rebellion: Popular Politics and Culture in England, 1603–1660* (Oxford: Oxford University Press, 1985).

van der Wee, Herman, "Money, Credit, and Banking Systems," in *The Cambridge Economic History of Europe,* vol. 5, E. E. Rich and C. H. Wilson, eds. (Cambridge: Cambridge University Press, 1977).

van Eeghen, I. H., *Amsterdamse Boekhandel, 1680–1725,* 6 vols (Amsterdam: N. Israel, 1978), vol. 5–1.

van Horn Melton, James, *Rise of the Public in Enlightenment Europe* (Cambridge: Cambridge University Press, 2001).

Veblen, Thorstein, *Theory of the Leisure Class* (1899; reprint, New York: Penguin, 1967).

Vickery, Amanda, *Gentleman's Daughter: Women's Lives in Georgian England* (New Haven: Yale University Press, 1998).

——, "Golden Age to Separate Spheres? A Review of the Categories and Chronology of English Women's History," *HJ* 36:2 (1993).

Wahrman, Dror, "*Percy*'s Prologue: From Gender Play to Gender Panic in Eighteenth-Century England," *P&P* 159 (1998).

Walkowitz, Judith, "Going Public: Shopping, Street Harassment, and Streetwalking in Late Victorian London," *Representations* 62 (1998).

Wall, Cynthia, "English Auction: Narratives of Dismantlings," *ECS* 31:1 (1997).

Walvin, James, *Fruits of Empire: Exotic Produce and British Taste, 1660–1800* (Basingstoke: Macmillan, 1997).

Watt, Tessa, *Cheap Print and Popular Piety, 1550–1640* (Cambridge: Cambridge University Press, 1991).

Wear, Andrew, "Early Modern Europe, 1500–1700," in *Western Medical Tradition 800 BC to AD 1800,* Lawrence I. Conrad, Michael Neve, Vivian Nutton, Roy Porter, and Andrew Wear, eds. (Cambridge: Cambridge University Press, 1995).

Weatherill, Lorna, *Consumer Behaviour and Material Culture in Britain, 1660–1760,* 2nd ed. (Routledge, 1996).

Weber, Max, *Protestant Ethic and the Spirit of Capitalism,* trans. Talcott Parsons (1904–5; reprint, New York: Scribners, 1958).

Webster, Charles, "Alchemical and Paracelsian Medicine," in *Health, Medicine, and Mortality in the Sixteenth Century,* Charles Webster, ed. (Cambridge: Cambridge University Press, 1979).

——, "Benjamin Worsley: Engineering for Universal Reform from the Invisible College to the Navigation Act," in *Samuel Hartlib and Universal Reformation,* Mark Greengrass, Michael Leslie, and Timothy Raylor, eds. (Cambridge: Cambridge University Press, 1994).

——, *Great Instauration: Science, Medicine and Reform, 1626–1660* (Duckworth, 1975).

Weeks, Jeffrey, *Sex, Politics and Society: The Regulation of Sexuality Since 1800,* 2nd ed. (Longman, 1989).

Weil, Rachel, "Sometimes a Scepter is only a Scepter: Pornography and Politics in Restoration England," in *Invention of Pornography: Obscenity and the Origins of Modernity,* Lynn Hunt, ed. (New York: Zone, 1993).

Westfall, Richard S., *Science and Religion in Seventeenth-Century England* (1958; reprint, Ann Arbor: University of Michigan Press, 1973).

Westhauser, Karl E., "Friendship and Family in Early Modern England: The Sociability of Adam Eyre and Samuel Pepys," *Journal of Social History* (1994).

Whitaker, Katie, "Culture of Curiosity," in *Cultures of Natural History,* N. Jardine, J. A. Secord, and E. C. Spary, eds. (Cambridge: Cambridge University Press, 1996).

——, *Mad Madge: Margaret Cavendish, Duchess of Newcastle* (Chatto and Windus, 2003).

Whyman, Susan, *Sociability and Power: The World of the Verneys, 1660–1720* (Oxford: Oxford University Press, 2000).

Williams, J. B., "Newsbooks and Letters of News of the Restoration," *EHR* 23 (1908).

Williams, Rosalind H., *Dream Worlds: Mass Consumption in Late Nineteenth-Century France* (Berkeley: University of California Press, 1982).

Wilson, Charles, *England's Apprenticeship, 1603–1763* (Longman, 1965).

——, "Trade, Society, and the State," in *Cambridge Economic History of Europe,* vol. 4, E. E. Rich and C. H. Wilson, eds. (Cambridge: Cambridge University Press, 1967).

Wilson, Kathleen, *Island Race: Englishness, Empire and Gender in the Eighteenth Century* (Routledge, 2003).

——, *Sense of the People: Politics, Culture, and Imperialism in England, 1715–1785* (Cambridge: Cambridge University Press, 1995).

Winslow, Cal, "Sussex Smugglers," in *Albion's Fatal Tree: Crime and Society in Eighteenth-Century England*, Douglas Hay et al., eds. (New York: Pantheon, 1975).

Wood, A. C., *History of the Levant Company* (Frank Cass, 1935).

Woodhead, Christine, " 'The Present Terrour of the World'? Contemporary Views of the Ottoman Empire c. 1600," *History* 72 (1987).

Woolrych, Austin, "Introduction," in *Complete Prose Works of John Milton*, vol. 7, Robert W. Ayers, ed., rev. ed. (New Haven: Yale University Press, 1980).

Wootton, David, "Ulysses Bound? Venice and the Idea of Liberty from Howell to Hume," in *Republicanism, Liberty, and Commercial Society*, David Wootton, ed. (Stanford: Stanford University Press, 1994).

Worden, Blair, "Harrington's 'Oceana': Origins and Aftermath, 1651–1660," in *Republicanism, Liberty, and Commercial Society, 1649–1776*, David Wootton, ed. (Stanford: Stanford University Press, 1994).

——, *Rump Parliament, 1648–1653* (Oxford: Oxford University Press, 1974).

Wrightson, Keith, "Alehouses, Order and Reformation in Rural England, 1590–1660," in *Popular Culture and Class Conflict, 1590–1914*, E. Yeo and S. Yeo, eds. (Brighton, 1981).

——, *Earthly Necessities: Economic Lives in Early Modern Britain* (New Haven: Yale University Press, 2000).

——, "Politics of the Parish in Early Modern England," in Paul Griffiths, Adam Fox and Steve Hindle, eds., *Experience of Authority in Early Modern England* (Basingstoke: Macmillan, 1996).

——, "Puritan Reformation of Manners with Special Reference to the Counties of Lancashire and Essex, 1640–1660" (Cambridge University, Ph.D. diss., 1973).

Wrigley, E. A., "A Simple Model of London's Importance in Changing English Society and Economy, 1650–1750," in his *People, Cities and Wealth* (Oxford: Blackwell, 1987).

Zahediah, Nuala, "Making Mercantilism Work," *Transactions of the Royal Historical Society* 9 (1999).

Zook, Melinda, *Radical Whigs and Conspiratorial Politics in Late Stuart England* (University Park: Penn State University Press, 1999).

Index